# THE ATONEMENT IN HISTORY AND IN LIFE

## A VOLUME OF ESSAYS

EDITED BY THE REV.

## L. W. GRENSTED, M.A., B.D.

FELLOW AND CHAPLAIN OF UNIVERSITY
COLLEGE, OXFORD

LONDON
SOCIETY FOR PROMOTING
CHRISTIAN KNOWLEDGE
NEW YORK AND TORONTO: THE MACMILLAN COMPANY

*First published in 1929*

PRINTED IN GREAT BRITAIN

# FOREWORD

By the Right Rev. the Lord Bishop
of Chelmsford

The doctrine of the Atonement has always been a subject upon which widely divergent opinions have been held in the Christian Church. It is probably true to say that the opinion of scholars in recent years has definitely inclined in the direction of those theories of the doctrine which may roughly be called " subjective." Beyond doubt, this has been in considerable measure the outcome of that impressive work of the late Dean Hastings Rashdall : *The Idea of Atonement in Christian Theology.*

Nevertheless, there are, and always have been, competent authorities who are by no means prepared to regard all that is commonly understood as the " objective " side of the Atonement as a mere example of crude thinking or as a survival of pre-Christian or sub-Christian religion. The very fact of this survival seems to testify to the existence of a core of truth, overlaid, it may be, by bad and even repellent forensic theories.

This volume of essays arose from the dissatisfaction which a group of friends felt at the unceremonious way in which, so it seemed to them, the whole Anselmian view, which had become popularised in the Evangelical movement of the last century, and which had been the main theme of Mission preaching, and the driving force in much of the missionary appeal of former times, had been tossed aside as finally disproved and discredited.

We felt that there was a call to gather together a group of writers who would examine the whole doctrine in a fairly thorough fashion. No attempt was made to secure writers who were all in even general agreement in their theory of

A                                    1

the Atonement, but clearly, the inclusion of any thorough-going " Subjectivist " would have stultified the whole object we had in view.   We wished to secure the co-operation of those who could not be satisfied that the whole content of the Atonement was exhausted by all those theories which are commonly called " Subjective."

I was asked to act as Editor of the volume, and the responsible duty was mine of securing the writers and contributing an essay as well as editing the book.

All the essays but three had come to hand, my own contribution was half completed, and a publisher had been secured, when the call to the Bishopric of Chelmsford came.

It was quite clear that other hands than mine must take the matter over, for even the completion of my own essay had now become impossible, and much more was this the case in regard to the difficult and important duty of editing the book.

It was at this stage that I turned to the Rev. L. W. Grensted, and he most kindly undertook to take charge of the book.   I am bound to say that this has turned out for the real advantage of the volume.   It was clear to me a long time ago that the essays needed the oversight of a trained scholar, and this benefit they now enjoy through unexpected circumstances.   It is my belief that the publication of this book will be a valuable contribution to this department of Christian Theology, and will provide a steadying influence in the consideration of the doctrine which is the centre of gravity of the Christian religion.

HENRY CHELMSFORD.

*Bishopscourt,*
*Chelmsford,*
*May 16th,* 1929.

# CONTENTS

3

# CONTENTS

# INTRODUCTION

## By L. W. Grensted

The Bishop of Chelmsford, in the Foreword which he has so kindly contributed to this volume, has explained the circumstances under which it came to be written. He has, indeed, minimised the very considerable amount of work which he had himself done in securing writers and in collecting the majority of the essays, before the present Editor took over the task of completing the book. The scheme, as he conceived it, has not, in fact, been fully carried out. But the essays here collected, despite certain obvious gaps in the treatment, covered so much ground that they seemed likely to serve as a useful introduction for the student and for the general reader, both to the history of the doctrine and to the problems which it raises for the theologian of the present day. In the hope that they may render this service they are now sent upon their way.

Resting upon such an inheritance of work already done, the Editor's task has been a light one, and it has been still further eased by the patience and forbearance of his fellow-contributors, by the wise and fatherly oversight of Dr. Lowther Clarke, and by the skill and accuracy with which the printers have done their part. To each he hereby renders grateful acknowledgment. It only remains to add a few pages of introduction which may serve to guide the reader in his study of the more detailed essays which follow.

We may start by sparing the reviewer the fearful joy of discovering that there is no complete agreement among the essayists. Clearly Mr. Cross and Mr. Cripps are at variance both as to the prophetic attitude to sacrifice and as to the ultimate meaning of some of its characteristics. The Archbishop of Armagh, in his striking delineation of the " Divine Adventurer," would probably be followed, at least in his use of such a phrase, by few of his fellow-writers. Nor would all accept Mr. Shebbeare's stress upon tragic and

5

emotional values, or Mr. Chavasse's assurance of the primarily retributive aspect of punishment. If it had been possible to secure fuller collaboration between the writers at an earlier stage the resulting volume would almost certainly have shown more unity alike of treatment and of outlook. Equally certainly it would have been of far less real interest. For such value as it possesses does not lie in its presentation of a traditional theory, even supposing that any one complete theory existed with a special claim to traditional orthodoxy. It is mere platitude to remark that the Anselmic theory is now held by nobody in the exact form in which Anselm originally stated it. And the restatement of that theory in Penal terms by the great theologians of the Reformation is, in its literal form, even less tenable to-day.

But nevertheless it is a conviction shared by all those who have contributed essays to this volume, that these greatest of the classical attempts to expound that fact of Atonement which is the very basis of the Christian life, both individual and corporate, have at least this supreme value, that they view it as arising from an inner necessity of God's Being, and not merely as a change within the heart of man. They are essentially objective in character, and not subjective. They seek to explain the experience of the Christian who has sought and found release from his sins, but they do not find the explanation simply within that experience. For the doctrine of the Atonement is, first and foremost, a doctrine of God. It is not simply a doctrine of the Cross, and attempts so to restrict its scope have invariably resulted in failure. No discussion of the Cross can be adequate which does not rest upon an adequate conception of the Being of God, just as no study of the work of Christ can be adequate which separates the Cross from the Resurrection on the one hand and from the whole condescension and obedience of His Incarnate Life upon the other. But to say this is tantamount to saying—and in this all the contributors to this volume would agree—that it would be not merely optimism, but sheer arrogance, to suppose that the whole mystery of the Cross can ever lie bare to our understanding.

And in the second place, strictly in the second place, the doctrine of the Atonement is a doctrine of man. In the light of the Cross of Christ man stands revealed far more

sharply than he had ever done before. The age-long
shadow of cosmic evil, with its vague confusions of pain
and suffering and disorder and half-wilful, half-inevitable
disobedience, is resolved. Sin stands out clear. Human
nature is seen in all its strange moral grandeur, its terrible
prerogative of withstanding God, and in its woeful recalcitrance and shame. Man and man alone at once seeks and
denies the good. Man and man alone has crucified the
Lord of glory.

But this is no explanation of the dark mystery of the
origin of evil. In this connection Dr. D'Arcy's essay will
repay special study,[1] and those who find difficulty in his
conception of an " Adventurer-God " may well ask themselves whether they can present an alternative conception
of the Universe which is at once more living and more
coherent. And indeed there is a relationship by no means
remote between this conception of God and that preached
with such conviction by Barth, as set forth for us in Mr.
Shebbeare's essay,[2] the conception of a God who lies beyond
all conceptions, whose realm of Spirit is in the sharpest
contrast to the world of Flesh. Neither conception would
have seemed too bizarre or too venturesome for Luther. It
is in Luther, indeed, that language of this kind has found
much of its inspiration.[3] The conception of a " hidden
God," which he stressed against Erasmus, is identical, if
we interpret it in the sphere of knowledge, with Barth's
God whom we can only know as unknown, and, if we interpret it in the sphere of purpose, closely akin to the God set
forth by Dr. D'Arcy.[4] The ultimate inscrutability of God
and of His purposes has, in fact, been a commonplace of
Christian theology from the first. Of the relation of the
great fact of evil to those purposes we can say much, but
nothing final and adequate. The Christian solution, if it
can be called a solution, looks forward and not back. We
emerge from our study with curiosity still unsatisfied, but
with a good hope.

But though in these essays we thus stand by the belief

[1] See especially pp. 267 ff.
[2] See pp. 301 ff.
[3] See p. 220.
[4] The conception of the " Divine Adventurer " does not in the
least imply a God without a definite purpose, or that that purpose
can fail of fulfilment, even though the mode of its fulfilment be
unknown. See pp 278–280.

in God as transcending the puny attempts which human reason makes to formulate His Being, we do not therefore repudiate human reason altogether. We accept fully, as Christians, the belief in a Christian revelation, and where there is revelation there is knowledge. This point has been brought out especially clearly by Mr. Shebbeare, in his discussion of Barth's " Irrationalism." [1] We may further call attention to the writings of Karl Heim, which have had a wide circulation in Germany, and which, in their emphasis on the specific value of the religious judgment as a real mode of knowledge, form a valuable corrective to Barth and Otto.[2] The belief in an objective Atonement does, in fact, imply a definite claim to understand, at least in some degree, the ways of God and the meaning of His creation. And we make bold to declare that the key to this understanding is the Cross of Christ.

But such an assertion obviously cries aloud for explanation. The Cross as a fact of history is simply an atrocious example of a politico-judicial murder. Such things have been done before, and since, without producing any conviction in man that he thereby knows more of God.[3] We must look beyond the Cross to find its full significance, seeing it in relation to the Person who hung there, to His life among men, to His rising from the dead, and to the continued assurance of His presence in His Church. And above all we must approach it from the point of view of that living experience, emotional [4] and regenerating,[5] which has given it a unique and abiding place in human history. We do not, in fact, explain atonement by the Cross, but the Cross by atonement. In the forgiveness of sin the Cross passes beyond history and becomes a cosmic principle, available for time, space, and eternity, a principle adequate to meet the cosmic disaster of evil in all its aspects.

If this vision is indeed to correspond to truth we must be able to see in the Cross a real revelation of God, and herein is the vindication of all those who, from Abelard to Dr. Rashdall, have spoken of it as " an exhibition of love." It is easy to criticise theology of this kind, to condemn it as subjective and emotional, but this criticism deals with its

---

[1] See pp. 307 f.
[2] See especially Heim's *Glaubensgewissheit*.
[3] See p. 297.    [4] See p. 299 f.    [5] See p. 295.

incompleteness rather than with its truth. And, as we shall see, such theology need not be as incomplete as is often supposed.[1] But we must be able to see something more, to see that that which happened at Calvary passes beyond the limitations of history, within which it was a real fact, to a sphere in which it has eternal and cosmic truth. It tells us something about God, and God is more than history. For history passes, and God is.

Our argument then starts with the forgiveness of sin, and, in effect, these essays are all studies in that single theme. To say this is to admit that we make religious experience the basis of our inquiry, and the argument from experience is unfashionable to-day, since experience may be of many kinds, and cannot in the nature of things justify its own claim to religious and ultimate worth. Here, then, we must at the outset walk by faith, faith that in this experience of forgiveness we are not deceived. But this faith is not simply our own. It is the whole witness of the Church from the first days until now. It is faith that overcomes the world and brings peace. It is faith that is self-vindicating, and vindicated by its transformation of human history. More things changed than the turn of a calendar with the coming of Jesus Christ.

When we examine the New Testament to discover what exactly the Cross and Resurrection meant to the first disciples we find two things standing out clearly : the conquest of death and the forgiveness of sins. A study of the first Christian preaching as recorded in the early chapters of Acts (here is one of the gaps in our series of essays to which a reviewer might rightly call attention) brings this out clearly. But of the two messages the greater is the message of forgiveness. Had not Jesus Himself said that a mere gospel of resurrection would not avail—" neither will they be persuaded though one rose from the dead " ? [2] The possibility of a resurrection was indeed nothing very new or surprising. Nor in itself was it particularly comforting. The widespread belief that Nero might rise from the dead, and return as a destroying conqueror from the East, leading the Parthian hordes, was for many years a terror and not a hope. Foreshadowings of a resurrection appear, dimly enough, in the Old Testament. Enoch and Elijah, to whom traditional interpretation had added Moses, were recorded

[1] See p. 30.  [2] Lk. xvi. 31.

to have passed into heaven without dying. A general resurrection at the last day had become a characteristic tenet at least of the orthodox Pharisaic teaching,[1] and St. Paul on one dramatic occasion threw his accusers into confusion by a reference to the belief.[2] But the gospel of the possibility of forgiveness was new and startling. The sacrifices of the Old Testament were not designed to deal with wilful sin, but only with errors, accidental breaches of the Law, unwitting defilement. For sin committed " with a high hand " there was no forgiveness.[3] Even in the striking ethical teaching of the later Jewish Rabbis there is nothing comparable with the gravity of the Christian sense of sin : " They minimise the weight of the opposition in our existing human nature to the Divine will, and this leads them also to minimise the gravity of any atonement that can bridge the gulf." [4]

The teaching of Jesus Himself had been full of the gospel of forgiveness. No teacher had ever so emphasised the terrible reality of sin and its true source, as coming not from failure to observe the ordinances of the Law, but " from within, out of the heart of men." [5] No teacher had ever proclaimed the free forgiveness of God in such unqualified terms,[6] and though there were hints, and more than hints, that what is free to man may be of bitter cost to his Redeemer,[7] these do not in the least qualify the freedom of the offer. But Jesus went further. He bade men forgive, " not, until seven times : but, until seventy times seven." [8] The proclamation of the possibility of the forgiveness of man by man was received with frank incredulity by the disciples, though in deference to the Master they were prepared to make some small experiments in this direction,[9] and as a blasphemous piece of arrogance by the Jewish theologians. " Son, thy sins be forgiven thee " was an even harder saying than " Arise, and take up thy bed, and go thy way into thine house." [10] To the Christian it is almost incredible that

[1] First clearly stated in Dan. xii.
[2] Acts xxiii. 6.                          [4] See p. 98.
[3] See p. 60.                              [5] Mk. vii. 21.
[6] See especially the Parable of the Prodigal Son, and, on the whole subject, Dr. Tait's comments, pp. 124 ff.
[7] Mk. x. 45; xiv. 24 and the parallel passages. Dr. Rashdall's attempt to dispose of these sayings as not original is entirely unconvincing.
[8] Mt. xviii. 22.          [9] Mt. xviii. 21.          [10] Mk. ii. 5–11

the central commonplace of his faith should be to others
an astounding paradox. And yet no teacher save Jesus
could ever have framed the petition, "Forgive us our
trespasses, as we forgive them that trespass against
us."

The world, haunted by evil and tormented by its own
inability to forgive, has found no way out save the easy way
of the Jewish Rabbis, making little of evil and asking a
repentance, sincere enough, but wholly inadequate. And
current popular feeling to-day has gone even further along
the same path. Evil finds little real recognition. There is
much discontent and but little repentance. Man blames
anything—Nature, heredity, environment, psychological
complexes, or pathological conditions—rather than his own
erring will. And at the same time he finds it harder than
ever to forgive. Men may be slow to blame, but they are
still slower to pardon. The Cross of Christ was the sterner,
but the only true way.

For what the disciples discovered through the Cross was
the reality of forgiveness. The events of those last days
had shown them evil as it really is, and they had found it
not merely in the world but in themselves. They had
failed their Friend in every way, and through their failure
He had died. Their leader had denied Him. All had forsaken Him and fled. The wonder of the Resurrection was
not that He lived again, but that the old friendship was
restored, and restored as though the sin had not been.[1]
He was risen indeed, and had appeared unto Simon.[2] Suddenly He was with them in the upper room, with the old
friendly greeting "Peace be unto you."[3] So was the
message of the Cross made plain. It showed moral evil at
its fulness, and it met that evil with forgiveness, a forgiveness which not merely annulled the past but which brought
with it renewal and power. In such creative forgiveness
they could see nothing less than the hand of God Himself.

It is small wonder that the first preaching of the early
Church was an appeal to those who had shared in the wrong
of Calvary to repent and to enter into this new and triumphant
experience.[4] It was years before they worked out the
theology of it all. Not until St. Paul wrote his letter to
the Colossians is it stated in its full and cosmic significance,[5]

[1] See p. 146 f.     [2] Lk. xxiv. 34.     [3] Lk. xxiv. 36.
[4] Acts ii. 38; iii. 19; v. 31.     [5] Col. i. 19, 20.

but the essential truth is there from the first. And it is true for man because it is true of God.

Thus in one sense the starting-point of these essays lies in their presentation of the New Testament evidence. What is essential to any understanding of the doctrine of Atonement is to realise that the preaching of the forgiveness of sins is from the first a proclamation of something wrought by God and hardly even sought, still less achieved by man. It is therefore a statement about God, and a statement which claims objective truth. It offers to the world a key with which to unlock the ultimate mysteries, a key which the philosopher may refuse, but which even a child may turn if he will.

At this point we may call attention to another gap in our series of essays. It did not fall within the scope of any of the writers to deal with the Epistle to the Hebrews, a work which, despite its unknown authorship and its late acceptance by the Church as canonical, has been of outstanding importance in its influence upon Christian language and thought in this special connection. There are four main aspects of the teaching of this Epistle which concern us at this stage in our argument, and though there is probably nothing which cannot be found, at least by implication, in the writings of St. Paul and St. John, it will be worth while to state them here.

(1) It lays stress upon the uniqueness and finality of the Cross. That which was wrought there was wrought, so far as history is concerned, once and for all. It need not be, and cannot be, repeated. As a sacrifice offered by Christ it does away with the need and the possibility of any further sacrifice. It should be noted that there is no indication whatever in the Epistle that this self-offering of Christ upon the Cross continues eternally in heaven. It is a thing accomplished once, finally, and complete.[1]

(2) The key to this offering is to be found less in its sacrificial than in its ethical character. Or perhaps it would be truer to say that the essence of sacrifice is conceived not as an offering primarily of blood,[2] or " the ashes of an heifer sprinkling the unclean," [3] but as obedience. The Son " learning obedience by the things that he suffered,"[4]

---

[1] Heb. vii. 27; ix. 12, 25–28; x. 12, 14.
[2] Heb. ix. 23; x. 4.
[3] Heb. ix. 18.          [4] Heb. v, 8,

and declaring " Lo I come, in the volume of the book it is written of me, to do thy will, O God," [1] so by obedience makes valid those sacrifices which in themselves had availed nothing.

(3) This obedience, restoring the true relationship between God and man, gives the work of Christ its eternal significance. " He ever liveth to make intercession for them." [2] On the plane of history it was perfectly expressed upon the Cross, and in the perfect filial response to the Father's love it continues unceasingly in heaven, so becoming the channel through which the forgiveness of God is eternally operative in the lives of men.

(4) The whole of this conception is worked out upon the basis of Old Testament types, in which the writer sees man's vain attempt to do that which is now at last accomplished. That which Christ wrought upon the Cross was a sacrifice indeed (and in this St. Paul [3] and St. John [4] agree). As a result of that sacrifice Christ has entered into the Holy of Holies,[5] there to act eternally as our High Priest, after the order of Melchizedek,[6] in His office as intercessor not only for the sins of the Jewish people, but for all.

In this recognition of the function of the Old Testament development of religion all the New Testament concurs, and we need not here labour the point. It was to men deeply versed in the ideas of that dispensation that the Gospel was preached and it is in relation to those ideas that it must be understood. This is the connection of thought which leads to the inclusion in this volume of the first three essays.

The importance of the Old Testament for our understanding of the doctrine of Atonement to-day lies not in the details of the ritual of sacrifice, but in the development in the richness and adequacy of the knowledge of God. It is quite probable that certain aspects of the sacrificial system go back to primitive magical conceptions which have little if any religious value. The idea that the " sins " of the people could be by a ritual act transferred to the " goat for Azazel," and put away by the simple process of driving

---

[1] Heb. x. 5–10.     [2] Heb. vii. 25.     [3] 1 Cor. v. 7.
[4] It is the Fourth Gospel which makes the Crucifixion occur at the time of the slaying of the Paschal lambs. Cf. also Jn. i. 29; xix. 36.
[5] Heb. ix. 7, 12.        [6] Heb. vii.

the goat out into the desert, good care being taken that it did not return, has obviously no lofty conception behind it all, and it is for us only of archæological interest if we consider it apart from the far more adequate ritual setting in which it is found.[1] So again the ideas and practices connected with the blood of the sacrifices depend upon a primitive, pseudo-scientific identification of the blood with the life, and whether Mr. Cross is right in his exposition and explanation of these ideas or not, his interesting discussion of them sufficiently indicates the region in which an explanation must be sought.[2] What really concerns us here is that at every stage the dawning conception of sin and of the need for atonement, and the development of the ritual by which atonement is sought, depends upon the growing understanding of God Himself, and that at every stage it is God Himself who is conceived as making His claim upon man, not man who by searching finds out God. God understood as the creative principle in Nature is met by simple and joyous fertility sacrifices. Even the dedication of the first-born to Him had not, probably, in its origin the tragic implications of its later forms. God understood as the Warrior-leader of His people demands above all things a complete loyalty and obedience, any breach of which must be atoned for by sacrifices in which the characteristics of expiation and penal cost are prominent. God as the God of the Covenant, the Guardian of social integrity, Himself linked by Covenant with His people, demands sacrifice in which a prominent conception is an entry into union with the sacrificer, through, for example, such a ceremony as passing between the severed portions of the body of a victim, in which the idea appears to be that of union within that body.

At the very outset, then, we find in the study of sacrifice the principle of *necessitas* upon which Anselm lays such stress.[3] Man has never viewed God's dealings with him as arbitrary and inexplicable. Always there has been the sense that God, being what He is, must act in accordance with the law of His own being. Men interpreted God by the highest that they knew, and on that basis tried to understand His ways. Whether He is the God " that teachest my hands to war and my fingers to fight," or

---

[1] See p. 61, note.       [2] See p. 44 ff.
[3] See Dr. Whately's comments upon this, pp. 206 f.

Anselm's God whose inmost necessity is the immutability of His goodness, the principle of man's approach to God is still the same. The history of doctrines of Atonement is in the end the story of man's increasing knowledge of God, and to recognise, with Luther and Barth, that we do not know all does not invalidate such knowledge as we have.

It does, however, demand of us caution in accepting as knowledge conceptions of God which have not come to us through Jesus Christ. There are gods many and lords many, and of some we can only say that they are the shadows cast upon the world by the sin of men, of others that the truth is so confused by the shadows that it is hard to say what is of God and what is of man. Even of theologies that claim to be Christian this is true, and obviously we must be careful to criticise in the light of fuller truth the implications of the early history of sacrifice. It was the special function of the Old Testament prophets to supply this criticism in their own day, leading up to the still more drastic criticism of Jesus, criticism which, drastic as it is, never fails to recognise the positive values of these early attempts to understand and obey. The prophets, each in his own way, rise to visions of God unprecedented in the ancient world. The work of Moses and Elijah comes to a head in Amos, whose God of justice attains, for the first time, world-wide significance. And so for Amos and Micah, justice is more than sacrifice. To Hosea God is especially a God of mercy, and this vision not only profoundly influenced Jeremiah and the writers of the Deuteronomic School, but also received the special *imprimatur* of Jesus Himself.[1] And Hosea's God demands " mercy, and not sacrifice." The exact attitude of these prophets to the sacrificial system is not easy to discover, and the point is discussed, with some divergence of result, in the first two essays. What we have to notice here is that the God who comes into view in their writings is a God whose worship involved in principle the complete transformation of the older sacrificial system.

But when this transformation comes, in post-exilic Judaism, its principle is not that of which we have just spoken. The work of Isaiah, Ezekiel, and " Deutero-Isaiah " had brought to the front the profound conception of the Divine holiness, and it is in this that we must see the background of the priestly system, with its sin-offerings and

[1] Mt. ix. 13.

guilt-offerings.[1] God has become remote. Man can no longer partake even in the residue of the sacrifices. They are more costly, more irrational, but again they bear witness to part of the truth. There is cost as well as mercy in God's ways with man. But how great the cost and how wide the mercy was not seen as yet. Revelation stood still for a while, waiting for the Cross of Christ.

We have said enough to indicate the place of our two brief studies of Old Testament theology, and of Dr. Lukyn Williams' fully illustrated account of the later developments of Rabbinic thought, in our general scheme. For with the New Testament we pass to the revelation which is in Jesus Christ, and to its interpretation by men, who, with whatever imperfections of understanding, accepted it with all their hearts and minds as God's final word to men. And here we have to notice that, while the central teaching of God's forgiveness of sins was new in itself and new in its direct association with the Cross of Jesus, the theological expositions of that teaching were inevitably based upon conceptions drawn from current Judaism. Greek thought comes in later, as the Church became predominantly Gentile, but there is little in the New Testament itself that is not drawn from the circle of Jewish ideas.[2] The great difference now is that man is no longer looking anxiously for something which God may do, but rejoicing in the assurance of something which God has done. Whether we speak of it in terms of conquest, or redemption, or remission of sins, or sacrifice, or salvation, it is God's act in history, wrought by God Himself and utterly beyond man's achieving.

Faith came first, and then, since man if challenged must strive, if only for his own satisfaction, to give account of his faith, theology followed. And so we pass to the historical section of our inquiry.[3]

---

[1] See p. 58 ff.

[2] Whatever else Dr. C. F. Burney may or may not have proved in his *Aramaic Origin of the Fourth Gospel*, he has at least made its Semitic background of thought abundantly clear. And St. Paul is always the true disciple of Gamaliel, and even though his language may at times (mainly in 1 Cor.) show the influence of the mystery cults, his thought is Jewish throughout.

[3] It is perhaps here that the inevitable incompleteness of our volume comes out most clearly. Only a sketch, and that only of some of the more salient features in the history of theories of the Atonement, has been possible. I may perhaps venture to refer the reader who desires a fuller and more connected account, with citation

The student of the history of doctrines of the Atonement is apt to be perplexed at the outset by the difficulty of remembering the statements of an immense number of writers, whose opinions seem often to be divided only by the finest shades of emphasis. They are apt too to think, and sometimes with reason, especially in connection with the patristic writers, that historians of the doctrine draw very broad conclusions from isolated passages, frequently without any serious attempt to appreciate the whole context of thought within which these passages should be read. It is by quotation of this type that advocates of any particular point of view have sometimes claimed support from writers of every period. It is true, for example, that we can quote an Anselmic phrase from the *Epistle to Diognetus*, and another from the *De Incarnatione* of Athanasius, and yet it should be obvious that this cannot prove that a transactional theory of Anselmic type was generally current in the second or fourth century. It is only when we set such passages or phrases against the wider background of ideas about God and the universe that we can appreciate them at their true worth. And it is not easy for us to-day to put ourselves back into the mental attitude of the fourth century, or the twelfth, or even the sixteenth.

The Church set out upon its way with Atonement as an assured and accomplished fact, with a wide range of inherited ideas about God, and with the memory of the things which Jesus had said and done, a memory soon to be enshrined in the pages of the Gospels. The different theories of Atonement, as they arise, represent, not the questioning of the fact, but the testing in history of the inherited ideas about God, bringing them more, though ever imperfectly, into conformity with the God to whom Jesus, by His life and His teaching, bore witness. The Atonement had always a " transactional " character. It was something wrought by God. And never, apart from a few writers in the nineteenth

---

of the more important passages in the original language, to my own *Short History of the Doctrine of the Atonement*, and to Rivière's *Le Dogme de la Redemption*. The appendices to Rashdall's *The Idea of Atonement in Christian Theology* give very complete citations for the earlier part of the history, and there is also a useful catena of passages, selected in support of the substitutionary theory, in Dimock's *The Death of Christ*, a book not well enough known. There is nothing else in English even reasonably complete.

B

century, has it been regarded simply as something wrought
in man. The Church did not make the mistake of confusing
the work of Christ with the work of the Holy Spirit. Justification and sanctification, inseparably connected as they
are, were not one and the same thing. For it was seen
clearly enough that what God has done cannot have meaning
for man unless it has meaning for God Himself. It springs
from an inner necessity of His Being, and just so far as we
understand it, we understand Him.

The history of the doctrine is thus, fundamentally, the
history of man's efforts to read this inner necessity of God,
to understand His character in such a way that man's
experience of Atonement is seen to spring naturally from
it. In the development of this history there have always
been two focal points, the love of God and the Cross of
Christ.

There has never been any doubt in the minds of Christians
that Jesus revealed God as loving, One of whom only the
term Father, of all human or earthly analogies, could fit-
tingly be used. The shortest of all the Creeds, " God is
Love," [1] is at once the most adequate, the most intelligible,
and the most strangely profound. And its pictorial presentation, in the parable of the Prodigal Son, has always
been reckoned a very corner-stone of our Lord's teaching.[2]
How easy it would seem simply to interpret the forgiveness
of sins as the display of God's love, arousing by its fulness
and warmth an answering fire of love in our own hearts!
Such in effect is the so-called " moral " or " ethical " account
of the Atonement. Almost in these terms we find it in
Abelard's *Commentary on the Epistle to the Romans*, in Peter
Lombard's *Sentences*, and in a succession of modern writers,
finding its latest and most learned endorsement in Dr.
Rashdall's Bampton Lectures.

But theories of this kind have to reckon with the Cross.
They may be, and undoubtedly are, true, but they must
expect us to ask of them how and where the Cross can be
fitted into their scheme. For there is no escape from the
centrality of the Cross in the Christian tradition. It is no
accident that makes all the four Gospels lead up to the
Passion narrative, and tell the story that leads from the
Upper Room to the Cross in quite disproportionate detail.

[1] I Jn. iv. 8, 16.
[2] On this, and the difficulties involved, see pp. 124 ff.

And the Cross is no obvious display of the divine love. In itself it stands grim and challenging. If love be the key, as we believe, then we must show how love can make room for such tragedy as this.

Here we may note in passing that though the first disciples had good cause to connect the Cross with the forgiveness of sins, since it was in the very face of that disaster that they had been themselves forgiven, no subsequent generation of Christians has found that connection so natural and so immediate. The saint understands us well enough when we say that it is our sins, our own, here and now, that nail Jesus to the Tree, but for the ordinary, rather good-natured sinner to whom we preach the words have no obvious meaning. The cry of the old pagan, " Would that I had been there with my Goths," is the natural and not dishonourable answer. That the Cross can awaken the sense of sin is, of course, beyond all doubting. To connect it with forgiveness has been the problem of the theologian from the first. But every theology that has not at least attempted to make the connection has failed to hold the attention of men.

In the first phases of theological development the problem was solved simply enough. Had not Isaiah foretold One who should suffer unjustly, going unresisting to His doom, making His grave with the wicked, One who should bear the sin of many and upon whom the Lord has laid the iniquity of us all ? [1] " Those things, which God before had showed by the mouth of all his prophets, that Christ should suffer, he hath so fulfilled." [2] The argument from prophecy, based on passages convincing enough to the exegesis of the day,[3] was sufficient to secure the Cross its place in the purposes of God. Until late in the second century discussion of its meaning is practically confined to the debate with the Jews, in which the fulfilment in Christ of Old Testament prophecies, and the application to Him of such types as the brazen serpent, are the dominant theme.

The accommodation of theology to current Greek thought did not at first take account of the Cross, apart from Gnosticism, which at least deserves the credit for seeing that the Cross is fundamental to the problem. The earlier Apologists as a whole are concerned with the defence of

---

[1] See p. 81 ff.  [2] Acts iii. 18; cf. Acts xxvi. 22, 23.
[3] To our modern eyes it is not easy to find a suffering Messiah in the Old Testament. Isa. liii. is not primarily Messianic.

Christianity on other grounds, and only Justin has anything to say about the Cross. What is of more importance for our purpose is that these writers bring the Christian thought of God as far as possible into line with current Greek philosophical ideas, and the Christian conception of the world into line with current demonology. The Logos doctrine of St. John is taken up and developed by the aid of conceptions of the immanent and the creative Logos, borrowed from Stoicism, and the thought of God as the source of all being, creating, sustaining, regenerating, comes to be characteristic of what is commonly called the Eastern type of theology.[1] Together with this is the intense feeling of freedom from the powers of evil. God is understood as the God who is at war with evil, and His great antagonist, the devil, now comes clearly into the field, replacing, in the third century, the demons of whom Justin had spoken. Here we have, of course, a reversion to the New Testament and to later Jewish thought.

What then did the inner necessity of the being of such a God involve as its objective theory of Atonement? Primarily, undoubtedly, it is, in the Greek fathers, with whom we may reckon Irenaeus, the thought of a new creative act, making good the disaster of the Fall. There is, apart from Athanasius, very little sense of the real gravity of evil as a moral disorder of the human heart. It is rather that God's creative work has been marred, and that He alone, by a new creation, can restore it and bring it to completion.

This thought is, of course, true and profound, and it is wholly objective. It does make God the source of Atonement, but it has the weakness that it leaves the Atonement so achieved almost completely without content. That man is raised up to God means nothing very definite in actual life, if God is viewed as an ultimate creative mystery, only to be described in the abstract terms of Greek philosophy. But this conception does not stand alone. Side by side with it, and giving it positive content, is that of release from the power of the devil, which is found practically wherever these writers try to take account of the Cross.[2] The forms in which this victory is presented are sometimes bizarre enough, but their strangeness is simply due to the attempt to express this cosmic divine victory in terms of a

[1] But see p. 177, and on all this section Dr. Harold Smith's essay.
[2] See p. 183 ff.

fanciful exegesis of the description of Leviathan in the Book of Job. The underlying idea of the utter antagonism between God and evil, and the certainty of His victory, is none the less valuable because of the strange forms in which it is found. But here again the imperfection in the thought of the period is that this victory frequently has little moral or spiritual meaning for man himself. It is as much a victory over fear as over sin. The main interest, in fact, in the study of this period lies in the evidence which appears, more or less sporadically, of a richer conception of God and a correspondingly fuller and more intimate realisation of the nature of evil, preparing the way for the first really comprehensive treatment of Atonement by Anselm and the great schoolmen. It is in the light of this that the rather complex detail in Dr. Harold Smith's essay should be read. In particular the constant appearance of sacrificial language [1] is noteworthy. This rests upon the language of the Bible itself and hardly constitutes a new contribution of thought. And, as in the Bible, it always demands interpretation. The analogy of sacrifice is not in itself a theory of Atonement.

The most important of the conceptions which, almost from the first, comes in to enrich the conception of God is that of justice, or righteousness, or integrity.[2] As early as Irenaeus this thought is prominent. Even the devil must be treated as befits a just God. This emphasis is commonly regarded as specifically Western, and it is certainly dominant in the Latin fathers. We shall not be far astray if we see in it the influence of the great Roman Imperium, a rule which stood for order and for protection against the chaos of the barbarian world quite apart from the character of any particular holder of the Imperial throne. It appears, in fact, in various Eastern writers too, but the Roman Empire stretched East as well as West, and the great hopes which attended the transfer of the Imperial throne to Byzantium at the beginning of the fourth century are more than sufficient to account for the appearance of so-called Western conceptions in the world of Greek thought.

The great exponent of this approach to God is, of course, Augustine, and he is followed by Leo and Gregory the

---

[1] See p. 187 ff.

[2] It should be noted that the Latin *justitia* covers all three conceptions, a fact which has profoundly affected the Western statements of the doctrine.

Great. The immense influence here of Augustine's *De Civitate Dei* has not always been noted. Written at a time when earthly illusions as to the Roman Empire were crumbling before the barbarian invaders, this epoch-making work set up before men's mind the vision of the eternal City of God, the City of unfailing order and justice and righteousness. So far as God is likened to an earthly ruler at all, it is as perfectly just.

And so from Augustine on we find that God's dealings with men come more and more to be interpreted along the lines of such justice as man could understand. The great principles of Roman law, standing grandly dominant over Roman citizen and barbarian conqueror alike, even when the very fabric of the Empire was falling in ruins, seemed to men to be of the eternal order. God is just.

The application of this principle to the Cross was never very fully worked out, though obviously it underlies the passages [1] where Christ is spoken of as a substitute or equivalent for man. Only in Gregory the Great, the last great Latin father of the early period, is there any signs of its development into a formal penal theory. And after Gregory darkness falls upon the theological as well as upon the political world.

But before we pass on to Anselm we should notice that this justice of Roman Law is not in any way incompatible with love. In Augustine love and justice go together. Even in God's dealings with the devil both are to be seen. "The devil," he says, "is a stranger neither to His power nor to His goodness." [2] The point is important for the criticism, and for the vindication, of later restatements of the Penal Theory. The greatest failure of the Protestant divines was failure to bear it in mind. But the failure was unnecessary, and a fuller understanding of Augustine would have prevented it.

With the close of the eleventh century, and the gradual stabilising of the political world, the great age of theology dawns, with Anselm, Bernard, and Abelard. Bernard is theologically a simple-minded upholder of tradition, but he transforms the tradition everywhere by his intense mysticism. Abelard, intellectually a rebel, despite his great learning, makes bold to substitute love for all the traditional explana-

---

[1] See pp. 189 f.
[2] *De Trin.* xiii. 12. The whole passage should be studied.

tions, or rather to interpret them all in terms of love.  Misunderstood, and officially silenced, he nevertheless exercised an influence upon his age at least as great as that of his accuser, Bernard.  Anselm, the greatest of the three, dominates the theology of the Middle Ages for two reasons. In the first place he lays down clearly and finally the principle of *necessitas* as applied to God.  That which God does springs from that which God is.  Such is the faith which precedes reason, for reason rests upon it, and it is faith in a rational God, a God of whose doings we could, if we could carry our reasoning far enough, give account, a God, in a word, of whom theology is possible.[1]  This is the fundamental principle of scholasticism, of which the crowning glory is the *Summa* of Aquinas.  In the second place, and as involved in this *necessitas*, he sees that we must not refuse to think of God in terms of the highest conception of human personality available to us.  It was in the light of this principle that he transformed the doctrine of the Atonement by means of the conception of the honour of God.

To understand this change we must look to changed political conditions.  The new basis of order and security had come, these many years past, to rest not upon justice, embodied in a system or in a sovereign, but in personal loyalty to a leader.  The honour of the prince was his right to command and his due was implicit and willing obedience. It is simply the feudal principle, and in some ways it curiously recalls the days of the Warrior-God of Israel. But as against the principle of abstract justice it has the immense advantage that it is personal.  The thought of the justice of God in itself makes man tremble for his sin; the thought of God's honour brings him near to worship.  And worship is more than fear.

Such is the background of the Anselmic theory of satisfaction, expounded in Dr. Whately's essay.  It is another gap in our treatment of the subject, perhaps inevitable in a volume of this size, that the full discussion and development of this theory in the great schoolmen has not been given a place.  To attempt to deal here, in a few words, with so wide a subject is obviously impossible.  It must suffice to point out the guiding principle of that development, in the growing richness of the personal conception of God upon which it rests.  It is perhaps an accident that Anselm never

[1] See p. 208.

equates the necessity of God's action with His love, since
he goes so far as to see in it " the immutability of His goodness." In some ways, indeed, the conception of honour
goes further than that of love, since it leads us towards that
thought of holiness which is love and justice in one.[1] Anselm
does not carry us on this further step, with the result that
we find ourselves disappointed in his conception of sin [2] and
inclined to dispute his argument that the death of Christ,
even, as he insists, a death freely and gladly incurred for
God's honour, could really establish that honour or really
affect the status of sinful man. He is at his very weakest
in his account of the way in which the effects of the Cross
become available for us, by what appears to be almost the
accident that God's honour will not permit Him to leave
so great an offering unrequited, and that, since Christ already
has all things, the gift must be bestowed, in " fitness," [3]
upon man, whose life He has condescended to share.

The schoolmen, and most notably Bonaventura and
Aquinas, are freed from this lame conclusion to the Anselmic
argument, which in principle they accept, by their vastly
grander conception of God. In their writings the logic of
the scholar, trusting human categories as far as they will
go, blends with the awe and intimacy of the mystic. Sin is
viewed in its true light, as not only disobedience but an
outrage against love, and as the thought of God's honour
passes over into that of His supreme holiness, so the thought
of satisfaction merges in that of sacrifice, the only word in
which man has ever been able to rest content when speaking
of the Cross.[4] This interpretation of the Anselmic theory in
terms of sacrifice has been characteristic of Tridentine and
post-Tridentine Roman theology. It has been widespread
also in Protestant thought through Arminian influence, and,
resting as it does upon a broad basis of New Testament
evidence, it seems likely that when misunderstandings are
cleared away it will form part of that common ground in
theology upon which Christians of all schools and traditions
can meet.

The Reformers seem hardly to have been conscious that

[1] See p. 210.          [2] See pp. 201 f.
[3] The word *convenientia*, which plays a very important part in
Anselm's argument, in the end means practically the same thing as
*necessitas*, since it is impossible to suppose that God does what is
not fitting. See p. 207.
[4] See p. 293.

they were completely transforming the doctrine of Atonement once more. The Anselmic theory had been in form legalistic, and legalism comes again to the front through changes in the political world. Feudalism had gone, save for some local anachronisms, and Europe was passing through the birth-throes of the modern constitutional monarchies. Justice, national and international, stood higher than princes. Roman imperial law came to its own again, as the basis of new and living codes. Indeed it did more, as the whole idea of Law rises beyond the boundaries of nations and codes to sublime and almost mystical heights, a development in which the majestic structure of Canon Law played its part. In the period following the Reformation we find the influence of this conception everywhere. It is the era of the growth of international law, and Grotius, a great pioneer in this field, is also a pioneer in doctrinal theory, working out his conception of God and of Atonement upon lines of benevolent and constitutional government. It is the era in which, with the growth of science, the idea of natural law develops as an immense system, and, for the illumination of modern scientists be it noted, it would probably never have been called law at all if it had not been thought of as the law of God. In philosophy we have the movement of ideas which leads past Butler to Kant and his austerely magnificent vision of a moral law, so supreme that God Himself seems in its presence to become a mere postulate, brought in to guarantee its authority and finality. And in some early nineteenth-century writers, of whom Bushnell is a striking example,[1] the eternal law seems to stand even above God, who is its First Subject, teaching man through the Cross to obey that law which He Himself observes. In this period, of which Calvinism is the typical theology, the inner necessity of God's action is seen as justice, and the more personal aspects of the thought of Anselm and Aquinas, though they survive indeed in Luther,[2] pass out of sight in his successors. It is very striking to find Melanchthon using Anselm's argument practically

---

[1] Bushnell's *The Vicarious Sacrifice*, with its legal exposition of Atonement and its interpretation of the whole in terms of love, is one of the greatest books upon the subject ever written. Dale's bitter attack on it, in his *Atonement*, is based upon both misunderstanding and misquotation

[2] See p. 225.

without change, save that justice, and penal justice, replaces
satisfaction. Apparently he is quite unaware of the magnitude of the change in outlook which results.

For justice, viewed in this way, has become blind, impersonal, inexorable. It is criminal law, and it demands
and must have the full and exact penalty for sin. And as
in life " the sins of the fathers are visited upon the children,"
the innocent suffering for the guilty by the sheer operation
of natural cause and effect, acting by laws which seemed to
be the Law of God Himself, so there seemed nothing strange
in the belief that Christ should have intervened to take this
penal consequence upon Himself, and that God's judgment
upon sin should thereby be fulfilled and satisfied.

The Penal Theory of Atonement was, in fact, a new
theory, though there were, naturally enough, hints of this
way of thinking in many earlier writers,[1] though it nearly
came into existence in the seventh century instead of the
sixteenth,[2] and though Anselm refuted it in advance.[3] Its
great merit was its real sense of the gravity of sin and of
the righteousness of God. Its great fault was its loss of
personal values, which allowed the statement of a theory of
vicarious punishment with a bare literalness impossible to
modern thought. Unless Jesus is not merely one of us but
one with us, unless He is not merely God's Son, but very
God, the Penal Theory is untrue to the principles of justice
upon which it rests, and in its literal form it has rightly
been cast aside by the majority of thinking people to-day.
To the process of its transformation we must now turn, and
the story is simply the story of the re-assertion of personal
values.

Justice in the abstract is not only impersonal, but, if
put into practice, liable to become desperately cruel. Of
all periods in the history of the development of legal punishments the sixteenth and seventeenth centuries have an
unenviable supremacy in the barbarity with which these
punishments were inflicted and in their complete disregard
of the criminal as a human being.[4] The fact is not irrelevant
to the understanding of an age which could view with
complacency the doctrines of limited Atonement and of

---

[1] See especially pp. 189, 191.     [2] See p. 22.
[3] *Cur Deus Homo*, Bk. I. c. 8.
[4] I owe this comment to a great legal authority, Dr. W. Ash-
burner, in private conversation.

reprobation, involving the sheer, and apparently arbitrary, predestination of the greater part of humanity to eternal death. Happily for the credit of mankind, such a mood could not last, and the doctrine with which it was so closely linked went down before the decent feeling of a world awakening as from a nightmare. That there were real values in the doctrine is undoubted. It is the main purpose of this volume to assert those values. But if they are to be preserved they must be restated in terms of a newer and more enlightened mood, a mood which owes not a little to the influence of that New Testament which the Reformers themselves made available for its use.

Various factors can be traced in the coming of this better mind. There is the study of the open Bible, to which we have just alluded. There is the growing sense of personal and individual values, which led to a new political theory, that of democracy, of which the essence is not government by the many but government for the many. The modern civilised world is still working out experiments upon this theme, not always with success. There is the demand for a God who can be worshipped, a fundamental need of man to which the great Catholic tradition, loyally Anselmic, bore continuous witness throughout the whole period. And there is the development of free rational criticism, emerging, especially in the Socinians, from the great Humanist movement, itself one of the most worthy by-products of mediæval learning.

It is difficult altogether to separate these influences, but a few words must be said about them before closing this introductory chapter. We may take each of the four points in turn.

(1) The great Reformers followed the example of the Schoolmen in using the Bible to substantiate their theology. Indeed they exalted the authority of the Bible to an extent which has created real difficulty for their successors, since they tended to claim an inerrancy for the words of Scripture which frequently obscured instead of revealing its supreme spiritual value. And it is hardly unfair to say that they again and again interpreted Scripture from their theology, instead of building up a theology which used the whole of the Biblical material. The Bible has proved itself too great a book to be straitened by such usage. The Old Testament has gradually given up its secrets, until now we can trace

the progressive revelation of God, if not with certainty in every detail, at least sufficiently clearly to see in it a true preparation for the Gospel. And in the New Testament the figure of Jesus had stood out more and more clearly, until it can be said that we know Him, so far as records can give us that knowledge, better than any generation of Christians has done since the first.

But as this study of the Bible progressed, and long before it reached modern scientific accuracy, interest was turned from the death of Jesus as an isolated fact to the whole incarnate life of which it formed the climax. The Socinian from the first saw the Cross mainly as the prelude to the Resurrection. And the later movement of thought in Calvinism, with its rather dreary neo-scholastic debate about the active and passive obedience of Christ, is really the working out of this theme. It was not new. The stress on obedience in the Epistle to the Hebrews reappears in Anselm, and Anselm and Bernard alike agree in saying that it was not the death but the good-will of Him who died that was pleasing to God. But it was novel, and indeed bitterly contested, in the seventeenth century, until Turretin, the last of the great theologians of rigid Calvinism, practically, by his admissions, surrenders the case. Thus stress was laid once more upon the Incarnation, and not upon the Cross alone, and this stress again is wholly Anselmic.[1]

In the nineteenth century this tendency led to a series of attempts to recover " the Jesus of history," a movement in which the greatest name is that of Ritschl. Liberal Protestant theologians unveiled the figure of a great ethical teacher. And while emphasis was again laid upon the love of God, mysticism and the richer values of worship were at a discount as compared with simplicity and goodness. Christ's words and example stood, for these writers, higher than His death. And, correspondingly, in some writers of the so-called " Moral " school, Atonement seemed to vanish in sentimentality.[2]

Again the Bible has been too great for its exponents. Here the most important influence has been that of Schweitzer, who has forced us to see how interpretations can differ if they rest upon the presuppositions of critics.

[1] The *Cur Deus Homo* is primarily a treatise on the necessity for an Incarnation.

[2] On this whole section see the comments of Mr. Essex on Ritschl and Stevens, pp. 243 ff.

The whole tendency of the present day is away from an easy assurance that we can wholly understand Jesus by the record of His teaching, and back to the belief that it is in His dying that we know Him best. The Cross is coming to its own again, and therewith we find that men are tiring of subjective theories of Atonement. We are coming to see once more that for our salvation more than instruction, more than an example, is needed. We look to that which God has wrought for us in Christ, wrought doubtless in love, but wrought through the divine tragedy of Calvary.

(2) The preceding paragraphs have indicated a changing outlook which is closely paralleled in the social and political world. It began with Humanism and has developed into humanitarianism. The famous phrase of utilitarianism, " the greatest good of the greatest number," might be written as its motto. At the outset of the change stands Grotius,[1] with his conception of God as the benevolent Ruler, who governs through punishment, it is true, but punishment directed not to the vindication of justice, but to the general good of His subjects. Thus the deterrent, and later the reformative, aspects of punishment come into view.[2] This so-called Rectoral theory of atonement has influenced almost all later writers, though not in the form in which Grotius states it. Its general principle is that it uses the highest social relationship which man can recognise as the basis of man's interpretation of God. It has the great advantage over the Penal Theory proper that it makes possible a personal conception of man's relation to God, and it does not at all preclude a thoroughly objective account of Atonement as springing from that inner necessity of God's Being which this relationship involves.[3] In its later forms, under the direct influence of the New Testament, theories of this kind have looked rather to God as a wise and loving Father, and have striven to interpret the Cross on this basis.[4]

[1] See p. 237.

[2] The change has been conspicuous in law as well as in theology.

[3] It is this that distinguishes the position of Grotius from the " Acceptilatio " theory of Scotus, not elsewhere mentioned in these essays, as being irrelevant to their main purpose. Scotus regarded the worth of the sacrifice of the Christ as resting simply upon God's will to accept it, and not upon its own adequacy. But this introduces arbitrariness into the divine action, and therewith any approach to it by man's understanding becomes impossible.

[4] So especially Erskine, McLeod Campbell, Moberly, and Scott Lidgett. See pp. 247 ff.

It is clear that we come here very near to the heart of the whole matter, as we should expect, since we are using the language of Jesus Himself. For fatherhood is ideally the expression of a love that fulfils itself in sacrifice. And in such love there is nothing weakly sentimental. Of all things love can least ignore sin, or content itself so long as the sin is not put away. Love alone is wholly inexorable, and therefore wholly just. Love must punish, but the punishment is not the arbitrary equivalent for sin, imposed by a code. For in the governance of God love is that judgment upon sin which is the basis of the moral law itself, and love alone can judge sin adequately, since it is within the sphere of love that the truth of the sin lies and that the disaster of sin has been wrought.

And still we have to ask whether love is a better term than holiness, the word to which Barth and Otto are pointing us to-day. For love has been lowered in common usage by emotionalism and shallow optimism, and to many it has associations which make it in itself misleading. Nevertheless, without the aid of the conception of love, holiness is apt to remain impersonal, mysterious, lacking in ethical content. Probably, for men of to-day, it is best that the two stand side by side, with love still in the first place, since it was in holiness that men first came to worship God, but in love that Jesus first taught men to know the God of their worship.

(3) This last point reminds us that the impetus to worship had been characteristic of the Anselmic position. The thought of God's honour is not far removed from that of His holiness. And it cannot be denied that one result of the Reformation was very definite loss upon this side. It may be true that much mediæval worship was mingled with superstition and that reform was urgently needed, but in fact the whole trend of thought in the Reformation theology rendered true worship far more difficult. The God of penal justice was a God who could be preached, and who could be approached in prayer, and Evangelicals have ever been mighty in preaching and prayer. But the awe-stricken and yet loving approach of man in adoration to the God of holiness and love, which is the deepest need of his life, was little in evidence in the Churches which the Reformation touched or created. Evangelicals owe a debt here which they are only now beginning to recognise to the maintenance throughout the last three hundred years, by those who, with

most assurance and certainly with no ill claim, call themselves Catholic, of an ideal of worship as fundamental to the Christian life. On every hand this need is recognised to-day, as deeper and richer conceptions of God are touching man's imagination. And those who claim to re-interpret for this age Anselm's great thought of the honour of God, should be among the foremost in pleading and encouraging the return to a fuller conception of worship which that thought involves.

(4) The last of the great broadening principles with which we have to deal is that of the free and ever more rigorous use of reason. The great Scholastic system of thought breaks down with the indeterminism of Scotus and the nominalism of William of Occam. The Reformation was in no sense a philosophical movement, nor even, apart from Socinianism, liberal in its modes of thought, but it opened the way for the great modern developments of philosophy, claiming to interpret man, the world, and God in their own right and apart from theological presuppositions. To tell the story of this reconquest of the world of reason, even in headings, is obviously impossible here. We can only note one or two points which concern us more directly.

In the first place, Calvinism had the dignity of a great moral achievement, but it lacked inner coherence as a system. And from the first the new philosophic temper found it intolerant and inconsistent. Descartes and Pascal, seeking a rational God in a rational universe, the Cambridge Platonists, recovering the mystical avenue to truth, Lord Herbert of Cherbury and Locke, seeking that " Natural Religion " which is common to all men and for the confirmation of which revelation was given, all alike find Calvinism intolerable. Since those days philosophy has striven hard to come to terms with life, and the philosophical account of ultimate reality has taken many forms. The optimism of the eighteenth century saw in God the supreme and remote Creator-Mechanician, the Ordainer, in Leibniz' phrase, of pre-established harmony. Evil was an illusion, left to the Calvinists, and all was well, in the best of all possible worlds. The nineteenth century, shaken by the spectacle of pain, cruelty, and disorder in Nature, scared by the political chaos of the Revolution, and thwarted in its philosophical quest for an Absolute, a Deity in whom no contradiction is unreconciled, fell from optimism either to the moral pessimism of such writers as Schopenhauer and von Hartmann, or to the philosophical agnosticism of a

Matthew Arnold or a Herbert Spencer, looking for a vague
" Eternal which makes for righteousness," or erecting in
the darkness an altar to " the Unknown and Unknowable
God." Science meanwhile has gone upon its way, with its
mighty hypothesis of evolution, and its bitter disappointment at discovering how little evolution explains, either of
its processes or of its results. And now philosophy and
science, joining hands, are experimenting with conceptions
of emergent realities, each higher grade of being arising
unpredictable and unexplained from that next below it,
and revealing the meaning of that which has been in the
light of that which is.[1]

It is impossible to refrain from pointing out the close
parallel between this and the Logos conceptions of the later
Greek philosophy. The thought irresistibly suggests itself
that modern theology will be forced by the philosophers
to recover one last value which seemed to have been lost
in the long passage through the centuries, the idea of God
as Creator, restoring by a new creative act His own original
creation. We saw that in the patristic period this approach
failed to give adequate content to the idea of God. But
now the concepts of justice and holiness and love have
each been stressed in turn. The human figure of Jesus
glows and lives before us again. And we who now seek to
recover in worship the full sense of the holiness of God,
see in that holiness love more adequate than any human
love, and justice more perfect than any human justice.
But we may see still more. For holiness is no static un-
attainable glory, but the self-renewing and creative splendour
of the Creator-God. And as in the Cross we see love displayed to the uttermost in forgiveness of sins, and the
righteousness of God fulfilled to the uttermost in the condemnation of sins, so may we see the fulness of God's
creative purpose made manifest, the Incarnation complete
once and for all in the Person of His Son, God for man
conquering sin, and man in Man dying unto sin, that man
through Man reaching up to God by faith might rise in
holiness from the death of sin unto everlasting life.

Does this pass understanding ? Then let us worship the
more, for so, beyond understanding, comes the peace of
God.

[1] For an invaluable discussion of the Incarnation in the light of
such conceptions see L. S. Thornton, *The Incarnate Lord*.

# I

## SACRIFICE IN THE OLD TESTAMENT

### By L. B. Cross

ANY attempt to interpret the origin and meaning of sacrifice among the Hebrews which leaves out of account their conception of God and of his relation to themselves must necessarily be inadequate; for, whatever the ruling motive behind sacrifice may have been, no one can deny that it had as one of its objects the establishment of some kind of contact between the deity and the worshipper. This must, then, be our excuse for a brief survey of the fundamental religious beliefs of the Hebrews.

Much has been written on the conception of God in the Old Testament, and perhaps the most striking result of modern research on the subject has been the emphasis laid upon its evolutionary nature.[1] The early ancestors of the Hebrews, in common with all other people, began with very rudimentary conceptions, and advanced, through a period to be calculated not in hundreds but in thousands of years, to the ethical monotheism which we find expressed so beautifully in the Wisdom Literature of the last two centuries B.C.

Unfortunately, we cannot follow this evolutionary process from its beginning in detail, for with the Hebrews, as with other people, the art of writing came in comparatively late. We must therefore begin our survey with such ancient literary portions of the Old Testament as the sources J and E, together with other earlier fragments, where we may expect to find survivals of beliefs dating from the early period of the monarchy and even from more remote days.[2]

---

[1] See article on "The Religion of Israel," by E. Kautzsch, in *H.D.B.*, Vol. V.

[2] For an attractive and lucid exposition of the literary analysis of the Pentateuch see D. C. Simpson, *Pentateuchal Criticism (1924)*.

C

God to the Hebrew was primarily a War God.  Were not the title *Yahweh Sabaoth* sufficient to show this, we should have no hesitation in coming to this conclusion after examining some of the Old Testament war songs.  Of these the Song of Moses contained in Exod. xv. 1 is typical, " I will sing unto the Lord, for he hath triumphed gloriously :  the horse and his rider hath he thrown into the sea " ;  or again the Song of Deborah in Judges v. 4, " Lord, when thou wentest forth out of Seir, when thou marchedst out of the field of Edom, the earth trembled, the heavens also dropped, yea, the clouds dropped water."  In such passages as Exod. xiv. 25, which recounts the overthrow of the Egyptians, or Josh. x. 11, 12, where Yahweh assists in the battle of Beth-horon, and even as late as the time of Elisha and Isaiah, this same rôle is given to God by the Hebrew historians.

It might be asked, Why did Yahweh [1] fill this rôle ?  The answer is to be found in a further characteristic attributed to him—that of a landed proprietor.  He was ever ready to enlarge his borders at the expense of neighbouring peoples and gods, and he had to fight in order to gain and retain his kingdom.[2]  As a landed proprietor, he was also the God of productivity, giving to the earth her increase, making the folds full of sheep and the oxen strong to labour, and giving the former and the latter rains.  Within his territorial limits he was absolute, exercising the rights of a feudal lord, and commanding the service and support of his thanes and serfs ; but apart from the power of his sword he had no rights outside those limits.  On every side he was hemmed in by powerful rivals ever as ready to dispute his claims to the land as he was to challenge theirs.

This idea of local almightiness, however, had its limitations, for it made it necessary for the deity to be on good terms with his people.  If they were exterminated, or became apathetic towards him, it meant a corresponding decrease in his power, and the diminution of his territorial domain.  In consequence, a very close bond of union existed between the two.  He always ran the risk of becoming one of the jinn,

---

[1] This form of the divine name is supported both by philology and by ancient tradition.  *Jehovah* is philologically impossible, being a hybrid word, formed by combining the consonants of Yahweh with the vowels of *'Adonai* (' Lord ').

[2] See Judges xi. 24.

demon-possessed animals which inhabited desert places. This idea of the interdependence of Yahweh and his people survived, in popular religion at any rate, up to the time of Isaiah. In the early period there was always a mutual necessity for an at-one-ment.

Though this mutual obligation existed, the advantage was invariably on the side of the deity, owing to his superior power. In consequence, a man was at a corresponding disadvantage; he might rebel, but he was eventually forced into submission. Yahweh could always give or deny prosperity, he could shorten or prolong life. Hence the natural attitude to him was one of submission; there was a constant endeavour by the worshipper to produce in the mind of the deity an attitude favourable to health and prosperity. In return the Hebrew was mindful of his obligation; he had to fight for him. Patriotism and religion were synonymous. The best, and indeed the only way of expressing religious fervour was by feats of arms, or by other actions which were conducive to national, and therefore to divine prosperity. Individual lives were only of value in so far as they were efficient members of the nation; Yahweh exhibited his gratitude to the individual—a not disinterested gratitude—by granting a prolific progeny, to the Hebrew the acme of blessedness. Once a man had become senile, or a woman barren or beyond the age of bearing children, Yahweh had no use for them; there was no future life in store, but only a nebulous existence in Sheol, whither his active jurisdiction did not extend.

In consequence, sin, as failure to attain to high ethical and moral standards such as those inculcated by the eighth-century prophets, was not known. The greatest sin was apostasy, the next, refusal or inability to produce children. Disobedience to the will of the Divine Patron was likewise sin, but that will was not always moral in its volitions; it was invariably selfish, sometimes whimsical. This failure to appreciate sin as moral wrong, and the conception of God as a self-seeking tyrant, were responsible for the justification, in the name of religion, of brutal and barbarous deeds. Of these, the early sources of the Old Testament are full, especially such passages as recount the deeds of those who did exploits.[1] The revered Abraham was not above practising fraudulence, Moses was guilty of homicide which could

---

[1] See account of conquest of Canaan in Josh. i–xii

hardly be called justifiable, Joshua and Samuel of brutal cruelty; yet all acted in the interests of their deity.

Despite the basis of obligation on which the relations between Yahweh and his people were founded, these relations were not always confined to mere business transactions, though it would seem that most were prompted to a greater or less degree by this motive. Occasionally the veil of self-interest is lifted from the history of the Hebrews, and disinterested devotion flickers feebly forth; [1] but positive unselfish love, either on the part of Yahweh or his people, never illumines their somewhat dark national and individual records, until at any rate a late date. Fear was the main-spring of their religious zeal, and only when that was least prevalent, in times of victory, deliverance, and plenty, was there any note of joy or thankfulness expressed in their religious observances.

This lack of disinterested piety, and the prevalence of fear as the inspiration of their religious life, combined with unsuccessful campaigns, produced in the Hebrews a strong inferiority complex. This tended to increase their sense of dependence upon Yahweh, and in consequence encouraged the establishment of methods or channels whereby contact with him could be gained. These appear from the Old Testament to have been of two kinds, personal and impersonal, represented by the men of God on the one hand, by material objects on the other. Of the former it must suffice here to say that they were of two classes, the prophet and the priest, the one claiming to reveal Yahweh's present or future designs to the nation or the individual, the other administering and interpreting his ancient commands, or consuetudinary law.[2] It is with the second means of contact that we must deal fully, for that included sacrifice.

That sacrifice was a means of obtaining contact with Yahweh no one will dispute. The really vexed question to

---

[1] This may perhaps be seen in the obedience of Moses to the commands of Yahweh, Exod. iii. 10, *seq.*

[2] Buchanan Gray says, "The prophet spoke out of individual, direct personal experience; the priest out of the stored wisdom and collective experience of his class. The great personalities are to be sought among the prophets; the living force in times of crises is theirs; but the maintenance of a permanent ethical and religious tradition, which needed at times, no doubt, vivifying by the direct law and challenge of the prophet, was the task of the priest." *Sacrifice in the Old Testament*, p. 223 (*1925*).

which we must address ourselves is whether that contact was considered to have been established by means of bribing the deity, the sacrifice being the bribe offered, or by means of a sacramental communion, the sacrifice being the medium of that communion. These two interpretations of sacrifice, the gift theory and communion theory, represent two divergent schools of thought on the subject, championed in England respectively by Buchanan Gray and Robertson Smith. Neither writer is so extreme as to rule out the possibility of both ideas having been present, yet neither has any doubt as to which was the more primary.

In considering the meaning of sacrifice in connection with the early sources of Hebrew literature, there is nothing more misleading than the terminology used by the translators of the English Versions. The word *sacrifice* itself has, owing to post-exilic Jewish and later Christian influences, been associated with doctrinal beliefs which would seem to be wholly unwarranted by the narratives. Similarly, the word *offering* when used in compound words such as burnt-offering and peace-offering has no counterpart in the Hebrew text, and therefore has nothing to justify its inclusion in the English. It may be well, then, in view of any confusion which may arise owing to mistranslations, or the intrusion of later theological presuppositions, to discuss briefly the Hebrew terminology of sacrifice.[1]

The two words used most commonly of sacrifices are *'olah* and *zebaḥ*, translated respectively burnt-offering and sacrifice. Buchanan Gray in his careful examination of the meaning of these words shows that the former can bear no meaning other than " what ascends," or " what is burnt," and the latter " what is slain." Both refer not to the object of the sacrifice, but to its method of treatment. Another word, *shelem*, constantly used as synonymous with *zebaḥ*, is translated peace-offering, but this again would seem to be unwarranted, since its meaning is doubtful, and at the most we can only go so far as to say that it was something associated with requital. Of the other commonly used, but often mistranslated words, *minḥah* is the most important, and wherever used in pre-exilic literature, has the meaning gift, though it is not used exclusively of gifts to the deity. Other

[1] For a full exposition see Buchanan Gray, *Sacrifice in the Old Testament*, p. 3 *seq.*

sacrificial terms, such as sin-offering and guilt-offering, we shall not discuss here, since they are late in both usage and origin.   Hence we may conclude that, with the exception of one word (*minḥah*), practically no light is thrown upon the meaning of sacrifice by its terminology.   There is certainly no word which would, at any rate from the point of view of etymology, make us associate sacrifice with the idea of communion.   Since, then, terminology throws little or no light upon the meaning of sacrifice, let us turn to examine the occasions upon which sacrifices were offered, and then to the ritual employed.

Occasions of sacrifice may be divided into two classes : those which were specified, and those which were not.   This distinction seems to be so clearly marked that it would be as well to treat each separately.   According to the Code of the Covenant,[1] all Hebrews were compelled to present themselves before Yahweh at one of his sanctuaries on three occasions during each year : at the feast of unleavened bread, the feast of weeks or harvests, and the feast of ingathering.   At none of these feasts was a Hebrew to come before Yahweh empty-handed, but he was to bring on each occasion those firstfruits such as were connected with each of the three productive seasons.   These firstfruits would seem to have been of three kinds : firstfruits of man's male issue [2] and domestic animals, of his cereals, and of the fruits of the land.   Apparently all were to be presented at the altar, and handed over, either to the deity direct, or through his priests.   There were, however, two exceptions to this rule : the firstborn of man and of unclean domestic animals were not to be sacrificed, but were to be commuted for some clean animal which could be offered in the same way as, and along with, the other firstfruits.   What are we to infer from this wholesale presentation of firstfruits by every male Hebrew ?   Let us note two important considerations which are apparent from the narrative.   First, only man's own male firstborn, his livestock, and his agricultural products were presented ; there is no evidence that jewels, weapons

---

[1] Exod. xxiii. 15 ff.; cf. xxxiv. 18 ff.

[2] It is probable that human sacrifices were offered at one time by the Hebrews, see Gen. xxii.; Judges xi. 31; I Kings xvi. 34; cp. II Kings iii. 27.   Archæological research has shown that child sacrifice was common in Palestine.   The firstborn may, however, have been devoted to the local sanctuaries as prostitutes.

of war, or agricultural implements were included.[1]  Secondly,
what was brought to the altar was always in edible form,
though, as we have seen, in some cases commutation of the
original offering into an article of food was necessary before
it could be presented.  Surely there can be only one interpretation of these sacrificial acts : they represented the gift
to Yahweh of what he, as the god of productivity, had given
to man.  We have seen that the prevalent conception of
Yahweh in the early literature was that he was a god of war,
and that he gave or withheld the increase of all things ; such
a god was to be expected to need for his own use, at any rate
some portion of the things which he had given to his people.
But what was he to do with them ?  The nature of the gifts
would suggest that he would eat them, and that the Hebrews
thought he did is, to say the least, rendered likely by the
presence of a number of passages throughout the Old
Testament which suggest that Yahweh, like human beings,
ate ordinary food.[2]  Yahweh was essentially a god confined
to his own land, and passages implying his habitation in it,
and not in heaven, are not wanting.[3]  We may conclude,
then, that at any rate the most likely interpretation to be
given to these annual feasts is that they represented the
presentation to Yahweh of his portion of the increase which
he had been responsible for, and that, just as food was
necessary to the life of man, so too it was to that of the
deity.  These offerings would represent Yahweh's fixed
annual dues, and would insure his continued existence.

What of the occasions other than these specified ones
upon which similar offerings were made to Yahweh ?  These,
by their very nature, cannot so easily be collected together,
for they depended upon the particular circumstances of the
moment.  However, it would seem, from the accounts of
sacrificial offerings mentioned in the early sources, that they
may roughly be divided into three groups : occasions of
great national or individual crisis, occasions of special

---

[1] The golden gifts of I Sam. vi. 3 are Philistine, not Hebrew, and
those mentioned in Num. vii. and xxxi. 50 are late and represent
gifts for temple adornment.  The ornaments of Judges viii. 24 represent not gifts to Yahweh but contributions towards the manufacture
of an image.

[2] Gen. viii. 21; xviii. 5; Num. xxviii. 2; Judges ix. 13; I Sam.
xxvi. 19; other passages which repudiate the idea presuppose that
it was held by some, Ps. l. 12; Lev. xxvi. 31; Amos v. 21.

[3] See Gen. xxviii. 16, 19; Exod. iii. 4; Judges v. 4, etc.

thanksgiving, and occasions when treaties or covenants were being ratified.    On all occasions such as these, either a burnt-offering, or a burnt-offering and a peace-offering were presented, and in every instance the object offered was food.    Let us turn now to examine some of these non-specified occasions.

Examples of sacrifices at times of crisis are particularly interesting, and show that almost invariably they belong to the burnt-offering type,[1] though in one case a peace-offering accompanied the burnt-offering.[2]    These burnt-offerings alone were brought by Abraham in obedience to the whim of his Almighty Patron, by Balaam and Balak, by Gideon when embarking upon his new and great adventure, by Samuel when a Philistine invasion was impending, by Saul on a similar occasion, by Solomon at the outset of his reign, and by Elijah on Mt. Carmel.    Occasions of thanksgiving when burnt-offerings alone[3] were presented are to be found in Noah's sacrifice, in that of Jephthah upon his return from victory, in that of Manoah after he had been promised a son, and in that presented by the men of Beth-shemesh upon the return of the ark.    Burnt-offerings accompanied by peace-offerings[4] were presented by Jethro after the escape from Egypt, by Aaron when celebrating the inauguration of the Golden Calf cult, by Joshua after his first victories, by David when bringing the ark to Jerusalem and when building a new altar there.    Covenant sacrifices,[5] though not so common, may be noted as having accompanied the agreement between Yahweh and Abraham, that between Laban and Jacob, and the Covenant at Sinai.

From this representative but by no means exhaustive list of occasions upon which sacrifices were offered, it is clear that they were such as would well justify the presentation of gifts to the deity.    These may have been given either as bribes or as spontaneous thankofferings.    Furthermore, with the possible exception of the covenant sacrifices, there is no example in early Hebrew literature of an occasion of sacrifice which would demand an interpretation of it as an act of communion; every occasion mentioned is satisfactorily

---

[1] Gen. xxii.; Num. xxiii.; Judges vi. 26; I Sam. vii. 9; xiii. 12; I Kings iii. 4; xviii. 33.
[2] I Sam. xiii. 9.
[3] Gen. viii. 20; Judges xi. 31; xiii. 16; I Sam. vi. 14.
[4] Exod. xviii. 12; xxxii. 6; II Sam. vi. 13 ff.; xxiv. 10 ff.
[5] Gen. xv. 9; xxxi. 44, 46; Exod. xxiv. 5.

explained by the gift theory, and indeed demands it. We may, therefore, for the present at any rate, conclude that these offerings represented gifts from individuals, or groups of individuals, to the deity upon special but not specified occasions. Just as those offered at the three great festive seasons of the year represented Yahweh's annual dues, so these may be taken as having represented bonuses in return for his favour and protection in straitened circumstances.

Bearing in mind these tentative conclusions, we may now turn to the ritual employed upon the presentation of the offering at the sanctuary. This differed according to the kind of offering made. The burnt-offering, after the blood had been drained off and the hide and other apparently worthless parts discarded, was presented whole upon the altar and burnt; neither the offerer nor the priest retained any of the victim. The peace-offering, in like manner, was subjected to the blood ritual, but only a part of the animal, the fat, was burnt on the altar, the rest being appropriated and eaten by the offerer and his family after the priest, if any was present,[1] had taken his portion. What was the significance of this ritual?

According to Buchanan Gray, all Hebrew sacrifices in origin were primarily gifts, and this was especially so with the burnt-offering; but he makes certain reservations, especially in connection with the pouring out of the blood against the altar, the application of it, in some cases, to the offerer, and the eating of a part of the victim by the priest and the offerer in the ritual of the peace-offering. To quote his words,[2] " While what are called Jewish sacrifices were all of them certainly gifts and felt to be such, some of them were also something more. The fire-ritual to which nearly all gifts at the altar were subject has been, and may perhaps, without overstraining in the absence of clear indication to the contrary, be explained as organically connected with the conception of gift to God; by means of the fire the food presented was sublimated into a form which to developing conceptions of deity appeared more suited for consumption by the deity. In part, again, the ritual has been explained as a means of conveying to the deity the part of the victim

---

[1] It would appear that in many of the early examples of sacrifice no professional priest is understood to be present, e.g. Noah, Abraham, Isaac, Jacob, offer without. See Buchanan Gray, op. cit., p. 219.

[2] Buchanan Gray, op. cit., p. 32.

most valuable or acceptable for food; but though this again might, failing good evidence to the contrary, explain the tossing of the blood against the altar or pouring it down at its base, it cannot explain the application of the blood to the person of the offerer. Finally there is the ritual meal: what is burnt on the altar might, as already remarked, have been originally so treated in order to prepare food for the deity; and further, what was consumed by the priests might still be regarded, and indeed was regarded, as a gift to the deity passed on by him to his proxies, the priests; but what was eaten by the offerer cannot be fully explained in a satisfactory way as a gift to the deity."

Robertson Smith, in his comprehensive work on sacrifice, comes to an entirely opposite conclusion.[1] "The one point," he says, "that comes out clear and strong is that the fundamental idea of ancient sacrifice is sacramental communion, and that all atoning rites are ultimately to be regarded as owing their efficacy to a communication of divine life to the worshippers, and to the establishment or confirmation of a living bond between them and their god. In primitive ritual this conception is grasped in a merely physical and mechanical shape, as indeed, in primitive life, all spiritual and ethical ideas are still wrapped up in the husk of a material embodiment." Again he says, "The leading idea in the animal sacrifices of the Semites . . . was not that of a gift made over to the god, but of an act of communion, in which the god and his worshippers unite by partaking together of the flesh and blood of the sacred victim."

These conclusions are reached by Robertson Smith after a detailed and exhaustive examination of the subject from the point of view of comparative religion. At the outset of his book he draws attention to the closeness of relationship which, in primitive religions, was conceived as existing between the deity, his worshippers, and certain animals. The three shared a common life, and in consequence the sense of the numinous was highly developed. He draws examples from Arab and Semitic folklore, of places, objects, and animals which were closely associated with deities, and which were in some way or other capable of imparting the divine life to the individual. In particular, he emphasises the importance of an example of sacrifice such as that given

[1] *Religion of the Semites,* 3rd ed. (*1927*), edited by S. A. Cook, p. 439.

by Nilus, in which the Saracens are described as falling upon their victim as the morning star rose, slaughtering it, and devouring flesh, blood, and bones whilst still warm with their natural heat. This he takes as the example *par excellence* of the aim of sacrifice, namely, by eating the sacred animal, and in particular by drinking its blood, to absorb the divine life and so enjoy complete communion with the deity.[1] This idea he transfers to Hebrew sacrifices, and, though there can be found no examples in the Old Testament of a similar rite, he finds in the blood ritual and in the meal associated with the peace-offering a sufficient justification for this interpretation of them. Originally, he suggests, the Hebrews, like the Saracens of Nilus' day, ate the whole victim; but, for some reason or other, the drinking of blood and the eating of raw flesh became repugnant to their developing conception of God, and in consequence the blood was poured out, and the whole or part of the victim burnt upon the altar. Though the only relic of this gross and barbarous superstition to be found in the Hebrew sacrificial ritual is the meal of the peace-offering, nevertheless, the same experience of communion was realised as though they had devoured the whole in a sacramental manner.

Few would deny that among primitive peoples the idea of the numinous played an important part in the development of the conception of God, and there can be no doubt that among the Hebrews in particular this idea was strong from early times.[2] Where most students of primitive custom, however, would disagree with Robertson Smith is in the way in which he grafts on to a Hebrew stock present-day primitive and ancient non-Hebrew beliefs, despite the lack of real justification for doing so. It by no means follows that because later Arabs interpreted certain practices and customs in one way, the Hebrews interpreted similar ones in like manner. Surely we must leave room for at least some originality, and avoid

---

[1] Robertson Smith's contention that the Hebrews went through a stage of totemism, upon which his argument is largely based, can by no means be satisfactorily illustrated from the Old Testament. As A. Bertholet says, " It is therefore very unsafe to infer a previous stage of totemism in Israel from the existence of animal and plant names." See his treatment of the subject in his *History of Hebrew Civilisation* (*1926*), translated by A. K. Dallas, p. 130 *seq.*

[2] See a recent and concise treatment by J. W. C. Wand, *The Development of Sacramentalism* (*1928*), pp. 15–30.

forcing all religions into the same mould.  The comparative study of religions is invaluable in that it shows what numerous elements are common to all religions, but it must cease to be of any real value when it ties all religions down to stereotyped beliefs, and gives practices common to a number of religions an identical interpretation.  Again, it would seem that Robertson Smith's conception of communion is prejudiced by his own Christian presuppositions ; he credits the early Hebrews in particular, and primitive man in general, with a conception of God and his relation to man which, to say the least, is hardly consistent with the somewhat crude and materialistic means adopted for getting into communion with him.  He seems scarcely able to think that, what to him may appear to be an act of communion, may to others be nothing less than bribery or intimidation.

There are two points in particular connected with the ritual of Hebrew sacrifice which this communion theory fails satisfactorily to explain :  the practice of burning the victim, and the blood ritual.  It is difficult to see why, if at one time the Hebrews found in eating the victim and drinking its blood the apogee of communion with God, they should have found it necessary to forego this deep religious experience, the very acme of which was in the eating of the victim, and have stood aside to behold a blackening carcase of which they did not partake.  Similarly, in the blood ritual, why should they suddenly have ceased to drink this source of divine life, and instead have stood by to see it poured upon the ground ?  If we accept Robertson Smith's view of the origin and meaning of this custom, then it is impossible to understand the constantly recurring warning, that no Hebrew should drink the blood of either sacrificial or non-sacrificial animals.  We may justly ask, How could the poured-out blood be conceived of as transferring the divine life to the individual when in all probability he never touched it ; or, on the other hand, how could it have benefited the deity ?  Why should the Hebrews so carefully not only have refrained from drinking the blood which gushed forth naturally when an animal was slain, but also have been at pains to drain every drop from the carcase of the victim ? If the blood was the medium of communion with God, why, at any rate, in the burnt-offering should it have been let at all, and not rather have been burnt in, or with the carcase ? Similarly, Buchanan Gray in putting forward his arguments in favour of the gift theory fails satisfactorily to account for the blood ritual. If the burnt-offering was a gift solely to the deity, what prompted the complete separation of the blood? We can hardly think that the blood dashed on the altar was a mere disinfectant, "to rid what was naturally holy from intrusive contamination"; [1] it would have been more likely, as Robertson Smith argues, to have acted as a tonic.[2] Again, in the peace-offering, if the blood was a gift to the deity, why should it have been treated differently from the fat? Buchanan Gray, as we have seen, appreciates these difficulties, and is therefore forced into admitting that in the Hebrew sacrificial system "there is something more than, or something else as well as, gifts."

The meaning of the blood ritual would seem to be the most pressing question in our endeavour to trace the significance of Hebrew sacrifice, therefore no apology is needed for the somewhat lengthy treatment of this particular aspect of our problem.

According to Old Testament teaching, the blood of both man and animals was conceived of as the life principle.[3] In addition, there is another word *nephesh* which is frequently used as a synonym for blood,[4] and translated *life* in many passages. The precise meaning of this word is obscure, but it certainly does not bear that attached to the word *soul* whereby the English Versions translate it. In all probability it was originally associated with the breath, and, owing to the necessity of breath for sustaining life, it became closely associated with the blood, or life principle. If we may take this identification of the life of man and animals with their blood or breath, as representing a common belief amongst the early Hebrews, then we may ask, Where did that life go to after it had left the body? There could be only three alternatives: that it went to heaven, stayed on earth, or went to Sheol. The Hebrews had no clear conception of any supra-terrestrial dwelling-place of Yahweh, and certainly there is no suggestion that the ordinary human being departing this life went to him; the two exceptions to this rule, those of Enoch and Elijah,

---

[1] Buchanan Gray, *op. cit.*, p. 359, n. 1.
[2] Robertson Smith, *op. cit.*, p. 408 f.
[3] Note the Arab belief that when a man dies on the battlefield "his life flows on the spear-point," when he dies a natural death life departs through the nostrils. Ḥamasa, p. 52.
[4] Gen. ix. 4; Lev. xvii. 11, and *passim*.

prove that. That the spirits ordinarily remained on earth must be excluded by the presence of innumerable passages which presuppose that Sheol was the place of all departed spirits. Sheol, then, was the abode of the departed. The meaning of this word is doubtful; it may mean " the place of inquiry " from whence oracles were obtained, or it may come from the root meaning " to be hollow," hence it would be the hollow place under the earth.

Sheol was the abode of the departed in both Hebrew and Babylonian literature, and in the stories of both people there is exhibited a common conception of the state of the dead there, and of the place itself.[1] It was a land of but a shadowy existence, where all men were gathered together. Earthly distinctions of rank were kept, and though it had few attractions to offer to the ordinary mortal, those who lived there seem to have retained to some degree their consciousness. There is no direct evidence of the presence of animals in Sheol, though the fact that they shared the common life of man, together with the frequent mention in the Old Testament of uncanny doleful creatures, would suggest that they may have departed there at death too. This certainly would find parallels in other religions. Those who dwelt in Sheol had no communion with God, and no knowledge of the affairs of men upon the earth, their existence was one tedious round of semi-conscious inertia; the fear of going down into Sheol was the constant dread of the living, for once there, there could be no return. This was the ordinary view of Sheol, and it finds frequent expression in the later literature of the Old Testament. Oesterley upholds the theory, however, that this represented only the orthodox belief. He contends that in pre-exilic days there were two conceptions of life after death; according to one a return in exceptional circumstances was possible, according to the other, death meant eternal banishment. In proof of this he makes reference to Babylonian texts which mention occasions upon which men did return, and to the practice of ancestor-worship, burial and mourning customs, and necromancy among the Hebrews. It is true, he admits, that these practices were banned by orthodox religion and its supporters, but this necessity of legislating against them lends strong probability to his argument that they were an integral part of popular

[1] See W. O. E. Oesterley, *Immortality and the Unseen World* (*1921*), Chapter VII.

belief. They were banned because, leading as they must have done to a mere half-hearted trust in Yahweh, and to the promotion of ancestor-worship, they were subversive to the best interests of Yahwism. To quote him,[1] " The regard for and veneration of the departed involved practices which were incompatible with a true belief in Yahwe. It became, therefore, the duty of the religious leaders to ban ancestor-worship and all communication, or supposed communication, with the dead. And one of the most efficacious means to this end was what was regarded as a reformed teaching regarding the abode of the dead, Sheol."

Other considerations would go to show that this idea of parallel but mutually exclusive religious beliefs is not foreign to the literature of the Hebrews. Burney has suggested that from the time when those tribes who went into Egypt returned, there existed two forms of Yahwism, the one orthodox and the result of Moses' influence, the other unorthodox, and representing a synthesis of local Canaanite cults.[2] Buchanan Gray[3] has expressed the opinion that there was at one time confusion between the altars of Baal and those of Yahweh, the former being frequently used for the services of the latter, hence the insistence in the Code of the Covenant that altars must be made or built; apparently the old rock altars of Canaan were not to be used for offerings to Yahweh unless new ones made by hand were superimposed. The frequent lament of the editor of I and II Kings[4] that the high places were not removed, the complaints of Hosea[5] and his contemporaries that Yahweh and Baal were often confused, and the attempts of Elijah and Jehu to stamp out Baalism all lend support to this view. In addition, it should be noted that, as a result of the literary and historical criticism to which the Old Testament has been subjected during the last century, it is becoming more and more evident that Hebrew religion contained in its early stages beliefs and practices which were condemned by the later religious leaders. The most common method of condemning these beliefs and practices was by means of literary propaganda. Again and again the records of Hebrew history were edited and re-edited, until what we now possess is a record

---

[1] Oesterley, op. cit., p. 203.
[2] Burney, Journal of Theological Studies, Vol. IX., p. 321 f.
[3] Buchanan Gray, op. cit., p. 114 seq.
[4] I Kings iii. 2, etc.     [5] Hosea ii. 16.

of Hebrew religious history which has undergone the refining influence of the eighth-century prophets, and has been passed through the successive and increasingly fine-meshed sieves of the Deuteronomic and Priestly Schools. A second and natural method adopted was that of transforming what was ancient custom and usage to meet increasingly ethical conceptions of God, a process which has gone on in all religions as they have advanced, and one which has the advantage of retaining the devotional element in any one system, and at the same time providing an opportunity of developing the intellectual.

If, then, we admit the thesis illustrated by Oesterley—and there seems no adequate reason for doubting it—we may ask what was the attitude of the spirits which returned from Sheol towards living men ? There are numerous passages in the Old Testament which, having escaped the attention of the orthodox redactors, suggest that the departed were possessed of powers which were greater than those of the living. The story of the witch of Endor,[1] the existence of seers,[2] of those who had familiar spirits, and of those who chirped and muttered,[3] suggest that by means of occult processes the riddles of the present and the future might be solved. Again, the word Sheol, as already mentioned, may bear the interpretation of " the place of inquiry." But though there is evidence that the departed might be capable of helping the living by revealing secrets through a medium, there is also abundant evidence that they were capable of harming them. The care with which burial customs were carried out, and the constant mention of uncanny creatures which inhabited unclean or waste places, and which roamed abroad at night, well illustrate this.[4]

As there is every reason for believing that the Hebrews did practise the occult at both early and late periods in their

---

[1] I Sam. xxviii. 7. The woman's reply to Saul's question is particularly interesting, " I see gods coming up out of the earth." The whole scene might have been sacrificial.

[2] I Sam. ix. 6; *passim*.        [3] Isaiah viii. 19; *passim*.

[4] Note Hebrew custom of stoning an animal which had inflicted injury upon man; the stones were piled upon the beast to prevent the spirit of the animal from rising and continuing to do harm (Exod. xxi. 28). The enactment of Deut. xxi. 22 *seq.*, that a criminal should not be allowed to hang upon a tree all night, had behind it the fear that the man's roaming spirit might do harm. See A. Bertholet, *op. cit.*, p. 279.

history, and as the object of these practices was undoubtedly both to placate and enlist the aid of departed spirits, is it not possible that these unorthodox undercurrents of belief found expression in their sacrificial system ? Since the blood of both man and animals was identified with the principle of vitality, and since there was no idea of life after death with Yahweh, may not the blood ritual of sacrifice originally have been connected with some form of sacrificial offering to the departed ? [1]  In view of this possibility, let us now return to the ritual of sacrifice.

As we have seen in our discussion of Buchanan Gray's interpretation of the blood ritual, there remains at least one great difficulty to be explained in connection with it : why was it necessary in both the burnt- and the peace-offering to separate the blood from the victim, rather than to present it along with, either the whole carcase, or the fat ? In the case of Robertson Smith, with whom Buchanan Gray seems inclined to agree, why should the blood which was neither offered on the altar nor drunk by the people have been thought of as establishing a communion with the deity ? If, however, we suppose that the blood was separated from the victim for a purpose other than that of worshipping Yahweh, then we have an explanation of this puzzling and persistent ritual, and one which is in accord with similar occult practices mentioned in the Old Testament. A parallel example of the combined rites of the cult of the departed and the cult of Yahweh in one act of worship may perhaps be seen in the ritual of the Day of Atonement.[2] Here, two goats were brought to the priest, one being offered to Yahweh, the other being sent away into the wilderness to Azazel. Various attempts have been made to explain Azazel,[3] but the most feasible put forward is that he

[1] Early altars were undoubtedly of earth (Exod. xx. 24), and the sinking of the blood into the altar would certainly have suggested the idea of the life departing to Sheol; perhaps this gave rise to the later belief that souls of martyrs were retained under the altar, waiting for their blood to be avenged (see Rev. vi. 9, 10). Kittel, drawing attention to the subterranean hollows under many of the Canaanite rock-surface altars, suggests that these were the abodes of earth-housing deities. See his *Studien zur hebräischen Archäologie*, p. 152 (*1908*). These deities might easily have been identified with the departed and the practice taken over by the Hebrews.

[2] Lev. xvi.

[3] Buchanan Gray, *op. cit.*, p. 316 *seq.* Cheyne, art. in *Encyclopedia Biblica*, Vol. i. p. 394.

D

represented *in una persona* the prince of demons or spirits of the departed such as were condemned, along with necromancy in general, by the religious leaders of the Hebrews from the eighth century on. May not this be taken as an excellent example of the skill with which the more enlightened turned old superstitions and practices to new and more spiritual uses ?

Similarly both Buchanan Gray's and Robertson Smith's attempts to connect the ritual of the red cow and the young heifer slain and burnt away from the altar with the exclusive sacrificial blood ritual of orthodox Yahwism are singularly unconvincing. The red cow was slain, subjected to the blood ritual, and burnt outside the camp, and its ashes were used as an ingredient in the liquid prepared and used for the removal of uncleanness incurred by contact with a dead body. It would seem that the most natural explanation of this is that it was an attempt to placate the spirit of the departed, whether of man or animal, which might take vengeance on those who had last touched its body. In the ritual of the young heifer which was slain beside running water where an unknown murdered man had been found in the open country, may we not see an attempt to propitiate the departed spirit, whose blood, like that of Abel, was crying for vengeance from the ground ? The blood feud, which would have been settled in the ordinary course of primitive justice by the death of the murderer, had he been known, was in this way ended by offering, as an equivalent, the most valuable of animals.[1] In neither case is there any suggestion that the ritual was performed to appease the wrath of Yahweh or to re-establish communion with him, for the ceremonies were performed away from his sanctuary.

Another example of the blood ritual which the exponents of the gift and communion theories of sacrifice to Yahweh fail satisfactorily to explain, is that connected with the Passover meal prior to the Exodus. Most scholars admit that in origin it was older than the period to which it is assigned, and suggest that it was primarily an agricultural feast; hence its confusion later with the feast of unleavened bread. However this may be, the blood ritual is just such as that practised among other peoples for warding off or

---

[1] With these practices may be compared that of covering up the blood of animals slain in the chase. Lev. xvii. 13; Jer. ii. 34.

placating malevolous spirits, and so preventing them from exerting an evil influence among the inhabitants of the house or tent.[1]

Three customs definitely connected with the cult of the dead may also be mentioned with reference to the blood ritual : those of cutting the body,[2] polling the hair,[3] and the offering of fire for the dead.[4]    Blood-letting for the dead was evidently a common practice among the Hebrews, and is spoken of without condemnation by two of the sixth-century prophets, but is condemned in Deuteronomy and Leviticus.   According to Oesterley, " in its original form laceration of the body was probably practised over the dead so that the blood dropped upon the corpse ; this may have signified either that a blood covenant with the dead was effected, or, bearing in mind the ancient belief of life residing in the blood, it may have had the purpose of assisting the departed in his new life."   Similarly, the idea of helping the dead in all probability lies behind the custom of cutting the hair, and it is important to note, in considering this practice in relation to the whole question of offerings made to the dead, that the hair, as well as the blood, was conceived of as the seat of life.   Burnings for the dead are mentioned in several passages dealing with Hebrew history towards the end of the monarchy.   To quote Oesterley's words, " These burnings for the dead were remnants of a time when incense-offerings were offered in the firm belief in the continued life of the departed, who was thus propitiated." [5]   In none of these practices is there any suggestion that rites were being performed in connection with Yahweh.[6]

---

[1] For examples of the use of blood to ward off demons and evil spirits, see A. Bertholet, op. cit., pp. 137 seq., 349.

[2] Lev. xix. 28; xxi. 1–4, 5; Deut. xiv. 1; Jer. xvi. 6; xli. 5; Ezek. vii. 18.

[3] Lev. xix. 27; xxi. 5; Deut. xiv. 1; Jer. xvi. 6; xli. 5; xlviii. 37; Ezek. vii. 18; Mic. i. 16; Isa. xxii. 12; Amos viii. 10, cp. Virgil, Æneid, iv. 700–705, and see note in Robertson Smith, op. cit., pp. 325, 606.

[4] Jer. xxxiv. 5; II Chron. xvi. 14; xxi. 19.

[5] Oesterley, op. cit., p. 107.

[6] In the Odyssey, Ulysses speaks with his dead companions after resuscitating them with blood-offerings, Odyssey, xi.   The offering of blood to the departed underlies a great deal of Greek mythology connected with the Underworld.   In Theocritus ii. 12, Hecate is described as faring " through black blood and across the barrows of the dead "; in an Orphic Hymn she is described as αἱμοποτίς. Similarly Virgil, iii. 67; v. 78; vi. 248 connect blood-offerings with the departed.   Roman mythology has no parallels.

A further example of the significance of the blood may be found in the ritual connected with the forming of covenants. In the best known of these, Moses takes half the blood and sprinkles it upon the altar and half upon the people, saying, " Behold the blood of the covenant, which the Lord hath made with you concerning all these words." [1] Here and here alone in the early Hebrew literature does there seem to be any justification for a communion theory of sacrifice ; for the sacred blood applied to people and altar would suggest some kind of association between the two. But in view of the fact that these covenants were commonly concluded between individuals in the ordinary private and business affairs of life, it need represent nothing more than a bond which must never be broken on pain of death. There is certainly no idea present of a gift of the blood or life to Yahweh, and it is hardly giving the passage its natural interpretation if we take it as representing the communication of life or holiness to the people. In this blood ritual there may have been present a similar idea to that suggested in connection with the Passover ritual—namely, the placation of spirits which might conspire to frustrate the plans of the covenanters.[2]

These examples would suggest that the idea of making offerings to departed spirits was not foreign to the Hebrews, and that they were not averse to combining practices connected with the cult of the dead with those of the Yahweh cult, and we may now attempt to summarise the result of our inquiry into the origin and meaning of sacrifice in the early sources of Hebrew literature. As far as our records go, though we must remember that few are much earlier than the ninth century, the evidence bears witness to the great antiquity of sacrifice, and to its unchanged nature right from the beginning of Hebrew history.[3] These sacri-

---

[1] Exod. xxiv. 8.

[2] Note the Covenant of Gen. xv. 9 ff., where Abraham finds it necessary to drive away certain birds of prey (v. 11), and "the horror of great darkness" which fell upon him (v. 12), and the assurance that he should go to his fathers in peace (v. 15); the last two references are very reminiscent of Sheol, and the first might possibly refer to demons in the form of birds.

[3] According to P. sacrifice was not pre-Mosaic, but the Biblical tradition of J. and E. certainly traces it back to the very beginnings of the nation. P. in all probability had a pragmatic purpose in making Moses the founder of the whole sacrificial system, for thereby

fices were always offered at some place where Yahweh had appeared to men. They were of two types : those specified for the three fixed periods during the year, and those which were not specified but offered spontaneously on an occasion of crisis or thanksgiving. The sacrifices were presented to the deity as gifts, those on the specified occasions representing his annual tithes from the land to which he had given its increase, the non-specified ones being bribes or rewards for the express purpose of procuring and keeping his favour. The blood, though, according to our documents, a part of the whole sacrificial ritual of Yahwism at the beginning of the ninth century, was not necessarily a part of these gifts to Yahweh, nor a means of securing the essence of divine life, but may have been poured out to placate and nourish those countless demons or departed spirits whose power over the individual was as great as that of Yahweh, and who were not directly under his control. This may not have been the significance of the rite in the historical period, for the tendency among the more spiritually-minded leaders of Yahwism, as we have seen, was to discourage these occult practices, and either dissociate them from the cult of Yahweh, or so to transpose them as to destroy their original significance. So far as our evidence goes, there was no idea of communion in these early sacrifices in the sense of partaking of the divine life, for when the victim was slaughtered the life was poured out upon the ground or altar, and therefore not partaken of by the offerer or the deity. The clan or family meal associated with the peace-offering can best be explained as a gathering at which the deity shared with his people in a family meal, an act of social intercourse at which Yahweh, as the chief guest, was given the best part. The meal would certainly be looked upon as cementing a closer friendship between the participants, but not as an act of communion in the sense in which Robertson Smith would interpret it. It was a fellowship and not a communion meal.[1] Most of the offerings were propitiatory or placatory in character, attempts to bias the deity on the side of the

---

all the post-exilic legislation was given the prestige of his authority. The eighth-century prophets and Jeremiah suggest that sacrifice was not practised by Moses, and with this some modern scholars would agree. In this case the sacrificial practices of the Hebrews may have been Canaanite in origin.

[1] See Gen. xviii. 1 f.; Judges xiii. 15 *seq.*

worshipper in view of possible future calamity, or to turn
away his wrath when circumstances suggested that this
was necessary.    There is no evidence that the offerings
were made as a result of any consciousness of sin.    The
whole idea of atonement is one based on a system of barter.
Other gods were originally in all probability approached
sacrificially at times,[1] but the hosts of the departed had
always to be contended with, and therefore appeased with
offerings in addition to that of blood, as the burial and
mourning customs illustrate.

Upon leaving these early Hebrew sources, and turning to
those which represent the teaching of the eighth-century
prophets, we are at once struck by the complete change in
religious outlook.    Yahweh is no longer the god of war;
though he does sometimes cause enemies to punish his
people, he no longer delights in cruelty or in the multitude of
sacrifices brought to him.    Righteousness, love, and holiness
are the essence of his character, and it is in accordance with
these standards that he would have his people do him worship.
" He hath shown thee, O man, what is good; and what doth
the Lord require of thee, but to do justly, and to love mercy,
and to walk humbly with thy God ? "[2]    The war god has
given place to the law god.

In consequence of this new conception of God's character,
we find that the old religious practices were discredited, and
among these sacrifice.    The prophets direct a wholehearted
denunciation against the complete sacrificial system.    In
particular do they inveigh against the contemporary interpretation of it.    Their contemporaries offered sacrifice as a
means of bribing the deity, or of lulling him into a state of
torpor, whilst they found in the sacrificial feasts an excuse
for excesses and orgies such as rivalled those of their heathen
neighbours.    Their stern denunciations leave us in no doubt
as to whether the prophets objected only to the system of
sacrifice as it was practised in their day, or to the whole
system of sacrifice itself.    It is true that their condemnation
was directed primarily against the belief that Yahweh
wanted or accepted gifts; but it is important to notice that,
while they condemned this interpretation of sacrifice, they
made no attempt to give it a new one.    Communion with
God certainly was the essence of their teaching, but it was

---

[1] Exod. xxii. 20.                    [2] Mic. vi. 8.

not a communion through sacrifice, or one based wholly on the privileges which accrued to the Hebrews because they were a covenant people; it was a communion of the spirit. The people's sins, not Yahweh's whims, stood between them and their God, and no amount of offerings could blot them out; the prophets, as Yahweh's messengers, demanded a spiritual regeneration. Of this Amos, at any rate, had no doubt, and with him his contemporaries and successors concur. " I hate, I despise your feasts, and I will take no delight in your solemn assemblies. Yea, though ye offer me your burnt-offerings and meal offerings, I will not accept them : neither will I regard the peace-offerings of your fat beasts. Take away from me the noise of your songs; for I will not hear the melody of your viols. But let judgement roll down as waters, and righteousness as a mighty stream." [1]

Well may we ask, What called forth so strong a denunciation of the whole sacrificial system ? The answer is clear. Yahweh's people had been playing the harlot with customs and practices in which he had no delight; a synthesis of Yahwism and the local nature-cults had been made, and the religious ideas for which the prophets strove in the name of their God were in jeopardy. They were themselves idealists, and they wanted a nation of idealists to worship their King. Along with sacrifice they seem to have condemned the whole religious and political system; even their supposed colleagues, the prophets and the Nazirites, had been unfaithful to their vows. Though the prophetic literature does not set out to treat with the origin or meaning of sacrifice, its writers leave us without any doubt as to what they would have said had they been asked. Sacrifice in origin to them was at best a practice which had sprung up from a synthesis of the local nature-cults; they were even prepared to go so far as to say that it was not even Mosaic; it was certainly not the divine will. Nor do they leave any doubt as to the meaning attached to it by their contemporaries; it was offered as a gift to local deities masquerading in the name of Yahweh. They lend no direct support to the suggestion put forward when dealing with the earlier period of Hebrew history, namely that part of the sacrificial system was connected with the practice of the occult; but they do at least condemn necromancy, and show us that contemporary

---

[1] Amos v. 21 f.

Hebrew religion was full of undesirable perversions of what to them was true religion.[1]

From this uncompromising invective against the whole sacrificial system, we pass on to a literary source, which, if less idealist in outlook, was more optimistic towards organised religion. If we may take the popular religious practices and belief of the eighth century as representing the low water-mark of Yahwism, and the ideals of the prophets as the high, then we may say that Deuteronomy represents a compromise, an attempt to condemn what was completely bad in the system in vogue at the time, and to raise the remainder to a spiritual plane, not so high as that of the prophets, it is true, but one which was more practicable. This religious reformation was concerned chiefly with the local sanctuaries; these it completely abolished, centralising all religious practices in the one sanctuary at Jerusalem.[2] In consequence of this, the whole sacrificial system was upset, and legislation to re-organise it had to be introduced. Owing to the difficulty of taking sacrificial animals and other offerings long distances, all sacrifices were to be commuted into money, and equivalents bought at Jerusalem. There the offerings were to be made in the usual manner; practically the only difference from earlier usage being that the priests appear to have received a larger portion, one which represented a more suitable payment for their services.

We may note, however, two important points in connection with the reformed sacrificial system as portrayed in Deuteronomy. In the first place, what was offered was still a gift, but not one of the type we have noticed in the earlier sources; there was no longer any idea of propitiation or atonement associated with it, nor was there a double purpose behind it. All sacrifice to the Deuteronomist was a thank-offering to Yahweh for his bounty, and for that reason its joyousness was emphasised. There is a tendency in the book to relate all offerings to the past redemptive work of Yahweh in the history of the nation, and so to introduce the idea of memorial offerings rather than that of tithings. Again, the tendency to give more to the priest, and to include

---

[1] See Chapter II, where the prophetic attitude is dealt with more fully.

[2] For different views upon the Deuteronomic Reformation, see A. C. Welch, *The Code of Deuteronomy*, and R. H. Kennett, *Deuteronomy and the Decalogue*.

with him the poor, the dispossessed Levites, the stranger, the orphan, and the widow shows that sacrifices were being looked upon as a recognition of Yahweh's bounty. The whole system of sacrifice corresponded more to our present-day Harvest Festivals than to the system of pre-Deuteronomic days. Thus Buchanan Gray sums up, "Though in Deuteronomy the belief that sacrifices are gifts to God is certainly not discarded, sacrifice is less regarded as a means to obtain God's favour than as an opportunity for acknowledging his goodness and the manifold benefits which he has bestowed. There is here some suggestion, more at least than in the prophets, of a re-interpretation of sacrifice, but a re-interpretation that does not return to or introduce the belief that actual participation in a sacrificial meal was a means to communion with God, but a re-interpretation which treats sacrifices as historical and memorial symbols." [1]

Secondly, we may note that a blood ritual was retained. It is evident that the Deuteronomic legislators were confronted with a difficult problem when they came to deal with the disposal of the blood. Apparently in pre-Deuteronomic days all animals, even those which had been used for domestic purposes only, had been taken to the local sanctuaries to be slain, and there the blood had been disposed of. However, now that these sanctuaries had been done away with, what was to happen to the blood ? That which belonged to the ordinary burnt- or peace-offerings they ordered to be offered with the flesh, apparently being poured out upon the altar.[2] Whatever the meaning of this ritual may have been, it certainly was not in any way connected with the communion motive, for, as we have seen, the Deuteronomic sacrifices were essentially the giving back to Yahweh of what he had given to his people. Perhaps we may gain some insight into the significance of the blood in the ritual prescribed for the slaughter of the non-sacrificial animal. Of this it is said, " Only ye shall not eat the blood; thou shalt pour it out upon the earth as water "; later is added the statement that " the blood is the life," and twice more the warning against eating it is repeated. There then follows an additional reason for not eating the blood, " that it may go well with thee . . . when thou shalt do that which is right in the sight of the Lord." [3] We may note

[1] Buchanan Gray, *op. cit.*, p. 47.    [2] Deut. xii. 27.

[3] Deut. xii. 16, 23–25.

also that similar words are used with regard to the ritual of the burnt-offering : "there thou shalt offer thy burnt-offerings, and there thou shalt do all that I command thee." [1] Surely here is the Deuteronomic legislators' interpretation of the blood ritual; it was Yahweh's command that the blood should not be eaten, it was man's duty to obey it. This, indeed, would seem to be their attitude towards all the offerings which were presented for disposal upon the altar : undoubtedly they would have preferred to give all to the Levites, the orphans, the strangers, and the widow. They were far keener upon inculcating moral principles, upon putting forward their doctrine of retribution, upon establishing a feeling of brotherhood which was even to include the stranger, and upon emphasising the joyousness of religion. The paucity of references to sacrifice apart from those at the three great annual festivals, the meaning of which was perfectly clear to them, suggests that had they not believed that Yahweh had, through Moses, founded the sacrificial system, they would have been only too pleased to drop it. [2] They did the next best thing—they regulated it by bringing it under strict control and supervision at Jerusalem. Thus they attempted to shut out from the Jewish sacrificial system unorthodox practices and suspicious rites.

When we turn from the happy atmosphere of the Deuteronomic legislation to the somewhat austere one of the Priestly code, [3] we find that the whole rationale of sacrifice is changed. We saw that the former tried to regulate sacrifice; the latter succeeded in making it into a hidebound system carefully regulated by a priestly hierarchy of Aaronic descent. The number and relative importance of occasions of sacrifice are changed, the three agricultural festivals which were so prominent in Deuteronomy recede into the background, and a new and far more significant day of fasting appears for the first time—the Day of Atonement, the day on which the whole congregation assembled before

[1] Deut. xii. 14, 28.
[2] At a later date Philo exhibits a strong tendency in Judaism to disregard the altar of burnt-offerings with the things offered upon it, and to emphasise in its place the golden altar of incense. His contemporaries found no explanation for the sacrificial system other than that it was the will of God. See Buchanan Gray, *op. cit.*, pp. 46, 51.
[3] Leviticus and parts of Exodus and Numbers. See D. C. Simpson *op. cit.*

their God to afflict their souls and to obtain absolution from their sins. The somewhat haphazard system of the non-specified sacrifices of the early sources has given place to an elaborately regulated scheme in which the sacrifices vary not only according to the occasion, but also with regard to the gifts offered. The new legislation includes within itself a full manual of worship for the offerer, and one for the priest.[1] It provides for the consecration of the members of the priesthood,[2] and regulates the paraphernalia of the great Tent of Meeting upon a most elaborate scale,[3] and claims for itself Mosaic origin.

The basis of this re-organisation of the sacred things was one of holiness; Yahweh was holy, and therefore his people were to be holy too.[4] It was, however, a holiness which was far from spiritual, and practically synonymous with exclusiveness. Perhaps owing to the influence of Ezekiel's conception of the ideal Jewish theocracy,[5] or perhaps as the outcome of that exilic influence which inspired Ezekiel—namely, the desire to be for ever freed from the contamination by heathen neighbours—post-exilic Judaism settled down to relate itself in an almost physical way to a holy deity on the one hand, and an unholy heathen on the other. The centre of this holiness was in the Holy of Holies, the fringe of it among the nations; in between were gradations of holiness which embraced every Jew and his possessions. They were a holy people, and they possessed holy things. Hence, the old system of offering only the firstfruits of the land was insufficient, and in consequence a new system of tithing, one far more elaborate than that of Deuteronomy, was introduced, and a definite poll tax of a half shekel demanded from each of Yahweh's children.

All these additional statutory offerings were in the nature of obligatory gifts,[6] not bribes, as in the earliest sources, nor spontaneous offerings, as in Deuteronomy, but taxes imposed by Yahweh for the upkeep of his Temple and its priesthood.

---

[1] Lev. i.–vi. 7; vi. 8–vii. 38.
[2] Lev. viii.–x.      [3] Exod. xxv.–xxxiii., xxxv.–xl.
[4] See Lev. xvii.–xxvi.      [5] Ezek. xl. *seq.*
[6] Post-exilic legislation introduced a new word to describe all offerings brought to the Temple, *Ḳorbanim*. The old word used to express gift (*minhah*) had been given a new and specific meaning, being used with reference to the meal-offering alone; for its old use see Gen. iv. 3 ff. and I Sam. xxvi. 19; for new use see Lev. ii. 1. For Ḳorban see Mk. vii. 11.

In addition, there were the gifts presented whenever a sacrifice was offered by an individual Jew, gifts varying in number and value according to the social and financial status of the offerer, and according to the reason for which he offered them. These were simply and solely fines inflicted for breaches of the Law. They represented an elaborate system of penance, and, like the statutory offerings, went towards the upkeep of the Temple and its priesthood.

What, then, was the object of orthodox Judaism of the post-exilic period in formulating such an elaborate system of sacrifice? This Driver sums up succinctly when he says, " The aim of the priestly legislation is to maintain, by a detailed and comprehensive ceremonial, the ideal holiness of the theocratic community." [1] In constant opposition to this ideal were the facts of experience, and these convicted the nation and the individual of sin. Such a system appeared superficially to be deeply religious, but it was at fault in its conception of what sin was. It divided sin into two classes : sins which were committed wittingly, which it called sin with a high hand, for which there was no forgiveness, and sins committed unwittingly; for these latter the sacrificial system was provided. It interpreted sin as a physical and not as a psychological and spiritual fault.

This emphasis upon sin by the post-exilic priesthood is well illustrated by the introduction of two new and important kinds of sacrifice, the sin-offering and the guilt-offering.[2] In the ritual of the sin-offering, the victim was an unblemished animal; this was presented by the offerer, who laid his hands upon its head, apparently at the same time confessing his sins, killed it, and gave it to the officiating priest, who manipulated the blood, burnt the fat upon the altar, and appropriated the remainder to himself, eating it in the court of the Holy Place. This was the chief offering on the Day of Atonement, when the ritual was substantially the same, differing only in the fact that the part not burnt upon the altar was burnt in a clean place outside the sacred area.

---

[1] Article on " Expiation and Atonement " in the *Encyclopædia of Religion and Ethics*, p. 657.

[2] Buchanan Gray thinks that the sin- and the guilt-offerings were prior to P., as they were apparently known to Ezekiel, and he gives one passage, II Kings xii. 16, where they are mentioned; but even if we accept this, they were late introductions as part of the sacrificial system, and were certainly not known to the Deuteronomic legislators. See Buchanan Gray, *op. cit.*, p. 57 f.

The guilt-offering differed from the sin-offering in that it atoned only for sins against God and man which could be estimated and therefore compensated. The ritual employed differed from that of the sin-offering in that the blood was not offered, compensation having already been made to the offended party, and therefore forgiveness obtained.

The significance of the ritual of the sin-offering seems to have been in the laying on of the hands and in the manipulation of the blood. Traditionally, the laying on of the hands has been associated with the transference of the sins of the offerer to the victim; [1] but this cannot be so, otherwise the animal would in that way have been rendered unclean, and in consequence not acceptable to God. There can be no doubt that the laying on of the hands symbolised proleptically the identification of the offerer's life with the blameless life of the animal. This life, which was identified with the blood of the victim, made atonement for sins through its presentation to Yahweh.

Much has been written on the etymology of the word for " atone " (*kipper*), but whatever its original meaning may have been, in the post-exilic period it certainly conveyed the idea of " wiping away " or " expiating," and was always connected with sin.[2] Hence, in the ritual of atonement, the blood, as representing the life of the animal, brought expiation from sin. But its operation was by no means meant to be mechanical. The ritual was based upon the supposition that the offerer was primarily repentant, otherwise he could not have identified his life with the perfect life of the victim. The whole ceremony was symbolical; the perfect life was such as the offerer knew his own ought to be. It represented the re-consecration of his life to Yahweh, who, accepting the

---

[1] The only example of the victim bearing away sins is that of the goat offered to Azazel in the ritual of the Day of Atonement. It is important to note that the goat was not offered to Yahweh, and that it was not killed. The practice is a survival of an ancient Hebrew custom connected with exorcism, and has many counterparts in Sumerian and Babylonian texts. See article by S. Langdon on " Atonement and Expiation " in the *Encyclopædia of Religion and Ethics*. As has already been suggested, it may originally have been connected with the practice of making offerings to maleficent departed spirits, and is an excellent example of the way in which later religious reformers converted old non-Yahwist practices to their own use.

[2] See articles in the *Expository Times* by S. Langdon and C. F. Burney, Vol. XXII., No. 7, p. 320.

blood, the perfect life of the animal, as a symbol of what the man's life was going to be in the future, re-admitted him into the fellowship of his holy people. It was certainly presupposed that the offerer in this act of re-consecration was prepared to put forward a new effort; the whole act was one of repentance and penance, the latter having been done in the purchase of the animal. Justification followed, but not in the sense that the offerer was made righteous, but in the sense that Yahweh accounted him righteous. There is no suggestion of vicarious suffering, nor any thought of the victim being substituted for the offerer to bear the punishment he ought to have borne; the animal was in the first place a fine, and in the second place the symbol of perfection. No doubt the whole system soon developed into a somewhat mechanical means of justification, but that was not the original intention of its framers. As a means to an end the system was capable of being salutary, but it broke down completely when it became the end in itself. In addition, as we have seen, it was based upon a wrong conception of sin, and in consequence was bound to become superficial and of decreasing spiritual value.

We may now attempt to summarise the results of our examination of the Hebrew sacrificial system as portrayed in the three chief literary sources of the Old Testament. Foremost among these results is the extraordinary influence which the constantly changing conception of God had upon the motive of sacrifice. At first, when Yahweh was a war god, sacrifices were for the most part bribes, though in some cases they appear to have been thankofferings. Later, when Yahweh ceased to be primarily a war god, and became more closely associated with love and righteousness, though sacrificial offerings were still gifts, they were no longer given for the purpose of biassing the deity on the side of the worshipper, but as expressions of grateful hearts, and in recognition of the divine munificence. In the priestly legislation, where the deity has become so completely transcendent, and his awful holiness his only characteristic, sacrificial offerings ceased any longer to be gifts, and became fines, fines for transgressing the ritual and ceremonial of the Law, which itself had been built up to ensure the holiness of the Jewish nation.

Whatever may originally have been the significance of the blood ritual in the sacrificial system, there does not seem to be sufficient evidence to warrant the conclusion that it was the means of establishing a sacramental communion with the deity. It may in origin have been connected with some form of ancestor-worship, or, on the other hand, it may merely have represented an attempt on the part of primitive man to assist the escaping life to the abode of the dead. The fact that the blood ritual was connected with practices which in themselves do not appear to have been connected with the sacrificial system, would lend support to either of these views. The Deuteronomic legislators do not seem to have appreciated its significance, but continued it because they thought it was Yahweh's command. The Priestly legislators were the first to make any real attempt to interpret it.[1] For them, it was the symbol of a perfect life which rose up before Yahweh in heaven, thus giving him the assurance that the worshipper was repentant, and desired once more to be admitted within the holy Church of Judaism.

There is no evidence in the Old Testament that sacrifice was ever connected with sin in the sense of moral wrongdoing.[2] As has been already said, such an interpretation of sin was not recognised among the early Hebrews; hence, though there are innumerable examples of moral lapses and the grossest cruelty, in no case is there any recognition of sin, nor an attempt made to gain remission of it through sacrifice. Even in Deuteronomy, where the sense of sin has developed considerably, there is no connection between it and the sacrificial system. In the Priestly legislation, real sin, sin with a high hand, is not included among those things for which sacrifice can make atonement; the whole system is for the expiation of ceremonial and ritual offences. The inadequacy of the sacrificial system, where moral as opposed to ceremonial offences are concerned, is illustrated by the

[1] Even they were really at a loss for an adequate explanation of the sacrificial ritual, and we find frequent passages which explain it as the will of God and therefore the duty of man. Jochanan ben Zakkai represents God as saying, " I have decreed a decree : no man is allowed to transgress my decree : it is written, This is the ordinance of the law : and that is sufficient reason for performing the ritual." See Buchanan Gray, *op. cit.*, p. 51.

[2] The passages I Sam. ii. 27–36 and iii. 14, where the sense of sin as moral wrongdoing is developed, are evidently of a later date than the setting in which they are found. The point of the passage comes in ii. 35, where the new and superior Zadokite priesthood of a later date is introduced.

tendency exhibited in the Apocalyptic and Wisdom Literature to substitute other means of obtaining forgiveness, and by the fact that, though the sacrificial system is presupposed, it plays a very inconspicuous part.   Almsgiving, prayer, good works, fasting, repentance, and the cultivation of wisdom are the chief means of gaining forgiveness; sacrifice is mentioned only occasionally.[1]   This is the more surprising in view of its prominence in the Priestly legislation, and suggests that the motive of sacrifice in post-exilic Judaism was in some way connected with the priestly hierarchy's attempt to protect and further its own vested interests.   If sacrifice played such an important part in the whole scheme of salvation in the last two centuries B.C. as is usually supposed, this lack of appreciation in contemporary popular literature is surely extraordinary.

[1] See Chapter III.

ADDITIONAL NOTE.—In the vast literature of Sumer, Babylonia, Assyria and of the Hittites, blood is only twice mentioned in connection with sacrifice. One passage forbids the drinking of blood (see S. Langdon, *Babylonian Wisdom*, p. 83, § 18), the other says that the Sun God feeds upon the fat tail of the sacrificed sheep, but the earth drinks the blood (unpublished text of epic poem, " Etana and the Eagle ").

# II

# THE CONTRIBUTION OF THE PROPHETS OF ISRAEL

## By Richard S. Cripps

### A—The Prophetic Teaching upon Sacrifice

From our sources of information it is clear not only that sacrifice was an institution as ancient as the Israelite tribes, but also that its history may be traced back to an antiquity even more remote. A problem, however, arises when a precise explanation is being sought as to the purpose of such sacrifice. In the opinion of the present writer it seems probable that, at least originally and in its essence, sacrifice was regarded as a means of establishing communion with the deity rather than of placating or propitiating him. These latter uses of the rite would develope naturally out of the root principle of communion. Sacrificial offering may have found a place in Mosaic religion, as, of course, the Pentateuch represents to be the case.[1]

In the middle of the eighth century B.C., however, men began to arise in Israel who criticised their compatriots in the matter of their use of sacrifice. These prophets claimed that Yahweh [2] had sent them, and had even ' revealed his secret ' to them.[3] Doubtless they could appeal to earlier teaching and traditions in support of their startling utterances,[4] yet the opinions which they expressed, and expressed

---

[1] But see below, pp. 68, 69.

[2] In this essay the Sacred Name of the God of Israel is spelled *Yahweh* only for the sake of uniformity of usage. Whether the pronunciation of the Name familiar to Christians as ' Jehovah ' should be *Yahweh* (or *e.g. Yahoh* or *Yahu*) may be a matter of opinion. In any case, in the mouths of the great prophets the Name had a far richer significance than in the speech of the average Israelite before their day.

[3] Amos iii. 7; cf. Jer. xxiii. 22.

[4] As Professor Kennett points out, the Rechabites, since they took no part in agriculture, could not have joined in the three great sacrificial festivals (*Deuteronomy and the Decalogue*, p. 13). This scholar holds that Moses himself taught a non-sacrificial religion.

so forcibly, were obviously out of accord with the general religious beliefs of their day.

First Amos says, in ironical language :

> ' Come to Beth-el, and transgress,|to Gilgal, and
>     multiply transgression ;
> And bring your sacrifices every morning| . . .
> For this liketh you, O ye children of Israel.' [1]

Again, he declares, as the words of Yahweh :

> ' I hate, I despise your feasts,| . . .
> Take thou away from me the noise of thy (sanctuary-)
>     songs ;|for I will not hear the melody of thy viols. . . .
> Did ye bring unto me sacrifices and offerings|in the
>     wilderness forty years, O house of Israel ? ' [2]

The form of this last question in Hebrew indicates that the answer is that the people did not bring sacrifices to any God.[3]

Hosea takes up the teaching :

> ' For I desire mercy, and not sacrifice ;|
> And the knowledge of God more than burnt offerings.' [4]

Isaiah, in stirring language, classes all sanctuary institutions as observed by the people of Judah in one category of things obnoxious to God : [5]

> ' To what purpose is the multitude of your sacrifices
>     unto me ?|saith the LORD :
> I am full of the burnt offerings of rams,|and the fat of
>     fed beasts ;
> And in the blood of bullocks, or of lambs,|or of he-goats
>     I delight not.
> When ye come to appear before me,
> Who hath required this at your hand,|to trample my
>     courts ?
> Bring no more vain oblations,'|etc.

Even more striking are the words of Micah, the contemporary of the great " Evangelical Prophet." This poet-preacher does not content himself with contrasting sacrificial acts or institutional religion with the claims of

---

[1] iv. 4 and 5b.   [2] Amos v. 21a, 23, 25.
[3] The interrogative particle in the Hebrew is attached, not to the word ' me,' but to the word ' sacrifices.'
[4] Hos. vi. 6.   [5] Isa. i. 11–13a.

morality in daily life, but he even denies that Yahweh
' requires ' sacrifice at all.   In one and the same class he
places offerings which are commanded in the Pentateuch,
and a type of offering forbidden therein to Israelites.[1]

> ' Wherewith shall I come before the LORD,|and bow
>     myself before the high God ?
> Shall I come before him with burnt offerings,|with calves
>     of a year old ?
> Will the LORD be pleased with thousands of rams,|or
>     with ten thousands of rivers of oil ?
> Shall I give my firstborn for my transgression,|the fruit
>     of my body for the sin of my soul ?
> He hath shewed thee, O man, what is good ;|and what
>     doth the LORD require of thee,
> But to do justly, and to love mercy,|and to walk humbly
>     with thy God ? ' [2]

The student of the Old Testament, when reading such
utterances, is compelled to ask himself : To what precisely
are these great prophets objecting ?   Nor is the answer to
this question so simple as at first it might appear.   (a) The
evil in Israel, or, rather, the chief evil, is not polytheism, for
such prophetic outbursts occur even in connection with the
worship offered at the Jerusalem shrine, worship of the true
God.   (b) Further, in the passages cited above, idolatry
is not so much as mentioned.   (c) The view commonly
held is that in general the prophetic condemnation of
sacrificial worship is to be explained as a reaction from the
popular attitude.   This would seem to be the main point.
The prophets were placing themselves in opposition to the
crass, unthinking, worship of the average Israelite ; who,
moreover, failed to conform his daily life as a citizen to the
ethical standards which worship of Yahweh should carry
with it.[3]   (d) It is doubtful, however, whether this supplies
the whole explanation of the problem.   " Sacrifice," in the
prophetic utterances, is something more than a synonym

---

[1] Lev. xviii. 21, xx. 2, comparing Exod. xxxiv. 20 : ' All the firstborn of thy sons thou shalt redeem.'

[2] Mic. vi. 6–8.   It is not absolutely necessary to regard the passage
as emanating from a prophet later than Micah's day.   Human
sacrifices took place in the reign of Ahaz (II Kings xvi. 3).

[3] Sir G. A. Smith well puts this in *The Book of the Twelve Prophets*,
1st ed., pp. 156 ff.

for " worship at the shrine." Why should sacrifice be singled
out so insistently and with so much elaboration of language ?
It is true that Isaiah, in the passage quoted, does include in
his condemnation the people's observance of sabbath, new
moon, and even (public) prayer. But in this Isaiah stands
almost alone. Speaking generally, it is a fact that the
prophets fasten on one thing and one thing only. That they
were dissatisfied and distressed with the people's use of
sacrifice is abundantly clear. Are we justified in going
further and asserting that they, or some of them, were
opposed to sacrifice as an institution ? Amos says that the
people did not sacrifice in the wilderness; Micah classes
sacrifice among the things not ' required ' by Israel's God.
But clearer than this, the last of the great pre-exilic prophets
declares that, in his opinion, Yahweh never spoke one word
about sacrifice in the day of Israel's redemption from
Egypt : [1]

> ' Thus saith the LORD of hosts, the God of Israel :
> Add your burnt offerings unto your sacrifices, and
> eat ye flesh. For I spake not unto your fathers, nor
> commanded them in the day that I brought them
> out of the land of Egypt, concerning burnt offerings
> or sacrifices : but this thing I commanded them, say-
> ing, Hearken unto my voice, and I will be your God,
> and ye shall be my people : and walk ye in all the
> way that I command you, that it may be well with
> you.'

Undoubtedly Jeremiah, when using such words as these,
shews that he is opposed to sacrifice *in toto*. It may be a
matter of opinion with us whether he was right in taking
up this attitude. And it may be questioned whether his

---

[1] Jer. vii. 21–23. The prophet's collocation of ' sacrifice ' and
' burnt offering ' amounts to this : ' Do not waste your meat in a
whole burnt offering; use it all in sacrifice in which you, as the
worshippers, will enjoy a big share as a meal—*eat ye flesh* ! ' Cf.
Kennett, *Sacrifice*, p. 28, note 2. The irony is to be compared with
that of Amos in Amos iv. 4, 5.—As regards the passage from Amos v.,
cited above, it may here be stated that the prophet, it would seem,
does not necessarily go so far as does Jeremiah. Amos v. 25 may
not mean that God did not command sacrifice, but only that in the
wilderness the people did not, as a matter of fact, offer it, and that
this did not interfere with the Divine favour towards them. After
all, there were no holy places in the wilderness except Sinai and,
perhaps, Kadesh.

statement with reference to Yahweh's part in the sanctioning of sacrifice is in all senses to be regarded as the last word. Obviously Yahweh may not have spoken about sacrifice.   A good deal turns upon what is to be understood generally by such an expression as ' God spake.'   Probably the prophet desires to make no distinction between ' speaking ' and ' intending ';   God never actively wished sacrifice to be offered.[1]   But even in this, Jeremiah may be exaggerating. On the other hand, sacrifice was an institution dating from times far anterior to the Exodus, and it may well be that God did not consider that it was practicable, or even perhaps advisable, that it should be uprooted from the religion of the descendants of Jacob.   It is obvious that sacrifice upon any large scale must have entailed a vast amount of cruelty, but the instinct to offer it was capable in the course of time of being guided into channels productive of good.   ' For your hardness of heart Moses wrote you this commandment ' is true of not a little in ancient Hebrew legislation.   The duty of the law-giver was to regulate and, if possible, to refine existing institutions—not always to abolish them.   But, of course, this is not what Jeremiah's words plainly meant. To him the only law from the mouth of Yahweh was moral, not sacrificial :   ' but this thing I commanded them, saying, Hearken unto my voice . . . and walk ye in all the way that I command you . . .'   (vii. 23).

It is important for us to notice that, consistent with the objection of the prophets [2] to the people's use of sacrifice, and in some cases to the institution as such, the prophets' call to their audience is to repent, not to repent and bring offerings.   Similarly, on God's side, forgiveness is represented

[1] For a collection of the opinions of thoughtful " pagan " writers upon the inadequacy or futility of sacrifice, the writer may perhaps be allowed to refer to his *Critical and Exegetical Commentary on the Book of Amos*, S.P.C.K., pp. 345–348.

[2] The opposition is a very definite one, but this does not mean to say that certain great prophets, at some time in their life, may not have looked more favourably upon the institution of sacrifice, or at least may not have referred to the offering of sacrifice (in the general sense of worshipping God) approvingly.   See Hos. iii. 4, viii. 13, Jer. xvii. 26, xxxiii. 18, Isa. xix. 21, Mal. i. 11.   These last two passages are post-exilic, and, indeed, the other five may be later additions to the original texts.   The prophet Ezekiel does not speak slightingly of sacrifice.   It may be questioned, however, whether he was responsible for drawing up the sacrificial regulations found in the last part of the book which bears his name (xliii. 13–xlvi. 24).

as being in no way conditioned by, or even remotely related to, any system of sacrificial rites.[1]   Passages which are the glory of the Old Testament will come at once to the reader's mind :

> ' Seek ye the LORD while he may be found,|call ye upon him while he is near :
> Let the wicked forsake his way,|and the unrighteous man his thoughts ;
> And let him return unto the LORD, and he will have mercy upon him ;|and to our God, for he will abundantly pardon.' [2]

So says a prophet at the close of the Exile.   Earlier, another had entreated his people to ' return unto the LORD,' suggesting a confession to be put into their mouths :

> ' Take away all iniquity,
> And accept that which is good :|so will we render (as) bullocks (the offering of) our lips.
> Asshur shall not save us ;|  . . . .

To such words of repentance God hastens to respond :

> ' I will heal their backsliding,|I will love them freely.' [3]

How are these considerations to influence our doctrine of the atonement of Christ ?   If the present writer may be allowed to transgress beyond the limits of prophetic religion, he would sum up this part of the subject as follows.   Undeniably, the study of the prophets brings out the fact that we Christians would do well to use with extreme caution the terminology of the sacrificial institution, when we seek to describe for ourselves what we believe to be the spiritual value and the eternal effects of the passion and death of the

---

[1] For a doubtful exception, see pp. 87, 88.   The symbol and seal of Isaiah's own forgiveness was not a priestly offering, but a hot stone brought from the only fire that was near.

[2] Isa. lv. 6, 7.

[3] Hos. xiv. 2b–4.   Stress cannot be placed on the expression ' as bullocks,' as if the prophet is definitely contrasting repentance and confession with *sacrificial offerings*.   The LXX reading (quoted also in Ep. Heb. xiii. 15) may well be right ; so Nowack.   Some critics would place the chapter later than the time of the prophet Hosea.   This hypothesis, however, appears to be difficult in view of the many points of contact between ch. xiv and the body of the book.

For other passages of a similar character, cf. Dan. ix. 9, Jonah iii. 9, 10.

Son of God. Such expressions as 'sacrifice,' 'propitiation,' 'satisfaction,' [1] 'offering,' and even 'atonement' itself, may suggest ideas which are not really helpful when we are trying to think out, and to proclaim, the redemptive work of the One Saviour. Assuredly, the great prophets were not the only men in the Divine counsel; none the less, their theory of religion and their contribution to eternal truth are so invaluable, that we should be wise not to employ too lavishly language with which these great teachers would feel out of sympathy, were they alive to-day.

Some theologians will go further, and, building on Jer. vii. 21–23, will feel that in Christian theology the idea of any atonement is not to be entertained. They will say that it is contrary to Jeremiah's view which was that no kind [2] of sacrifice had any part in the Divine order.

But are we bound to this, even if Jeremiah and the prophets were entirely right? The Christian doctrine of the Atonement may well be related, for example, more to the conception of vicarious suffering given in Isa. liii than to the theory of animal sacrifice. But, in any case, it would seem not altogether out of the question that certain refined sacrificial ideas should be taken into account in the understanding of the redemptive work of Christ. Much, however, of what the prophets taught was forced from them as a result of the particular circumstances of their age, when, in popular religion, mechanical acts of ritual were everything. After the Captivity the moral life of Israel tended slowly to improve. The introduction of the use of piacular sacrifices, as distinct from " clan " and " placatory " ones, would serve a useful purpose in contributing in course of time to the training of an *individual conscience*, as well as in providing a recognition of the sovereignty of the moral law of right.[3] Had the great prophets lived in the age succeeding the Exile, their language upon the subject of sacrifice, and even their ideas, might have been different. Whether this be so or not, surely Christians

[1] The phraseology of the Prayer of Consecration in the English Liturgy and of Article XXXI would appear to be chosen not so much to suggest an ideal theory of the objective work of Christ as to make clear the position of the Church of England with regard to a certain doctrine held by the Church of Rome.

[2] Whether the (earlier) clan feast and the placatory offering, or the (later) piacular.

[3] For a development of the general argument of this page, cf. the writer's *Amos*, p. 341.

may be permitted, if they wish, to find in the best elements of the sacrificial institution truth which is summed up ultimately in the work of the Redeemer.   Care, however, must be taken not to exaggerate the importance which New Testament writers attach to the conception of Christ's death as an oblation.[1]   Similarly, it must be remembered that there is no hint in the Old Testament law that anything in the sacrificial institution was pointing forward to a Saviour to come.   The fact is that Christ's redemptive work has more analogies than that of Old Testament sacrifice, one of which comes up now for consideration.

## B—THE PROPHETIC TEACHING UPON ATONEMENT

It would seem that the great prophets before the Exile preached a simple gospel of human repentance and Divine pardon without reference to atonement either on God's part or on man's.   Moreover, the general attitude which they adopted towards the institution of sacrifice might suggest that any idea of atonement was precluded from occupying a place in their theology.   However, there is to be found within the prophetic writings a doctrine tending in quite a different direction.   It centres around the conception of *vicarious suffering* enunciated within the book of one of the most wonderful of all the Old Testament prophets—the great Unknown Prophet of the Exile.[2]   The teaching came to the prophet (so it would appear) not as a corollary to ideas of institutional sacrifice, but from a contemplation of the age-long problem of the suffering of the comparatively innocent.   The great passage in question is, of course, the fifteen verses—poetic quatrains—of Isa. lii. 13 to liii. 12 upon the career and work of the righteous, but afflicted, servant.[3]

It is hardly too much to say that such a theory of adversity

[1] See Professor C. Anderson Scott, *Christianity according to St Paul*, pp. 85–97.

[2] Of all the conclusions of modern criticism one of the most assured is that Isa. xl.–lv. does not represent the teaching of the son of Amoz. Even the late Professor Orr was inclined to concede this point (*Problem of the Old Testament*, edn. 1906, p. 458 *ad init.* and footnote 1).

[3] Called ' my servant ' in lii. 13, and in liii. 11, as the text stands, ' my *righteous* servant.'

as that which underlies Isa. liii. 4–12 is something absolutely new in Israel.[1] The prophet is musing, perhaps upon the humiliation of his people at the hands of idolators, or else upon the martyrdom of some revered compatriot, probably a teacher; and he feels not only that earlier generally accepted explanations of the reason for suffering have broken down, but also that there may be circumstances which demand another and an entirely fresh solution. In developing his new theory of suffering, at the same time this great prophet comes near to exhibiting the Divine means both of eliciting genuine repentance from man, and (especially) of furnishing the atonement by which sin may be forgiven. Thus he supplements in important, indeed vital, particulars a magnificent theological conception of the earlier prophet Ezekiel—' And I will sprinkle clean water upon you, and ye shall be clean. . . . A new heart also will I give you ' (Ezek. xxxvi. 25–27).

The doctrine of vicarious suffering is evolved, in an attempt to help the men of his generation, by a spiritual genius under the influence of the Spirit of God who, as Christians believe, ' spake by the prophets.' Such an ideal once conceived cannot fall, or drop out of history. Indeed, it must be carried further than the limited historical circumstances (whatever they may have been) in which it originated.[2] Christians see in the redeeming work attributed by the prophet to the Suffering Servant something of the atonement wrought by the passion of the only Saviour. It might be said that for the purpose of Christian theology all that is absolutely necessary in the present essay would be to elaborate the teaching of the great prophetic preacher. But Christian doctrine cannot be formulated on the basis of Israelite theology until the latter has been considered in its

[1] This does not mean that the ground had been in no way prepared. Both Jeremiah's deep distress, occasioned by the guilt and the coming doom of his people, and his office as a suffering intercessor, are very significant. The important expression used in Isa. liii. 12 ' he bare the sin of ' had, in a sense, already been anticipated in the words of Ezek. iv. 4, 5 (though the meaning is different), ' thou shalt bear their iniquity.'

[2] Cf. the words of the late Professor Skinner : " It is one of the marvels of the Old Testament that the idea of vicarious suffering, which was but imperfectly illustrated in the history of Israel, is so clearly and profoundly apprehended by this prophet that only ' the immeasurable step of the Incarnation ' could reveal the perfect life in which his creation is realised " (*Isaiah XL–LXVI*, 1st edn., p. 236).

historical setting.   A brief attempt will therefore be made at such a consideration, in spite of the well-nigh baffling nature of the conflicting evidence, and, indeed, the elusiveness of the servant-idea itself.

Some Christian interpreters, to be sure, regard this page of the Hebrew Bible not as history but as prophecy concerning a distant future.   William Paley in 1794 placed Isa. lii. 13–liii. in the forefront of his argument from prophecy, believing it to be " of Old Testament prophecies interpreted by Christians to relate to the Gospel history . . . the clearest and strongest of all." [1]   As a direct prophecy of the Messiah the elder Delitzsch understood the poem.[2]   And so to-day does that fine Roman Catholic Old Testament scholar Albert Condamin.[3]   With these might be classed in a measure the interpretations of Sir G. A. Smith [4] and the late Professor Burney.[5]   But in no wise may the passage be legitimately

[1] *Evidences of Christianity*, Part ii, ch. i *ad init.*

[2] *The Prophecies of Isaiah*, Eng. transl., Vol. II., pp. 303, 304, 340–342.

[3] *Le Livre d'Isaie*, pp. 340–344.   " The ancient tradition of the Church and the majority of interpreters have been right in recognising in the Servant of Jehovah the Messiah of the Gospels, and in seeing in the four passages in question a direct prediction of His work, sufferings, death and universal reign."   (The four passages are given below, page 78.)

[4] *The Book of Isaiah*, Vol. II., edns. 1890 and 1927, chs. xvi and xx.

[5] *The Old Testament Conception of Atonement fulfilled by Christ*, pp. 9–14.   " The Servant of Yahweh . . . in Isa. lii. 13–liii. 12 represents primarily Israel as a nation. . . . To myself, however, as to many others, the boldness of the lines in which the Servant is depicted *as an individual* makes the conclusion well-nigh irresistible that it was *already revealed to the prophet* in some mysterious way that his conception was to find fulfilment in one great *Person*, the Redeemer of the world."   (The italics *already . . . prophet* are not Burney's.)   Cf. this writer, in the *Church Quarterly Review* (April 1912, p. 125), " Since the ' many nations ' and ' kings ' of lii. 15 are apparently pictured as commenting upon the meaning of the servant's fate *after the event* the employment of the past tense is inevitable." For a similar view, which takes the servant-sections as conscious prophecy (influenced by Babylonian mythology), see G. H. Dix in *The Journal of Theological Studies*, April 1925, pp. 251–255.   It may be remarked that it is not surprising that the Jewish Targum should interpret the passage messianically, at least those parts of it where the Servant is described as glorified.   The Targum of Jonathan renders Isa. lii. 13, 15, ' Behold, my Servant, the Messiah, shall prosper ; He shall be high . . . so will He scatter many peoples.' And again in liii. 10, ' They shall look on the kingdom of their

regarded as being a reflection before the time, an exact antedated *replica* of New Testament events and doctrine. It is hardly too much to say that no such prophecies exist. What appears to be an insuperable difficulty in the way of regarding the verses under consideration as pure prediction is the fact that the tenses in which they are written are only in part futures, mainly they are historic.[1] Practically speaking, it may be said that the poet's point of view is after the death of the Servant and before his resurrection, vindication, and success. In other words, the Servant's afflictions are past by the time of the prophet (Isa. liii. 1–10*a*); it is only the consummation of his work to which the prophet

---

Messiah.' Cf. also Isa. xlii. 1, 'Behold, my Servant the Messiah.' In the Babylonian Talmud occur these words : 'The Messiah— what is His name ? . . . Shiloh . . . Menahem . . . and the Rabbis say, The leprous one ; they of the house of Rabbi [Judah] say, [The sick one] is his name, as it is said, Surely He has borne our sickness . . . smitten of God and afflicted ' (*Sanhedrin* 98*b*). This opinion is as early as the date of the Targum above, *viz. c.* A.D. 180. See, further, Driver and Neubauer, *The Fifty-third Chapter of Isaiah according to Jewish Interpreters*, 1877, Vol. II., pp. 5–7. It may be said, with all respect to these ancient Bible-lovers, that their use of passages as prophecy was too often lacking in accuracy. In *The Testaments of the XII Patriarchs* a reference occurs which reflects the Jewish belief in a Messiah the son of Joseph, and which contains a reminiscence of Isa. liii. 12. ' In thee [Joseph] shall be fulfilled the prophecy of heaven, that a blameless one shall be delivered up for lawless men, and a sinless one shall die for ungodly men ' (*Test. Benjamin*, III. 8). It may legitimately be questioned, however, whether the passage belongs to the original of *c.* 100 B.C. and is not rather a post-Christian addition. To sum up : if Isa. liii. were entirely predictive prophecy there should be much more evidence that the Jews took it as such ; and, moreover, there would be no explanation available of the fact that a crucified Messiah was ' unto Jews a stumbling-block ' (I Cor. i. 18, 23).

[1] Condamin maintains that the tenses are ' prophetic past ' and some support may be claimed for this in Driver's *Tenses*, §§ 14, and (especially) 81, where the passage is cited. Cf. the same writer's *Isaiah, his Life and Times* (p. 179), " Such is the figure which the prophet projects upon the future." But the phenomenon of ' prophetic past,' though particularly frequent in Hebrew, is never sustained in any one passage over more than a very few verses. See, *e.g.*, Joel ii. 21–23, Isa. x. 28–31 and *perhaps* ix. 1–6 (but this also may be the past tense of history, cf. Kennett, *Schweich Lectures*, 1909, p. 70). Moreover, the abrupt introduction of ' And (not ' for ' as R.V.) he grew up ' in liii. 2 is hardly consistent with the meaning ' and he *will* grow up ' !

bids his audience look forward (Isa. lii. 13, 15 and liii. 10b–12).[1]

Who, then, was this Servant of Yahweh ? The expression is applied in the Old Testament both (i) to certain individuals, and (ii) to the nation Israel personified.

(i) A view held by some Jewish interpreters in Christian times has been to identify him with Jeremiah, who silently suffered at the hands of his people [2] and interceded on their behalf.[3] If an individual whose name is known in Israelite history is to be sought, Jeremiah alone would seem to be that person.[4] But evidence that he met with a martyr's death is entirely lacking. And the beginning of the sixth century B.C. would be somewhat early for so developed a picture as the poem, at least in its present form, affords.

If the Servant be an individual, it is far more probable that he was some Jew of the period towards the end of the Captivity or of the earlier years of the Return, a teacher perhaps, at any rate a man of exemplary piety, who met with shameful treatment. This unknown sufferer made a profound impression upon his contemporaries, and the poem is the result of the meditation of a disciple. If the poet's

---

[1] The only exception occurs in v. 10a. ' When (or, if) thou shalt make his soul an offering for sin.' See p. 88, footnote 2. In liii. 11 the phrase ' by his knowledge *shall* my righteous servant justify many ' probably refers to his post-resurrection service to mankind. But some would emend the Hebrew text to *perfect*. In liii. 12 the R.V. has rendered rightly the Hebrew idiom (of *imperfect* tense after a *circumstantial clause*) as : ' and made (not ' maketh ' or ' will make ') intercession for the transgressors.' It is difficult to accept the view of Professor C. C. Torrey that the redemption (to be wrought by the nation Israel) lies entirely in the future at the time of the poet. Torrey places the composition of Isa. xl.–lxvi. including the Servant Poems at c. 400 B.C. (*The Second Isaiah : a New Interpretation*, 1928, pp. 410, 109).

[2] Jer. xi. 19, ' I was like a gentle lamb that is led to the slaughter.'

[3] Jer. xiv. 7–xv. 9 ; cf. II Macc. xv. 14. But Isa. liii. 12 may not refer to intercession ; see below, p. 83 and footnote 2.

[4] Attempts to find the Servant in Jehoiachin, Zerubbabel, and Moses appear to break down hopelessly. After all, it is not very remarkable that either of these last two should happen to be described in Scripture as Yahweh's ' servant ' (Hag. ii. 23 ; Deut. xxxiv. 5). The hypothesis that the Servant is the great prophet, the Deutero-Isaiah himself, has been all but abandoned. Bertholet's identification with Eleazar the Maccabaean martyr has more to recommend it. See below, the reference p. 77, footnote 3.

words imply the *death* [1] of the sufferer, he confidently expects him to rise from the dead and to bring his service for God and man to a triumphant conclusion.[2]   Such an hypothesis is carefully worked out by Dr S. A. Cook in Vol. III of the *Cambridge Ancient History*.[3]   Upon the whole, this approach would seem to the present writer to offer the most satisfactory solution of the historical problem.   The martyr may have suffered wholly at the hands of his own countrymen, or his death may have been caused by a foreign power

[1] See *v.* 8*b*, ' he was cut off out of the land of the living,' *v.* 9*a*, ' And they made his grave with the wicked, and with the rich in his death,' and 12*a*, ' he poured out his soul unto death.'   It is extremely difficult to believe that these expressions are intended to refer to anything but physical death.

[2] Cf. lii. 13, 15; liii. 10*b*–12*a*.   In truth he will ( ?) ' startle many nations,' kings listening to him.   He will win converts : all will issue in his ' justifying many.'   It is the tacit assumption of the existence before the second century B.C. of the doctrine of the resurrection which supplies the strongest argument against an individualistic interpretation of Isa. liii.

[3] Cf. more fully an article by the same writer in *Expository Times*, Vol. XXXIV., pp. 440 ff.   See also one by Professor W. Rudolph, of Tübingen, in the *Zeitschrift für die alttestamentliche Wissenschaft*, 1925, pp. 90–114, " Der exilische Messias."   Rudolph, however, seems to hold that a single personality lay behind all four of the famous Servant passages.   (See below p. 79.)   This person, the prophetical writer looks upon as a sort of Messiah, whose career has been cut short by violent death after arrest and judgment, but whose resurrection will enable his work to be brought to a successful issue.   While Rudolph, however, believes that the historical incident, or rather the entire cycle of events, belongs to the Exile, Cook allows for the placing of it (or them) somewhat later than the Zerubbabel period; and whereas the German scholar styles the Servant ' Messiah ' (with qualification, however, in *Z.A.W.*, 1928, p. 162), the British maintains " The Servant himself is . . . not a Messianic figure. . . . Indeed, he is more than that; he is at once prophet and priest, missionary and intercessor; and his attributes make him almost more than human.   He is mysterious; ' spectral,' he has been called " (*Cambridge Ancient History*, Vol. III., pp. 494, 495). C. C. Torrey allows for variableness in interpreting the figure of the Servant.   To him Isa. liii speaks of the nation, Isa. xlix of an individual (*op. cit.*, p. 138).

For the idea of the efficacy of a martyr's death in making atonement for the sins of his contemporaries, the following extracts from Jewish writings of the first century B.C. and of the first century A.D. should be noted.   ' But I, as my brethren, give up both body and soul for the laws of our fathers, calling upon God that he may speedily become gracious to the nation; . . . and that in me and my brethren may be stayed the wrath of the Almighty, which hath been justly brought upon our whole race' (II Macc. vii. 37 f. R.V. mg.).   ' Thou

with the connivance or active help of the Jews.[1] The language of the entire passage is very individualistic, and certainly there is no parallel in Israelite literature to the sustaining over fifteen verses of the linguistic phenomenon of personification.

(ii) The alternative to the above treatment of the subject is to conceive of the Servant of Yahweh as being the *nation* under some aspect. This method of exegesis has been presented in three main forms. (*a*) Perhaps the most widely accepted view is that which sees the historic nation Israel in all parts of Isa. xl.–lv. in which any ' servant of Yahweh ' is referred to. In the generality of passages the ' servant ' is Israel as he existed, even Israel failing in his duty : ' Who is blind, but my servant ? or deaf, as my messenger that I send ? ' [2] According to this hypothesis, even in the four great passages in which reference is made to the Servant in the opposite way as successful and fulfilling his duty, it is still the nation [3] that is meant. The poems alluded to are, of course, xlii. 1–4, xlix. 1–6, l. 4–9 and lii. 13–liii. 12.[4]

---

knowest, O God, that though I might have saved myself, I die in fiery torments for thy Law's sake. Be merciful to the people and be content with our punishment on their behalf. Make my blood a purification for them and take my life as a ransom (ἀντίψυχον) for their life. Saying this the holy man [Eleazar] died nobly under his tortures, enduring torments even unto death by the power of Reason for the Law's sake ' (IV Macc. vi. 27–30). ' They became as it were a ransom for our nation's sin, and through the blood of these righteous ones and their propitiating death [τοῦ ἱλαστηρίου θανάτου, cf. Rom. iii. 25], the divine Providence preserved Israel which before was evil entreated ' (IV Macc. xvii. 22).

[1] As, *e.g.*, was the death of Onias III.; cf. p. 96.

[2] Isa. xlii. 19, 20, cf. xliii. 8. This Servant is personified as ' formed from the womb,' xliv. 2 and 3. In Num. xx. 19*b* the nation of tribesmen can say concerning itself, ' If we drink of thy water, *I* and *my* cattle, then will *I* give the price thereof : let *me* only, without doing anything else, pass through on *my* feet.'

[3] Note the presence of the name ' Israel ' in xlix. 3, and (with ' Jacob ' also) in the LXX version in xlii. 1. The national interpretation is adopted by the Jewish commentators Rashi (born 1040 A.D.), Ibn Ezra and Kimkhi. (The references are shown conveniently in Driver–Neubauer, Vol. II, pp. xlv and xlvi, 43–48, 49–56 respectively.) For a criticism of the Jewish interpretation, see Dr. A. Lukyn Williams, *Christian Evidences for Jewish People*, Vol. I, pp. 160–169.

[4] These four poems are sometimes styled by modern scholars " The Servant Songs." The title is convenient, but the word " song " in English does not seem very appropriate to the poem upon the Servant's passion.

In the last one, the peoples, many of whom have ill-treated Israel, are represented as coming to recognise that, in comparison with themselves, the Hebrews are innocent.    This is after Israel, having suffered for many generations at the hands of its neighbours, has ' died ' in the sense of having become through exile extinct as a nation.[1]   The prophet suggests that the foreign nations are led to look upon its afflictions as having a value in expiating their own so much greater sin.   The day will come when Israel will rise from its death and will fulfil its mission.   One of the most distinguished exponents in this country of such an exegesis is Professor Peake : [2]   " The Servant is Israel, but regarded from an ideal point of view."   Similar also is the interpretation of Professor Wheeler Robinson ; it is the actual Israel who suffers, " not an ideal though an idealised Israel."[3]

(b) Other scholars, notably Skinner, regard the Servant in the four servant-poems as the ideal Israel, or perhaps the genius of the nation.   This theoretical Israel is conceived of as suffering for, and as destined to redeem, the actual Israel—' my people ' of liii. 8.   So the paradox of xlix. 6 is explained ; it is ideal Israel that saves the nation Israel.[4] A like exegesis is suggested by Davidson, Driver and Kirkpatrick.   The strength of theories (a) and (b) is that the four " servant-poems " are expounded together [5] and brought into definite connection with the experiences of the Exile, to which period in history the composition of Isa. xl.–lv. is generally held to belong.

[1] Ezekiel describes the captivity as a death to Israel, Ezek. xxxvii. 1–14.

[2] See *The Problem of Suffering in the Old Testament*, pp. 34–72, 180–193, and (in a summary form) *The Bible and Modern Religious Thought*, March 1927, pp. 8–15.   For an interesting modification of this view, see L. E. Browne, *Early Judaism*, pp. 19–22.

[3] In *The Cross of the Servant*, 1926.   Of course, if the Servant is taken to be the literal Israel, it becomes necessary to make the (simple) emendation of the text of liii. 8 to '*ammîm*, ' peoples.'

[4] *Op. cit.*, 1st edn., pp. xxxii–xxxvii, and Appendix, note 1 ; but especially in the edition of 1917, Appendix, note 2 (pp. 263–281). For criticisms of this position see Peake, *op. cit.*, pp. 191–193.   The present writer cannot help feeling that the hypothesis of an ideal Israel belongs to the mind of a Platonic philosopher rather than to that of a Hebrew prophet.

[5] Some who adopt the " individualistic " interpretation apply it to all four servant-poems (cf. above p. 77, footnote 3), but obviously this exegesis is called for more with the fourth poem than with the first three.

(c) Some scholars have suggested that ' Israel ' in the four great poems stands for the godly nucleus or remnant of the nation, either in Exile, or at a period some centuries subsequent.[1] One advantage of (b) and (c) over (a) is that an atonement is provided for the sins of Israel which appears to be entirely lacking by interpretation (a).

Thus far an attempt has been made, with all possible brevity, to discuss the place in history to which the great passage concerning the Suffering Servant is to be assigned. Lacking in conclusiveness the matter will, perhaps, always appear. The event which forms the background of the chapter belongs (from the standpoint of our own day) to such a dim and distant past. Only, however, as we strive to reconstruct the original historical setting can we possibly explain those divergences in matters of detail between the portrait of the Servant and the actual facts of the life and passion of the Son of God. Jesus Christ was not characteristically marred by sickness,[2] His grave was not with the

---

[1] The difficulty about this theory in regard to Israel in Exile is that the godly, though they may have suffered more than their worldly compatriots, did not die while the others survived.

An extremely attractive theory, however, is that associated with the name of Professor Kennett. He believes the Servant to be that body of descendants of Israel who at the time of the persecution by Antiochus Epiphanes (168–165 B.C.) were martyred for God's sake. The martyrdom of the *Hasidœans* was indeed voluntary, cf. below, p. 85. The poet seeks to explain the sufferings of this group of great and noble saints as having a vicarious value for the whole nation. And it was at this period that the doctrine of the coming-to-life-again of the individual appears first for certain in the history of Hebrew religion (Dan. xii. 2, 3). There is a difficulty in holding that the four servant-sections were thus inserted into the Hebrew text after the year 200 B.C., but the difficulty is not insurmountable. See *The Servant of the LORD*, 1911, especially pp. 103–122, *The Composition of the Book of Isaiah*, p. 72.

With regard to the general problem as to whether the four servant-poems are by the same writer as the rest of Isa. xl.–lv., it may be said that a decisive answer is impossible. While it is simplest to suppose that the text is homogeneous (considerations of language and style are, to say the least, not against it) yet it is true that the four servant-passages seem to lack cohesion with their respective contexts; at any rate, this is the case with the fourth one. The four passages may be : (1) older poems deliberately inserted by the writer of the book, or (2) additions to it made either by a disciple of the great prophet or comparatively late in history. Professor Kennett holds that a very considerable portion of the Book of Isaiah is, in fact, of Maccabæan date.

[2] See R.V. marg., Isa. liii. 3, 'acquainted with sickness'; *v.* 4,

' wicked ' [1] but was that of a good man. If ' he opened not his mouth ' implies that He did not converse with His judges, the Fourth Gospel, at least, gives a very different story of Jesus. [2]

If, therefore, the Suffering Servant had an existence at a definite time in Old Testament history, what is the theological doctrine enunciated by the great poet-prophet at that time, as he mused upon the Servant's evil treatment? He presents it as truth which, as it were, forces itself upon the consciences of the contemporaries of the Sufferer. It will be seen that there is unfolded teaching extremely profound, even for the utterances of this great prophetic writer.

The sinful make the following confession : [3]

---

' he hath borne our sicknesses '; cf. ' yet we did esteem him stricken, smitten of God '—which word ' stricken ' the Vulgate renders ' a leper ' (*et nos putavimus quasi leprosum*). For leprosy as a punishment for sin, cf. II Kings xv. 5. The passage Isa. liii. 10 declares ' he hath made him sick ' (so the Massoretic text); and Isa. lii. 14, ' his visage was so marred more than any man and his form more than the sons of men.' The Lord Jesus was not sick, leprous, nor plaguestricken. It could not be said of Him that men hid their faces from Him (liii. 3), or that He had no ' form,' ' comeliness ' or ' beauty ' (liii. 2). It may be held, however, that, while the terms (employed in E.VV.) ' grieve,' ' grief ' are not possible as renderings of the Hebrew root *ḥālāh*, yet the representation of the Servant as a sick man is a figurative one. Cf. Staerk, in *Z.A.W.*, 1926, vol. 3/4, p. 255, "bildlich."

[1] See Isa. liii. 9, ' And they made his grave with the wicked, and with the rich in his death; *although* (cf. Job xvi. 17) he had done no violence. . . .' No one reading the Hebrew page would suppose that the ill-used Servant is represented there as being honoured by burial in the grave of a *good* man (Lk. xxiii. 50, 51)—of one who could be described as a ' disciple ' (Mt. xxvii. 57). The parallelism suggests *wicked* rich; in fact, the construction is precisely that of Zech. ix. 17b, *viz.*, *divided parallelism*. In old Hebrew literature ' the rich ' stood for the oppressing class, even as the term ' poor ' is used almost as a synonym for godly. The discrepancy between Isa. liii. and the Gospel story is still more obvious if the simple emendation be adopted ' and with the *doers of evil* in his death ' (*wᵉ 'eth 'ōsē ra' bᵉ mōthāw*).

[2] Isa. liii. 7. Contrast Jn. xviii. 19–23 (before Annas), 33–38 and xix. 8–11 (before Pilate). But perhaps the original verse means merely that the accused did not answer back maliciously. G. A. Smith seems to take the words as referring to the sufferer's attitude towards God (*op. cit.*, 1st edn., p. 360, 2nd edn., p. 375).

[3] It is probable, though not quite certain, that the prophet (unlike the writer of Hosea xiv.) includes himself among those who are making confession.

F

That the sufferings of the Servant were not due to any sin of his own, though at first his contemporaries had thought such to have been the case.

> liii. 4*b*. ' We had accounted him stricken,|smitten of God and humbled.
>
> *v*. 4*a*. Surely (however) it was our sickness(es) that *he* bore [1] :|it was our pains that he carried.
>
> *v*. 5. But pierced [2] he was because of rebellions that we (not he) had committed :|he was crushed [3] because of our iniquities.
>
> Upon him was the chastisement which was to produce our welfare [4] :|and it is with his scars [5] that there has come about healing to us.
>
> *v*. 6. All of us like sheep went astray :|each to his own way we turned,
>
> While Yahweh on his part has caused to rest [6] upon him|the iniquity of us all.'

Again, the prophet puts the truth in his own words in summary form :

> *v*. 8*b*. Because of [7] the rebellion of my people the stroke was upon him.[8]

[1] The Hebrew *nāsā'* could be rendered *took away*, as in Mic. ii. 2. Although in the context the sense comes somewhat near to this (cf. also *v*. 12*b*), it is hardly justifiable to translate so; for the parallel word *sābhal* means simply ' he carried ' (cf. again *v*. 11).

[2] The Hebrew perhaps means, merely, ' slain.'   It is not the same word as occurs in Zech. xii. 10 (see below, p. 95).   Cheyne (in *Sacred Books of the Old Testament*) and others, prefer Aquila's text, and read *mᵉhullāl*, ' dishonoured.'

[3] As by stoning to death.

[4] The Hebrew *shālôm* signifies ' health and happiness,' not ' peace ' in a theological sense, as *e.g.* the opposite of ' enmity with God.' Many manuscripts, however, read *shillûmēnû* with the resultant meaning ' our *retributive* chastening.'

[5] *I.e.*, the weals caused by flogging.

[6] The margin of the A.V. ' Heb. *hath made . . . to meet on him* ' suggests an idea not contained in the original.   The iniquity does not meet *together* or focus upon him, but meets, *i.e.* alights, upon him.   Cf. the use of the noun in Job vii. 20 ' a mark ' *i.e.* where the arrow *strikes*.   At the close of the verse one word has fallen out of the text, but with no loss, apparently, to the sense.

[7] ' Because of ' (Heb. *min*) signifies in this verse and in *v*. 5, not merely ' arising from,' but *through*, *for;* (cf. E.VV. and Cheyne's note in *The Prophecies of Isaiah*, II, 3rd edn., pp. 47, 48).   The teaching of the second half of *v*. 5 is final upon this point.

[8] Or, ' was he stricken to death '; so LXX, Lowth, Duhm, Cheyne (*Sacred Books of the Old Testament*).

And yet again (God is represented as saying) :

    *v.* 11. By his [1] [prophetic] knowledge will my (righteous) servant make many righteous :|while it is he who will carry their iniquities.

    *v.* 12. Because he poured out his soul to death :|and with rebellious ones was numbered,
    While it was he who bore the sin of many,|interposing [2] for the rebellious ones.'

Such statements amount to this. The people, or peoples,[3] moved to penitence by contemplation of the Servant's passion, realise that the sufferings were wholly unmerited as regards any sin of his. Further, by a new conception in Hebrew religious thought, the prophet represents the people as holding that the afflictions which ended in death were such as had been deserved by the Servant's fellows : a passion indeed *on their behalf*, in fact instead of them.[4] In this view God Himself is shewn as concurring (*vv.* 11, 12). Be it noted how far-reaching is the new doctrine of vicarious suffering. There is no question here of the relatively just being involved with the wicked in some general calamity. The context supplies no hint that the Servant's contemporaries are anything but well and prosperous. He is the one victim. Nor, again, is it a

---

[1] The Hebrew expression is extremely difficult. The *genitive* should be subjective or possessive, *i.e.* defining the knowledge of God which the Servant has. See Skinner's and Cheyne's notes *ad loc.* The last verses of the chapter are in a bad state of preservation textually. One conjectural emendation (not very convincing) is ' by his evil ' *i.e.* ' by his [the Servant's] suffering.'

[2] The same Hebrew word in Isa. lix. 16 is rendered in R.V. marg. ' none *to interpose.*'

[3] *I.e.* if the ' Servant ' is the *nation* whose sufferings the foreign peoples are contemplating. See above pp. 78, 79. Undoubtedly the individualistic interpretation of Isa. liii (as of a literal death) is that which leads on most naturally to the doctrine of Christ's atonement. But by the other interpretations also the Servant's passion points forward to the redemption of Christ.

[4] A refined " substitutionary " idea is strong in the expressions ' the iniquity of us all ' (*v.* 6) and ' he bare the sin of many ' (*v.* 12). The Greek rendering of the latter verse runs, ' his soul *was delivered over* unto death . . . and he himself bore the sins of many, and on account of their iniquities he was delivered over.' Some scholars trace directly to this passage the famous saying of our Saviour reported in Mk. x. 45 ' to give his life a ransom for many.' See Rashdall, *The Idea of Atonement*, pp. 31–36; cf. Rawlinson, *St. Mark*, p. 147, " The phrase (in Mark) sums up the general thought of Isa. liii."

case of only a sympathetic bearing of his neighbour's troubles, valuable in its place as such might be.   The bearing of sicknesses, sorrows, wounds, bruises, smiting, stripes, chastisement culminating in subjection to judicial murder, is the taking of the consequences of sin to which the Servant was a stranger.[1] The rebellions, iniquities and sins were committed by them. In the original the antithesis between ' him ' and ' us ' throughout the confession is very prominent.   Indeed, the repetition of the pronominal suffix ' our ' is so marked as to produce a phenomenon—extremely rare in Hebrew—*viz.* that of rhyming poetry.   Furthermore, it would appear that the Servant's passion, at least as regards his fate at the hands of his judges, was (so far as this can be so even in the case of a willing martyr) voluntary on his part : cf. liii. 7 and 12, ' yet he humbled himself,' [2] ' he poured out his soul [3] unto death.'

[1] It is incorrect to employ the term ' sinless ' in connection with the Servant of the Old Testament passage.   Even if the word ' righteous ' is part of the true text in liii. 11 (which is extremely doubtful) the word is probably used with only a relative meaning. It is, surely, not saying too much to assert that *absolute* righteousness is a theoretical idea unknown to the ancients, except perhaps (in the mind of certain Hebrew prophets) as an attribute of Yahweh. It would appear that Skinner goes too far, in commenting on liii. 9*b*, " While absolute sinlessness is not explicitly predicated of him, but only absence of ' violence ' and ' deceit,' yet the image of the lamb led to the slaughter, and his patient resignation to the will of God, strongly suggest that the prophet had in his mind the conception of a perfectly sinless character."

On the question of the genuineness textually of  the adjective ' righteous ' in *v.* 11 the comment of Bishop Lowth may be quoted : " Three MSS. (two of them ancient) omit the word *ṣaddîq*; it seems to be only an imperfect repetition, by mistake, of the preceding word. It makes a solecism in this place ; for, according to the constant usage of the Hebrew language, the adjective, in a phrase of this kind, ought to follow the substantive : and *ṣaddîq 'abhdî* in Hebrew would be as absurd as ' shall my *servant righteous* justify,' in English. Add to this, that it makes the hemistich too long."   To these remarks, made nearly two centuries ago, modern critical study has little to add.

For the title in the New Testament ' the Righteous One,' see Acts vii. 52, xxii. 14; cf. I Pet. iii. 18.

[2] The Hebrew *niph'al* voice here probably has a reflexive force, as in Exod. x. 3, ' How long wilt thou refuse to humble thyself before me ? '

[3] Literally, ' made bare,' or ' emptied.'   Possibly it is a mere equivalent of ' died,' the metaphor being of the emptying out of the ' soul ' in the sense of the blood or strength; cf. Gen. xxxv. 18, Ps. cxli. 8 (where the *pi'el* voice of the verb ' *make bare* my soul ' = ' cause me to die ').   More probably, however, the phrase under discussion is intended to suggest a voluntary death.

But more than this. To quote the words of Skinner,[1] " The essence of the Servant's sacrifice lies in the fact that, whilst himself innocent, he acquiesces in the Divine judgment on sin, and willingly endures it for the sake of his people."

What is meant by the prophet when he says ' The LORD hath laid on him the *iniquity* of us all,' and again, ' he bare the *sin* of many ' (liii. 6, 12) ? Not a few Christian commentators understand the phrases to refer to a transference of guilt from the sinful to the Servant; but it is more than doubtful whether such a theological conception would be possible to an Israelite mind.[2] The truth is that in Hebrew the same word may be used both of an act and of its natural result. Thus the terms *'āwôn*, ' iniquity,' and (in a measure) *ḥēṭ*, ' sin,' mean also ' punishment ';[3] and these clauses should be interpreted in the light of this usage. Moreover, as this servant-chapter does not describe transference of guilt in the abstract, so it is highly improbable that it exhibits any (converse) doctrine of the transference of righteousness to the guilty. The fact seems to be that the statement (in Isa. liii. 11) ' my servant, a righteous one, makes many righteous, bearing their iniquities,' adds little to what has been said earlier in the chapter. *V.* 11, taken as it stands, appears to mean that the Servant will ' make righteous the many ' in the sense ' will bring about their acquittal.' The Hebrew verb occurs again in Isa. v. 23, with reference to unworthy judges, ' which justify the wicked

[1] Commenting on liii. 12 (p. 134, *ad fin.*)

[2] Is it not a fact that the entire idea of *guilt* being passed on to another is illogical ? From the nature of the case, guilt, being personal, can be neither entailed nor transferred.

[3] See Gen. iv. 13, Isa. v. 18, xl. 2.   Cf. Kennett, *Hebrew Conceptions of Righteousness and Sin*, pp. 1–18. The word *'āshām*, rightly rendered in Isa. liii. 10 ' an *offering*-for-sin,' is used also of sin in the abstract. It is doubtful how much theological doctrine should be made to evolve from the Saviour's quotation upon the Cross of the highly poetical cry of the Psalmist (Ps. xxii. 1); the metaphors of Hebrew poetry are apt at times to be exceedingly bold, as *e.g.* in the phrase, ' Awake, why *sleepest* thou, O Lord ? ' (Ps. xliv. 23). See Kennett, *In our Tongues*, pp. 19, 20.

The present writer, in alluding to aspects of the doctrine of the Atonement which arise in the New Testament or in later theology, is in no way seeking to prejudge questions which belong rather to other essays in this volume. Allusions to the later history of the subject are sometimes necessary in order to explain the contents, and the limits, of Old Testament doctrine.

[*i.e.* the guilty] for a reward, and take away the righteousness of the righteous from him,' (*i.e.* they send him to
prison).

Although it must not be supposed that the theology is
one of "punishment at all costs," yet some doctrine of
substitution is here enunciated.   The martyr, or the afflicted
nation, was consumed with voluntary, silent, vicarious
suffering.   This was his calling on behalf of the souls of
men ; who, as a result, will be freed from the load of their
sin.[1]   As we saw above, the verses imply that, while the
Servant's contemporaries by their sins deserved stripes,
the Servant received stripes which were due to them.
There is substitutionary suffering, vicarious atonement, but
yet the passage does not provide any theory ; it does not
say why God should forgive sinners because the innocent
has suffered.[2]

It is possible that the atonement doctrine underlying
Isa. liii. is best explained upon the basis of the metaphor
of the tribunal.   But many scholars see in the passage, in
greater or less degree, atoning *sacrifice*.   " The idea of the
efficacy of sacrifice—here of one that is physically tainted,
but ethically supreme—is elevated from the animal into
the human plane, though in a sense it is a reversion from
the animal to the human victim ; and, just as a holy place
was ' sanctified ' by a sacrifice (and perhaps even a human
sacrifice), so it may be said that this sacrifice ' sanctified '
and gave new life to Israel." [3]   Such is a refined conception
of sacrifice.[4]   And it is possible that this is a true line of
approach to the problem.

However, indeed great is the gulf between the two con-

---

[1] Cf. Professor W. Staerk in *Z.A.W.*, 1926, vol. 3/4, p. 251 *med.*
Davidson (working on the idea of institutional sacrifice in which in
later times the death of the creature was of the nature of a penalty
by the exaction of which the righteousness of God was satisfied)
puts the idea, perhaps somewhat crudely : " These two points
appear to be stated (in Isa. liii) that the sins of the people, *i.e.* the
penalties for them, were laid on the Servant and borne by him ;
and, secondly, that thus the people were relieved from the penalty,
and, their sins being borne, were forgiven " (*Theology of the Old
Testament*, p. 355).

[2] W. H. Bennett, *The Post-Exilic Prophets*, p. 327.

[3] S. A. Cook in *C.A.H.*, Vol. III, p. 497.

[4] Approaching more to the modern meaning of the word " sacrifice."   The Hebrew term signifies *ritual slaughtering :* cf. the writer's
*Amos*, p. 169 and the references given there in footnote 2.

ceptions, (1) the voluntary death of a human being of more or less perfect character, and (2) the slaughter of a brute beast. An important point in the picture in Isa. liii. is that the Servant gave himself willingly. This is just what a sacrificed animal did not do. Moreover, it would seem that, if the basis of the prophet's ideal had rested in Semitic sacrifice, he could not well have avoided the use of its technical terminology, e.g. ' to atone,' ' blood,' ' wrath of Yahweh.' (In liii. 7 the reference to the ' lamb led to the slaughter ' has no connection with sacrifice, any more than have the comparisons with the ' sheep before her shearers,' etc., in v. 7, and the 'straying sheep ' in v. 6.)[1] We seem to miss also a clause indicating that God ' looked upon ' or ' accepted ' the sacrificial offering.

Our treatment of this aspect of the subject may be influenced by the question of the genuineness or otherwise of the expression in v. 10, ' an offering for sin,' and by the stress to be given to it if genuine. Oehler, dealing with this chapter, speaks of " one who, not for his own sins, but as the substitute of the people and for their sins, lays down his life as an 'āshām, a payment in full for the debt."[2] And, similarly, a modern continental scholar interprets the clause : " The Servant's sad lot is placed under the sacred idea of sacrifice, for the atonement of the guilt of others."[3] In Hebrew the term 'āshām can be used either of the money-payment which makes compensation for an offence (Num. v.

---

[1] A similar expression is used also by the prophet Jeremiah with reference to his own submission to his persecutors ; see above, p. 76. It is interesting in connection with the above argument to refer to the method by which St. Paul seeks to explain the atoning work of Christ. Nothing would seem to be clearer than that the Apostle made the Scriptural basis of his doctrine ultimately the general theological conception of Isa. liii. In the passage Rom. iv. 25, παρεδόθη διὰ τὰ παραπτώματα, he is obviously quoting v. 12b of the chapter, διὰ τὰς ἀνομίας αὐτῶν παρεδόθη ; cf. p 83, footnote 4. On the other hand, it is noteworthy in how limited a way St. Paul's theology of the Atonement is made to depend upon the technical ideas and formulæ of institutional sacrifice ; cf. above, p. 72. For a different view, cf. Principal Maldwyn Hughes, What is the Atonement ? pp. 61-79.

[2] Theology of the Old Testament (Eng. transl.), Vol. II., p. 426.

[3] Staerk, op. cit., p. 252 ; and so perhaps G. A. Smith, " It is in this sense that the word ('āshām) is used of the Servant of Jehovah, the Ideal, the Representative, Sufferer. Innocent as he is, he gives his life as satisfaction to the Divine law for the guilt of his people," 1st ed., p. 364, 2nd ed., p. 380.

7 and 8), or of the ram of the guilt offering which *makes satisfaction* (Lev. v. 15).   It is uncertain what is its exact meaning in the present passage, as the expression in connection with Israelite law is employed only in the very late strand of the Pentateuch.[1]   In the history of I Sam. vi. 3–17 the term is applied to the golden mice which the Philistines rendered as compensation when they returned the ark.   In any case, it is never employed of either the slain victim or the goat which went free in connection with the ceremony of the great day of atonement (Lev. xvii.).

The Hebrew half-line presents difficulties, to obviate which various emendations have been suggested; and all of them have the effect of dropping out this particular word.[2] Even if *'āshām* stands, the clause is a hypothetical one— ' if his soul should constitute a guilt offering ' (cf. R.V. marg., and Torrey's translation); or ( taking the reading of the Vulgate, as Cheyne) ' if he should place his soul [3] for a guilt offering.'   Thus the idea is introduced (whether the ordinary text or the Vulgate be read here) as a mere hypothesis, and it seems to come in incidentally rather than to form the central theory of the chapter.   Principal Wheeler Robinson, retaining the word *'āshām*, and assigning to it a very simple meaning, sees in Isa. liii. 10 the thought that the voluntary suffering of the Servant is *not* substitutionary or penal, but that it provides " the costliest of gifts " with which the

---

[1] Viz. ' P.'   The Levitical sin offering and trespass offering are not once mentioned before the Captivity, W. Robertson Smith, *Old Testament and the Jewish Church*, p. 263, cf. p. 229.

[2] Thus Marti reads, ' And rescued his soul from misery,' Duhm, unconvincingly, ' To let his old age blossom afresh.'   Ball (quoted by Professor Box, *The Book of Isaiah*, p. 273) has the second half-line, ' With sickness his soul *was wasted*.'   It is extremely tempting to take the word *'āshām* as having arisen, by the scribal error known as dittography, out of the preceding word *tāsîm*.   Box prints the entire verse as a later addition to the original servant-poem.   In any event, the rendering adopted by the English versions is, surely, utterly improbable; for the *second* person is not employed in the poem, and the abrupt introduction in the Hebrew of a second person singular (not plural) would be particularly strange.   Further, such a translation seems to imply that the verb could signify something like ' take to oneself,' which is not the case.   Besides, how could the prolongation of the Servant's ' days ' (*v.* 10*b*) be conditioned by the action of any Israelites ?   Or, should the ' thou' be taken as Jehovah ? (Elmslie).

[3] Or, ' lay down his life ' : cf., precisely, the Greek expression used in Jn. x. 11.

repentant may approach God.[1] Elsewhere, this scholar emphasises the " subjective " value of the sufferings of the Servant in producing contrition, but he freely allows also a God-ward significance in the passion.[2] The late Professor Burney held to the word *'āshām*, and sought to use it in connection with his own conception of the theory of the sin offering, as " typical of a perfect sinless life which God consents to accept in place of the imperfect life of the wor-shipper." [3] But is it not difficult to understand how the prophet should have been so impressed with a spiritual theory of sacrificial offering ? Normally, with the exception of Ezekiel, canonical prophets before his time spoke of the institution of sacrifice somewhat slightingly.[4] Indeed (though too much stress must not be laid upon this point) the very prophet amidst whose chapters the servant-passages are found, if he does not disparage sacrifice, at least calls attention to the fact that God dispensed with it during the Exilic period : ' I have not made thee to serve with offerings, nor wearied thee with frankincense.' [5] Does it not seem more probable that the author of Isa. liii. approached his subject as a problem presented by silent, voluntary, innocent

[1] *Religious Ideas of the Old Testament*, p. 147.

[2] *The Cross of the Servant : A Study in Deutero-Isaiah*, pp. 46–50. Some further words should be quoted to explain Dr. Wheeler Robin-son's meaning. " The principle of substitution is indeed here, not in the cold and repellent setting of a mere transaction, but in a transformed moral relation, which robs the figure of all formality. The atmosphere is an essential part of the doctrine, and the atmo-sphere is the creation of moral and religious emotion, on the one hand, and of poetic imagination, the highest form of truth, on the other. Without this atmosphere, the principle of substitution becomes easily a barbarous and mechanical injustice ; with it, to suffer freely for others becomes, as with the later Maccabæan martyrs, the glory of a life, whether of individual or nation."

[3] *Op. cit.*, p. 19. Burney's sermon, referred to also above in footnote 5 to p. 74, is worthy of study by those who, like the writer of this essay, hold that an " objective " value attaches to the death of Christ. One may venture to criticise, however, Burney's theory of the ideal holiness of a sacrificial animal ; why should an animal, any more than a human being, be so thought of ?

[4] See the references on pp. 66–68, above.

[5] The section Isa. xliii. 22–25 is highly obscure, but it seems to belong to the category of Amos v. 25 ; see Skinner's note. Dr. Melville Scott's treatment of the passage is attractive : he suggests that ' not ' and ' neither,' in *v*. 23, and ' no ' and ' neither,' in *v*. 24, are later additions. See *Textual Discoveries in Proverbs, Psalms and Isaiah*, pp. 213–218.

suffering, having also in his mind certain elements in the teaching of Jeremiah and Ezekiel ? [1]   But doubtless there is room for more views than one.

It is worthy of note in connection with some theories concerning the death of Christ that, though a " subjective " importance attaches to the passion of the Old Testament Servant, this is not, in the context, prominent.   It is true that a large portion of the poem is cast in the form of a confession made by Israel (or the nations), which confession has been brought about by a contemplation of the sufferings of the Servant; yet the doctrinal theory of the poet is that the sufferings had an " objective " value.   While the passion of the Servant provides the process, a dynamic perhaps, by which men are brought to repentance [2] (and even in this the prophet represents an advance upon his predecessors), yet there is no sign on the Hebrew page that, in the opinion of the prophet, the repentant are being forgiven and restored to spiritual health by anything short of the objective value in the sight of God of vicarious atonement.   Nothing could be clearer than the words ' with his stripes we have been healed.'

The God-ward aspect of the Servant's task, as we have seen, is not indicated in any language of the sacrificial institution.   None the less, the vicarious sufferings which the Servant has borne are represented as being, in some real sense, recognised by God (who is shortly to bring about his exaltation, lii. 13, liii. 12a, and whose pleasure throughout he will do, liii. 10b) and as being counted by Him to have been suffered in the place of the Servant's sinful contemporaries.   It is God who announces ' he bare the sin of many ' (liii. 12b).   However, too much, perhaps, must not be made out of the Hebrew expression ' The LORD has caused to rest on him the iniquity of us all ' (liii. 6), as if God Himself actively, so to speak, transferred the penalty. The ancients believed everything [3] to be the work of the Deity, especially death.   Isa. liii. 6 may, in modern speech, mean simply that when death *came* to the Servant it was not on account of any sins of his, but because he was bearing

[1] Cf. above, p. 73, and footnote 1.

[2] " Subjective " is the interpretation of Isa. liii. suggested by J. W. Povah, who compares the phenomenon to " Transference " in Psycho-therapy (*The New Psychology and the Hebrew Prophets*, pp. 202, 203).

[3] Cf. the writer's *Amos*, pp. 289, 290.

the punishment due to others. Many expositors, however, see a definite God-ward aspect expressed in the very wording of this particular verse.[1]

In bringing to a conclusion this brief analysis of " the most dramatic of all Old Testament passages," some of the results arrived at may be summarised, and the connection of the passage with our Divine Saviour and His work may tentatively be suggested. (1) The sufferings and death of the Servant were past when the great prophet of the Exile (or after) uttered his teaching. The reanimation of the Servant was in the future, though apparently expected more or less immediately. (2) The prophet idealised the value of the Servant's passion, both in any effect it might have towards God, and in its results in bringing about an immediate repentance and confession from sinful people. (3) The Servant himself is elusive indeed. (a) If, by 'the Servant,' Israel as an historic *nation* was meant, then (so it is supposed) there is an atonement provided for the sins of foreign peoples. A weakness in this position is that the prophet would have no means of redemption for the wicked majority of Israel itself. (b) If the Servant be an Israelite (whose death at the hands of idolators was brought about with, or without, the aid of influential Israelites), it is then possible for us to see how the prophet might interpret the martyrdom as having a spiritual value alike for his own nation and heathen. (4) In linking to the Servant the great doctrine of vicarious redemption, the prophet was right only in a very limited degree; the sins of mankind (or even their effects) could not be borne by a fellow human being, even if he were comparatively righteous, and actually willed to bear them. (5) The probability is that the Hebrew expressions used imply the idea of the transference of punishment, and not of guilt in the abstract. (6) Though it may be legitimate to see in the poem an idealised doctrine of atoning sacrifice, this is not clear with regard either to

---

[1] Staerk, who adopts the sacrificial interpretation of Isa. liii., goes so far as to say, with reference to the Servant's work, that atonement is an office appointed by God, and an action following the Divine will (*op. cit.*, p. 256). Such an initiation of it by God is not, to the present writer, very clearly to be detected in the narrative, nor, indeed, is it to be expected. It must always be remembered that the Old Testament poet is still, as it were, groping after truth. The real solution of his problems, as also the fact which he was unconsciously seeking, could of necessity be found only in Christ.

the section as a whole or to Isa. liii. 10 in particular. (7) While it is true that the confession of the sinners in Isa. liii. 4–6 is produced by a contemplation of the Servant's passion, the work of the Servant is something altogether more than " subjective." (8) The prophet represents that the work of the Sufferer is recognised by his exaltation at God's hands; and, further, the passage *perhaps* implies that the atonement which he wrought is accepted by God. (9) A careful study of Isa. lii. 13–liii. 12 does not justify us in concluding that the " Evangelist of the Old Testament " formulated any precise theory of vicarious atonement, but it does warrant us in saying that his theory was an " objective " one. The ideal of vicarious suffering is too wonderful to fall for ever with the passing of the prophet who first enunciated it. Indeed, it seems natural that it should be carried further and be raised on to a plane still higher. In place of a comparatively innocent martyr, an absolutely righteous sufferer must come. Instead of a figure, the degree of the voluntariness of whose suffering was (of necessity) conditioned by events, Someone might yet arise whose atoning work should be wholly voluntary. Though it was apparent to neither the prophet nor his listeners that the ideal would thus be carried further, Christians cannot help realising that the partial doctrine was destined to have a fulfilment infinitely richer than the original circumstances of its formulation admitted. Alike on the one hand by the limitations of the prophet's time and historical circumstances, and, on the other, by the true greatness of the ideal upon which he had laid hold, his doctrine could not be substantiated until the advent of Jesus, the Son of God, " who only could unlock the gate of heaven, and let us in." As Skinner says, " What we observe in the servant-poem is the creation of an entirely new religious idea, arising in the deepest mind of the nation—an ideal which was to remain unrealised until it found its response and fulfilment in the soul of Jesus of Nazareth." [1] An early Christian teacher

[1] *Op. cit.* 2nd ed., p. 279. Cf. the words of S. A. Cook (in *C.A.H.*, Vol. III, p. 497), " The ideas reached out further than men could follow; they were greater than the man himself in whom they were incarnated. The exegesis of twenty-four centuries proves that the writers of Isa. xl. *sqq.* had an insight into spiritual truths which remained unsurpassed in Israel. The height, once reached, was never regained in Judaism; the history of interpretation moved westwards——" Ed. König sums up a very considerable discussion

was asked, ' Of whom speaketh the prophet this ? '   It is not recorded that Philip gave a direct answer to the question upon a point of history ; nor may *we* be able to do so, but, none the less, like the deacon, we may ' from the same scripture ' preach unto the Jews and unto the world Jesus [1] and His vicarious, redemptive, work.   The past history was, we may say, that of a martyr of Old Testament days : the doctrine is that of Christ.

In God's economy there is provided substitutionary atonement.   As we have said, Isa. liii. is not a direct prophecy ; nor is it, necessarily, a page of Christian doctrine which happens to be found within the Old Testament.   At times the Old Testament exhibits religious thought which will be well-nigh, or quite, perfect as long as the world lasts ; but, obviously, we do not as a rule look for final truth in the pages of the Old Covenant Scriptures.[2]   It does not lie within the scope of an essay upon the prophetical doctrine of Atonement to discuss ethical and metaphysical problems raised by a great prophet's new doctrine, or by any of the several elements which may be detected in that doctrine. For the present purpose it suffices to draw out the teaching itself.   The questions, (1) whether it provided the basis upon which the Early Church interpreted the redemptive work of Jesus of Nazareth, (2) whether even it was also in the earthly consciousness of the Son of God Himself, must be left to the later essays.

The idea of vicarious atonement, so fully developed in Isa. liii., does not appear again in the Old Testament.   There are a few passages, however, the theme of which seems to stand in some sort of relation to that of the great servant-poem.   Psalm xxii., whether it refers to Israel or to an individual, exhibits the same divisions of (1) suffering (in the

---

with the remark that the Servant of Isa. liii. (Israel) is one of the buds of the Old Testament.   It is only a bud, yet as such it contains the fruit in itself, and the bud was to develop into the fruit, *Das Buch Jesaja*, 1926, p. 481, *ad init.*

[1] Cf. Kennett, *The Servant of the LORD*, pp. 116, 117 : "It would scarcely be possible to sum up the work of Christ more tersely than in the words of the great prophecy : ' He was wounded for our transgressions . . . ; and with his stripes we are healed.' "

[2] One advantage arising from the historical treatment of Isa. liii. is that by it we are freed from any absolute necessity to hold the doctrine in all its details to be final for all time.

present, or the immediate past), (2) success and exaltation to come.

The influence of Isa. liii. is perhaps to be seen in Zech. ix. 9. Here the prophet announces in words so familiar to us :

> 'Behold, thy king cometh unto thee :|he is just, and having salvation;
> Lowly, and riding upon an ass,|even the foal of an ass.'

This ruler of Jerusalem will have a realm as large as Solomon's, and will inaugurate an era of peace. The expression ' he is just ' may be but an echo from such passages as Isa. xi. 4 and 5, ix. 7, xxxii. 1–8, Jer. xxiii. 5, in which the king to come is pictured in the light of an ideal administrator and judge. Others prefer the rendering ' righteous,' interpreting it as a (more or less conscious) quotation from Isa. liii. 11*b*.[1] The phrase ' having-salvation ' or ' -victory ' (R.V. margin) implies the provision of Divine help (cf. Deut. xxxiii. 29, Ps. xxxiii. 6), and, perhaps, that the king feels a special sense of dependence upon God.[2] The term ' lowly,'[3] *i.e.* ' meek,' undoubtedly suggests a contrast with the *usual* royal " Messiah." This fact is still more apparent if the word be translated, as it almost certainly should be, ' poor ' or ' afflicted.'[4] Lastly, as regards the phrase, ' riding upon an ass, even upon a colt, the foal of an ass,' while it is far from certain that in itself

---

[1] This assumes that the word *ṣaddîq* was by this time in the Hebrew text of the great servant-poem. See above, p. 84, note 1. The verb ' *declares-righteous* ' occurs in one of the other servant-poems, Isa. l. 8.

[2] The Hebrew *nôshā*' is a *niph'al* (or passive) voice, literally, ' saved.'

[3] Hebrew '*ānî*. In the LXX and the Gospels πραύς, but in the Vulgate more correctly, ' poor,' *ipse pauper*.

[4] As, *e.g.* in Isa. liv. 11, ' O thou afflicted,' Ps. lxix. 29, ' I am afflicted and in pain ' (E.VV. ' I am poor and sorrowful '). If the king whose advent is predicted is to be from among the *Ḥasîdîm*, the use of this adjective in Zech. ix. 9 is very apposite. It is generally agreed that the last six chapters of the book belong to a period considerably later than the Return. C. H. H. Wright, who in matters of Biblical criticism seemed consistently to take the traditional view, makes the significant admission : " If the date of the book were to be determined by clear references to facts of history, it would have to be assigned to a period not earlier than the time of the Maccabees " (*Bampton Lectures*, 2nd ed., p. 369).

it implies a humble station and attitude,[1] yet, taken with the other features of the picture, and contrasting Jer. xvii. 25, it perhaps carries on the idea of unostentatious royalty. Such a modification of the traditional delineation of a future king can hardly be independent of the description of the Servant in Isa. liii.[2]  But still, there is no suggestion in the Zechariah prophecy of the king as suffering, still less as working redemption or atonement.

The prophet has no more to say concerning the poor king. Another figure appears in Zech. xii. 9–14,[3] where a very elaborate reference is made to the death of someone whose decease all Judah, high and low, will lament :

> *v.* 10 : ' And I will pour upon the house of David,|and
> upon the inhabitants of Jerusalem,
> The spirit of grace [perhaps, *kindness*] and of
> supplication ;|
> And they will look unto him [4] whom they have
> pierced| [5] and they will mourn for him,' etc.

Obviously there is an allusion here to the martyrdom, or at least the murder, of someone.   The circumstances are known

---

[1] The wording of Zech. ix. 9, 'a colt, the foal of an ass,' seems to be intended definitely to carry the reader back to the royal ' sceptre ' prophecy of Gen. xlix. 11.   And, as in that passage, the kingship possesses the attribute of peace.   In times of peace, at least in the early period of Israel's history, nobility rode on asses (Judges v. 10, x. 4, xii. 14, II Sam. xvii. 23, xix. 26).   Cf. the verse following in Zechariah :  ' And I will *cut off* the chariot from Ephraim, and *the horse* from Jerusalem . . . and he shall speak peace . . .'

[2] Cf. the description of the Servant also in Isa. xlii. 2 and 3.   The allusion, further, in Zech. ix. 10 to a wider mission of the king than one to his own people, reminds the reader of the delineation of the Servant in Isa. xlii. 1*b*, 4*b*, and xlix. 6*b*.

[3] The section chs. xii. 1–xiii. 6 forms the second part (according to Sellin) of the middle portion of the Deutero–Zechariah.   It is not perfectly certain that the writer is the same as in the section ix. 1–xi. 3, quoted above.

[4] The common reading ' me,' though strongly attested, can hardly be correct.   The third personal pronoun is found in forty-five Hebrew MSS., and is supported by a considerable amount of Jewish evidence.   Further, it is the only reading known to New Testament writers (Jn. xix. 37, cf. Rev. i. 7).   It is not out of the question that the present Hebrew *'ēlai 'ēth* is, as a matter of fact, all that remains of the martyr's name ' unto *\*Y"TH\** (whom they pierced).'

[5] The Hebrew *dāqar* usually means ' to pierce,' but it occurs in the simple sense of ' to slay ' in Zech. xiii. 3, Judges ix. 54.

to the prophet's hearers, and, clearly, they themselves have had a responsibility in the death. The Divine spirit, however, will change their attitude towards him who has been slain, and there will be a widespread mourning. Possibly the prophet pictures that the death of the Sufferer will thus, indirectly, bring about a reform in what is wrong in the nation's life and morals; cf. xiii. 1, 2. It is too much to assume that 'the fountain for sin and for uncleanness'[1] points to any "objective" value in the victim's death; but it does declare (what the whole context, indeed, implies, *viz.*) that the sins of the people will be forgiven by God. The crime referred to may be the murder of the priest Onias III[2]; or it may be that of the very same martyr whose passion, according to Isa. liii., was believed by the Deutero-Isaiah to be about to work such wonderful results. Historically all is obscure. But from the point of view of theology, the writer seems to be keeping alive something of the teaching of the great servant-poem; and thus he unconsciously continues the preparation for the coming of Him who will in fact work the supreme redemption. It may be added that, were it not for such passages as Ps. xxii. 1–21, Zech. ix. 9, xii. 10, as well as Isa. liii., it would be difficult to understand how the early Christians so quickly came to the conclusion that the passion of Jesus could be proved to be a part of the Divine mind—'according to the Scriptures.'[3] In short, these portions of the Old Testament formed the basis of what was destined to be the characteristically Christian, as distinct from the Judaic, theory of a Messiah.

[1] xiii. 1. Cf. the general promise in Ezek. xxxvi. 25, 'I will sprinkle clean water upon you.'

[2] See II Macc. iv. 32–38; if so, Zech. xii. 10, 12–14 implies that the descendants of David have taken some definite part in the anti-Puritan movement; cf. Kennett, *Old Testament Problems*, p. 234.

[3] *E.g.* Acts iii. 18, 'by the mouth of *all* the prophets,' I Cor. xv. 3, 'Messiah died for our sins, according to the scriptures,' Acts xvii. 3. Our Lord Himself makes similar references, Mk. ix. 12, xiv. 49.

# III

# ATONEMENT IN JEWISH LITERATURE FROM
## c. 400 B.C. TO c. A.D. 200

### By A. Lukyn Williams

The present essay is concerned with the period which is known in popular language as " between the Books." For whatever the ideas of atonement may be which were held by the writers of the New Testament, it is of great importance to know what those were which were floating round them, and in which they were brought up.

This involves the study of some of the later books of the Old Testament (in spite of the popular term), the Apocrypha, the Pseudepigraphic writings, and certain other Jewish documents, which, though written later than the New Testament, contain not only post-Christian and even anti-Christian doctrines, but also many which are pre-Christian.[1]

The attitude of Jews during this period to the idea of atonement is so very different from our own that it is hard for us to grasp it, and so to make use of it. But our present purpose is to point out the principal illustrations of that attitude in the writings under consideration, and to state what appears to be their teaching. It may be said at once that the clue to their meaning is that God's mercy is over all, and provides means for the restoration of sinners to His favour, while there is no suggestion that the exhibition of His mercy is only for the purpose of leading sinners to thank and love Him. In other words, the thought of the Jewish conception of atonement during our period is *not* that the sinner is to be reconciled to God by any act of love on God's part, but that God is to be reconciled to man by the means

---

[1] In the many quotations throughout this essay reference has always been made to the original texts (so far as these exist), or to the nearest representations of these, save in Ethiopic and Slavonic, but in the case of those books which are contained in Dr. Charles' invaluable *Corpus* of *The Apocrypha and Pseudepigrapha of the Old Testament*, 1913, the translations found there are generally followed.

He has mercifully devised for this purpose. The pious Jewish thinkers of this period regarded atonement for sin as something made objectively, not merely subjectively and within the heart.

When, however, we speak of atonement for sin, we must not forget that the sense of sin during this period was far from being that of the Christian Church. The Psalmist, indeed, might say, " Behold, I was shapen in iniquity, and in sin did my mother conceive me," [1] and suggest that sin was in his nature from the very moment of his conception. But this was not grasped by Jewish scholars. To them sin is not anything inherent in fallen human nature, but rather the commission of this or that action, positively or negatively, which is displeasing to God. They think of sins rather than of sin. They minimise the weight of the opposition in our existing human nature to the Divine will, and this leads them also to minimise the gravity of any atonement that can bridge the gulf.

Ezra, indeed, might confess the sins both of his own generation and of that of his forefathers,[2] and in the Apocalypse attributed to him plead that God may not look upon His people's sins, but on them that have served Him in truth,[3] but even here there is a hint that the righteous do not require mercy, a thought which is plainly stated a little further on : " For we and our fathers have passed our lives in ways that bring death ; but Thou, because of us sinners, art called compassionate. For if Thou hast a desire to compassionate us who have no works of righteousness, then shalt Thou be called ' the gracious One.' For the righteous, who have many works laid up with Thee, shall out of their own deeds receive their reward." [4] Yet the author does acknowledge that even the righteous are not perfect : " For in truth there is none of the earth-born who has not done wickedly, and among those that exist who has not sinned." [5] In agreement, again, with the failure to appreciate the depth in which sin is planted, Issachar is made to say in the *Testaments of the Twelve Patriarchs*, " I am a hundred and twenty-two (*var. lect.* six) years old, and I am not conscious of having committed any sin unto death." [6] Similar, but

---

[1] Ps. li. 5.    [2] Ezra ix. 6–15; I Esdras viii. 74–90.
[3] II (IV) Esdras viii. 26.    [4] *Ibid.*, *vv.* 31–33.    [5] *Ibid.*, *v.* 35.
[6] *Test. Issachar* vii. 1.    The words " unto death " are omitted by MS. α.

not quite so strong, is the *Testament of Zebulon :* " I am not conscious that I have sinned all my days, save in thought. Nor yet do I remember that I have done any iniquity, except the sin of ignorance which I committed against Joseph." [1]

On the other hand, the writers of this period have passed beyond the outlook of the Pentateuch. For in the Law those sins which admit of atonement are such as we Christians hardly call sins at all. They are unwitting infractions of ceremonial laws connected with what we call external observances. But for wilful transgression of the Ten Commandments, for example, no atonement is provided. The sinner is left to the judgment of God. Anxiety about such sins is useless; the question of atonement for them is pointless. In our period this is not the case. The definition of sins is so widened as to include moral as well as ceremonial sins. Atonement is considered in relation to sins of all kinds.

What means, then, asked the Teachers of our period subconsciously, have been appointed by God for bringing about the At-one-ment between Himself and the sinner? Primarily, it must be acknowledged, the stress is laid not on means as such, but on the character of God. It is God's lovingkindness that prompts Him to forgive. Grieved and even angry though He may be, yet His mercy overrules His wrath, and His heart turns in love to the sinner in spite of his sin.

One can hardly lay too much stress on this, for it rests at the basis of all Jewish thought about God, as in fact also of all New Testament teaching. The Jewish word, indeed, is mercy (*chesed*), the Christian is love ($\dot{a}\gamma\dot{a}\pi\eta$), and it may well be the case that the latter connotes to us more than the former because of St. John's phrase, " God is Love." To our minds the sentence " God is Mercy " does not reveal to us so much of God's nature as does " God is Love." For it suggests only a potential attribute called into action by the need of man, instead of that essential quality which from all eternity has moved Him to bestow and to impart.[2]

However this may be, the thought of God's mercy and loving-kindness extending over all His works, even to the

---

[1] *Test. Zeb.*, i. 4, 5.

[2] Yet something of the loss inherent in the word " mercy " may be due to the failure of any English term to convey the full meaning of *chesed*.

unthankful and the evil, is a root idea in the theology of our period. Without that fundamental attribute in God there would be no encouragement to serve Him, or reason to think At-one-ment possible.

God, indeed, is all-powerful, but His very perfection in power enables Him to pardon. "Thou, being sovereign over Thy strength, judgest in gentleness. . . . Thou didst make Thy sons to be of good hope, because Thou givest repentance when men have sinned. . . . While therefore Thou dost chasten us, Thou scourgest our enemies ten thousand times more, to the intent that we may ponder Thy goodness when we judge and when we are judged may look for mercy." [1] There is also this pathetic appeal : "We do not present our supplication before Thee, O Lord our God, for the righteousness of our fathers and of our kings. . . . O Lord Almighty, Thou God of Israel, the soul in anguish, the troubled spirit, crieth unto Thee. Hear, O Lord, and have mercy; for Thou art a merciful God : yea, have mercy upon us, because we have sinned before Thee." [2]

Akin to this are the statements in the *Zadokite Fragments :* " In accordance with the covenant which God established with the forefathers, in order to pardon their sins, so shall God pardon them." [3] " He shall have mercy upon them as a father upon his children, and shall forgive all that have incurred guilt." [4]

Somewhat similarly, though with no direct reference to forgiveness, Philo writes : " God, by reason of His love for mankind, did not reject the soul which came to Him, but went forward to meet it, and showed to it His own nature as far as it was possible that he who was looking at it could see it." [5] " It is His goodness and His power combined with mercy that is the harmony and uniter of all things." [6]

Joshua ben Chananja (*c.* A.D. 90–130) in particular insists on God's freedom in forgiving. Does not Isa. lii. 3 say : " Ye were sold for nought; and ye shall be redeemed without

---

[1] Wisd. xii. 18–22.
[2] I Baruch (Greek) ii. 19; iii. 1.
[3] vi. 6.
[4] xvi. 2.
[5] *De Abrah.,* xvii. Yonge, Vol. II. p. 413.
[6] Ἁρμονία γὰρ πάντων ἐστιν ἡ ἀγαθότης καὶ ἵλεως δύναμις αὐτοῦ (*Vit. Mos.,* iii. 14. Yonge, Vol. III. p. 101).

money "?—*i.e.* freely, and not by repentance and good works.[1]

Yet, in spite of R. Joshua ben Chananja's phrases, it was never supposed that God's mercy was shown towards sinners irrespective of their character. Sins demand Repentance if there is to be atonement. This is always implied, and often definitely expressed. The Jews can, indeed, find no language too strong to tell of the value, the necessity, and the effect of Repentance. Naturally, one must not take here, any more than in other subjects, the earnest pleadings of the Jewish preacher—whether in spoken word or in written exposition—as the weighed and considered utterances of a dogmatic writer. There is nothing answering to the *Summa* of Aquinas or the *Institutes* of Calvin in the Judaism of our period. The sayings, however strongly they may be expressed, are but the impassioned exhortations of the popular orator, or the earnest utterances of the godly expositor. But they occur so often, and in so wide a range of authors, that there can be no doubt that they represent the accredited thought of the time.

Zophar said truly enough to Job, however much he misunderstood Job's position : " If iniquity be in thine hand, put it far away." [2] And the compiler of the book of Proverbs tells us : " He that covereth his transgressions shall not prosper : but whoso confesseth and forsaketh them shall obtain mercy." [3] The Son of Sirach warns us : " Count not upon forgiveness, that thou shouldest add sin to sin. And say not, His mercies are great, He will forgive the multitude of mine iniquities." [4] And again, " In the time of sins show repentance." [5] For Repentance is the aim of God's long-suffering : " Thou hast mercy on all men, because Thou hast power to do all things, and Thou overlookest the sins of men that they may repent." [6] So in the *Prayer of Manasseh* : " Thou hast appointed repentance unto me that am a sinner." [7] And the *Prayer of Azariah* says : " In a contrite and humble spirit let us be accepted, like as in the burnt offerings of rams and bullocks." [8]

[1] T. B. *Sanhed.*, 97b. Cf. *Psalms of Solomon*, vii. 5(6)–9(10); II (IV) Esdras vii. 132–140.

[2] Job xi. 14.

[3] Prov. xxviii. 13.

[4] Ecclus. v. 5 *sq.*

[5] *Ibid.*, xviii. 21.

[6] Wisd. xi. 23.

[7] *Prayer of Manasseh, v.* 8. See all *vv.* 7–13, also the interpolation in *v.* 7.

[8] *Prayer of Azariah, v.* 16.

It is hardly necessary to say that such Repentance includes not merely the open confession of sins, but also sincere grief for having committed them, together with the determination to leave them, and to live a life well-pleasing to God.

The author of the *Psalms of Solomon* chants : " Unto whom art Thou good, O God, except to them that call upon the Lord ? He cleanseth from sins a soul when it makes confession, when it maketh acknowledgment." [1] Eliezer ben Hyrcanos (*c.* A.D. 90–130) therefore, when arguing with R. Joshua ben Chananja (*vide supra* p. 100) insists on it in every case.[2]

For, after all, the first step towards goodness is more effective than the one step outside the City of Refuge which caused death.[3] So also Eliezer ben Jacob (*c.* A.D. 130–160) says : " Repentance and good works are as a shield against punishment." [4] It was therefore accepted by the Rabbis that it was not sackcloth, nor fasting, that wrought forgiveness, but repentance and good works—as the account of Nineveh shows.[5]

Yet Repentance alone, however openly expressed and however real, was not sufficient. Sacrifices (in the legal meaning of the term) of one kind or another always had been demanded, and were still regarded as the normal way of making atonement. Job, for example, offered sacrifices for his sons, in case they had sinned during their festivities,[6] and his three friends were bid offer sacrifices for themselves, and Job was to pray for them.[7] Judas Maccabæus sent two thousand drachmas of silver to Jerusalem for a sin-offering for those dead Jews who had trusted in their pocket-idols as mascots, all the survivors " beseeching that the sin committed by them might be wholly blotted out . . . wherefore he made the propitiation for them that had died, that they might be released from their sin." [8] Again, in the morning and evening sacrifices " they shall seek forgiveness on your behalf perpetually," [9] and these sacrifices were to be main-

---

[1] *Psalms of Solomon,* ix. 11 (6).
[2] T. B. *Sanhed.,* 97b, 98a.
[3] R. Eleazar ben Azariah (*c.* A.D. 90–130) in *Siphre* on Num. xxxv. 26, § 160 end.
[4] *Aboth,* iv. 13 (15).
[5] Jonah iii. 10 ; T. B. *Taan.,* 16a.
[6] Job i. 5.                                  [7] Job xlii. 8.
[8] II Macc. xii. 38–45.
[9] *Jub.* vi. 14 ; cf. xxi. 7–20.

tained even on the sabbath, " that they may atone for Israel
with sacrifice continually." [1]  One side, indeed, of the value
of sacrifices is brought out in the *Letter of Aristeas :* " He
who offers a sacrifice makes an offering also of his own soul
in all its moods." [2]  More normal is the saying in II Enoch :
" Blessed is the man who in his patience brings his gifts
with faith before the Lord's face, because he will find
forgiveness of sins." [3]

The position of sacrifices in the doctrine of atonement is
clearly defined by Philo : " God therefore here (in Lev. v. 7,
11, 12) is propitiated by three different kinds of repentance,
by the aforesaid beasts, or by the birds, or by the white flour,
according, in short, to the ability of him who is being purified
and who repents." [4]  Yet Philo also insists that the perfection required in the sacrifices was a figure of the perfection
required in those who offered them : " God designed to teach
the Jews by these figures, whenever they went up to the
altars, when there to pray or to give thanks, never to bring
with them any weakness or evil passion in their soul, but to
endeavour to make it wholly and entirely bright and clean,
without any blemish, so that God might not turn away with
aversion from the sight of it." [5]

In the *Siphre* we find on Num. xv. 25, " *And the priest shall
make atonement for all the congregation of the children of Israel,
and they shall be forgiven,*" R. Eliezer (ben Hyrcanos,
c. A.D. 90–130) saying : " This passage implies that the sins
of the community as a whole (in contrast to the sins of the
individual), even when done wilfully, are reckoned as
though done unintentionally." [6]  One can understand the
more easily from this that " if the proselyte was in the tribe
of Judah he received atonement in the tribe of Judah (*i.e.*
by Judah's share in the sacrifices); if in the tribe of Benjamin, he received atonement in the tribe of Benjamin." [7]

The Mishna connects the atoning value of the Sacrifices
on the Day of Atonement closely with personal confession
of sins.  The High Priest lays his hands on the bullock

[1] *Jub.* l. 11.                          [2] § 170.
[3] *Secrets of Enoch*, lxii. 1.
[4] *De Mut. Nom.*, § 41.   Yonge, Vol. II. p. 285.
[5] *De Animal. Sacrif. Idon.*, § 2.   Yonge, Vol. III. p. 212.
[6] *Siphre*, § 111, p. 32a.
[7] *Siphre* on Num. x. 29, § 78 end, p. 21a, referring to Ezek.
xlvii. 23.

assigned to him and says : " O God,[1] I have erred, I have transgressed, I have sinned before Thee, I and my house, and the sons of Aaron, Thy holy people. O God, atone now for the errors and transgressions and sins in which I have erred and transgressed and sinned before Thee, I and my house and the sons of Aaron, Thy holy people, as it is written in the Law of Thy servant Moses, ' For on this day shall one make atonement for you,' etc. (Lev. xvi. 30). And they answer him, ' Blessed be the Name of the glory of His majesty for ever and ever.' " [2] So also the High Priest lays his hands on the Scape-goat, and makes the same confession over it, save that he here speaks of the sins of the whole people.[3]

Animal sacrifices, then, were the normal way of making atonement. No doubt the Jews, like the Christians, often understood that they were in themselves inadequate to this purpose, but sacrifices at least represented some loss to those who, by the very fact of offering them, displayed willingness to bear privation, if only their sins could be put away. The sacrifices, then, were an outward and visible expression of Repentance. So Philo tells us : " My good man, God is not pleased even though a man bring hecatombs to His altar; for He possesses all things as His own, and stands in need of nothing. But He delights in minds which love God, and in men who practise holiness, from whom He gladly receives cakes and barley, and the very cheapest things, as if they were the most valuable, in preference to such as are most costly. And even if they bring nothing else, still when they bring themselves, the most perfect completeness of virtue and excellence, they are offering the most excellent of all sacrifices, honouring God, their Benefactor and Saviour, with hymns and thanksgivings." [4]

So far as men entered into the spirit of the service of the scape-goat, putting their hands (through the High-Priest) on it, to signify the laying of their sins there, so far sacrifices represented an offering which carried away sins—" bore them," as the Baptist says of Christ. In other words, sacrifices became looked at, in certain cases, as means of atonement, due, in the first instance, to the promptings of

---

[1] He really uses the sacred Name; see *Yoma*, vi. 2 (3).
[2] *Yoma*, iv. 2.
[3] *Yoma*, vi. 2 (3).
[4] *De Sacrificantibus*, § 3; Yonge, Vol. III. p. 232.

Repentance, but receiving on themselves the guilt of the
actions for which Repentance was being expressed. Sacrifices thus became a means external to the sinner of procuring his atonement. This appears to have been at least
one of the thoughts connected with sacrifices from time
immemorial, and, however much the meaning of sacrifices
was spiritualised, this was never quite forgotten.[1]

The capture of Jerusalem, however, and the destruction
of the Temple by Titus, brought the whole sacrificial system
to an end. What was there to take its place ? Preparation
for such a catastrophe had, all unwittingly to the Jewish
leaders, been provided by the formation of synagogues, and
already men had begun to see that sacrifices were not the
only means of showing the reality of their devotion to God,
and of securing At-one-ment with Him. The doctrine of
Merit was not limited to what was obtained by sacrificial
offerings. It extended far wider. R. Jochanan ben Zakkai
had perhaps already given a lead to this : " As sin-offering
and guilt-offering atone for Israel for the world to come,
so almsgiving and mercy atone for the Gentiles in this
world." [2] Again, " R. Jochanan ben Zakkai was once
walking, and R. Joshua (as his pupil) was running behind
him. R. Joshua said : ' Woe to us that the House of our
very life, the Place which used to make atonement for our
sins, has perished ! ' R. Jochanan said to him : ' Fear not,
we have another atonement instead of that.' ' What is it ? '
said he, ' I will have mercy and not sacrifice ' (Hos. vi. 6)." [3]

First, Merit was seen in the very desires and intentions of
the heart. No doubt the definition of " merit " is not easy.
One must beware of attributing to the word more than it
contains. Like " merit " in the mediæval Christian sense,
it wavers between what is merely congruous to a certain
state of mind and behaviour and what positively claims
reward and blessing. This latter meaning cannot be

[1] The Mishna says : " Sin-offering and guilt-offering atone for a
definite transgression (in contrast to one that may possibly have
been committed). Death (vide infra, p. 112) and the Day of Atonement atone together with Repentance. Repentance atones for light
transgressions of a positive or of a negative commandment, but in
the case of severe transgressions it suspends (punishment) until the
Day of Atonement comes and makes atonement " (Yoma, viii. 8).

[2] T. B. Baba Bathra, 10b (Munich MS.).

[3] Aboth d'R. Nathan., B. viii.; Schechter, p. 22; slightly longer
in A., p. 21.

excluded in the period under consideration. "*A God of faithfulness* : As He repays in the world to come the reward of the perfectly righteous man with the reward of a commandment done in this world, so He repays here the perfectly wicked man with the reward of a little command which he did here. And as He punishes in the world to come the perfectly wicked man for a transgression which he committed in this world, so He punishes here the perfectly righteous man for a transgression which he committed here. *And without iniquity* : When a man departs from this world all his actions come one by one before him, and He says to him, Thus didst thou on a certain day; dost thou acknowledge these things ? He says, Yea, yea. God says to him, Set thy seal, etc." [1]

Evidence of the Merit of Intentions may be seen as early as Prov. xvi. 6 : " By mercy and truth iniquity is atoned for, and in fearing the LORD is avoidance of punishment." [2] Compare : " To do justice and judgment is more acceptable to the LORD than sacrifice." [3] Here, too, may perhaps be placed the saying in Ecclesiasticus : " He that honoureth his father shall make atonement for sins." [4] So again, " To depart from wickedness is a thing pleasing to the Lord, and to depart from unrighteousness is a propitiation." [5]

Closely akin to such good intentions is the determination to learn as much as possible of the will of Him whom the man is desirous of pleasing. Hence the study of the Law is of great importance, and procures a kind of " merit." The study of the Laws about the sacrifices, says indeed a later teacher, R. Chanina bar Pappai (*c.* A.D. 300), is like offering the sacrifices themselves.[6] Hillel (died *c.* A.D. 10) used to say, " He who has acquired for himself words of the Law has acquired for himself the world to come." [7]

Intentions issue in action, and the actions themselves become meritorious. This is so much the case that they can be weighed against acts of contrary character which have been committed by the same person. Nothing is commoner throughout post-Biblical Jewish history than to find

---

[1] *Siphre* on Deut. xxxii 4, § 307, p. 133a, compared with *Yalqut.*
[2] This is probably the meaning of the second clause.
[3] Prov. xxi. 3.
[4] Ecclus. iii. 3. Cf. Oesterley, *in loco.*
[5] Ecclus. xxxv. 3 (5).
[6] *Pesiqta d'Rab Kahana*, Buber, 60b.     [7] *Aboth*, ii. 8.

statements to the effect that a man's future is decided by the relative amounts of his good and evil acts. If the latter prevail over the former he is condemned, if the former are greater he is blessed. If indeed it happens that the sets of actions are equal, then, according to some authorities, God's mercy inclines the scale of a man's merits in his favour,[1] or, according to other authorities, other merits than his own are reckoned as his.[2] In any case, a man's actions are regarded as having, so to speak, an entity of their own, and, when performed, as existing outside of himself, and therefore are considered to be an external means of atonement for his past sins. To those thinkers who hold such opinions atonement is no subjective thing, consisting in the reconciliation of the sinner with God, but the result of external actions bringing about the reconciliation of God with the sinner. Not the change alone in the man's heart, but the due performance of certain actions, wins for him his acceptance with God. Atonement is not subjective, but objective.

" Do good to a godly man," says the Son of Sirach, " and thou shalt find a recompense; and if not from him, yet from the Most High."[3] "The righteous," adds the Syriac *Apocalypse of Baruch*, " justly hope for the end, and without fear depart from this habitation, because they have with Thee a store of works preserved in treasuries."[4] Again, " For behold the days come and the books shall be opened in which are written the sins of all those who have sinned, and again also the treasuries in which the righteousness of all those who have been righteous in creation is gathered."[5] And the Greek *Apocalypse of Baruch* says of the great vessel that Michael was holding : " This is where the merits of the righteous enter, and such works as they do, which are escorted before the heavenly God. And as I was conversing with him, behold angels came bearing baskets full of flowers. And they gave them to Michael. And I asked the angel, Lord, who are these, and what are the things brought hither from beside them ? And he said to me, These are angels who are over the righteous. And the archangel took the baskets, and cast them into the vessel. And the angel said to

---

[1] So the School of Hillel (c. A.D. 25), referring to Exod. xxxiv. 6, and all Ps. cxvi. Tosephta, *Sanhed.*, xiii. 3. So also R. Eliezer (ben Hyrcanos) in *Pesiqta d'Rab Kahana*, Piska xxvi. p. 167a.

[2] *Vide infra*, p. 113. Cf. further *The Testament of Abraham*, Longer Recension, §§ xii–xiv. (Box, 1927, pp. 19–25); *Pesiqta d'Rab Kahana*, Piska 23, § 54, p. 153b.

[3] Ecclus. xii. 2.  [4] II Bar. xiv. 12.  [5] *Ibid.*, xxiv. 1.

me, These flowers are the merits of the righteous." [1]  " Work
righteousness, therefore, my children," says Levi, " upon
the earth, that ye may have it as a treasure in heaven." [2]
The writer of II Enoch may indeed be altogether too late for
us, but his words at least illustrate the thought of our
period :  " Blessed is the man who does not direct his heart
with malice against any man, and helps the injured and
condemned, and raises the broken down, and shall do charity
to the needy, because on the day of the great judgment
every weight, every measure, and every make-weight (will
be) as in the market, that is to say (they are) hung on scales
and stand in the market, (and every one) shall learn his own
measure, and according to his measure shall take his
reward." [3]  " For all these things will be laid bare in the
weighing-scales and in the books, on the day of the great
judgment." [4]

Again, in the *Apocalypse of Ezra* we read :  " For the
righteous who have many works laid up with Thee, shall
out of their own deeds receive their reward." [5]  So, a little
later, in a passage where perhaps a Christian thought has
been interpolated, we find :  " And every one shall then be
saved, and shall be able to escape on account of his works,
or of his faith by which he has believed." [6]

R. Tarphon (*c.* A.D. 130) bids :  " If thou hast learned
much Torah, they will give thee much hire; and the Master
of thy work is faithful, who will pay thee the hire of thy
labour; for know that the giving of the hire of the righteous
is for the time to come." [7]  So R. Aqiba (killed *c.* A.D. 132)
says in his figure of the tradesmen :  " The account book is
open, and the Hand writes . . . and the judgment is a
judgment of truth." [8]  And we read in the same collection
of moral sayings :  " Ben Hê-Hê (*c.* A.D. 1) said : ' According to the toil is the pay.' " [9]

R. Aqiba again says that the lack of one good action may
incline the scale to condemnation.[10]  R. Eleazar ben R.
Simeon ben Jochai (*c.* A.D. 190) says :  " Let a man always
consider himself as half meritorious (*zakkai*) and half
guilty.  If he performs one good deed (*mitzvah*), blessed is

[1] III Baruch xi. 9 to xii. 5.                [2] *Test. Levi*, xiii. 5.
[3] *Book of the Secrets of Enoch*, A., xliv. 4 *sq.*        [4] *Ibid.*, lii. 15.
[5] II (IV) Esdras viii. 33.            [6] *Ibid.*, ix. 7.
[7] *Aboth*, ii. 20 (19).      [8] *Ibid.*, iii. 20 (25).      [9] *Ibid.*, v. 26 (33).
[10] T. J. *Qidd.*, I. 10, p. 61d., with a play on Isa. v. 14.

he ! For he has placed himself in the scale of merit. If he commits one transgression, woe to him ! For he has placed himself in the scale of guilt." [1]

Now it is evident that such acts may be of different kinds, some more fraught with merit, some less. Among the greater and more important are those which help other people, particularly by gifts of money. So much is this the case that one of the forms of the Hebrew words for " righteousness " (*zedaqah*) is applied to almsgiving so constantly that it is sometimes difficult to say whether " almsgiving " or " righteousness " is intended. It was this dubiety of interpretation, no doubt, that led to the famous various reading in Mt. vi. 1, where our Lord's phrase " Take ye heed not to do your righteousness before men " was interpreted as " not to do your alms," and the proper word for alms (ἐλεημοσύνη) was even interpolated in the text. But, be that as it may, this false reading is thoroughly in accord with the Jewish thought of the time. " Righteousness " was almost synonymous with " almsgiving," and almsgiving was one of the surest ways of increasing one's merit before God.

So we read : " For the relieving of thy father shall not be forgotten : and instead of sins it shall be added to build thee up. In the day of thine affliction it shall remember thee ; as fair weather upon ice, so shall thy sins melt away." [2] " If thou have little bestow it, and be not afraid to give alms according to that little : for thou layest up a good treasure for thyself against the day of necessity : because alms delivereth from death, and suffereth not to come into darkness." [3] " It is better to give alms than to lay up gold : almsgiving doth deliver from death, and it purges away all sin. They that do alms shall be fed with life." [4] " When man clothes the naked and fills the hungry, he will find reward from God." [5]

R. Jochanan ben Zakkai's words about the effect of almsgiving have already been quoted.[6] R. Meir (*c.* A.D. 150) used to say : " If a heathen objects and says to you : ' If your God loves the poor, why does He not feed them ? ' Tell him, ' That by them we may be delivered from the

---

[1] Tosephta, *Qidd.*, I. 13 ; T. B. *Qidd.*, 40 a.b.
[2] Ecclus. iii. 14 *sq.*  [3] Tobit iv. 8–11.  [4] *Ibid.*, xii. 8 *sq.*
[5] II Enoch lxiii. 1 A., or " he shall find forgiveness," B.
[6] *Vide supra,* p. 105.

judgment of hell.' " [1] So the School of R. Ishmael (c. A.D. 130) taught : " Every one who cutteth off his necessities and useth them for alms is delivered from the judgment of hell. For if two ewes try to cross a river, one shorn and one unshorn, only the former will succeed." [2] " Greater," said R. Eleazar (ben Pedath, c. A.D. 180) " is he that doeth alms than all the sacrifices," adding a playful reference to Prov. xxi. 3.[3]

" Whence do we know," said R. Eleazar in the name of R. Jose (c. A.D. 150), " that almsgiving and kindly actions are a great advocate (" paraclete ") and great peace between Israel and their Father who is in heaven? Because it is said, ' Thus saith the LORD, Enter not into the house of mourning, neither go to lament, neither bemoan them : for I have taken away My peace from this people, saith the LORD, even mercy (chesed) and pity (rachamim, Jer. xvi. 5). ' Mercy ' means kindly actions, and ' pity ' means alms. It teaches us that alms and kindly actions are a great advocate and peace between Israel and their Father who is in heaven." [4]

The saying of Prayers, again, has always tended to become meritorious, although there does not appear to be any express statement to this effect belonging to this period. Hence our Lord warned His hearers against the mere repetition of prayers, or perhaps against even the heaping up of synonyms in prayers.[5] Philo, however, very nearly attributes such meritorious value to prayers when he speaks of Jews on the Day of Atonement " propitiating (ἱλασκόμενοι) the Father of the universe by holy prayers, by which they are accustomed to solicit pardon for their former sins, and the acquisition and enjoyment of new blessings." [6] The same thought perhaps underlies his words : " The High Priest of the Jews . . . is accustomed to propitiate (ἐξευμενίζειν) the Governor of the world by supplications and prayers, beseeching Him to give a portion of His own merciful and humane nature to the things which He has created." [7]

Similarly with Fasting. It, too, became regarded as an

---

[1] T. B. *Baba Bathra*, 10a.    [2] T. B. *Gittin*, 7a.
[3] T. B. *Sukkah*, 49b.
[4] Tosephta, *Pea*, iv. 21 ; T. B. *Baba Bathra*, 10a, is nearly identical.
[5] Mt. vi. 7.   Cf. *infra*, pp. 116, 118.
[6] *De Vita Mosis*, ii. 4 ; Yonge, Vol. III. p. 79.
[7] *De Monarchia*, ii. 7 ; Yonge, Vol. III. p. 197.

act which possessed a certain amount of meritorious weight in the balance of good and evil actions. For the human heart always seeks something by which it may win God over to its side.

Thus in the *Psalms of Solomon* we find : " He maketh atonement for (sins of) ignorance by fasting and afflicting his soul." [1]

But of all the means of making atonement none is so effective as that of Suffering, especially suffering culminating in death. A man's sufferings, whether borne in the course of nature, or brought upon him by his faithfulness to religion, have a peculiar power in winning the favour of God. The following examples may be noted.

One passage in the *Psalms of Solomon* has been mentioned already, for " affliction " is there joined with " fasting." [2] Another passage in the same book is : " Happy is the man whom the Lord remembereth with reproving, and whom He restraineth from the way of evil with strokes, that he may be cleansed from sin, that it may not be multiplied." [3] Another is : " The Lord spareth His pious ones, and blotteth out their errors by His chastening." [4] So also we read that when R. Eliezer ben Hyrcanos was ill, four elders visited him. Three of them praised him, but the fourth, R. Aqiba, was glad at his chastisement. ' Raise me up,' said the dying man, ' that I may hear what Aqiba says ; . . . Why do you say this ? ' Aqiba reminded him that it was chastisements that led King Manasseh into blessing." [5]

In the *Mechilta* we find, apparently as spoken by R. Aqiba, " A man should rejoice in chastisements more than in prosperity, for even if a man stays in prosperity all the days of his life, he gets no pardon for the transgressions he has

[1] iii. 9 (8). So Buchanan Gray's translation in Charles' *Corpus* ii. 635. Ryle and James' version (1891) does not connect Fasting so definitely with making atonement. Later Rabbinic utterances on the subject are very strong; *e.g.* Rab Sheshet (third century) used to pray : " Now that I have been fasting, and my fat and my blood have been diminished, may it be Thy will that my fat and my blood which have been diminished may be accounted as though I had offered them before Thee upon the altar, and do Thou accept me " (T. B. *Berakoth*, 17a). On the whole subject see especially Isr. Abrahams, *Pharisaism*, Vol. I. pp. 121–128; Vol. II. pp. 197–199.
[2] *Psalms of Solomon*, iii. 9 (8).
[3] *Ibid.*, x. 1.
[4] *Ibid.*, xiii. 9 (10).
[5] T. B. *Sanhed.*, 101 ab. Cf. *Pesiqta d'Rab Kahana*, ix. beginning.

committed. How, then, does he get pardon for his transgressions? By his chastisements." [1] R. Nehemiah (*c.*
A.D. 150) says : " Precious are chastisements, for as sacrifices appease (God) so do chastisements (cf. Lev. i. 4;
xxvi. 41). And chastisements appease even more than
sacrifices, because sacrifices cost money, and chastisements
cost pain of body (cf. Job ii. 4)." [2]  " Which is the way,"
said R. Simeon ben Jochai (died *c.* A.D. 160), " that brings a
man to the world to come? It is chastisements." [3] Further,
R. Ishmael (died A.D. 135) says that in certain sins chastisements atone for one third.[4]

If, however, sufferings as such are effectual in drawing
God's favour toward us, much more effective is suffering in
its extremest form of Death. What more can a man give?
What more can he do than offer up his life? Surely this is
the ideal means by which God may be reconciled to him!
Observe, again, that a man's death is not regarded in our
period merely as a means by which a man shows his love
for God, or the reality of his repentance for past sin, but as
an act which God considers in itself, that He may apply the
value of it to bridging the gulf between Himself and the
sinner. The sinner, no doubt, deserves punishment, but the
fact of his death, especially if that death be brought about
because of his faith on God (*i.e.* if he is a martyr), is sufficient
in God's sight to outweigh his sins. A low, mechanical, and
carnal notion of atonement, no doubt, even though repentance is always presupposed, but there it is, and the literature
of our period is full of it.

A strange passage in the Greek and the Peshitta of
Ecclesiasticus seems to affirm this. Samuel, it says, " after
he died was enquired of; he declared unto the king his way,
and he lifted up his voice from the earth, to blot out iniquity
by prophecy." On this Box and Oesterley (in Charles'
*Corpus*) comment : " The reference is to the fact that by
announcing the approaching death of Saul, Samuel prophesied
the blotting out of the sins of his people, of whom Samuel
was the representative; Saul's death atoned for the sins of
the people as well as for his own sins." [5] But the absence of

---

[1] On Exod. xx. 23. Friedmann, p. 72b; Weiss, p. 79b; Horowitz,
p. 240.    [2] *Ibid.*    Similarly in *Siphre*, Deut. vi. 5, § 32, p. 73b.
[3] *Siphre*, Deut. vi. 5, § 32, p. 73b. The whole passage is instructive.
[4] Tosephta, *Yoma*, v. (iv.) 8. Cf. Mishna, *Yoma*, viii. 8.
[5] Ecclus. xlvi. 20.

the words "to blot out iniquity" from the Hebrew text makes the interpretation doubtful. So in I Enoch the Holy Ones in heaven pray "on behalf of the blood of the righteous which hath been shed . . . that judgment may be done unto them."[1] The Mishna bids the criminal make confession just before he is stoned, and, if he does not know how to make confession, to say: "May my death be an expiation of all my sins."[2]

R. Aqiba said that a guilt-offering was to be brought for one who needed atonement, but a dead person did not need it, "for his own soul had (*i.e.* in his death) already offered atonement."[3] And it is said in the *Siphre* again, "All the dead are atoned for by their death," save those who persist in sin without repentance.[4] Further, "It is a good sign," says R. Nathan ("the Babylonian," latter half of the second century A.D.), "for a man when he is punished soon after his death. If he dies without being lamented, or being buried, or if a wild animal devours him, or storms come down upon him—this is a good sign, for he is being punished soon after his death."[5]

The merit of Death, however, especially of a martyr's death, brings us very close to the question whether men's merits may not be of use to others as well as to themselves. Yet here, more than elsewhere, we must be careful not to over-estimate the value placed upon merits. For example, the phrase "the merits of the Fathers" is continually upon the lips of Jews. What does it mean? Properly and originally it was perhaps harmless. It meant that God, as He looked at the Jewish nation, regarded it with a peculiar and personal love, because He could never forget the moral worth of its great ancestors and leaders. The Patriarchs in particular, and Moses, had served Him with such whole and perfect service that it was only natural and proper that when the nation showed a very different, and indeed degenerate, spirit He should bear with it in consideration of their "merits." It was but congruous that He should do so. But it can hardly be denied that in the popular mind the idea far outstripped this. Treasuries of the good works of the pious now existed, and God could, if He would—and He certainly would always so desire—use

[1] I Enoch xlvii. 2.
[2] *Sanhed.*, vi. 2 (4).
[3] *Siphre* on Num. v. 9, § 4 end, p. 2b.
[4] *Ibid.*, Num. xv. 31, § 112, p. 33a.
[5] *Ibid.*, p. 33b.

H

such merits for the benefit of others.   No one, it was thought, was obliged to be more than moderately good.   If he was, so to say, extra good, his own superabundant merits could be applied to other cases.   There was not, to be sure, as in the Roman Church, any thought that this application lay within the power of a man—for Judaism never attributed such power to its priests even when it possessed them; [1]—but the superabundant merits were stored up, and God would not be likely to let them be wasted.

These superabundant merits were generally considered to be the result of the lives of the pious of earlier ages, but sometimes the idea was applied to certain extraordinarily good people in relation to their contemporaries.   In other words, the question of time as such was accidental, not inherent, in the theory of the effectiveness of the merits of outstanding saints in helping those who had a deficiency.

The better side of this theory may be seen in Philo's representation of value of " the just man " to others : " Let us pray . . . that the just man may be firmly established in the human race for the relief of all diseases; for while he is in vigorous health, one must not abandon all hope of complete safety, as through the medium of him, I imagine God the Saviour, extending His all-healing medicine, that is to say, His propitious and merciful power, to His suppliants and worshippers, bids them employ it for the salvation of those that are sick . . . spreading it like a salve over the wounds of the soul. . . . And a most visible example of this is the righteous Noah." [2]

Something of this kind perhaps lies in the words of comfort addressed by all the people to a High Priest who is mourning : " We are thy atonement," i.e. we are prepared to share thy suffering, bearing it for thee.[3]

As examples of the more definite teaching the following may be noted.   When Eleazar, according to the author of IV Maccabees, was cast into the fire by the command of Antiochus, he prayed : " Thou, O God, knowest that, though I might save myself, I am dying by fiery torments for Thy

---

[1] In one sense Judaism still has " priests," all, presumably, who have the surname of Cohen, but their power seems to be limited to giving the blessing at fixed occasions, and even this is dependent on their observing certain taboos.   See the *Jewish Encyclopædia*, Vol. IV., p. 144; Vol. X., p. 197.

[2] *De Migr. Abraham*, § 22; Yonge, Vol. II. pp. 70 *sq.*

[3] *Sanhed.*, ii. 1 (2).

Law.   Be merciful unto Thy people, and let our punishment
be a satisfaction in their behalf.   Make my blood their
purification, and take my soul to ransom their souls." [1]
And at the end of his book the author writes : " These men
(*i.e.* the seven martyrs), therefore, having sanctified themselves for God's sake, not only have received this honour, but
also (the honour) that through them the enemy had no
more power over our people, and the tyrant suffered punishment, and our country was purified, they having as it were
become a ransom for our nation's sin." [2]

The author, however,[3] of II Enoch expressly warns his
readers not to trust in the prayers of the departed.   " And
now, my children, do not say, Our father stands before God,
and prays for us (to be released) from sin; for there is no
person there to help any man who has sinned." [4]   Gamaliel
III. (*c.* A.D. 250) rather later, indeed, than our period, says :
" Let all who labour with the congregation labour with them
for the Name of Heaven, for the merit of their fathers
upholds them, and their righteousness stands for ever.   And
God will reckon reward to you yourselves as if ye had done
it." [5]

Besides the reliance on the merits of the Fathers in general,
special mention is made of those of Phinehas, and, again,
there are various examples of trust in the work of Angels.

After speaking of Aaron, including his reconciling work
as High Priest, the Son of Sirach goes on to praise Phinehas,
who " made reconciliation for Israel (Num. xxv. 13; Ps.
cvi. 30 *sq.*), therefore was there a covenant of peace established for him." [6]   In itself this might seem to be merely
historical, but in the *Siphre* we find that Phinehas' work is
regarded as still effective.   " *And he atoned (waykappēr) for
the children of Israel*; because he poured out his soul unto

[1] IV Macc. vi. 27–29.

[2] *Ibid.*, xvii. 20 *sq.*   The fact that the author makes no sharp
distinction between the temporal and the eternal effect of the
martyrs' death does not diminish the force of his words as attributing
merit to it.

[3] A passage in I Baruch (in our Apocrypha) iii. 4 would be of
importance if its text were certain.   For it runs : " O Lord Almighty,
Thou God of Israel, hear now the prayer of the dead Israelites "—
implying that their death gave them special reason for supposing
that their prayers would avail.   But probably the lost Hebrew
original had not " the dead Israelites," but only " the men of Israel "
(*Mthê*, not *mêthê*).

[4] II Enoch liii. 1.          [5] *Aboth*, ii. 2.          [6] Ecclus. xlv. 23 *sq.*

death (Isa. liii. 12). It does not say here " to atone "
(*lkappēr*) (*i.e.* once for all), but *ykappēr*; for until this
present time he hath not moved from his position; but he
stands and atones, until the time when the dead shall live
again." [1] So, too, Enoch is called " Redeemer of the sins
of man." [2]

There are also several references to the work of Angels.
In the book of Job itself, when a man is in danger of death,
if only " there be with him an Angel . . . to shew unto man
what is right, then he is gracious unto him and saith,
Deliver him from going down to the pit, I have found a
ransom." [3] It is not clear, indeed, whether the speaker be
the angel, or the supreme Judge Himself—probably the
latter—nor again whether the ransom is something wholly
external to the man, or some act of his own which is discovered to be in his favour. But in any case it is an angel
who takes his part.[4]

So is it plainly stated in the *Testament of Levi* : " I am
the angel who intercedeth for the nation of Israel that they
may not be smitten utterly [for every evil spirit attacketh
it]. And after these things I awaked (says Levi), and
blessed the Most High, [and the angel who intercedeth for
the nation of Israel and for all the righteous]." [5]

So again in the *Testament of Dan* the writer insists on the
power of the Angel to help Israel against all other spirits.[6]

More to the point is the *Testament of Levi*. There are
" the archangels (or " the angels of the presence of the
Lord ") who minister and make propitiation to the Lord
for all the sins of ignorance of the righteous, offering to the
Lord a sweet-smelling savour, a reasonable and a bloodless
offering." [7] In I Enoch Michael is bidden by the Most
High : " Cleanse thou the earth from all oppression, and
from all unrighteousness, and from all sin, and from all
godlessness : and all the uncleanness that is wrought upon

---

[1] *Siphre* on Num. xxv. 13, § 131 end, p. 48b.
[2] II Enoch lxiv. 5 A.        [3] Job xxxiii. 23 *sq.*
[4] See T. J. *Qidd.*, i. 10, p. 61d. R. Eliezer, son of R. Jose the
Galilean (c. A.D. 130), said : " If 999 angels pronounce a man guilty,
and one declares his merit," the Holy One accepts the verdict of
the latter.
[5] *Test. Levi*, v. 6 *sq.*, but there is some doubt about the genuineness
of the words in square brackets.
[6] *Test. Dan*, vi. 1–6.
[7] *Test. Levi*, iii. 5 *sq.* The text here also is doubtful.

the earth, destroy from off the earth.    And all the children
of men shall become righteous, and all nations shall offer
adoration and shall praise Me, and all shall worship Me." [1]

It must, however, be pointed out that sometimes God
Himself is thought of as coming for propitiation and deliverance.    In the *Testament of Simeon* we find :  " Then the
Mighty One of Israel shall glorify Shem, for the Lord God
shall appear on earth,[2] and Himself save men." [3]    In the
*Testament of Levi* an angel tells Levi :  " By thee and Judah
shall the Lord appear among men, saving every race of
men." [4]    And in I Enoch we have :  The righteous " shall
have no honour through the name of the Lord of Spirits,
yet through His name shall they be saved, and the Lord of
Spirits will have compassion on them, for His compassion
is great." [5]

Yet is there in the non-Christian writings of our period no
expectation of the atoning work of the Messiah ?    We
should naturally have supposed that the Jews would have
regarded Him at least as the very flower of the human race,
with actions so superabundant in goodness as to fill a whole
treasury which might be applied for the benefits of others
who are less perfect.

There is, it must be acknowledged, very little evidence to
this effect.    In the *Testament of Levi* we read :  " Then shall
the Lord raise up a new priest. . . .   In his priesthood shall
sin come to an end, and the lawless shall cease to do evil . . .
and Beliar shall be bound by him, and he shall give power to
his children to tread upon the evil spirits." [6]    Philo, again,
in one passage seems to come verbally near the Christian
hope when he writes, apparently of Moses, " It was indispensable that the man who was consecrated to the Father
of the world should have as a paraclete his son, the Being
most perfect in all virtue, to procure forgiveness of sins, and
a supply of unlimited blessings." [7]    But, if the passage is
not a Christian interpolation, the " son " presumably refers
to Aaron.    Or, possibly, Aaron may be the first, and
Phinehas the second.[8]

[1] I Enoch x. 20 *sq.*
[2] The MSS. here add " as man," but Charles is probably right in
supposing this to be a Christian interpolation.
[3] *Test. Sim.*, vi. 5.                    [4] *Test. Levi*, ii. 11.
[5] I Enoch l. 3.
[6] *Test. Levi*, xviii. 2, 9, 12.
[7] *Vita Mos.*, III. 14.   Yonge, iii. 102.    [8] *Vide supra*, p. 115.

It is no doubt true that as it was predicted of Michael [1] so also it was foretold of the Messiah, that, in the beginning of his reign, " the heart of the inhabitants of the world shall be changed, and be converted to a different spirit.   For evil shall be blotted out, and deceit extinguished ; faithfulness shall flourish, and corruption be vanquished ; and truth, which for so long a time has been without fruit, shall be made manifest." [2]   So again :  " And it shall come to pass, when He (Messiah) has brought low everything that is in the world, and has sat down in peace for the age on the throne of His kingdom, that joy shall then be revealed, and rest shall appear. . . . And judgments, and revilings, and contentions, and revenges, and blood, and passions, and envy, and hatred, and whatsoever things are like these, shall go into condemnation when they are removed." [3]

But in these passages there is no thought whatever of either the holiness or the sufferings of Messiah availing anything towards atonement between God and man.   The first indication of any such suggestion on the part of non-Christian writers comes in the very end of our period, about A.D. 200, when the School of R. Judah the Prince said in homiletical and Midrashic language that the name of Messiah was " The Leper of the House of Rabbi (Judah), for it is said, Surely He bore our sicknesses, and as for our sorrows, He carried them and we esteemed Him stricken (with leprosy), smitten by God, and afflicted." [4]   R. Judah himself, we are told by a later authority, had suffered illness for thirteen years, thus atoning for his people's sins, and thus his School was the more easily inclined to attribute the same kind of virtue to suffering in the case of the Messiah ben David.[5]

It is therefore improbable that during our period there was any thought of attributing merit to the sufferings of the Messiah, much less to His death.   That post-Christian Judaism (until at least very late in its history, and then only in writings which suggest a mediating attempt to bridge the

[1]  *Vide supra*, p. 116.
[2]  II (IV) Ezra vi. 26–28.
[3]  II Baruch, the Syrian Apocalypse, lxxiii. 1, 4.
[4]  T.B. *Sanhed.*, 98b.
[5]  See further Strack and Billerbeck on Lk. xxiv. 26, p. 286.   It may be noted that no atoning power was ever attributed to the death of Messiah ben Joseph (*ibid.*, p. 297).   Messiah ben David is not killed in Jewish Haggada.

difference between Judaism and Christianity) shrank from saying anything likely to encourage faith in a Messiah whose personal merits should avail for others, is but natural. But even in the Judaism of the earlier part of our period (*i.e.* before the rise of Christianity made the Rabbis suspicious) there is no certain trace of such a doctrine. We Christians in general rightly interpret the great text, " With his stripes we are healed," of the sufferings of the Messiah for others, but in books written between the Return and the Incarnation there seems to be no trace of the belief that this referred to Him. In fact, the Messiah seems never (in our period) to have been regarded as the One who was to make atonement for sin. He was to remove sin, no doubt, and to cast out sinners, and so to purify the nation and all nations that would be under His rule. But either to bear sin on Himself,[1] or to form a treasury of merits from which the merits of repentant sinners should be increased, are thoughts quite unknown to the Judaism of the three or four centuries before, and the two centuries after, His actual coming.

This is disappointing. We should have liked to have been able to say that the Coming of the Messiah was desired because He was to make the great Atonement between God and ourselves. But there seems to be no trace of such an expectation. The notion of atonement is there; but it is not connected with the Messiah. For, after all, He has never held in Judaism the all-important position which we Christians naturally suppose Him to have held. He was expected to be God's instrument for ruling the world during a certain limited time. But that was all.

That, however, the Jews did look for atonement, and that they regarded this not primarily as effecting a change in themselves in relation to God, but as bringing about a change in the attitude of God towards them—of this there seems to be no doubt.

And surely they were right. The means they had in mind were, to be sure, hopelessly inadequate. For they thought that a man's actions could provide the remedy for himself, and in some cases even partially for others. We Christians know better. We know that God in His love did not shrink from the extremity of self-sacrifice—for surely this is the essence of the doctrine—in order that He might make the

[1] As in Jn. i. 29.

Atonement.  We do not pretend to explain the method, or the peculiar value of the method, for we are hampered by our poverty of thought, and therefore of expression, in explaining Divine relations.  Nor can we forget that such terms as " Satisfaction," " Redemption," " Ransom," " Washing in the Blood," and such like, are but figures of incomprehensible because transcendent truths.  We suppose indeed that some kind of demonstration of self-sacrifice was necessary for the well-being of the unseen powers.  But in any case we lay hold of this truth, that God is Love, and that Love in the last instance shrinks from no self-sacrifice to win others.  To say merely that the Father sent the Son is inadequate.  It was God who came to sacrifice Himself, in that Divine " Person " (for we must use human language) who had always been in touch with Creation.

# IV

# THE ATONEMENT IN THE SYNOPTIC GOSPELS

## By A. J. Tait

THE title which is prefixed to this and several of the
other essays in this book raises at once a question. Are
we justified in thinking and speaking of the Atonement, with
a suggested and intended distinction of meaning from
atonement ?

No one who entertains any kind or degree of faith in
our Lord Jesus Christ as the Saviour of men could hesitate
for a single moment in assenting to the belief that He lived
and died for the purpose of bringing men to God, of effecting
at-one-ment between men and God, and that He did and
does this through His teaching, His example, and the constraining power of His love and obedience unto death.
Moreover, no question would be raised about man's way to
this atonement being the way of faith in God, repentance,
discipleship of Jesus, and participation in His character and
outlook. The idea of atonement, viewed as the effected
reconciliation of God and man, is an indispensable accom-
paniment of any conception of the life of the Lord Jesus,
which can be regarded as Christian.

The phrase " the Atonement," however, is generally used
to connote more than this, and it is around this something
more that diversity of thought has arisen. Indeed for very
many Christians it has been, and still is, just this something
more that constitutes the first message of the Gospel. In
other words, before the individual man enters into the
picture, with his repentance, faith and self-surrender, the
Lord Jesus rendered the Divine forgiveness possible. He
made, or was, or is (the conception is expressed in different
ways) the Atonement : and it is only because of this fact
that there can be realised atonement in the experience of
men.

Some conception of objective Atonement had dominated

Christian thought until the reaction set in which is a marked feature of present-day theology. The question now has to be faced as to whether, in reacting from the particular ways in which the idea was expressed, we are in danger of abandoning a fundamental element of truth, when we ought rather to be seeking a truer way of expressing the truth which was inherent in the old conception. We must not cast away a jewel because we do not like its setting. This question has been ceaselessly before my mind in the examination of the evidence of the Synoptic Gospels.

It is well at the outset that we remind ourselves of the limited content of the evidence with which we are now concerned. If we were to say that we are restricted to the recorded teaching given by our Lord during His earthly ministry, we should not have determined sufficiently the limited scope of the inquiry. We shall get a truer definition of the limits if we say that we are now confined almost entirely to the public teaching given by our Lord during the periods of His Galilean ministry.

This is an important point, because it would be contrary both to evidence and to reason to demand that the complete articulation of the Gospel must be found in the records of our Lord's public ministry. Such a conception would not be justified by the evidence of the New Testament. The teaching which our Lord gave even to the Eleven was confessedly incomplete, and they were bidden to wait for the illumination of the Spirit of truth. "I have many things to say unto you, but ye cannot bear them now." The opening words of the Acts of the Apostles tell us that the Lord during the forty days that elapsed between His Resurrection and Ascension gave to His disciples teaching about the Kingdom, of which there is but scanty record in the Synoptic Gospels. Without falling into the snare of reading into those words everything for which we wish to claim the authority of the Lord, we can and must at least accept them as demonstrating that the complete articulation of the Gospel did not come within the scope of His Galilean preaching and teaching.

Further, it would be contrary to reason to suppose that we can find the full presentation of the Gospel in the Synoptic records. It is obvious that our Lord had to practise marked reserve in His teaching on several matters which later became part of the web and woof of the Apostolic Gospel.

He was compelled to accommodate His message both to the necessities of His mission and to the conditions and circumstances of His hearers.   Let us suppose, for the sake of argument, that our Lord did regard His mission as including the making of atonement for the sin of mankind, even so we could not reasonably demand that He must have proclaimed such a message.   If He had done so, He would have raised a barrier to the accomplishment of His earthly ministry as surely as if He had openly declared His Messiahship or the passing of Judaism.   Even His teaching about the Holy Spirit, as given in the Synoptic Gospels, bears no comparison with that which is recorded in Jn. xiv.–xvi.   The difference provides no argument for an adverse judgment upon the historicity of the Fourth Gospel, but it does illustrate the accommodation which the Lord had to exercise in His public ministry.

The reasonable position to adopt is that the teaching given by our Lord during His earthly life is the foundation, and the Apostolic teaching given under the inspiration of the Holy Spirit is the superstructure.   The Gospels and the Epistles are not mutually independent.   To accept the Epistles in separation from the Gospels would be to lose the foundation;   to accept the Gospels in separation from the Epistles would be to do without the building.   If the four Gospels seem to be inarticulate on some theme which formed an essential and central element of Apostolic teaching, it would be precarious to reject the teaching on that ground, and still more so if the reference were to the Synoptic Gospels alone.

On such a theme as the atoning work of our Lord the utmost that we could reasonably expect to find in the records of the Synoptists would be some hints, some adumbrations of the truth which at the time and under the circumstances of the Lord's earthly ministry could not be fully declared.

Such anticipations we do find of the truth of the Messiahship of Jesus, of the Holy Spirit, and of the catholicity of the Church;   and, to the mind of the present writer, we find anticipations likewise of the truth of the atoning mission of our Lord.   There could not have been anything more than anticipations, for the following reason :   if the Lord was unable fully to declare the truth about His Person and office, He must have been equally debarred from fully declaring truth that was based upon it. For the fact is that no conception of the Atonement has any foundation apart from the belief that the Lord Jesus is God-man. The Church never entertained the thought that a mere man could make atonement for the sins of mankind. It was only because of, and in consequence of the belief that Jesus Christ is God-man, that the belief in the Atonement became possible.

At the very threshold of the inquiry with which we are now immediately concerned, we are faced with the fact that our Lord was constantly teaching about the forgiving love of the Father, without reference to any condition saving that of man's repentance and faith. Could He have avoided speaking about the need of the Atonement, if the satisfying of that need was an essential element of the Gospel of forgiveness?

This question seems to be raised in its most acute form by the parable of the Prodigal Son, and it will be well for us to examine it on that ground. It is undoubtedly true that there is not the slightest hint in this parable of any necessary condition for the bestowal of the father's forgiveness, other than the son's repentance, return and confession. On the other hand, we must remind ourselves that the argument from silence is precarious, and in this instance inapplicable. No parable can be supposed to illustrate every aspect of the truth to which it is related. There is nothing, for example, in this parable about the necessity for exercising the forgiving spirit as a condition of remaining in the grace of forgiveness. That is a truth which was illustrated in the later parable of the Unmerciful Servant.

There is, moreover, a still stronger reason for rejecting in this case the argument from silence. If pressed, it would entirely rule out the mission of the Lord Jesus; and we should be carried to the conclusion that the Incarnation itself was unnecessary, and that the life and death of Jesus Christ had nothing to do with bringing men to repentance, because there is nothing in this parable which gives the slightest hint of His redeeming work.

The plain fact is that the parable of the Prodigal Son provides the most moving picture of the welcoming and forgiving love of God, but has nothing whatever to contribute about His redeeming love. That did not enter into its purpose. Hence the argument would be as inimical to the position of Abelard as to that of St. Anselm.

We find hints of the redeeming love of God in the parables of the Lost Sheep and the Lost Coin; but to admit that is to allow that the parable of the Prodigal Son may not be regarded as a complete presentation of the Divine love. Even in those two parables there is no suggestion that the redeeming activity of God necessitated the Incarnation; and the point of their teaching which the Lord Himself stressed is not so much the redeeming love as the joy in heaven over one sinner's repentance.

It seems clear, then, that the only sound method of interpreting the Lord's parables is to note their positive teaching, and to avoid basing any inferences upon the argument from silence. The parables which illustrate the Divine forgiveness lay down for us several cardinal truths; and the utmost that we can say on matters which lie outside their purpose and scope is that nothing may be introduced into the doctrine of the Atonement which is inconsistent with those governing principles.

The framework of the doctrine must certainly include the following positions :

1. Forgiveness is the outcome of the unmerited love of God.

2. Forgiveness is a new relation to God into which He brings men : a new relation, in which the forgiven man is treated as though he had never gone astray and had never transgressed 'God's will.

3. This new relation depends upon man's co-operation, through his change of mind and attitude, which manifests itself in faith in God, repentance, confession of sin and self-surrender to God.

4. The change must be abiding, the abiding response to the forgiving love. Man cannot earn forgiveness, but he must fulfil the purpose for which he has been forgiven, which is that he should himself participate in the forgiving character and all that it involves.

These fundamental positions are clearly set forth in the Lord's parables of the Divine forgiveness, but there is nothing in them which precludes the inquiry as to whether the process of bringing men into this new relationship to God cost God anything. Every Christian allows that it did cost Him the very utmost : but was that cost wholly required in order to bring constraint to bear upon men ? Is there any sense in which God had to meet a necessity arising out of His relation to the sinner, as well as the necessity of constraining the sinner to return to Him ? For our immediate purpose the question resolves itself into the inquiry as to whether in the Synoptic Gospels there is any presentation or anticipation of the content of such words and phrases as " Propitiation," " Offering for Sin," and corresponding statements which are freely used in the Epistles to describe our Lord's redeeming work.

What was the meaning of the submission of our Lord to the Baptism of John ? Could He have allowed Himself to be baptised into repentance unless He was conscious of His representative capacity ? He took a great risk in doing so, and the quite remarkable thing is that in spite of it He was able to produce the conviction in men that He was sinless. If He was sinless, what could His offering of Himself for John's Baptism mean but that He was making a representative act of repentance ? Undoubtedly it was also an act of self-dedication, but that consideration does not cancel the significance of the fact that He was submitting to the ordinance of repentance.

If the Atonement is exclusively related to the Lord's sufferings on the Cross, and those sufferings are interpreted as God's penalty inflicted upon Jesus for the sins of mankind, the representative act of Jesus in His baptism will be regarded as irrelevant to the subject. If, however, the redemptive value of the death of Jesus is found in the fact that it was the final and supreme manifestation of the self-offering which underlay His entire incarnate experience, then the act whereby He publicly took upon Himself man's obligations, and gave up His life to the fulfilment of them, is strictly relevant, and the Synoptic records can be regarded as providing evidence in their earliest pages of the Lord's consciousness of His atoning mission at the outset of His public work.

We have here raised a question which must be faced, even if it takes us away for a while from our immediate quest. The question is, Does this interpretation of our Lord's atoning work as the representative fulfilment of man's obligations require any straining of the Apostolic emphasis upon His death ?

The interpretation certainly involves the rejection of the penal theory of our Lord's death, but it retains the conception of the Atonement as something over and above the realised at-one-ment which follows man's repentance. There is a good deal that can be said for refusing to be tied up to the alternative theories usually associated with the names of St. Anselm and Abelard, and for regarding each of those great teachers as standing for a complementary aspect of the truth. St. Anselm stands for the position that the Atonement was made on man's behalf by the death of the Lord Jesus Christ; Abelard stands for the position that the Lord Jesus Christ lived and died on our behalf in order that He might bring us into at-one-ment with God. The two men were at variance in the way in which they expressed themselves; but if we get behind the form to the substance, we can make a synthesis of their positions.

Rejection of the idea of the Atonement is always due to a reaction from a particular doctrine or explanation of it. Let it once be granted that there is no necessity for regarding our Lord's Crucifixion as the Divine penalty for man's sin, that God's requirement from man is obedience and self-offering to Him, that the Lord Jesus in our name completely fulfilled this requirement and was offering Himself to God during the whole of His incarnate life, that the particular form of the final and supreme manifestation of His self-offering was demanded by His enemies, and that the Atonement was effected by His perfect and representative self-offering and obedience to the will of God—let all this be granted, and the reason for the reaction seems to be removed.

But can all this be granted in view of the Apostolic statements about our Lord's death? There appears to be no reason why we should not, and every reason why we should, regard the Lord's submission to the Cross as the culminating expression of His life of self-offering rather than as the isolated and exclusive act of offering. We pay particular honour to the memory of the men and the women who died for our sake in the Great War, but the fact remains that every man and every woman who voluntarily faced death for the cause laid down his or her life in so doing, whether it involved actual death or not. If that self-offering did involve death, we naturally think of it in terms of death, because the dying was the supreme expression of the offering; but so to think and so to speak do not mean that the self-offering was exclusively related to the dying, or even that it would have been incomplete without that price having been paid.

This illustration may help us to recognise how entirely natural it was that the Apostles should constantly speak of the Lord's atoning work in the terms of His death, if the act of dying gathered up into itself, in a culminating expression, all the self-sacrifice of His life. They would naturally speak as though the death were by itself the whole atoning work, and say that " Christ died for our sins," without in the least meaning that He was doing nothing for our sins until the moment of His death. We are entirely free to believe that the Lord was called upon to endure the agony of the Cross because the Jews demanded that death as the price of His obedience to His Father, and that on account of their hostility His self-offering had of necessity to take that final form. " He was obedient unto death, yea the death of the cross."

The late Dr. Dale, in his great work, *The Atonement* (p. 26), wrote : " It is impossible to exhibit the testimony of the Gospels to the truth by a mere enumeration of the passages in which Christ speaks of the nature and purpose of His death." Yes, and his argument would have been infinitely stronger if he had related the atoning work of Jesus to His whole incarnate life of obedience and self-offering, and not merely to His Crucifixion; for then he need not have been on his defence about the sparcity of the interpretation of our Lord's death. The argument of Dr. Dale and all whom he represents is seriously weakened by this insistence upon the isolated act of dying : and when the Lord's death is interpreted as the Divine penalty for sin, the position becomes repellent. The death of Jesus has been spoken of as "fully satisfying the Divine requirements." It has been asserted that " the justice of God demanded it," and that " not suffering but death is the penalty of sin " (J. B. Oldroyd, *Doctrine of the Atonement*, pp. 47, 73). Is that so ? Can it be, then, that our Lord has not, after all, saved us from the penalty of sin ? Physical death still remains the lot of man : in what sense have we been saved from it by the atoning work of Jesus ?

When the particular mode of our Lord's death is regarded as an essential element in the Atonement, and the Crucifixion is stressed as the Divine penalty for man's sin, the position becomes even more difficult; for we cannot attach any meaning to the conception that our Lord has saved man from crucifixion. Indeed the carrying of the cross, in the only sense in which we can carry it, is the condition of discipleship (Mt. x. 38, xvi. 24 and parallels). The Lord has not saved us from it : He has called us to it. Could anything be more eloquent of His thoughts about His approaching sufferings than that ? He evidently regarded the carrying of the cross as self-oblation, and not as Divine penalty; and self-oblation, no matter what form it might have to take, He regarded as incumbent both upon Himself and upon all men who would be His disciples.

To return, then, to the question which gave rise to this digression, the fact that our Lord's death gathered up into itself His whole life of self-oblation provides ample reason for its being spoken of as though it were by itself the atoning work; and there is no necessity for our regarding it as the penalty inflicted by God, and as the isolated and exclusive means whereby the Atonement was effected.

We pass now to the consideration of another line of evidence which is available in the Synoptic Gospels, and that is our Lord's teaching about the fulfilment of the Law. He asserted that the Law was to be fulfilled in its entirety, that not one jot or one tittle should pass away until all had been fulfilled; and He claimed that He had come to fulfil it (Mt. v. 17 f.; Lk. xvi. 17). It is true that the immediate reference of the claim was to the moral code, but the phrase " The Law or the Prophets " suggests entirety, and there is no evidence for our regarding the propitiatory system which lay at the very centre of the Law as being excluded from the Lord's reference.

This claim of Jesus exactly corresponds to the teaching of the Epistle to the Hebrews, in which the author sets forth Jesus as having brought to its appointed goal the whole propitiatory system of the Levitical Priesthood, and as having annulled it. It would not be unreasonable to believe that it was just that claim of Jesus which was the basis of the teaching of this Epistle.

Now, if there was one characteristic more pronounced than any other of that part of the Law, it was the setting forth of atonement as objective, something that had to be done on behalf of man, the removal of a barrier which had been raised between God and man by the fact of man's sin, and its removal not merely through man's repent-

I

ance and confession, but also through the oblation of a substitute.

Here again we are faced with the question that arises from the emphasis which is laid in the Law upon the death of the substituted animal. " Apart from blood-shedding there is no remission." What is the value in spiritual terms of that blood-shedding ? The word " blood," when propitiatory value is attached to it in the Holy Scriptures, undoubtedly signifies death. True, the blood is the life, but there is all the difference between life retained and life poured out : and in the Law " blood," with propitiatory association, always signifies life given up, laid down, poured forth. In what other way, we may ask, could the life of the substituted animal be offered to God ? But we must not confuse form and substance. The form of the type consisted in death, the substance of it was the offering of the life. The emphasis which was laid upon the nature and the quality of the victim confirms the belief that this was the central significance of the type. When we look for the fulfilment of the type in our Lord's incarnate experience, it is the substance rather than the form that we must keep in mind. We find the fulfilment in the perfect self-oblation of the perfect representative man. That self-oblation was being made during the whole of the Lord's incarnate life. It had to culminate in the Crucifixion because of the demand of His enemies, and consequently there was a literal correspondence to type in the actual blood-shedding : but the Atonement which brought to an end the Levitical system was the complete fulfilment of man's obligations through the representative life of perfect obedience, which was all gathered up into its supreme expression on the Cross. The Cross will always be the symbol of the atoning work of the Lord because His self-offering on Calvary was the final and supreme manifestation of the perfect obedience, which fulfilled and abrogated the propitiatory system of the Law (Heb. x. 5 ff.).

In the early part of this essay reasons were given for our not expecting to find in the Synoptic Gospels any clear pronouncement about our Lord's atoning mission. Hints of it we might with reason expect, and such anticipations we have found in the fact and significance of our Lord's baptism, and in His teaching about the fulfilment of the Law. But the evidence of the Synoptic records is more specific than that : they preserve for us sayings of Jesus which may contain something more than a hint.

One of the occasions of strife among the disciples about precedence, which was caused by the request of the wife of Zebedee and her two sons, led Jesus to speak about His own life and mission. " The Son of Man came not to be minis- tered unto but to minister and give his life a ransom for many " (Mt. xx. 28; Mk. x. 45). These words have been freely quoted in connection with the subject that is before us, as justifying belief in the objective Atonement, and in the Atonement as having been effected exclusively through our Lord's death. The word " ransom " (as also the word " redemption ") has been interpreted as signifying payment, and the phrase " to give his life " has been interpreted exclusively of His death.

It is worthy of note that in Ephes. i. 7 the word translated " redemption " comes from the same root as that which is here translated " ransom," and it is explained by St. Paul as meaning " the remission of sins." Hence, while it would be exceedingly precarious to base upon the use of the word the idea of bearing a penalty, it would be reasonable to interpret it as signifying that the Lord's self-offering was related not merely to the bringing of men to repentance, but also to the Divine gift of forgiveness. Further, the words " for many " (ἀντὶ πολλῶν) suggest that in His self- offering our Lord was the representative of men, and the substitute, in the sense not of saving men from crucifixion, but of being the perfect representative of all who bear the cross after Him.

No one wishes to deny that the redemption which our Lord wrought for man includes the delivering of men's minds from every form of spiritual bondage (Wendt, *Die Lehre Jesu*, Vol. II., pp. 510–517), or that this is a true sense in which He gave His life a ransom for many. In this con- nection, the saying ascribed to our Lord in the recently discovered manuscript of the Gospels (The Freer Manuscript, now in Washington) should be noticed. After Mk. xvi. 14 occur these words : " For the sake of those that have sinned was I given up to death, that they may return unto the truth and sin no more, but may inherit the spiritual and incorruptible glory of righteousness in heaven."

Whatever their source may be, these words should serve as a caution against interpreting assertions about the Lord's

death as excluding reference to His life, and against interpreting " ransom " or " redemption " as necessarily involving the objective Atonement : for the Lord's earthly
ministry was related in its entirety to the bringing of men
into light and life, and the idea of " ransom " is certainly
present in the words " for the sake of those that have
sinned was I given up to death." On the other hand, the
phrase " ransom for many " (λύτρον ἀντὶ πολλῶν) in Mt.
xx. 28, Mk. x. 45 is in itself distinctly suggestive of objective
Atonement,[1] and in the light of other evidence may be
regarded as including the idea.

The narrative of the Last Supper, as given in St. Matthew's
Gospel, seems to provide the clearest statement of the Lord's
atoning mission that can be found in any of His recorded
utterances. We pass over St. Luke's version of the words
used in the blessing of the Bread (" my body which is given
for you "), because their meaning would be amply realised
by any service which Christ rendered to man through His
self-offering ; but the words used in the blessing of the Cup,
as given in St. Matthew's Gospel, are explicit : " This is
my blood of the Covenant which is shed for many unto
the remission of sins." To interpret these words as meaning
" I am about to shed my blood in order that I may bring
many to repentance, and those who repent will be forgiven "
would not satisfy an unprejudiced mind. The phrase
" blood shed unto remission of sins " must have conveyed a
quite clear and definite idea to minds trained in the Jewish
tradition. That idea would have no direct relation to
man's repentance, it would be immediately related to the
Divine forgiveness. Jesus was about to die in order that
remission of sins might be granted to men.

To people who think in the exact terms of the propitiatory
system of the Law, the words may suggest that the Lord in
dying was bearing the divinely appointed penalty for sin :
but for those who penetrate the form in order to discover
the substance, the physical blood-shedding will stand for
the perfect self-offering, which reached its final manifestation in the supreme sacrifice that was demanded by the
enemies of Jesus as the price of His obedience.

To the mind of the writer of this essay, it was that perfect
self-offering in the entirety of its manifestation that constituted the objective Atonement.

---

[1] Cf. ἀντίλυτρον ὑπὲρ πάντων, I Tim. ii. 6, where the idea is introduced in the noun rather than in the preposition.

# V

# THE PAULINE VIEW OF THE ATONEMENT

## By D. Dawson-Walker

" The Son of God, who loved me, and gave Himself up for me." [1] " I determined not to know anything among you, save Jesus Christ, and Him crucified." [2] These combined passages express at once the origin and the content of St. Paul's gospel.

The limits assigned to this essay do not permit a survey of the theories that have been advanced about the origins of St. Paul's religion; more especially of that distinctive teaching about the Person and Work of our Lord which it is customary to call " Paulinism." It is possible that the particularity of Paulinism has of late been unduly emphasised, and that we should do well to insist more on the convictions which the Apostle held in common with that earliest Christian community of which he became a member. " I delivered unto you," he says to his Corinthian converts, " *that which also I received,* how that Christ died for our sins according to the Scriptures." [3] He and the Jerusalem community were at one in connecting the death of Christ with human sin, and in finding the key to its interpretation in the Old Testament Scriptures; and, however much they afterwards criticised him, we have no evidence that they disagreed with him, or he with them, on these fundamental points.

And yet, along with this general agreement, there is something distinctive in St. Paul's attitude and in his presentment of the matter. There is the personal element, the ardour of personal devotion that rings through the words " who loved me, and gave Himself up for me." The Apostle could never forget—never wished to forget—the call that came to him, particularly, by name, on the road to

---

[1] Gal. ii. 20.  [2] I Cor. ii. 2.  [3] I Cor xv. 3.

Damascus, with its haunting accents of tender reproach :
" Saul, Saul, why persecutest thou Me ? "   At that moment
his heart was captured and held.   The other Apostles, with
the Old Testament in their hands, may have fortified and
instructed him.   But the flame of passionate love, kindled
by the fire of God's love to him—the love revealed in the
life and death of Christ—was something peculiar and distinctive.   The love of God in Christ was at once the constraining and the inspiring power throughout his life.

It is quite beside the point to seek for the formative
influences on St. Paul's religion in Gentile Christian circles
at Antioch, or in the still more remote influences of contemporary mystery religions.   Personal experience of Christ
interpreted in the light of Old Testament Scripture would
seem to be a sufficient basis for the structure of Pauline
teaching as to the meaning of the death of Christ.

The question may be raised—has, indeed, in recent times
been raised—whether St. Paul's views about the significance
of Christ's death can be harmonised with the teaching of
Christ Himself ; whether the Apostle inserts into his system
of thought many conceptions that are alien to the mind of
the Master—Christ bringing a gospel of free forgiveness, and
St. Paul one of sacrificial propitiation—so that the New
Testament contains, at least, two irreconcilable gospels, the
one a direct antithesis to the other.

Dr. Denney has dealt faithfully and adequately with this
question in his book *Jesus and the Gospel*.   He there shows
that, from the beginning, Christians regarded Christ as the
object of their faith, the Redeemer of men from sin and
their Reconciler to God through His death on the Cross ;
and that this attitude on their part was the only one consistent with the Self-revelation of Jesus during His life on
earth.

There are, doubtless, in the New Testament, contrasts.
It was not unnatural that our Lord should dwell on the
depth and freeness of the Father's love ; and it was also not
unnatural that sinners, on realising that love, should
magnify the cost, to God, of carrying out His purpose of
love.   But these contrasts are relative, not absolute.   To
oppose them, the one to the other, as two conflicting gospels,
is to misread and to misrepresent the whole tenor of the
New Testament writings.

To put the point in this way is to attempt a vindication

of St. Paul's teaching, at any rate to the extent of maintaining that it is not out of harmony with the teaching of Christ. Such vindication, however, if called for at all, may be left to the end of our survey. Our more immediate task is to attempt an account, in outline, of what St. Paul actually has to say, reserving for the conclusion any words of comment. The account must either be given in his own words, or be justified by constant reference to them.

The student of his writings does not need to be reminded that these writings are letters; that they are largely " occasional " in the sense that they are concerned with the particular needs and interests of the Church to which, or the individual to whom, he happens to be writing, and that some of the clearest expressions of his most profound convictions come in quite an incidental way. In the first eight chapters of the Epistle to the Romans he approaches most nearly to something like a systematic exposition of his " gospel." But in Galatians and II Corinthians—each an epistle largely occupied with the Judaising controversy— we have passages of central importance about the reconciling work of Christ. In fact the closing verses of II Cor. v. may almost be called the *locus classicus* on the death of Christ in the writings of St. Paul.

Without laying down any rigid lines of treatment, we shall do well to follow generally the presentment of his thought in Romans, with supplementary reference to his other writings as they touch upon the points that arise.

Fundamental to all St. Paul's thinking and to all his teaching is his belief in God, the personal God, who created the world, called Abraham, chose Israel, inspired and enlightened the Psalmists and Prophets; who upholds and controls the whole Universe, natural and spiritual, and whose beneficent purpose is being accomplished in the history of humanity. In accordance with the writings of the Prophets, St. Paul conceived this God to be supremely a God of righteousness—perfectly righteous Himself, and requiring righteousness in those who would be in communion with Him. The " righteousness of God "[1] is one of the determining factors in St. Paul's thought.

And over against this thought of God stands the spectacle of human sin. In Rom. i.–iii. St. Paul pictures this as universal in its scope, degrading and destructive in its

[1] Rom. i. 17.

effects. On certain ultimate problems which exercise the moral philosopher, about the origin of sin in a world created and upheld by God, St. Paul does not touch. He probably accepted as sufficient the narrative in Gen. iii. He believed wholly in a righteous God, and he realised the fact of sin, both in its wide extent and in its deeply seated presence in the heart of man.

It is, possibly, the recognition of this virulent presence in the heart that explains his employment of the term " flesh." That our bodies, with their appetites and desires, are essentially evil St. Paul does not say. But the body is the living instrument of the personality. And when he says that " the flesh lusteth against the spirit " ; [1] that " in me—that is, in my flesh—dwelleth no good thing " ; [2] and that " they that are in the flesh cannot please God " ; [3] it is his way of expressing not only the universality, but the ingrained, deeply seated character of sin. It has so completely established itself in us, taken possession of us, that it has become, as it were, a second nature.

And what is God's attitude towards this sin ? It is indicated by the word " wrath." [4] " The wrath of God " is also one of St. Paul's fundamental conceptions. Like others, it is supplied to him by the Old Testament. The conception of God's wrath there may be traced through an upward process of moralisation till there is reached the idea of the Divine righteousness in its relation to the universal sin of man. There seems to be, in our time, a tendency to shrink from this idea as unduly anthropomorphic. To St. Paul, with his intense belief in God as living, personal and righteous, there would be nothing unacceptable or incongruous in the conception that God's attitude to sin is one of " wrath." It was the natural and reasonable way of expressing the reaction of Divine righteousness to human sin.

He expresses the thought—again employing Old Testament conceptions—in terms of eschatology. The wrath of God was, indeed, to be seen in the condition of the contemporary Gentile and Jewish world. The depravity of the Gentile world in particular was in itself a revelation of God's wrath ; [5] but the final and decisive manifestation would be " in the day when God shall judge the secrets of men," [6] " the day of the Lord," or, as he frequently expressed it,

---

[1] Gal. v. 17.  [2] Rom. vii. 18.  [3] Rom. viii. 8.
[4] Rom. i. 18.  [5] Rom. i. 18.  [6] Rom. ii. 16.

" the day of Jesus Christ." St. Paul taught clearly that a day of God's judgment would come, when His wrath against sin would be finally revealed, and it is significant, in this connection, that he speaks in one of his earliest writings of " Jesus, Which delivereth us from the wrath to come." [1]

The account which St. Paul thus gives of the general situation is not that of the dispassionate, speculative observer. It is based on personal experience, on his intense awareness of the workings of his own inner consciousness. When he says : " In me—that is, in my flesh—dwelleth no good thing," [2] he means, not the physical, sensuous, part of him, but the whole of his personality as it actually was. And when he says : " O wretched man that I am, who shall deliver me ? " [3] he is expressing the general situation as one of which he is intimately and practically aware.

This, then, was the condition of things as he viewed it : a righteous God, a sinful world, exposed to God's inevitable wrath against sin, and moving onwards to the day of judgment, when God's wrath would be fully and finally declared. Was this situation hopeless and irremediable ? Could the broken harmony be restored ? Could men be reconciled to God and put in a right relation to Him again ? Is man left to himself, or has God undertaken on his behalf ?

It is the centre and heart of St. Paul's gospel that God has so undertaken. He " reconciled us to Himself through Christ, and gave unto us the ministry of reconciliation ; to wit, that God was in Christ reconciling the world unto Himself, not reckoning unto them their trespasses, and having committed unto us the word of reconciliation." [4]

Here we meet with a distinctive " contribution " of St. Paul, the conception of " reconciliation." At any rate the noun and its corresponding verb occur only in his Epistles in the New Testament writings, and in this connection they are limited to Romans and II Corinthians. It is the natural— may we not say, the inevitable—word to express readjustment between a personal God and responsible personal human beings. If such beings are estranged, there must be a process of reconciliation, and St. Paul conceived the message of the Gospel to be that the necessary means for this reconciliation have been provided and offered to men by God. It must needs come from God's side, for man was

[1] I Thess. i. 10.    [2] Rom. vii. 18.
[3] Rom. vii. 24.    [4] II Cor. v. 18, 19.

powerless to initiate it. But it *has* come from God's side;
and what God has provided it is for man to accept. In
Jesus Christ " we have now received the reconciliation." [1]

In Rom. i.–iii. we have another aspect of the truth presented. It does not contradict the idea of reconciliation; it
supplements it. What man sorely needs is " righteousness."
He must be righteous if he is to be at peace with God. And
to him, in his need, is made available " God's righteousness."[2]
Students of Romans are familiar with the debate that has
been held as to the respective merits of the Authorised
Version and the Revised Version renderings of the Greek
expression in this passage. Those who favour the A.V.
rendering, " the " righteousness of God, regard the words as
referring to the righteousness which is God's eternal attribute;
and they regard the expression as indicating that this
righteousness is an energising force; that it is active, not
passive; that, by its very nature, it tends to create, to
produce, righteousness. Those who favour the R.V. rendering, " a " righteousness of God, hold St. Paul's idea to
be that in Christ is made available a righteousness such as
man in his lost condition needs, a righteousness that will
exactly meet his case.

Both conceptions are true, and it would be rash to assert
that either was absent from the mind of St. Paul when he
used the expression. He would be familiar enough with
the conception of God's righteousness as an active force
issuing in salvation, and would be readily aware of the
passages in Psalmist and Prophet in which this great thought
is expressed. But that thought might have been developed
without any reference to Christ; and what St. Paul is
declaring is a gospel to sinful and sin-stricken men; a gospel
that in the crucified Christ alone is offered to men a
righteousness, which originates from God and is sufficient to
meet all His requirements, a righteousness of God adequate
to the needs of sinners exposed to the wrath of God.

In his earlier reference to God's righteousness,[3] he simply
indicates its availability as proclaimed in the Gospel, and
declares that the condition of its availability is " faith " on
the part of man. To discuss adequately St. Paul's use of
the term " faith " would take us far outside our present
limits. It must suffice here to say that by " faith " he means
the attitude of complete dependence on God, the receptive

[1] Rom. v. 11.　　　[2] Rom. i. 17; iii. 22.　　　[3] Rom. i. 17.

attitude, the attitude of one who trusts to the uttermost, who depends entirely on what God has done, both for pardon of past sin and for strength to conquer future temptation. Faith is the attitude which lays hold on God and clings to Him. It is such a faith as this that, on man's side, receives the gift of righteousness which God bestows.

In the later reference [1] he defines the idea more fully. The righteousness of God is available for all; " for all have sinned "; that is, it is coextensive with human need. It is " through faith in Jesus Christ . . . whom God set forth *to be* a propitiation, through faith, by His blood, to shew His righteousness." What St. Paul seems to say here, if we may venture on reverent paraphrase, is that the true nature of God's righteousness is seen, its essence and its demands, in the crucified Christ, whose death is to be viewed as a propitiatory offering.

The word that St. Paul uses to express the idea of propitiation has been the subject of great debate. It only occurs elsewhere in the New Testament in Heb. ix. 5, where it is a substantive unquestionably meaning the " Mercy-seat." In the Romans passage it may also be a substantive, and the question is whether, as in Hebrews, it also means the Mercy-seat, and St. Paul is consequently correlating the death of Christ with the sprinkling of the victim's blood by the High Priest, in the Holy of Holies, according to the Levitical ritual.

Dr. Deissmann, in recent times, has protested warmly against this correlation, and holds that, as the word which St. Paul employs is used in the Septuagint with reference to other objects than the Mercy-seat, it is not to be so restricted, and has the more general meaning of " object " or " means " of propitiation. He emphasises the fact, too, that the word was in contemporary usage in the pagan world, in inscriptions on monuments erected as votive-offerings to placate the gods or to win their favour. More recently, Dr. Anderson Scott, in his book *Christianity according to St. Paul*, has indicated the Old Testament, but not the Levitical ritual, as the place of origin, finding the analogue to Rom. iii. 25 not in any form of Jewish sacrifice, but in the Brazen Serpent.

A partial solution of the problem may be found if it be the case that St. Paul is not using the word as a substantive at all, but as an adjective (the form admits this possibility),

[1] Rom. iii. 22.

and that he simply means to say that God " set forth " Christ in a propitiatory character, to effect a work of propitiation. In so conceiving the matter he is not unique and alone. We remember the cognate word used by St. John and translated by the same English word " propitiation." " He is the propitiation for our sins." [1]  " Herein is love, not that we loved God, but that He loved us, and sent His Son *to be* the propitiation for our sins." [2]  The writer of Hebrews, too, is moving in the same region of thought when he says : " Wherefore it behoved Him in all things to be made like unto His brethren, that He might be a merciful and faithful high priest in things pertaining to God, to make propitiation for the sins of the people." [3]

We note here a fact of profound interest for the understanding of St. Paul's thought. He most certainly viewed our Lord's death as sacrificial in character. In emphasising the category of sacrifice he is not peculiar. Space does not admit of extended quotation from other parts of his writings,[4] or from St. Peter, St. John and the writer of Hebrews, to confirm this assertion. And such quotation is needless because the point is generally admitted, though with interesting modifications in more recent times.

The tendency now is, while admitting the analogy, not unduly to stress it. The reference, it is held, is more general than particular ; and it is only one along with other comparisons employed by New Testament writers. At the time of our Lord and of St. Paul, sacrifice with the Jews was really a survival. Except for occasional pilgrimages to Jerusalem, the religious life of Judaism was more intimately associated with the Synagogue than with the Temple. Sacrifice " was prescribed in the law, and obedience to the law was a matter of conscience ; but while in some vague sense all sacrifices, and not merely the sin or trespass offerings of the Old Testament were probably regarded as having propitiatory power, there was no doctrine of sacrifice, or of the way in which it took effect." [5]

Any reference to sacrifice, even in the most general terms, is somewhat suspect at the bar of much present-day thinking. It is held to be an obsolete category, of historic interest, but quite unable to find a place in any truly moral

---

[1] I Jn. ii. 2.   [2] I Jn. iv. 10.   [3] Heb. ii. 17.
[4] Cf. Rom. viii. 3, I Cor. v. 7, II Cor. v. 21, Eph. v. 2.
[5] Denney, *The Christian Doctrine of Reconciliation*, p. 160.

conception of God. Our present task is not to examine this —possibly superficial—point of view, but to offer a suggestion as to the origin of this sacrificial conception in the earliest Church.

If we may trust our records, it seems not unnatural to suppose that the primary source is to be found in the words of our Lord at the Last Supper, when He spoke of " My blood of the Covenant which is shed for many," [1] or, as St. Luke expresses it, " the New Covenant in My blood, even that which is poured out for you." [2] Our Lord is here referring, in the first instance, to the new covenant spoken of by Jeremiah.[3] He declares that God is now entering into this new covenant with His people, of which Jeremiah spoke; but His words further imply that this covenant, like those of the Old Testament, is ratified by sacrifice. The outstanding instance in the Old Testament narrative is that of Exod. xxiv. 7, 8. Our Lord associated the New Covenant with the sacrifice of Himself.

The other possible source for the sacrificial conception of Christ's death is Isa. liii. It is admitted that the " Servant " as there depicted profoundly influenced the thought of the earliest Christians about Christ; and what is there portrayed is, undeniably, not only sacrifice, but substitution too. Those who learned to regard our Lord as the fulfilment of that prophetic picture were thereby taught to regard Him as One who saved them by the sacrifice of Himself.

It is interesting to bear in mind that both our Lord and His followers went to the Old Testament for conceptions to explain the significance of His reconciling work, and it is perhaps a matter for question how far we are justified in discarding as archaic and obsolete what they found so adequate.

Before leaving this crucial passage in Romans, it should be noted that we encounter in it another of the great conceptions, chiefly characteristic of St. Paul, under which the work of Christ is presented—that of " redemption." [4] The word means originally " ransom "—that is, redemption effected by the payment of a price. And it will be remembered that there are passages in which St. Paul quite definitely operates with this idea of price. " Ye were

[1] Mk. xiv. 24; Mt. xxvi. 28. [2] Lk. xxii. 20. [3] Jer. xxxi. 29 ff.
[4] Rom. iii. 24; viii. 23; I Cor. i. 30; Eph. i. 7, 14; iv. 30; Col. i. 14.

bought with a price." [1]  It is, however, now a matter of
fairly general agreement that the idea of price is not to be
pressed in the word " redemption "; that it means simply
" deliverance," and may rightly be understood of the rescue
from guilt and sin which Christ effects.  But the passages
in which he speaks of price are not to be dismissed as intract-
able elements in his thought.  They do serve to keep before
our minds the thought that our redemption was a costly
thing, that it cost God something to send His only-begotten
Son to the Cross.

The view has sometimes been held that the matter, as St.
Paul presents it here, is open to the charge of being presented
as a fiction—a legal fiction, indeed, but still a fiction.  That
God should " justify the ungodly," that He should treat, or
regard, as righteous those who are not actually righteous, is
held to be unthinkable.

This misconception—for such it is—only becomes possible when chapters iii and iv in Romans are separated from
chapter vi.  It may be admitted that there is a contrast;
that in chapters iii and iv we have the more legal aspect of
the gospel, in which St. Paul, with his zeal as a Pharisee for
" righteousness " and his lofty conception of Law, is mainly
concerned with the question how unrighteous man may be
put right with God who is not only his Father, but also his
Judge.  And it may also be admitted that in Rom. vi. we
have the more " mystical " aspect of the matter : the
work of Christ within the heart; the Christian in union
with Christ, reproducing, as it were, in his own consciousness
those very stages of Christ's redeeming work—death, burial
and resurrection—with the result that he shares the resurrection life of Christ.  And here St. Paul was doubtless
drawing on the contents of his own experience.  But both
these aspects are portrayed by the same Apostle.  We do
him injustice when we actually separate where he only
distinguishes, when we describe as contradictory what, for
him, was joined together by the bond of a living personal
experience.  He believed profoundly that Christ had done
for him a work of reconciliation; he was intensely aware of
the presence and power of Christ in his own heart.  And he
conceived that Christ's work *for* him was the basis and
pre-requisite of Christ's work *in* him.  It is simply impossible to follow the track of St. Paul's thinking without the

[1] I Cor. vi. 20; vii. 23

clue of a sympathetic insight into his experience.    For him, the corollary to Christ's work on the Cross is the work of the crucified and risen Christ in the heart.    And his experience in this respect may be said to be the normal experience of the genuinely Christian life.

Reference has already been made [1] to II Cor. v. 14–21, as a passage of central importance for St. Paul's view of Christ's reconciling work.    It should be read carefully, with due weighing of every word, for the candid reader cannot escape the obligation—in face of all the conflicting explanations that have been set forth—of deciding for himself what he thinks St. Paul meant to express by his words :  "The love of Christ constraineth us ;  because we thus judge, that One died for all, therefore all died.    And He died for all, that they which live should no longer live unto themselves, but unto Him who for their sakes died and rose again." [2]

An attempt at paraphrase may help to bring out the meaning of these words.    "Christ's love has a constraining power on us, a leading and controlling power over us ;  and it has this power because He died for us—that is, He died a death which was our death, a death which we should have had to die if He had not died.    He saved us from dying by dying our death.    But what He did was no mere work of substitution, to be regarded as having fulfilled its purpose when the death had been died.    It had a further object in view—and it was the necessary and inevitable preliminary for the obtaining of that object—that we should be drawn into such intimate communion of love with Him, our Saviour, that His life should be our life ;  that we, inspired and enabled by that Divine power which in Him triumphed over sin and death, should share in the same triumph."

This paraphrase seems to do justice to the Apostle's words. It certainly prepares the way for the subsequent words : "Wherefore if any man is in Christ, he is a new creature : the old things are passed away ;  behold, they are become new." [3]    He then, in the immediately following words, declares categorically that the whole redemptive work originates with and proceeds from God :  "All things are of God, who reconciled us to Himself through Christ, and gave unto us the ministry of reconciliation ;  to wit, that God was in Christ reconciling the world unto Himself." [4]    This

[1] See p. 135.       [2] II Cor. v. 14, 15.
[3] II Cor. v. 17.       [4] II Cor. v. 18, 19.

" ministry of reconciliation " he straightway proceeds to exercise in his appeal : " We beseech you, on behalf of Christ, be ye reconciled to God," [1] and he indicates, in terms most solemn and mysterious, the central fact on which the possibility of that reconciliation for which he pleads is surely based : " Him who knew no sin, He made to be sin on our behalf ; that we might become the righteousness of God in Him." [2]

These words, briefly, but quite decisively, supply St. Paul's *rationale* of the Cross. They certainly do not mean that God made Christ to be a sinner. But what they do seem to mean is that on the Cross the Sinless was treated as sin. The consequences of the sin of mankind were appointed to Him by God, and were accepted by Him. It has been suggested that when he wrote these startling words, St. Paul had in his mind the picture of the scape-goat over whose head Aaron was commanded to confess " all the iniquities of the children of Israel, and all their transgressions, even all their sins . . . and the goat shall bear upon him all their iniquities into a solitary land." [3] It is also suggested that Isa. liii. was present to his thoughts. Either or both of these suggestions may be true. That Christ suffered for us, even instead of us, is evidently his meaning ; and he regards this suffering of Christ as a perfect manifestation of God's judgment on sin, more adequate for God's demand and man's need than all other judgments could be. In order that God might carry out His loving purpose of enabling us to become " the righteousness of God," there was a Divine necessity that He should make His Son " to be sin " on our behalf. He made Him, " on our behalf," to realise and to exemplify in His own Person, in willing obedience, the consequences of sin, the Divine judgment on sin. The Son obeyed the Father's will to the uttermost, and He did it for us—to save us. To save us He became our substitute.

The words we are considering are often treated in close connection with the similar expression of Gal. iii. 13 : " Christ redeemed us from the curse of the law, having become a curse for us." It may be admitted that these words are primarily connected with anti-Jewish controversy, and that they are intended, by a reference to Deut. xxi. 23 " to give a reason " to the Jewish opponent or inquirer why Christ should have endured the death of

[1] II Cor. v. 20.  [2] II Cor. v. 21.  [3] Lev. xvi. 21, 22.

crucifixion.  It is also to be remembered that St. Paul, in quoting his text, omits the words " by God."  It may simply have been that he abbreviated; or it may be that he would not say that Christ was " cursed by God."  The resulting expression which he does use is not unlike that of the Corinthian Epistle, " He made Him to be sin," and each expression conveys alike the meaning that Christ saves us by becoming our substitute.

Many other allusions to the central theme of " Jesus Christ, and Him crucified," might be gathered from other places in St. Paul's writings; but they only corroborate and supplement the passages with which we have tried to deal.

When, in later years, he wrote to the Colossians, he said : " For it was the good pleasure *of the Father* that in Him should all the fulness dwell; and through Him to reconcile all things unto Himself, having made peace through the blood of His cross; through Him, I say, whether things upon the earth, or things in the heavens." [1]  Here Christ's redemptive work is viewed not only in its relation to humanity, but also to the Universe.

In writing to the Philippians he views the matter more particularly from the side of Christ : " Who, being in the form of God, counted it not a prize to be on an equality with God, but emptied Himself, taking the form of a servant, being made in the likeness of men; and being found in fashion as a man, He humbled Himself, becoming obedient *even* unto death, yea, the death of the cross." [2]

And in the encyclical letter which we call Ephesians he speaks of God's grace, " which He freely bestowed on us in the Beloved : in whom we have our redemption through His blood." [3]  In whatever ways, and on whatever topics, further experience of life may have modified St. Paul's views about God's way of dealing with man, and the particular methods of His providence, we have no evidence of any change at all in his conception of God's way of salvation, by the sending of His Son " unto death, yea, the death of the cross," thereby " reconciling the world unto Himself, not reckoning unto them their trespasses." [4]

It is not an easy task to summarise in a few pages what has received from many distinguished writers the fuller treatment embodied in whole volumes of patient and learned

[1] Col. i. 19, 20.    [2] Phil. ii. 6–8.
[3] Eph. i. 6, 7.    [4] II Cor. v. 21

K

investigation. Still, the attempt must now be made to indicate, in rapid outline, but in coherent form, St. Paul's conception of the way in which God deals with the problem of human salvation.

Before beginning to do this, reference may again be made [1] to a problem, raised from time to time, from the side of moral philosophy in the alleged interests of a true and worthy conception of God. Why, it may be said, if St. Paul believed in a God who is both good and loving, does not his doctrine of redemption culminate in a free forgiveness ? " If God is Love, why cannot He forgive and forget ? "

The words of Dr. Maldwyn Hughes, in his reply to this query, are well worth quotation : " Forgiveness means the reconciliation of persons. But there can be no reconciliation between persons by ignoring the deep-seated ground of offence. This must be eradicated and destroyed if the reconciliation is to be deep and lasting. If God and man are to be reconciled, it cannot be by the simple expedient of ignoring sin, but only by overcoming it. We cannot overcome it of ourselves, and if we had to depend on ourselves alone, sin would always remain a barrier between us and God, and we should never be reconciled to Him. But when the righteous, loving God suffers in Christ on account of sin and on behalf of sinners, and in the very act by which He shows forth His mercy also pronounces His severest condemnation of sin, puts forth all His moral resources against it, and works such a transformation in those who have faith in Him as causes them to re-affirm His judgment of sin— then reconciliation takes place not by ignoring sin but by overcoming it. . . . In the Cross God's resistance to sin reached its climax and culmination. In Christ He put forth all the resources of His holiness and love and resisted even unto death. The Cross is the revelation in one focal act in time and on the field of history of what God is from all eternity. And it is not merely a revelation, it is a mighty work. It is Christ's crowning achievement in suffering and travail on behalf of sinful man." [2]

Dr. J. K. Mozley, too, has suggested possible lines of answer to this question : " Why cannot God freely forgive ? " He points out [3] that whereas forgiveness can deal

[1] Cf. pp. 134, 140.      [2] *What is the Atonement ?* pp. 146, 147
[3] *The Doctrine of the Atonement,* pp. 70, 71.

with the situation caused by sin in connection with the individual, it cannot do so on the greater scale of humanity as a whole. In relation to the whole human race sin is not a number of isolated acts, but an organic whole, and it perpetuates itself as guilt. An individual sinner may be forgiven. But guilt is a corporate thing ; it implies a dislocation of that moral order of the universe which is God's order, and the problem of salvation is the problem of saving a guilty world. Again, just as forgiveness, which is applicable to the individual, does not solve the problem of the world's guilt, neither does it in itself give assurance of future power. If we limit ourselves to the idea of forgiveness, we may say that by it the guilt of humanity as a whole is not rolled away, nor is any new principle introduced which can work towards the moral transformation of humanity. And, finally, if we limit ourselves to this idea of God's freely forgiving the repentant sinner without the intrusion of any other factor or consideration, then we seem to lack adequate explanation of the life and death of Christ. If God could have done, and does, as a matter of fact, do all that is necessary on the sinner's behalf, without any reference to Christ, we seem to be driven to the conclusion that what He did in Christ was—one shrinks from using the word " superfluous "—but at any rate it could have been done in some other way. Of any such conclusion it must be said that, whatever be its merits, it has the great demerit of being wholly alien to the New Testament conception of the work of Christ. St. Paul certainly viewed the death of Christ as God's way of bringing salvation to a guilty world.

And we have no evidence that he contemplated any alternative possibility. He held that Christ died because Christ must die, if sin is to be conquered and sinful men set free from the fetters of their sin. The assertion that Christ would have come even if the world had been sinless, and the proffered ground for this assertion, that the Divine must, by a necessity of Its own nature, reveal Itself, are propositions that do not appear to have entered into St. Paul's conception of the matter. He dealt with the existing situation. He regarded Christ as saving a world of sinful men exposed to the righteous wrath of God.

Insistence, then, on the question : " Why may we not suppose that God freely forgives, without any reference to the death of Christ ? " appears to rest on an inadequate view not only of forgiveness, but also of the deeper issues involved in man's position as sinful.

It may be noted, too, that in discussions that arise in this connection the word " transactional " appears to be somewhat of a bugbear. It is, of course, a word that may be employed in the interests of less worthy and less defensible theories. But if it is taken to mean simply that Christ did something for us which had to be done, and which we could not do for ourselves; in other words, that there is a truly objective aspect of Christ's work, to be taken into consideration and allowed its due place, along with the subjective appeal to our hearts—then the word seems to express a conception that was fundamental to New Testament thought about the work of Christ.

In attempting now to present St. Paul's *rationale* of the Atonement, we must reaffirm the point that it all rests on the belief in a personal, holy, loving God. If this be questioned or denied, the whole fabric of the Apostle's thought collapses. All the work of salvation—the salvation needed by a world of sinful men—originates from Him. Any " transactional " theory, in the sense of an offended Deity being placated by the intervention of One more merciful in character than He, has no place whatever in St. Paul's thinking. " All things," he says, " are of God, who reconciled us to Himself through Christ." [1]

The idea of " salvation " is perhaps the most inclusive and far-reaching one with which he operates. He held that God sent His Son to " save " men, in the widest sense of the term : from guilt, from the power of sin, from the onset of those personal spiritual forces of evil in whose existence St. Paul, in agreement with the thought of his age, thoroughly believed. It was to men entangled and enslaved in " this present evil world " that God sent His Son to bring salvation. And the salvation would reach on to the end; it would be effective in the day of God's judgment : Christ " delivereth us from the wrath to come."

He also employs the idea of " reconciliation." If sinful man is to be saved he must be reconciled to God. And what God has done for us in Christ is a work of reconciliation, a work which He has done and which we receive. He has done this work by making " Him who knew no sin to be sin on our behalf." Christ, for us, and in obedience to His

[1] II Cor. v. 18.

Father's will, not only endured the utmost consequence of sin, but also submitted to God's judgment on sin, acknowledging, in His submission, the absolute rightness and fitness of God's doom on sin. Some such meaning as this would seem to be implied by the mysterious reference to Christ's being made " sin."

On the ground of this passage, and the other one in which He is said to become a " curse " for us, the assertion may fairly be based that St. Paul clearly held the thought of substitution. Christ acted for us, took our place, endured our lot. Whatever may have happened to the idea of " substitution " in more recent thought, it cannot be eliminated from the thinking of St. Paul.

It is in accordance with this, and equally clear to the candid student of his writings, that he regards the death of Christ in the light of " sacrifice," an idea closely allied with that of " redemption." Christ redeems man by the sacrifice of Himself—He reconciles us to God by being our substitute, a propitiatory sacrifice offered on our behalf.

The terms employed should not be over-pressed into too great minuteness of detailed application. We need not inquire too closely into the object of propitiation, though on the analogy of general usage it would seem most naturally to apply to God. It seems unnatural to speak of propitiating sinful man. If the point be pressed, the reply must be made that it seems most reasonable to interpret " propitiation " in the light of " reconcilation." If St. Paul can say that God was in Christ reconciling the world to Himself, he may go on to say that Christ's part in the work of reconciliation was that of propitiation. And it must be remembered that here, too, the initiative in the great transaction lies with the loving God. It was He who " set forth " Christ to be a propitiation in His blood.

We may have to admit that language almost fails St. Paul adequately to express the profound issues which he struggled to set forth, as, indeed, all human thought and speech may fail in the effort to portray transcendent mysteries; but it must be reaffirmed with emphasis that he conceived Christ's death as a propitiatory sacrifice, the willing sacrifice of Himself, whereby the reconciliation of man to God is effected.

And, further, he employs the idea expressed in English by the term " Justification." He believed in a God who

" justifieth the ungodly." [1] The word " justification " perhaps conveys to our minds associations of law and legal procedure, associations not so closely connected with St. Paul's word in the original, where he is speaking of God as righteous, and the need of putting man " right " with the righteous God. He believed in the supremacy of that moral order, which is the expression of the mind and being of God —a moral order that could neither be altered nor evaded, the demands of which must, always and everywhere, be fully met; an order which God Himself, the God of love, could not abrogate, repeal, or cancel. And the essence of the Gospel which he believed and proclaimed was that, in Christ, the loving Father had done this miraculous thing— maintained and vindicated His own righteousness, upheld in all its majesty His moral order, and yet brought redemption and release from sin to a sin-stricken world of men, so that He is " just and the justifier of him that hath faith in Jesus." [2] And the result of this justification is that the justified " have peace with God through our Lord Jesus Christ." [3]

The question has been raised and often debated whether St. Paul, in regarding the crucified Christ as our substitute, regarded Him as bearing our punishment, and so being Himself punished by God. Here we must go cautiously if we would not misrepresent the Apostle's thought. On the one hand, he seems to think of a penal element in the Cross. He says that Christ was made " sin " for us, and " a curse " for us; and words like these appear to mean that Christ on the Cross endured what mankind had to expect. And yet, vicarious suffering such as His—that of the righteous for the unrighteous—cannot have had the same quality, the same character, as ours would have had, if we had under-gone the doom of God's judgment on unforgiven sin. And, for this reason, it would be rash categorically to assert that Christ bore our punishment. It would be a truer present-ment of St. Paul's thought to say that our Lord's work " is not one of atonement and expiation through punishment, but rather of expiation instead of punishment." [4] He held that on our behalf and for our redemption Christ suffered, but not that He was punished.

Finally, in justice to St. Paul's thought, we must never forget his teaching as to the ultimate purpose of this redemp-

---

[1] Rom. iv. 5.    [2] Rom. iii. 26.    [3] Rom. v. 1.
[4] Mozley, *The Doctrine of the Atonement*, p. 73.

tive work of Christ—that we " might walk in newness of life," [1] " alive unto God in Christ Jesus." [2]  Such criticism as approaches the matter *ab extra* has here found a logical hiatus in his thinking, and has been unable to discover any necessary connection between an objective redemption, wrought by Christ, and subsequent growth in righteousness, on the part of the redeemed.  Justification, as conceived by St. Paul, and Sanctification have seemed to lack the bond of any ascertainable link, and St. Paul's view of the Christian as " in Christ " and living in Christ has been treated as his " mysticism," a thing interesting, but incapable of being brought into relation with his other forms of thought.

For him, at any rate, the difficulty did not exist.  Christ was all in all to him, and the Christ who was the object of his love was the Christ who had been crucified, who " had made peace through the blood of His cross," who had risen from the grave and was alive for evermore.  The Christ who had died for him was the same Christ who now possessed him so completely in the intercourse of mutual love that he could say :  " I live, and yet no longer I, but Christ liveth in me." [3]  To put it very simply, it was unthinkable for St. Paul that any one who had experienced the redeeming love of Christ could do other than submit himself wholly and gratefully to the law and will of Christ.

It has been said, and repeated, in the course of this essay that St. Paul's view of the Atonement rests wholly on his conception of God.  It should be added here that it rests equally on his conception of Christ as the Son of God.  His particular conception of the Person of Christ and of Christ's relation to God belongs to other fields of investigation.  But the general tenor of his writings testifies that he conceived Christ to be Divine—the Son of God, " His own Son," whom God sent " in the likeness of sinful flesh and as *an offering* for sin." [4]  The work of atonement was not done by any human personage, or demi-god.  " God sent forth His Son, born of a woman, born under the law, that He might redeem them which were under the law, that we might receive the adoption of sons." [5]  " God was in Christ reconciling the world unto Himself." [6]

The essence, then, of St. Paul's belief and teaching seems to be this.  God, who is a God of love and righteousness,

[1] Rom. vi. 4.          [2] Rom. vi. 11.          [3] Gal. ii. 20.
[4] Rom. viii. 3.          [5] Gal. iv. 5.          [6] II Cor. v. 19.

has brought into being a race of men, to be the objects of His love, and to give to Him love in return. To enter worthily into this relationship of love they must be free moral agents. They have employed their freedom in the interests of self-seeking and rebellion rather than in the interests of obedience to the Divine Will. They have become sinful, and, as such, objects of the Wrath of God. But His loving purpose for man is not defeated. In love, He has sent His Son to declare God's righteousness, to meet and maintain all its requirements by the willing sacrifice of Himself to do the Father's will, and to win men to gratitude and love, by the appeal of His own loving sacrifice on their behalf. This loving work and sacrifice of Christ is the work and sacrifice of God. It is the manifestation under conditions of time and space, on the field of human history, of the eternal passion of the heart of God, the love that saves to the uttermost, that will not let us go.

St. Paul, as we have seen, views and expresses this in terms of salvation, redemption, sacrifice, reconciliation, justification, sanctification. By all this he means that Christ died for our sins on the Cross, and now reigns in glory; that what He did for us must be appropriated by a corresponding experience in the consciousness of each; the Christian must die to sin and must rise to the new life of triumphant power in Christ.

How does Christian thought, to-day, regard this teaching of St. Paul?

It has been regarded as overlaying the simple gospel of Christ, that God loves and forgives, with archaic forms of thought, and conditions now outworn and obsolete, in such a way as to obscure the truth and beauty of Christ's message and involve it in the meshes of quite alien ways of thinking. The logical outcome of this appears to be that we must discard St. Paul, if we would really appreciate and love his Master.

It has also been regarded, with somewhat greater appearance of sympathy, as corresponding really to the truth as it is in Jesus. It is said that St. Paul had really learned, and does pass on to us, the message of God's love in Christ; but that, as Jew and Pharisee, he had inevitably conceived it, as did other early Christians, under forms supplied by ancient Hebrew Scriptures. It is a case of the kernel and the husk. If we, for our part, would penetrate to that kernel of Divine truth which the heart of St. Paul had really grasped, we must strip the husk off of his particular presentment of it.   We must make allowances and discriminate.

It is also possible, still, to hold that in interpreting the death of Christ " for our sins according to the Scriptures," St. Paul, and those who thought with him, were following the lines laid down by Christ Himself, and that, so, their thoughts were really in touch with ultimate reality; that, when we speak of the righteousness of God, the wrath of God, the reconciling work of God in Christ, we are not dealing with transient conceptions which conceal rather than reveal the truth; we are in touch with eternal reality, with things as they are; that the Christ understood as St. Paul presents Him is the true Christ, the only Christ that meets our need.

What the ultimate verdict of Christian thought will be we cannot tell.   But it may be safely said that it is the Christ of whom St. Paul said : " He loved me and gave Himself up for me," who still wins the hearts of seeking men and makes His love triumphant in their lives.

# THE ATONEMENT IN THE JOHANNINE WRITINGS
## By W. H. Rigg

### I

#### The Gospel and the Epistles

THE writings to which the name of John is attached present critical problems which have baffled scholars for more than a century, and are still the subject of debate. We must content ourselves with outlining certain positions, the full proof of which would carry us beyond the limits of this essay. It is generally accepted that the Fourth Gospel and the First Epistle of St. John were written by the same person. Hence in our consideration of the Johannine view of the death of Christ and its significance our attention will not be confined to the Gospel, but full use will be made of the Epistle. They must both be taken together.[1]

It is otherwise with the Apocalypse. With regard to this book we are tempted to adopt the words of Origen respecting the Epistle to the Hebrews, that who actually wrote it " God only knows." The doctrine of the Atonement, as found in the book of the Revelation, must receive separate treatment.

Who wrote the Gospel? Although serious difficulties have been urged against the traditional view of its Apostolic authorship, we consider that they are not decisive ; but for our purpose it is best to leave the whole question in abeyance. We would merely urge that the writer had been in

---

[1] Professor Scott in his book on *The Fourth Gospel, its Purpose and Theology*, pp. 88, 94, considers that there are strong proofs that the Epistle was written by a different author, but such liberal critics as Windisch and Baumgarten ascribe the Gospel and the First Epistle to the same person, as do also Archdeacon Charles and Dr. Brooke in our own country.

direct contact with our Lord when He was on earth. This is supported by the opening words of the First Epistle of St. John : " That which was from the beginning, which we have heard, which we have seen with our eyes, which we have looked upon, and our hands have handled, of the Word of life . . . we bear witness unto you " (I Jn. i. 1 ff.). To explain them away on the ground that they are a record of mystical experience necessitates a very forced interpretation of the expression " and our hands have handled," and favours that Docetic view of Christ's Person which it was the chief purpose of the author to refute. A far more serious question confronts us : Are the contents of the Gospel, including the recorded sayings of our Lord, historical ? Although Canon Streeter admits that the Fourth Gospel contains genuine tradition, must we assert with him that it belongs " neither to History, nor Biography, but to the Library of Devotion " ? [1] Or shall we say, " Christ lives and breathes in the Fourth Gospel, because ' manifested in remembrance ' reflected from the faithful mirror of a mind at once accurate and devout " ? [2] Undoubtedly our sympathies are with the latter alternative, but we prefer to content ourselves with the statement that St. John's Gospel is the inspired interpretation of a disciple of Christ who knew His mind and heart as few, if any, have ever known Him. Let it be freely admitted that if, as some think, the Evangelist has given us a less literal report of what the Lord actually said, he is more spiritual, and therefore a truer interpreter of His words, work and Person, than are the writers of the other three Gospels. It is a well-known fact that a portrait drawn by a skilful artist will convey a truer impression of the original than will a photograph, although the latter may be more correct in matters of detail. This applies in a pre-eminent degree to the Fourth Gospel.

From St. John's own words we may conclude, if the present tense πιστεύητε rather than the aorist πιστεύσητε is read in xx. 31, that his object was to strengthen the faith of believers, and that their faith might grow. A true view of the Atonement must take into account the Johannine interpretation of that great subject, his special contribution, his special emphasis.

The differences between the Synoptists and the author of

[1] *The Four Gospels*, p. 365.
[2] Cf. *The Fourth Evangelist*, by C. F. Nolloth, p. 115.

the Fourth Gospel have frequently been observed by theological writers. Both in the selection of his subject matter and his treatment of the teaching and work of Jesus Christ the Evangelist pursues a distinctive line of his own. This aspect of the question, however, may easily be exaggerated, as it has been by some modern writers, and in particular when they set forth the Johannine teaching of the death of Christ. It will therefore be our endeavour to show that St. John's teaching makes *explicit what is implicit* in the Synoptic account of Christ's life and death; further, that his teaching is in perfect harmony with the Pauline view of the Atonement, at the same time fully recognising that he approaches the Cross of Christ from a somewhat different angle, in the light of his long experience of intense communion with the exalted Christ, and as one alive to the needs of his own generation.

As also in St. Mark, the description of the Lord's earthly life begins in the Fourth Gospel with the account of John's baptism in the River Jordan. What is peculiar to St. John is the exclamation which falls from the lips of the Baptist as he sees Jesus approaching, " Behold the Lamb of God which taketh away the sin of the world " (Jn. i. 29). Thus does St. John strike the sacrificial note at the very outset of the Lord's public life, giving us the motive and meaning of all that follows. As is the case with his predecessors, St. John devotes a considerable portion of his Gospel to the incidents of the Passion, thereby testifying that the death was the climax of the Lord's life. It may be that the Synoptic and Johannine dating of the Last Supper cannot be made to harmonise; if so, the Johannine rather than the Synoptic mode of reckoning is to be preferred.

The Evangelist regards our Lord as the true Paschal Lamb, His death taking place on the day of the preparation of the Passion (xix. 14; cf. I Cor. v. 7), and he alone amongst the Evangelists is careful to observe that when the soldiers came to Jesus " they brake not His legs," thus fulfilling the Scripture (Exod. xii. 46; Jn. xix. 33, 36).

The account of the institution of the Eucharist is not given in the Fourth Gospel, but, in accordance with the majority of scholars, we may assume that there is a direct reference to it in the discourse on the Bread of Life. It is highly significant that after Jesus had ascended a mountain it is stated that " the Passover, a feast of the Jews was nigh " (vi. 4). This is more than merely a note of time, for, as Lagrange rightly observes, " If John had only wished to append a chronological direction, he would have placed it at the beginning of this narrative " [1] (cf. v. 1; vii. 2; x. 22; xiii. 1).

From the Synoptists we learn that at the Last Supper the Lord celebrated the Passover with His disciples (Mk. xiv. 12 ff.; Lk. xxii. 7 ff.). The Lord's Supper was intended to be a memorial of the Paschal Lamb whose blood was to be shed for many on the morrow. The phrase " the Lamb of God " would have more than one meaning attached to it by the Evangelist, since it is a favourite practice of his to express himself in a manner which he intends his readers to understand in more ways than one.[2]

We may be sure that he wishes them to see in Christ the suffering Servant of Jehovah, who, as the Lamb of God, would be brought to the slaughter, on Him being laid the iniquity of us all. That this is not a mere conjecture on our part we may see from the fact that in the latter part of chapter xii, where the Evangelist is summarising the general impression made by the Lord's life, and where, outside the actual narrative of the Passion, more allusions are made to the Lord's death than anywhere else in the Gospel, our Lord is actually identified with the suffering Servant of Yahweh (cf. xii. 38 and Isa. liii. 1 ff.). There is no doubt that the Evangelist was giving the true interpretation to the meaning of Christ's Person and work as realised by Himself (cf. Lk. xxii. 37). So, then, whatever the words may have been from the Baptist's lips, to the Evangelist Christ was both the Passover Lamb and the Lamb mentioned in the Second Isaiah.[3]

---

[1] Cf. *Evangile selon Saint Jean*, deuxième édition, p. 161.

[2] Cf. ἐγείρειν, to build up and raise from the dead (ii. 19–21); ὑπάγειν, to go away and go home (xiii. 33; xiv. 28); ἄνωθεν, again and from above (iii. 5–8); εἰς τέλος, to the end and to the uttermost (xiii. 1), etc. Cf. Bauer, *Das Johannes-Evangelium, Zweite Auflage, S.* 46.

[3] In the saying of the Baptist what is in dispute is the saying ascribed to the verb translated in our R.V. " taketh away," αἴρων (i. 29). Taken in this sense it means " to remove sin," but in the margin of the R.V. another meaning is given, " beareth sin " (cf. Isa. liii. 6). In favour of the first rendering αἴρειν in the Fourth Gospel signifies not " to carry," but " to lift up " in order to remove something (cf. ii. 16; x. 18; xi. 39, 48; xv. 2; xix. 31). The Greek words used in the LXX of Isa. liii. 4, 11, 12 of the Suffering

It is striking that at the very threshold of his Gospel, after proclaiming the coexistence of the Son with the Eternal Father, and His creative energy, he unites with it (after a short interlude, *vv.* 19–28) His redemptive, His sacrificial work. To this Evangelist the Creator is of necessity Saviour also, the Lamb slain from the foundation of the world. As the Passover Lamb He takes away the sin of the world in the sense that He delivers the sinner from the burden of his sin by " lifting it away," and the offender, being thus forgiven, is delivered from the thraldom of evil (cf. Jn. viii. 35, 36) and looks upon Christ as his victorious deliverer. In harmony with the other writers of the New Testament, St. John regards the death of Christ as a sacrifice [1] upon which centres man's reconciliation with God and assurance of the Divine forgiveness. This is most prominent in his

---

Servant bearing our sins are φέρειν and ἀναφέρειν. As Strack and Billerbeck allow in their exhaustive discussion on the passage, the verb αἴρειν in the LXX never has the meaning of " bearing sin." (Cf. *Kommentar zum neuen Testament aus Talmud und Midrasch*, ii. *S.* 367.) Hence the primary meaning of the passage, at least as understood by the Evangelist, must refer to the Paschal Lamb. Now the Paschal Lamb was not a piacular sacrifice. But is the other rendering thereby excluded? Our answer is in the negative. The identification of the suffering Servant of Isaiah with our Lord was made very early in the Primitive Church (Mt. viii. 17; Acts viii. 32), and in our belief was derived from our Lord Himself (Lk. xxii. 37; xxiv. 26), as Dr. Estlin Carpenter allows, "The Evangelist —making the same citation as the Apostle Paul, shows that he, too, accepted the current recognition" (Jn. xii. 38; Rom. x. 16). Cf. *The Johannine Writings*, p. 408.

Besides this, the Lamb of God, ὁ ἀμνὸς τοῦ θεοῦ, goes back to Isa. liii. 7 (cf. Jer. xi. 19), and is the meaning which the Baptist would give. Bishop Headlam suggests that "the thoughts and ideas of John, as of Jesus, are derived from a fresh and intimate study of the prophets, and that Jesus from the beginning of His Ministry thought of Himself as the Servant of the Lord, and applied to Himself these passages. . . . There is nothing in the words put into the Baptist's mouth which he might not have learnt from the Book of Isaiah, and applied to Him who already felt Himself to be ' the Servant ' with all that it implied." (Cf. *The Life and Teaching of Jesus the Christ*, p. 153, and Strack–Billerbeck, *op. cit.*, *S.* 369.)

[1] Jn. xvii. 19. "For their sakes I consecrate Myself." The word translated consecrate (ἁγιάζω) has a twofold meaning. Our Lord is dedicating Himself to the service of God, preparing Himself for the supreme act of obedience (cf. Jn. x. 36), but, as St. Chrysostom in Joann. Hom. LXXXII. says, "What is, I sanctify Myself? I offer to Thee a sacrifice (προσφέρω σοι θυσίαν)." It is often used in this sense in the LXX., *e.g.* Exod. xiii. 2; Deut. xv. 19; II Sam. viii. 11).

First Epistle (I Jn. i. 7–9; ii. 1–2), and appears in the threefold witness mentioned towards the close of his letter. " This is He that came by water and blood, Jesus Christ, not in the water only, but in the water and blood. And the Spirit is that which beareth witness, because the Spirit is the truth. Because three are they that bear witness, the Spirit and the water and the blood " (v. 6–8). Difficult as these verses are, being intended to convey more than one meaning, the coming by water refers to the Baptism of Jesus, and His announcement as the expected Messiah, the Lamb of God, and the coming by the blood to the death on the Cross. The sacraments of Baptism and Holy Communion are the perpetual witnesses in the Christian Church to the cleansing and redeeming activity of Jesus. This passage in the Epistle carries us back to what the Evangelist relates that he saw after the piercing of the Redeemer's side, at the Crucifixion by one of the soldiers, " and forthwith came there out blood and water " (Jn. xix. 34), testifying to the reality of the Lord's sacrificial death, and also to the source of the new life of the Christian. The giving by the Father of His only-begotten Son for the salvation of the world carries with it the giving unto death (iii. 14–16). Without the death the Lord's life work would remain unfinished (xii. 24, 25), and by means of it will He draw all men unto Himself (*ibid.*, *vv.* 32–33).

In the discourse on the Bread of Life, although Dr. Zahn declines to see a single allusion to the Lord's death,[1] yet in vi. 51, " I am the Living Bread which came down out of heaven : if any man eat of this Bread he shall live for ever : yea, and the bread which I will give is My flesh, for the life of the world," it is surely referred to, since we may compare the preposition ὑπέρ, used of His flesh being given for the life of the world, with what St. Mark says of the blood of the covenant being shed for many (τὸ ἐκχυννόμενον ὑπὲρ πολλῶν) (xiv. 24. Cf. Lk. xxii. 20; I Cor. xi. 24, and Jn. x. 15, xv. 13).

The Evangelist would also have his readers to understand by the words " Except ye eat the flesh of the Son of Man, and drink His blood, ye have no life in you "[2] that a death by violence is understood. The distinct terms " flesh " and " blood " imply that mankind cannot partake of the

[1] Cf. *Das Evangelium des Johannes,* *S.* 352.
[2] vi. 53.

Bread of Heaven apart from the self-sacrifice of Christ on the Cross.

The laying down of the Lord's life as the culminating point of His mission and work is often referred to as " the hour." The expression " the hour cometh " is used of a particular time determined of the Father, independent of man's will (cf. ii. 4; iv. 21; v. 25, 28; xvi. 2, 25), but in many instances the hour of the Lord's death is intended. More than once it is stated that violent hands were not suffered to be laid upon Jesus, for " the hour had not come " (vii. 30; viii. 20), and when it drew near it was viewed by Christ with dread. " Father, save Me from this hour," He prays, and then adds that the purpose of His coming was for this hour (xii. 27). The agony of Gethsemane was not only experienced in the garden, but continually the weight of the Cross pressed heavily upon Him (cf. Mk. x. 32; Lk. xii. 50). Nigh unto the feast of the Passover our Lord knew that the destined hour had virtually arrived when He should depart to the Father (Jn. xiii. 1), and in the upper room He informs His disciples that " the hour was coming when they will be scattered each to his own home, and He will be left alone " (xvi. 32), and in His High Priestly prayer He prays His Father to glorify Him, " for the hour has come."

In a consideration of the Atonement from St. John's point of view, it is advisable to consider his conception of sin. It has been maintained that the conception of sin which enters into the essential structure of John's theology is far from according with that which is found in the Synoptists, that sin is regarded by him not so much as a positive principle but rather as a privation, a limitation. Consequently it has been pointed out that deliverance from sin to the Evangelist consists " in the opening of a door that has hitherto been closed." [1] Emphasis is laid on St. John's view, that the natural man cannot of himself become the possessor of the higher life, which is a gift from above, and that only after the coming of Christ were men answerable for remaining in the outer darkness, the way of freedom having been opened to them.

Now we do not deny that St. John is preoccupied with the attitude which men take towards Christ, Who is the touchstone of belief and conduct. Hence in the Fourth

[1] Cf. Scott, *op. cit.*, pp. 220, 221.

Gospel the gravity of sin lies in the rejection of the Incarnate Son and of the Father who had sent Him (xv. 24), and one of the principal objects of the Holy Spirit's work is to convict men of sin because of their failure to believe in Christ (xvi. 8, 9; cf. viii. 19–21; ix. 39–41). Although this view does not receive the same emphasis in the Synoptists as it does in the Fourth Gospel, yet it is by no means absent from them. Man's ultimate destiny depends upon his open profession or denial of Christ (Mt. x. 32, 33; Lk. xii. 8, 9). Hence by implication the rejection of Christ is regarded as fraught with the gravest consequences. Eternal life, one of the great doctrines of the Fourth Gospel, corresponds very closely to the " Kingdom of Heaven " of the Synoptists. In the latter the Kingdom of Heaven as taught by our Lord is both a gift to be received and a life to be lived. To receive His Kingdom we must become as little children (Mk. x. 15; Mt. xviii. 3), the word receive clearly denoting the granting of a gift. Nicodemus in the Fourth Gospel also must become a little child, repentance and cleansing being necessary in his case, as he cannot *enter*, as distinct from *seeing*, the Kingdom of Heaven unless he is born of water and the Spirit. Redemption in the Johannine thought brings positive blessings, fulness of life, light and love, but we cannot confine it to the view expressed above. The Evangelist also teaches that Christ liberated man from the power of indwelling sin, and overcame his most powerful antagonist, the Prince of Darkness. He declares that sin is universal, that it is every kind of sin—sin in all its forms— which is cleansed by the blood of Jesus (I Jn. i. 7–10). This involves the removal of sin as the ruling principle in the believer (I Jn. ii. 1), although a continual confession of sinfulness must be made (I Jn. i. 8, 9), and a daily cleansing is necessary (Jn. xiii. 10). The ultimate goal of the Christian disciple must be the reproduction in his own life of the purity of his Master. Effort there must be on his part, he must purify himself even as He is pure (I Jn. iii. 3). He must abide in Christ, and in so far as he abides in Him, to that extent he will not sin (I Jn. iii. 6). He will not fall short of the standard of righteousness (I Jn. i. 9; v. 17. Cf. Jn. vii. 18). Sin is regarded as lawlessness (I Jn. iii. 4), it actively operates against the work of Christ, deriving its force and energy from the Evil One, the great antagonist of God (Jn. xiv. 30), under whose domination the world for

L

the most part lies (Jn. xii. 31; I Jn. v. 19), and who has
nothing in common with Christ (Jn. xiv. 30). The Christian
knows that he must wage a perpetual warfare against evil,
both from outside and from within. Our Lord prays that
those who belong to Him may be kept from the Evil One
(Jn. xvii. 15; cf. I Jn. v. 18), and the Evangelist encourages
his readers by reminding them that they have One within
them who is greater than he that is in the world (I Jn.
iv. 4). Against the evil in their own hearts, the weakness
which comes from their bodily nature, the love of beauty
divorced from the love of goodness, the pride which comes
from worldly possessions, the children of God must ever be
on their guard (I Jn. ii. 15, 16). Such emphasis is laid on
the alienation of the world from God that some have considered that the Evangelist entertained a dualistic view of
the universe, but the opposition is ethical, not metaphysical,
The world is ever the object of the Divine love (Jn. iii. 16).
and all created things derive their existence from Him who
is the Word, who was with God, and is God (Jn. i. 1 and 3).
He is God and is the Light of the World (viii. 12). Instead
of regarding sin merely from the negative point of view,
St. John affirms that it is a positive evil, the overcoming of
which devolves on the Christian, and is rendered possible by
the triumph of his Master.

Further, the guilt of sin is implied. St. John states the
need of all to be cleansed from sin, amongst whom he
classes himself. He takes care in the very same sentence
to mention, previous to the cleansing, " the taking away of
sin," and the metaphor used is in the cancelling of debts.[1]
Before the cleansing process can be effected, the guilt must
be removed (I Jn. i. 9). The Evangelist assumes on the
part of his readers that they have experienced the forgiveness of sins through the name of Christ (I Jn. ii.
12; cf. Lk. xxiv. 47), and in the great commission to
His Church the Risen Lord entrusts her with the gift
of the Holy Spirit and with the power to absolve from
sin (Jn. xx. 22, 23).

The criticism has often been made that the Fourth Gospel
affords no parallel to the Synoptic records of the intercourse
of Jesus with sinners. The Saviour of sinners is Synoptic,
one finds it most in Luke, and least in John. In Lk. xix. 10

[1] Cf. the Johannine Epistles in the International Critical Commentary by A. E. Brooke, note on I Jn. i. 9, p. 20.

Jesus seeks the lost, in Jn. iii. 16; vi. 39; x. 28; xvii. 12; xviii. 9 much rather does He care, that none of those who are already His " should be lost." [1]  This opinion provokes our strong dissent, since it ignores such conversations as that with the woman in Samaria, in which her past life is brought to light, and to whom the offer of the Living Water is freely given.  It ignores the miracle wrought at the pool of Bethesda on the man who had been lame for thirty-eight years, and whose disease had been caused by his own sin (v. 14).  Moreover, general invitations were given by our Lord to all sorts and conditions of people to come to Him (iii. 14, 15; vi. 35; vii. 37), with the promise that " him that cometh unto Me I will in no wise cast out " (vi. 37).

But the giving of the Son is not exclusively associated with the Cross; His death is not viewed in isolation from the rest of His life, it is organically connected with what goes before as well as with that which follows after.  The gift of the Son was not confined to one specific event (iii. 16.  Cf. I Jn. ii. 1, 2; iii. 5, 8; and especially iv. 9 ff.), but all through His life He was giving Himself.  As we follow the record of the Lord's life and teaching, we learn to see the nature and being of the Father as revealed in and by Him, the Divine attitude towards sin, and the quality of eternal life which salvation bestows upon the disciple.  Thus gradually there is borne in upon us the inevitableness of the Cross, as the crown and completion of the Saviour's work, the hour must come when it is expedient that He " should die for the people " (xi. 50).  The perfect surrender to His Father's will, even unto death, was always exhibited in the days of His ministry, so that He could say on the eve of His Passion, " I have glorified Thee on the earth : I have finished the work which Thou gavest Me to do " (xvii. 4), and on the Cross, " It is perfected," it is finished (xix. 30).

According to St. John, the Cross is connected with the Resurrection and the Ascension.  This is brought out by the double meaning of the word " lift up " in iii. 14, " And as Moses lifted up the serpent in the wilderness, even so must the Son of Man be lifted up, that whosoever believeth in Him should not perish, but have everlasting life," and in

[1] Cf. H. J. Holtzmann, *Neutestamentliche Theologie*; *Zweiter Band* S. 522.

two other passages, namely, viii. 28 and xii. 32, 33. In all three references there is involved the lifting up on to the Cross and the lifting up into heaven. The connection of the Resurrection and the Ascension with the Crucifixion makes the Cross a present power, and guarantees the continued activity of the Redeemer's work (xvii. 26, " and will make Thy name known "). It transforms an apparent defeat into a glorious victory. It excludes the idea that salvation may be regarded just simply as a past event or an outside transaction; it translates it into an inward process effected by the Ascended Christ through His Spirit. The Christian will reproduce his Master's death and life (xii. 24, 25).

To St. John the Cross was glory, exaltation, " lifting up." To St. Paul the Cross was the supreme limitation of the Son of God (Phil. ii. 5–8). Glorying as he did in it, yet he could never forget the shame and degradation inflicted by man upon the Son of God, and in which, in a very real sense, he felt he had himself taken an active part. St. John, on the other hand, viewed the Crucifixion from quite a different aspect. Thus when the Greeks come with the request to see Jesus (xii. 20 ff.) the Lord exclaims that " the hour is come that the Son of Man should be glorified." Already He beheld the first fruits of that wonderful harvest, resulting from the death of the corn of wheat. The sheep outside the fold of Judaism would be brought, and together with God's chosen people, constitute one flock under one shepherd (x. 16). The pent-up activities of Jesus would be released, and rendered accessible to those who " having not seen yet have believed." The external Presence of Christ would be changed into an abiding manifestation within the hearts of those who should accept His gift of eternal life, and become united to Him, and He to them. The saving effects of Christ's redeeming love would become interwoven with the very fibres of the believer's life. From the Ascended and glorified Christ there would ever issue forth power and strength, cleansing him from all sin. His disciples would actually be enabled to do greater works than their Master, because of His departure to the Father.

Shining through the betrayal, desolation, mocking and scourging, St. John beholds the glory. No sooner has the traitor Judas left the upper room than the Lord exclaims, " Now is the Son of Man glorified, and God is glorified in

Him." The Cross is in sight, and our Lord freely accepts all that it involves. There is no turning back. The procession to Calvary is a triumphal march. "Art Thou a King, then ? " asks Pilate. "Thou sayest that I am a King," is the quiet answer. From now onwards Christ would be enthroned in the hearts of His countless multitudes ; they would ever behold in Him " the Man," the ideal Man and the Son of God. If, as we believe, St. John had been an eye-witness of the scenes of the Passion,[1] it was the regal dignity of the Son of Man which stood out in his memory. Notwithstanding all efforts made to humiliate Him, they had produced the contrary effect. Not from the centurion only was the involuntary confession drawn that " this man was a Son of God " (Mk. xv. 39). The Evangelist could add his own personal testimony, " We beheld His glory as of the Only Begotten of the Father full of grace and truth." For St. John Calvary was the scene of a Transfiguration, when the holiness of Christ shone forth as the dazzling sun breaks through the thick and heavy thunder-clouds. The Kingship revealed on the Cross carries through to its ultimate end the Lord's conception of the Messiahship and His Kingdom, and the saying, " I am among you as He that serveth," receives its most impressive confirmation. His self-sacrificing love would be henceforth the law of His realm, and the only mark of distinction would be that of service.

We have seen that the phrase " the Lamb of God taking away the sin of the world " carries with it also the secondary meaning of " bearing the guilt or sin of the world upon Himself," and thus removing it. The breaking down of the barriers between God and man was in some way effected by Christ taking upon Himself man's sin. This view is reinforced by the teaching given in the First Epistle, when it is definitely stated that Jesus Christ in His own Person is a propitiation [2] not for our sins only, but for the sins of the

[1] It is interesting to note that Professor Percy Gardner, who does not accept the Apostolic authorship of the Gospel, says that " the account of the last days is in the Gospel so very much more ample and detailed than any other part of the biography, while at the same time it has not at all the air of mere invention, that one is compelled to think that the Evangelist regarded this part of his work as in a special degree founded upon the testimony of an eye-witness " (*The Ephesian Gospel*, p. 70).

[2] What is the object of propitiation ? Two very distinct answers are given. Some assert that it is God. Others strongly deny this

whole world (I Jn. ii. 2), and is given and sent by God for that very purpose (I Jn. iv. 10). Nevertheless, this teaching is only an amplification, or rather a development, of the Lord's words concerning His mission, " The Son of Man is come to seek and save them that are lost " (Lk. xix. 10; Mk. x. 45; Mt. xx. 28). His whole life was spent in ministering to others, and its outcome would be that of a ransom for many, consisting in the offering of Christ's spotless life and His death in the place of many. The Beloved Disciple, like St. Paul, enables us to say that it had a Godward direction. That in our relationship to God and His relationship to us Christ accomplished a work on our behalf which we, left to our own resources, could never have performed,

---

and say that it is not God, but man. Before discussing these views, it should be noted that ἱλασμός, propitiation, is only used in the New Testament in this Epistle (ii. 2; iv. 10), and once in the Epistle to the Romans, where ἱλασμός is not actually used, but ἱλαστήριον. It is agreed that the ideas governing the usage of both writers must be derived from the Old Testament, and not from Hellenic thought. The late Professor Driver's article on " Propitiation " in Hastings' *Dictionary of the Bible*, Vol. III., pp. 128–132, is in all probability the most authoritative discussion in our language of the Old Testament conception. The ritual term " Kippurîm," usually rendered " coverings," is the Hebrew word translated " propitiation." Hence in the approach to God the sins committed by the community or the individual were covered. The question we have to determine is, Does the Old Testament favour the view that the *sinner only* felt it was impossible to enter into communion with the most High God unless his sins were covered, or does it include the Divine standpoint, that no sinner could draw nigh to God unless his sins were covered ? Dr. Driver's warning has often been disregarded, that " Kipper " is a difficult word to represent satisfactorily in English. " Cover " or " wipe out " is too colourless. Whilst admitting that " to make propitiation " accentuates somewhat unduly a particular side of what is involved in " Kipper," yet Dr. Driver considers that this is, on the whole, the best rendering. Difficult as it may be to explain, the Johannine teaching demands that, whilst God's love is unalterable, His holiness, which is one side of His flawless love, needed absolute vindication in order that the relation between Himself and sinful man should be restored, and this was effected in the person of Christ. Our chief concern here is not whether this conception can be made intelligible to the modern man, but what the teaching of St. John was. To say, with Dr. Wendt, that propitiation only means " forgiveness," or, with Bishop Westcott, that such phrases as " propitiating God " or " God being reconciled " are foreign to the language of the New Testament, cannot be maintained. At the same time, it is true to say that the barrier against reconciliation is on our side, not on God's (cf. II Cor. v. 19, 20).

is a true and correct interpretation of the Lord's life and
sacrifice on the Cross.

Love is one of the great words of St. John. More than
an attribute of God, it is His nature and essence. He *is*
Love, but the writer does not shrink from speaking of the
wrath of God, which is the reaction of holy love in contact
with sin (Jn. iii. 36),

> " Thou judgest us : Thy purity
>     Doth all our lusts condemn,
> The love that draws us nearer Thee
>     Is hot with wrath to them "
>
> (Whittier).

and is expressed by the necessity, that in order to destroy
the works of the Devil, the Son of God should lay down
His life.

The condemnation of sin was proclaimed by the very act
of forgiving love. Judgment is the shadow cast by the
brightness of the Divine love. Although the Son of Man
came not to judge the world, but to save the world (xii. 47),
yet judgment flowed from His very presence. By the very
attitude men adopted towards Him were they judging
themselves, and the Cross was the supreme judgment
of sin. The ruler of this world, the prince of darkness,
made assault after assault upon Christ (Col. ii. 15), and
though it was his hour (Lk. xxii. 53), and he appeared at
times to triumph, yet all unwittingly he proclaimed his own
downfall, and brought judgment upon himself and those
identified with him. The evil one is cast down (Jn. xii. 31;
cf. I Cor. ii. 6–8). In the condemnation of, and victory
over the devil by the Cross and resurrection of Christ were
expressed God's attitude towards sin and His absolute
triumph over it. The honour of the Father has been vindicated by the pouring forth of Christ's soul unto death,
enabling the world to recognise that God's love and justice
are one. Throughout the whole of His life our Lord never
sought His own honour (viii. 50), but the supreme motive
inspiring His work was God's honour; all that He said,
did and experienced was governed by that overwhelming
purpose.

The Divine background to the saving work of Christ is
only occasionally seen in the Synoptists; in the Johannine
thought we are never allowed to lose sight of it. The
Saviour is regarded as the gift of the Father to a sinful

world. " In this was manifested the love of God in us,
because that God sent His only-begotten Son into the world
that we might live through Him " (I Jn. iv. 9, 10). He
was the supreme exhibition of the Divine love and purpose,
for His whole life embodied the character and nature of the
Father, " He that hath seen Me hath seen the Father "
(Jn. xiv. 9), and in the great High Priestly prayer delivered
in the upper room He could say, " I manifested Thy name
unto the men Thou gavest Me out of the world " (xvii. 6).

And more than a manifestation of Himself, the giving of
His Son was also a most costly gift : " God so loved the
world that He gave His only-begotten Son, that whosoever
believeth on Him should not perish, but have eternal life "
(Jn. iii. 16), the most inspired reflexion ever given to the
world as to the significance of the life and work of the Son
of God. The giving in this verse, as we have already seen,
must be interpreted of the Lord's life as a whole, His life
and His death. Thus we see in the Incarnation not only
the unveiling of the Eternal God in terms of humanity, but
also the expression of God's self-sacrificing love, and in this
thought of the sacrifice inseparable from the Divine bestowal
of the Son of God, we light upon a truth brought out by
St. John more clearly than by any other writers of the
New Testament. This same truth meets us in the First
Epistle of St. John : " Herein is love, not that we loved
God, but that He loved us, and sent His Son to be the
propitiation for our sins " (I Jn. iv. 10). " Behold what
manner of love the Father hath bestowed upon us that we
should be called the sons of God " (I Jn. iii. 1).

The thought of suffering existing in God is not only
congenial to modern minds for the reason that it enables
us the better to realise the depth and range of the Divine
sympathy, " in all their afflictions He was afflicted," but it
also renders for ever impossible the doctrine of the existence
of a dualism within the Divine nature. No theory of the
Atonement can be entertained which would represent God
the Father as the fountain of justice and righteousness, and
God the Son as the source of love and pity averting His
wrath. If Christ loved His own to the uttermost, so also
did the Father. Here we have the perfect union between
the Father and the Son.

The late Baron von Hügel [1] has protested against the

---

[1] *Essays and Addresses on the Philosophy of Religion. Second
Series*, Essay VII. *Suffering and God*, pp. 189 ff.

idea of suffering as applied to God, and it must be admitted that we often speak too glibly respecting the Divine nature and experience, " for His thoughts are not our thoughts, nor His ways our ways," but in von Hügel's discussion, penetrating and searching as it is, his reference to the Fourth Gospel seems most inadequate.   No allusion is made to such texts as Jn. iii. 16 and I Jn. iv. 9, 10, neither does he face the undoubted truth that sin not only calls forth the Divine resentment, but must also be a sorrow to God, on account of the love which transcends all human love. That the sacrifice of Christ was the sacrifice of God does not involve Patripassianism as signifying that the Father suffered in the same manner as the Son suffered.   The mother who gave her son to fight for his country sacrificed herself though she had to remain at home whilst he suffered in the trenches.

The greatness, the costliness of the Divine Gift to the world is not a truth superimposed by St. John on the original Gospel, which proceeded from the lips of Jesus. It underlies the teaching conveyed in the parable of the husbandmen found in the first three Gospels.   " Having yet, therefore, one Son, His well-beloved, He sent Him last unto him saying they will reverence My Son " [1] (Mk. xii. 6; Matt. xxi. 37; Lk. xx. 13), and is by no means absent from St. Paul's epistles (cf. Rom. v. 8; viii. 32).

Throughout this Gospel stress is laid upon the universal character of the redemption wrought by Christ.   In the prologue it is stated that Jesus came to His own people, " and they that were His own received Him not.   But as many as received Him, to them gave He the right to become the children of God " (i. 11, 12).   The purpose of His coming was of world-wide significance, " to save the world " (iii. 16, 17; cf. iv. 42; I Jn. iv. 14).   He was to take away its sin (i. 29; cf. I Jn. ii. 2).   The bread which He will give is His Flesh for the life of the world (vi. 51).   On behalf of the other sheep who do not belong to the Jewish fold He will lay down his life, and they, together with the chosen people who have heard His voice, shall become

---

[1] Cf. Gen. xxii. 16 (LXX).   Klostermann, *Das Markusevangelium Zweite Auflage, SS.* 11 und 136, says, " ἀγαπητός equals μονογένης, ' The only Begotten,' cf. Mk. i. 11; ix. 7." Cf. Dr. Armitage Robinson's note on " the Beloved as a Messianic title " in his *Commentary on the Epistle to the Ephesians.*

under Him one flock (x. 15, 16). Quite unconscious of its
deep meaning, Caiaphas, the High Priest, prophesied that
it was expedient that Christ should die for the people, and
not for that nation only (xi. 50, 52). In these words the
Evangelist saw that the saving benefits of the death of
Christ would be extended to " all the children of God
scattered throughout the world." After Christ had spoken
of the casting down of the prince of this world, He pointed
to His death as of universal import : " I, if I be lifted up,
will draw *all* men unto Me " (xii. 32, 33). The episode of
the Greeks coming to Jesus is related as foreshadowing the
bringing nigh to God of those far off, through the death of
Christ. Thus is granted to Him authority over all flesh
(xvii. 2).

On the other hand, the Synoptic representation of the
Lord's death may seem to be at variance with the Johannine
view of Christ dying for mankind. No direct reference is
made to its universal significance ; His saving activity was
restricted to His own race. When the Lord found it necessary to go into the borders of Tyre and Sidon, it was
altogether contrary to His wish that any publicity should
be given to His presence in those parts (Mk. vii. 24).

Even when He acceded to the request of the Syro-
phœnician woman, and healed her daughter, His work of
mercy is entirely exceptional in character ; it remains " a
crumb which has fallen from the children's table " (cf. Mt.
xv. 24). Previous to this incident the Twelve had been
sent on their first missionary journey, with the special
injunction not to go " into the way of the Gentiles or into
any of the cities of the Samaritans " (Mt. x. 5).

In answer to this plea it should be observed that in the
Johannine representation of our Lord's work and ministry,
His activities are entirely confined to His own people.
Christ does indeed pass through Samaria, but the conversation with the woman by the well is not premeditated ;
we might almost say that it came about by chance, were it
not that a Divine necessity underlay all the Lord's words
and actions. Besides, Christ was careful to point out to
the woman that " salvation is of the Jews " (iv. 22).
Amongst the Synoptists, however, there are intimations
that the self-imposed restrictions of our Lord's work were
of a temporary character. Even in the case of the Syro-
phœnician woman St. Mark states that though our Lord

apparently at first refused her request, He did not deny it altogether, but said, " Let the children first be filled." Hence it is not surprising that both Professor Bacon and Dr. Rawlinson [1] consider that the spiritual meaning of the story as related by St. Mark is " the promise of the children's Bread to the Gentiles." When the children first have been fed, it will then be the turn of the Gentiles. Later on in St. Mark's Gospel, when speaking of His second coming, our Lord declares that before that great event " the Gospel must first be preached to all nations " (xiii. 10; cf. xiv. 9). In the first (Mt. xxviii. 19) and third Gospels (Lk. iii. 6; vii. 1 ff.) there is even more evidence to show that Christ did not conceive of His mission as for ever bound by the limits of time or race. In this, as in other matters, St. John unfolds what is implicit in the Synoptic Gospels. With perfect justice the claim may be made that, whilst the Fourth Gospel makes its own contribution to the meaning of the death of Christ, it in no wise conflicts with the Synoptic account of His spirit and teaching. Eternal life is obtained by belief in Jesus, not alone as the Son of God, but also as the Christ (xx. 31), the suffering Servant of God foretold centuries ago, who, as a willing offering for us men and our salvation, laid down His life, that He might take it again and bring us to God.

## II

### The Revelation of Saint John

The book of the Apocalypse, notwithstanding that its authorship is involved in considerable uncertainty, is yet, in its present form, in close literary relationship to the other Johannine writings.[2] A relationship exists also between the views held by the Seer and the Evangelist concerning our Lord's person and work.[3] We do not deny that there are differences between them extending even to the most fundamental of all beliefs, the doctrine of God, and, as must be evident to almost every reader, to the nature of eternal life. In the Gospel and the First Epistle eternal life is expressed from the point of view of a present

---

[1] *Commentary on St. Mark*, p. 100.
[2] W. Bousset, *Die Offenbarung Johannis, SS.* 177 ff.
[3] E. Lohmeyer, *Die Offenbarung des Johannes, SS.* 190, 191.

possession, in the Revelation it is projected entirely into the future. This may, however, be partly attributed to the very different objects pursued by the writer or writers.

The Revelation of St. John was probably written towards the end of Domitian's reign, between A.D. 93 and 96. At that time Cæsar worship was at its height, and no citizen living in Asia Minor could ply his trade or enjoy any social intercourse without of necessity paying divine honour to the Emperor (Rev. xiii. 16, 17). The Christian Church was singled out as the object of bitter persecution, owing to her refusal to participate in any form whatsoever of Cæsar worship. In order that the faithful might be confirmed in their allegiance to Jesus Christ, " the King of Kings and Lord of Lords " (xix. 16), the Seer wrote his book. He would vividly depict the heavenly background to the events of time. The terrible sufferings of the present age formed part of the eternal struggle between " the Lamb " and His servants on the one hand, and Satan and his followers on the other, ending in the complete overthrow of the Devil and his armies, and in triumphant Alleluias to " Him that sitteth on the Throne, and to the Lamb." Those on earth who had held fast to Christ's name, and sealed their testimony with their life's blood, would be called to the marriage supper of the Lamb, to reign with Him for ever. Hence it follows, as might be expected, that the aspects of Redemption on which most stress is laid are deliverance from demonic powers, its timeless significance and eternal victory.

The most exalted attributes are assigned to Christ. Though, as in the Fourth Gospel, He is subordinate to the Father (ii. 27; iii. 2, 5, 21), He shares with Him the throne of heaven (v. 6, 13; vii. 9, 10, 17; xxii. 1, 3). He is Alpha and Omega, the beginning and the end, the first and the last (i. 8, 11, 17; xxi. 6; xxii. 13). To Him are committed the keys of Hades and of death (i. 18; iii. 7), and to Him worship is offered, expressly forbidden to any other celestial being (xix. 10; xxii. 8, 9), and rendered alone to God. But His most frequent title in the Apocalypse is " the Lamb," which occurs twenty-nine times. We are at once reminded of the Fourth Evangelist's record of the words of the Baptist as he saw our Lord approaching : " Behold the Lamb of God which taketh away the sin of the world " ; and although the word for " Lamb " is not identical in the two books, being ἀμνός in the Gospel, and ἀρνίον in the Apocalypse, their meaning is the same. And here we have much the same conception as that of the first chapter of the Gospel—the Creator Saviour, whose part in time, as the Lamb of sacrifice, is in the Apocalypse transferred to the eternal Heaven of Heavens.

In the vision of the book with the seven seals the Seer beholds, " between the throne and the four living creatures and the elders, a Lamb standing as though it had been slain, having seven horns and seven eyes, which are the seven spirits of God sent out into all the earth " (v. 6). The Cross is, so to speak, never left behind. The Lord of Lords and King of Kings (xvii. 14) in highest Heaven still bears in His glorified body the tokens of His Passion. Not, indeed, that He is sacrificed afresh, for in that case He would not be represented as standing (xiv. 1), but as laid on the Heavenly altar, and in the new song, begun by the four Beasts and the twenty-four Elders, and taken up by the rest of the angelic host and by the redeemed whom Christ has purchased with His blood, their thoughts continually dwell on the sacrifice made once for all by the Lamb : " Thou wast slain " (the aorist) and " hast redeemed us." And though a completed sacrifice, its effects continue for ever (v. 12. τὸ ἐσφάγμενον). The fifty-third chapter of Isaiah was in the Seer's mind, for, as Swete [1] points out, the conception of chapter v, 8, 9, 12 is from Isa. liii. 7 (cf. Rev. xiii. 8). The Sacrifice on the Cross is regarded as a ransom [2] (i. 5; v. 9; xiv. 3, 4). The price that was paid was the Saviour's own blood. The nature of that ransom, and to whom it was paid, we are not told. He uses the Pauline word " redeem " (cf. I Cor. vi. 20; vii. 23; Gal. iii. 13; iv. 5; Eph. i. 7) as one fully understood by his readers and forming part of the current teaching of the Christian Church. Only those who have been purchased by the blood of Christ (xiv. 3) can " learn the new song."

The " Lamb " also bears a Paschal significance. He is the great Conqueror and Deliverer, and is the assurance of victory to those who trust in Him, since He has cast down " the accuser of our brethren " (xii. 10; cf. Jn. xii. 31).

---

[1] *The Apocalypse of St. John*, 2nd ed., p. 178; cf. Lohmeyer, *op. cit.*, SS. 51, 52.

[2] On Rev. i. 5 we prefer the reading λύσαντι (" loosed ") to λούσαντι (" washed "). The former has the support of the best manuscripts.

He enables those who bear His name to overcome the wicked one, and thus to have their names inscribed in His Book of Life (Rev. xii. 10, 11; iii. 5; xxi. 27). Endowed with the attributes of omnipotence and omniscience (v. 6), He will carry everything before Him, until all the Kingdoms of the world shall for ever own His sway (xi. 15). Salvation is ascribed to God and to the Lamb (vii. 10; cf. xii. 10; xix. 1), an expression rendered all the more impressive by the fact that the pagan people of Asia Minor hailed the Roman Emperor as " Saviour," but in this book it is carefully reserved for Him who sits upon the throne and to our Lord, its appropriateness also consisting in its double meaning of redemption and victory.

Notwithstanding the stress placed by the Seer upon the Christian's need of readiness in the time of persecution to lay down his life for his Lord, and upon the inspiration and help he derives from the example and power of Christ's victory, personal holiness is also demanded of him, and he must, before attaining the heavenly vision, be cleansed from the defilement of sin. To those who remain steadfast throughout, the white robes of victory are promised, probably " the spiritual bodies in which the faithful are to be clothed in the resurrection life " [1] (iii. 5, 18; vi. 11; vii. 9). These spiritual bodies manifest the inward character of those who receive them. As in the Church of Sardis, there are a few who have not defiled their garments, having led the Christian life (iii. 4), they will be permitted to walk with Christ in white. In contrast to these, the self-satisfied members of the Church of Laodicea, lukewarm in their allegiance to Christ, are counselled to buy from Him the heavenly righteousness to cover the shame of their nakedness (iii. 18). The unjust, the insincere and the impure are excluded from the heavenly vision (xxi. 27). On the other hand, the Church of God arrayed in fine linen, clean and white, " for the fine linen is the righteousness of the Saints " (xix. 7–9), will be adorned as a bride ready for her heavenly Bridegroom. How are these white robes obtained ? On the human side those who bear the name of Christ must come to Him, they must be washed and be made white, and this on the Divine side is effected in the blood of the Lamb (vii. 14). Through faith in the sacrifice of Christ

[1] Cf. *The Revelation of St. John*, by Archdeacon Charles, Vol. I. p. 82.

they will receive forgiveness of sin, by appropriating His life they will obtain His righteousness, and will be enabled to keep His commandments (xxii. 14). Their life will be hid with Christ in God, and they will remain unspotted from the world.

A very striking phrase occurs in connection with the vision of the beast rising out of the sea (xiii. 1). He will be allowed to make war with the Saints, and to overcome them. " All the dwellers upon the earth whose names are not written in the Book of Life of the Lamb slain from the foundation of the world ' will worship the Beast ' " (xiii. 8).

With Lohmeyer [1] we believe that the words " from the foundation of the world " apply both to " the Lamb slain " and to those " whose names are not written in the Book of Life of the Lamb," and we have presented to us the truth, as Archdeacon Charles observes that " the principle of sacrifice and redemption is older than the world : it belongs to the essence of the Godhead," [2] and thereby is expressed in another form the view found in the Fourth Gospel and the First Epistle, namely, that the giving of the Son was the sacrificial gift of the Father. From this passage in the Apocalypse it may be inferred that creation and redemption both alike formed part of the eternal counsels of God.

Seeing that the writer of the Book of the Revelation, in common with the other writers of the New Testament, viewed the sacrifice of Christ on the Cross as an essential part of the Everlasting Gospel, it may occasion some surprise that in the vision of the woman and the dragon (ch. xii) no allusion is made to the sufferings of her man-child.

Many explanations have been given of the omission, one being that the writer did not deem it necessary to make any allusion to the Lord's career upon earth, as the real point of the vision is the persecution of the woman by the Dragon. Be that as it may, the Seer would find no difficulty in speaking of the Messiah in this manner, as he would understand the rapture to heaven as including not only the Ascension, but also the Crucifixion and Resurrection. Just as in the Fourth Gospel these three events are taken together, and regarded as a single process, so also in this passage the same three events are looked upon as constituting the rapture of the man-child to Heaven. The Seer would assume that his readers understood this, especially as in the previous

[1] *Op. cit.*, p. 110      [2] *Op. cit.*, Vol. I. p. 354.

chapter, on the two witnesses, a direct reference is made to our Lord's Crucifixion in Jerusalem, " the great City, which spiritually is called Sodom and Egypt " (xi. 8), and soon afterwards, in chapter xii. in writing of the persecutions to be undergone by the Christian Church, the victory is ascribed " to the blood of the Lamb," Christ's death and conquest over sin (xii. 11).

Nearly two-thirds of the way through the Apocalypse a flying angel is mentioned, having " the everlasting Gospel to preach unto them that dwell on the earth " (xiv. 6). The contents of this Gospel are given : " Fear God and give glory to Him, for the hour of His judgment is come : and worship Him that made heaven and earth, and the sea and the fountains of waters " (v. 7). Here there is no allusion to the Atonement, and it ought also to be recognised that neither is there any reference to the Love of God, the first call of the Gospel being to repentance and to " holy fear," wherein is included the Atonement (cf. Mk. i. 15 ; Acts xvii. 30) ; this must be recognised by the heathen first of all. Nor need we conclude that more than the first portion of the Angel's message, the warning cry, is given here.

Perhaps there is no book of the Bible so difficult of interpretation as the Apocalypse ; it contains many things hard to be understood, its imagery of the eternal world appeals more to the Oriental than to the Western mind, but to all alike it presents a Christ reigning in glory, " the faithful witness and first begotten of the dead," who hath bestowed upon the sons of men the highest privilege ever conceived by human thought, even " to be Kings and priests unto God," and this promise is made sure because " He has loved us and loosed us from our sins in His own blood " (i. 5, 6).

# VII

## THE ATONEMENT IN PATRISTIC WRITINGS

### By Harold Smith

ONE great obstacle to bringing out the Fathers' doctrine of the Atonement is that no early writer deals specially with this, except as part of the work of Christ, which again is treated specially by very few writers, *e.g.* Athanasius, *De Incarnatione*, and Gregory of Nyssa, *Catechesis Magna*. The doctrine is dealt with incidentally; some aspect of Christ's work is brought out according to the subject in hand. The Fathers' main attention was directed to other subjects. Hence it is hard to discover the full view of many, or what elements or aspects others regarded as most important. In the case of those from whom we have little left, and that all of one character, *e.g.* the Apologists, it is very possible that we see only one side; if their writings on other subjects were preserved, we should find their ideas of Christ's work to be wider and deeper than they now appear.

Along with this absence of full discussion or exact statement of ideas, is the absence of precise modern distinctions, *e.g.* between representation and substitution. Hence a modern writer holding one of these views is likely to take various passages as clearly supporting his view, while others take them to support another.

A further difficulty arises from modern generalisations, often not too precise or accurate. Thus a distinction is commonly drawn between the Eastern or Greek and the Western or Latin views of the Atonement; this is but a rough division, as the so-called Western view is shared by many if not most of the Easterns. Again there is a tendency to call the whole theory of deliverance from the sway of the Devil the theory of *Ransom*, and to regard it as due to unduly pressing a metaphor; whereas the precise thought of Ransom in this connection is held by comparatively few, and distinctly repudiated by some who hold the general idea that the saving work of Christ largely consisted in delivering from the dominion of the devil and so from eternal death.

In the *Apostolic Fathers*, the most important passages are found in *Barnabas* and the *Epistle to Diognetus*. *Barnabas* (ch. ix.) sees in Christ's death the fulfilment of many Old Testament prophecies and types. "If the Son of God who is Lord and is to judge quick and dead has suffered, it is that His wounds might give us life. Let us believe that the Son of God could suffer only for our sake." "He had to offer His own body as a sacrifice for our sins." Thus Christ's Passion is with Barnabas of the highest importance, but he does not bring out *how* it saves.

The *Epistle to Diognetus* (ch. ix.) is much fuller. God allowed us to be carried away by sins, that we might be convinced of our inability to save ourselves, but be enabled by God's ability. "And when our iniquity had become complete, and it had become perfectly manifest that punishment and death were expected as its recompense . . . God hated us not nor rejected us . . . but in pity for us took upon Himself our sins, and Himself parted with His own Son as a ransom for us, the holy for (ὑπέρ) the lawless, the faultless (ἄκακος) for the evil, the just for the unjust . . . the immortal for the mortal. For what else than His righteousness could have covered our sins? in whom was it possible for us lawless and ungodly men to be justified save only in the Son of God? O sweet exchange, inscrutable operation, unexpected benefit! that the iniquity of many should be hidden in one righteous, and the righteousness of one should justify many lawless!"

This glowing passage is, however, capable of more than one explanation. It is noticeable that Christ's *death* is not distinctly mentioned. Salvation may be regarded as the result of the Incarnation itself; or of Christ's active obedience as our Representative, not necessarily as that of His substitutionary death.

The *Apologists*, as is only natural, regard the Lord almost exclusively as the Divine Teacher and the full Revelation of God. This holds good generally down to *Lactantius*, and *Clement of Alexandria* has practically the same limitation. *Justin* alone goes further, speaking repeatedly of the value of the Lord's Cross and Passion.

Two elements in Christ's work, prominent in the New Testament, are constantly recognised and brought out by the Fathers : His work as *Teacher* and as *Example.*   Early writers as well as modern recognise these two elements ; but they constantly see much more than these.   In what follows the constant recognition of one or both of these is taken for granted.

Apart from these, there are three main conceptions of Christ's work of redemption.   There is the conception of the bestowal of new life and power, through the Incarnation itself ; this means more than setting a perfect human example ; it may include stress on what later writers called Christ's active obedience.   There is the conception of deliverance from the dominion of the devil.   And there is the doctrine of the expiation of sin.   In both these last, as distinct from the first, Christ's *death* is the main thing.

The first view above is commonly called the Greek or Eastern view ; but it is far from being the only view held among the Greek fathers.   It is best presented by Irenæus, Athanasius, especially in his later writings, and Gregory of Nyssa ; in the West it is prominent in Hilary.   But in all of these other conceptions also occur ; thus Gregory has the fullest statement of the conception of *Ransom* from the devil.

Rivière [1] gives the general conception somewhat thus. Salvation consists in restoring to man his destiny, life immortal and divine.   Sin displays itself in its consequences, the worst of which is death.   The saving work of Christ therefore consists above all in destroying death ; that of the soul, by giving us the grace and friendship of God ; and that of the body, by promising us the future resurrection.   So humanity recovers the double immortality which was its original portion, and ascends again to the high degree of likeness to God where the Creator's goodness had placed it ; it is truly made divine.   The most frequent terms to express the salvation brought by Christ are life, incorruption, immortality, deification.   In this order of ideas the Saviour's *death,* without disappearing altogether, falls into a secondary place ; the most important point is the *Incarnation ;* for it was necessary that Jesus Christ, in order to accomplish His work of complete salvation, should be at once God and Man.   The deification of human nature

[1] *Le Dogme de la Redemption,* p. 118.

is accomplished by the fact of its union with the Logos; it will be brought about in all who unite themselves to Him by faith and obedience. Thus the Person of the Incarnate Word becomes not only the cause, but also the type and concrete realisation of salvation, and Redemption tends to be confounded with Incarnation. This theory has been called that of mystical or physical redemption.

With *Irenæus* a great thought is "Recapitulation" (ἀνακεφαλαίωσις). This starts from St. Paul's words, Eph. i. 10. It is a wide term, covering two ideas : the special and direct sense of "summing up" and the more general one of "restoration." Christ sums up, and as it were concentrates in Himself all humanity; but this is in order to restore it, re-fashion it, and bring it back to its origin. The solidarity of mankind is emphasised. Christ "recapitulates" man's nature, comprehending mankind in Himself as its true Representative; He passed through every stage of human life in order to consecrate it afresh to God. The work of Christ is the realisation of man's original destiny, and hence the abolition of the consequences of Adam's disobedience; *i.e.* the redemption of man from death and the dominion of the devil, and reconciliation with God. Irenæus emphasises Christ's obedience as repairing man's, especially Adam's, disobedience. Milton's antithesis, *Paradise Lost* and *Paradise Regained*, the latter by Christ's victory in the Temptation, might have been taken from Irenæus, who has the fullest discussion of the Temptation found among the ante-Nicene Fathers. Here we have the effect of Christ's "Active Obedience" as not only our Example, but our Representative.

Irenæus is far from ignoring the value of Christ's death, though its place in his general conception is not clear. Thus he says that the Son of God died for us, redeemed us by His blood; [1] and, speaking of the sacrifice of Isaac, "that God might be pleased to provide His own only-begotten and beloved Son as a sacrifice for our redemption." [2] He gives his fullest account of Christ's work in v. 1-2 : "The Lord redeemed us by His Blood, and gave His life (soul, ψυχή) for our lives and His flesh instead of our flesh; pouring out the Spirit of the Father to secure union of God and man, bringing God down to man by the Spirit and raising man to God through His Incarnation, and

[1] III. xvi. 9, Rivière, *op. cit.*, p. 207.   [2] IV. v. 4, *op. cit.*, p. 233.

securing and truly giving us incorruption through His advent, through communion with God." Rivière's comment is, " The doctrinal picture is complete, but it lacks perspective."

The full doctrine of *Athanasius* on this subject is best seen in the earlier chapters (iv.–x.) of his early work " On the Incarnation." Man, turning away from God, received the sentence of death; death and corruption were continually gaining new dominion. God, having ordained that man should die for his transgression, could not break His word; yet it was not worthy of God that rational beings made by Him should perish. Had God simply required repentance, this would not have maintained His truthfulness to His word nor restored the corrupted nature; so the Word took a body like ours. Because all were liable to the corruption of death, He delivered His body to death in the stead of all, presenting it to His Father, that, since all men were dead in Him, the law against man's corruption might be repealed, and that He might restore man again to incorruption. He took to Him a body capable of death, that the body partaking of the Word might be competent to die in the stead of all, and might, because of the indwelling Word, remain incorruptible, and that henceforth corruption might cease from all by the grace of the Resurrection. Offering His own shrine as an equivalent ($\dot{\alpha}\nu\tau i\psi\upsilon\chi o\nu$) for all, He fully met in death what was due, and so the incorruptible Son of God being present with all by reason of the likeness endued all men with incorruption by the promise of resurrection. By the offering of His own body He wiped away the death that had come in; He corrected men's carelessness by His teaching, and set right their whole condition by His power (cp. II Cor. v. 14–15; Heb. ii. 9 f.). Man had lost knowledge of God and likeness to Him; to restore this likeness the presence of its Original was needed. He resumes (ch. xx.) : " He had also to pay the debt due from all, viz. to die; this was the special object of His coming. He offered the sacrifice on behalf of all, delivering His own shrine to death instead of all, that He might set all free from the liability of the original transgression and show Himself stronger than death. . . . We believers in Christ no longer die the death according to the threatening of the Law, for such condemnation has ceased; but the corruption being ended and abolished by the grace of the resurrection, we simply endure dissolution as regards our mortal body at the time God has ordained for each, that we may be able to attain a better resurrection."

He adds (ch. xliv.) that God could not instruct and save men by a bare fiat (νεῦμα), for their corruption was inward and not merely outward; life had to be brought into the body.

Athanasius here makes Christ's death as important as His impartment of life. He came as Teacher and Example; He came to impart the life of God to us; but His great object in taking our nature was to secure ability to die. (This falls into the background in his later writings.) His death is representative or even substitutionary; He died the death which God had laid down as the penalty for sin. This was necessary in order to secure God's faithfulness; mere forgiveness would not have secured this, nor restored human nature from corruption.

Lidgett [1] says that here " Salvation is expressed in terms of the payment of death and the infusion of life, but with great prominence given to the physical side "; Rivière,[2] that we have here a mixture of two ideas, defining salvation and consequently the work of the Saviour, that of immortality or supernatural reconstitution of our nature, and that of expiation of our death. From other works of Athanasius, the first appears to be the principal idea. Man had lost by sin the incorruptible and divine life for which he was intended; Christ came to restore this to him. " He became man in order to make us divine." In these later writings Christ's death is no longer so prominent; but it may be held that these notices of His work are more incidental, and do not aim at completeness; and the thought of the need of His death is by no means wanting there.

The third great representative of this view is *Gregory of Nyssa*, in his *Oratio Catechetica Magna*, where, however, he also presents the view of Ransom from the devil.

God created man in love, to share in divine blessings, chief of which is immortality. But man fell. God in love sought means to restore him; hence the Incarnation. In answer to the question whether God could not have restored man by a simple act of will, he sets forth the benefits of the Incarnation. The Eternal Word clothed Himself with our nature in order to realise and fix for man the union of the two parts of our being, body and soul. The Saviour's

---

[1] *Spiritual Principle of the Atonement*, p. 451.   [2] *Op. cit.*, p. 146.

Resurrection is a principle of life for the whole of human nature. God united Himself to our nature in order to make it divine. By overcoming death He brings us with Himself to immortal life. By His Incarnation and Resurrection He has restored human nature. But the application and individual assimilation of this benefit proceed only on certain conditions, especially the Sacraments, faith and good works.[1]

The whole problem of salvation thus leads up to that of immortality. This was our original destiny, which we lost by sin; the Eternal Word came to restore it to us. Gregory conceives this in a very physical sense. Our human nature is made divine by the fact of its union with the Word in the Incarnation, and this process is consummated at the Resurrection. The whole system leaves out the redemptive death of Christ. But this is recognised in other of Gregory's writings, e.g. he speaks of Christ as having given Himself as an exchange for our death, and becoming for us sin and curse (*Contra Eunomium*, xi.).

Rivière[2] sums up, that both in Athanasius and in Gregory the idea of Redemption by the Cross does not dominate either their thought or their system; they do not, indeed, ignore it, but their chief attention lay elsewhere. This view of redemption is shared more or less by other Greek Fathers, and appears also in some Latin; but the above are the three best representatives of it.

The second main theory—that of Deliverance from the dominion of the devil—seems to us strange, if not grotesque and mythological. But spiritual powers, both good and evil, were great realities to the men of those days. This theory recognises fully the objective side of Christ's work, which is not merely something done within man. It takes two forms, often confused by modern writers: (*a*) The special conception of Ransom, held by Origen and some of his followers, especially Gregory of Nyssa; (*b*) the conception of Penalty for abuse of power, for unjustifiable claim; this is much more widespread, and is held e.g. by John of Damascus, who distinctly repudiates the idea of Ransom. The common basis of both is the idea that man by yielding to the devil had become lawfully enslaved to him; and God, being just, would not deliver man by force. (We seem to have here on a different plane the conviction that God could not restore man by a mere fiat.) Hence

---

[1] Rivière, *op. cit.*, p. 154.          [2] *Op. cit.*, p. 159.

the Incarnation. But while the first form naturally implies that the devil knew the Lord to be superhuman, the second implies that he did not.

It is not clear whether *Irenæus* comes in here. He lays stress on the vanquishing of the devil, and lays down the principle that he ought to be treated according to the rules of justice; but his inference is simply that he ought to be vanquished by man, as was, in fact, done by Christ.[1] Elsewhere he says that " the all-powerful Word of God, not lacking in righteousness, justly turned against the Rebellion itself, delivering His own from it, not by force . . . but by persuasion, as it was right for God to take what He would by persuasion, not force." [2] This fits in with the later view that God by a ransom persuaded the devil to release man; but this is not definitely stated here, and the meaning may be that *man* was persuaded to forsake the devil.

Thus the first clear upholder of this view is *Origen*. But it is not to be taken as his only or main view. As Mozley says,[3] " He sees the effects of the death of Christ in so many different ways that it is never possible to be certain that any one passage, however strongly worded, represents his dominating idea; while it is equally difficult, if not impossible, to make a synthesis of all the conceptions which he used." Hence very different estimates have been formed of his doctrine and influence. " Whenever he dealt with any passage in Scripture actually or conceivably bearing on the redemptive work of Christ he did it the fullest possible justice on its own lines; but how all these lines were to meet in one centre of unity was a problem that he never set himself to solve." [4]

He took his conception of *ransom* from Mt. xx. 28, " Give his life (soul) a ransom for many." Commenting on this passage, he says, " To whom did He give it ? not to God. Was it to the Evil One ? for he was holding us until a ransom for us was given to him, viz. the soul of Jesus. He was deceived in thinking that he was able to be master of it, not seeing that he would not bear the torment of holding it." [5] Origen quotes I Peter i. 18–19, adding, " We are then redeemed with the precious blood of Christ, and the soul of the Son of God has been given as a ransom for

---

[1] V. xxi. 3, Rivière, *op. cit.*, p. 319.    [2] V. i. 1, *op. cit.*, p. 292.
[3] *Doctrine of the Atonement*, p. 102.
[4] Mozley, *op. cit.*, p. 104.    [5] T. XVI. 8, Rivière, *op. cit.*, p. 726.

us. . . . Since His soul has been given as a ransom for many, but it did not remain with him to whom it was given as a ransom, He says (Ps. xvi. 10)." Origen repeatedly says that we became the slaves of the devil when we sold ourselves to sin; and gives a very commercial picture of his claims over us.

*Gregory of Nyssa* follows Origen here. But here again we must remember that this is not his only or his main conception of the work of salvation (see above). Justice required that God should not use violence to him who held us in his power. The way of justice was to give our master the ransom he desired. He asked for the man born of a virgin, who was working many miracles, unconscious of His Godhead, which was veiled by the flesh. Gregory meets the obvious objection that this view imputes deceit to God, by avowing that it was only justice that the deceiver should be himself deceived, and that it was for the ultimate good even of the devil (in whose eventual salvation Gregory believes). A weak point in his view is that the devil, while apparently regarding Christ as simply a wonderful man, sought Him as a ransom, and did not, as in the more general view, claim Him as his lawful prey.

The conception of Christ's death as a ransom to the devil is found also in *Basil*, *Ambrose*, etc. But *Gregory of Nazianzus* (*Oratio* xlv. 22) denies that the ransom was paid to the devil, which would mean rewarding him for his tyranny. What an outrage ! Nor was in strictness Christ's blood a ransom to *God ;* but He accepted it graciously as part of the plan of salvation, to sanctify and deliver us, vanquishing the tyrant by force. The idea of ransom was also repudiated by " *Adamantius*," *Eusebius* (*Ecl. Proph.*, iv. 22), and *John of Damascus*, who says, " Away with the thought that the blood of the Lord should have been offered to the tyrant ! "

But the usual line taken by the many who laid stress on Christ's work as delivering man from the dominion of the devil, drops the idea of *ransom* altogether, and should not be identified with it. The position is that the devil had obtained the right to put men to death because of their sins; regarding the Lord as merely man, and therefore subject to him like other men, he seized and slew Him. But since he had no right to Him, not only could he not hold Him, but in penalty for this usurpation he was justly deprived also of all mankind. This view comes out in *Chrysostom*,[1] who, commenting on " Now shall the prince of this world be cast out," says that if a tyrant who inflicts great sufferings on all who fall into his hands should attack the King or the King's son, and put him to death unjustly, that death may avenge all the rest. This view is shared by *Cyril of Alexandria, Theodoret,* and *John of Damascus.* But it comes out clearest in Western Fathers, with their Latin regard for law, *e.g. Ambrosiaster* and *Rufinus.* *Augustine* [2] says that while the devil had no right over man apart from God's permission, yet he was to be overcome and man rescued not by force, but by righteousness, viz. that of Jesus Christ. "How was he vanquished ? because whereas he found in Him nothing worthy of death, he nevertheless slew Him. And it is assuredly just that the debtors whom he was holding should be set free, believing in Him whom he slew without any debt."

*Leo* states this conception very plainly.[3] The devil believed Christ to be merely man, and, "knowing that he had infected human nature with his poison, believed that He whom he knew by many proofs to be mortal was not free from the first transgression. So he went beyond the bond on which he relied, claiming the penalty of iniquity from Him in whom he found no fault. Through the injustice of requiring too much, the whole debt is annulled ! "

This view, which runs through the Latin Fathers, is sometimes expressed in figures more forcible than tasteful, *e.g.* that the Lord's manhood was the bait in which the hook of His Godhead was concealed ; or that the Cross was a trap baited with Christ's blood. It was current till the times of Anselm, Abelard and Bernard. Anselm rejects it very cleverly by letting Boso, the interlocutor in his dialogue *Cur Deus Homo,* pile up objections against it, which Anselm leaves unanswered. Thus he does not in his own person oppose a view held by great predecessors ; yet he implies that he attached no weight to it.

The third main view is sometimes, not very happily, called the Realistic. It is also often called the Western or Latin, because the prevalent view among Latin Fathers, in opposition to the mystical view held by some representative Greeks. But this title is only partially appropriate, as it

---

[1] *John, Hom.* LXVII. 2-3.
[2] *De Trinitate*, XIII. xii. 16–17      [3] Serm. XXII.

does not appear clearly in the earliest Latin Fathers, and is found also in representative Greeks, including Origen, Eusebius, Chrysostom, and both Cyrils.

Tixeront [1] defines the Realistic view thus : " The sinner must expiate his faults and satisfy divine justice. Jesus Christ substitutes Himself for all men. . . . By His sufferings and death He pays our debt to God and ransoms us. He expiates our sins by undergoing the penalty due to us ; He satisfies justice, He appeases God's anger, and makes Him favourable. In a word, He offers to God the expiatory and propitiatory sacrifice, which blots out the sins of the world." But it must not be concluded that all those who take this general line hold exactly the same view ; or that some of their statements are not capable of other explanations ; or that they do not combine with this other conceptions of Christ's restoring work.

The first clear representative of the view is *Origen*, though, as we have seen, it is not his only view. As Harnack says, the redemptive work of the Logos is complex ; and Origen develops the saving value of the death of Christ upon the Cross with such abundance and detail as no previous theologian had employed. He left out no popular conception that seemed to have any moral value. The character of his teaching is strongly influenced by the fact that he is above all things a commentator and homilist upon Scripture ; hence he tends to keep close to Scripture, but deals with passages as he finds them in their immediate contexts, without holding, or at least showing, any connected system. His one systematic doctrinal work, *De Principiis*, " On First Principles," does not deal expressly with this subject. The great object of Christ's work is always with him " Restoration to fellowship with God " ; but this is brought about partly (as is emphasised exclusively by the Apologists and Clement) by revealing full knowledge of God, partly by faith in Christ's redeeming death.

He more than once illustrates the death of Christ by the stories of Greek and other heroes who sacrificed themselves to deliver their country, maintaining, however, that Christ's sacrifice has a far wider sphere and is far more efficacious. He sometimes connects this with the thought of ransom from the devil, but not always. One very striking passage is his comment on the prophecy of Caiaphas (Jn. xi. 48–52).

[1] *Histoire des Dogmes*, II  149

" He died for the people, a purer sacrifice than all animals.
He took our sins and infirmities, being able by taking to
Himself all the sins of the whole world to abolish, destroy
and consume it, since . . . He knew no sin.  He made
Him to be sin, who knew no sin, in that He who had sinned
in nothing took up the sins of all, and, to speak boldly, was
made more than the apostle the offscouring of the world
and the refuse of all (I Cor. iv. 13).   There are many stories,
Greek and barbarian, of men having sacrificed themselves
for the community.   But one able, in behalf of the whole
world, that all the world might be cleansed, to take death
upon Himselt, in order to cleanse what would have perished
had He not undertaken to die on its behalf, has never yet
been related nor can be related, since Jesus alone was able
to take upon Himself on the Cross the burden of the sin of
all, and to bear it (or ' take it away ') by His great might."
Origen now gives a running commentary on part of Isa. liii.,
" He bore our sins, and the punishment due to us was laid
upon Him." [1]

Or again, *Romans*, Book III. viii. p. 513.   Christ is our
Redemption and Propitiation.   " God is just, and the just
cannot justify the unjust ; therefore He willed the intervention of a propitiation that those who could not be
justified by their own works might be justified through
faith in Him."   " By the sacrifice of His body He made
God propitious to man."   Origen connects the term ἱλαστήριον
(Rom. iii. 25) with the " mercy-seat " or " propitiatory " of
the Ark ; this was a type of Jesus.   He is both mercy-seat,
priest and victim offered for the people. . . . In that He is
victim, propitiation is made by the shedding of His blood,
in that He gives remission of past sins ; this propitiation
comes to every single believer by way of faith.

There are also numerous shorter passages presenting the
same view.   Origen speaks of the sins of mankind being
laid on His head ; that He is the true High Priest who has
by His blood made God propitious to us, and reconciled us
to the Father.[2]   Sin requires propitiation ; this is made
only by a victim.   There is only one Lamb who could take
away the sins of the whole world ; hence other victims have
ceased.[3]   But Origen leaves a good deal unexplained, and
does not work his ideas and interpretations of Scripture
into a system.

[1] *John*, T. XXVIII. 18.      [2] *Leviticus*, Hom. I. 3.
[3] *Numbers*, Hom. XXIV. 1.

*Eusebius* takes the same line more definitely, though fully recognising other aspects and objects of the Lord's work. His lack of originality makes his witness all the more important, both as interpreting his master, Origen, and as reflecting the general view of his time. One important passage is *Gospel Demonstration*, IV. 10 f. The Word, at the impulse of God's love to man, not willing to leave mankind, which was dear to Him, to perish, intervened. He makes men know and love the Father; He procures remission of sins; He transforms hearts, leads men to eternal life. Eusebius gives several reasons for the Incarnation; these include: "That He might wipe away our sins, being pierced and made a curse for us." "That He might be offered to the Supreme God as a divine victim, a great sacrifice on behalf of the whole world."[1] In Book I, Eusebius has much on the sacrifices, regarding them as a means of substitution. The life of the victim was a substitute for the life of the sinner. So with the sacrifice of Christ. He is a substitute or equivalent (ἀντίψυχον) for all men; God has ascribed to Him the sin of us all.

At the beginning of Book X he applies to Christ the words of Ps. xli. 4: "Heal my soul, for I have sinned against Thee." Christ says this because He appropriates our sins to Himself. God made Him, the sinless, to be curse and sin, that He might be the equivalent (ἀντίψυχον) for us all, and that we might be justified in Him. We form with Christ one body; in virtue of this He has taken upon Him our miseries. "The Lamb of God, chastised and enduring for us punishment which was not His due but ours because of the multitude of our transgressions, is become to us the cause of the forgiveness of sins; having accepted death on our behalf, transferring to Himself stripes, outrages and disgraces, due to ourselves, having drawn upon Himself the curse assigned to us, and become a curse for us."[2]

Eusebius thus combines the ideas of penal substitution and expiatory sacrifice, which are separate in Origen. He frequently uses the word ἀντίψυχον, for which "*substitute*" is perhaps the best equivalent.

*Cyril of Jerusalem* in his Fourth Catechesis gives two short formulas: "Because of our sins, the Son of God came down from heaven"; "He was truly crucified because of our sins." The Incarnation and Passion have the same object, our Redemption. He begins the Thirteenth—on the

---

[1] x. 12, Rivière, *op. cit.*, p. 167                [2] Cf. also x. 8.

Crucifixion and Burial—by declaring the Cross to be the greatest glory of the Church. If Phinehas appeased God's wrath by slaying a wanton, shall not Jesus, who gave up Himself as ransom, remove the wrath against sin? If the blood of animals freed from sin, and brought salvation, much more that of the Lamb of God.

We were enemies of God by sin, and God ordained for the sinner to die. But in His wondrous wisdom He combined the maintenance of His decree with the working of His love. Christ took our sins in His body, on the Cross; "the unrighteousness of the sinners was not so great as the righteousness of Him who died for them; we did not sin so much as He who laid down His life for us did righteously." [1]

Later Greek writers generally include the mystical conception of redemption—that the Incarnation was to impart to us the life of God, to restore eternal life, to make man divine. But they fully recognise the special value of Christ's *death*, especially as an atoning sacrifice. So *Basil; Gregory of Nazianzus*, who says, "We need the incarnation and the death of God ($\theta\epsilon o\hat{v}$ $\sigma a\rho\kappa o\nu\mu\acute{\epsilon}\nu o\nu$ $\kappa a\grave{\iota}$ $\nu\epsilon\kappa\rho o\nu\mu\acute{\epsilon}\nu o\nu$) that we may live "; [2] and especially *Chrysostom*, who says that the Incarnation was that we might be made sons of God, but lays much more stress on the benefit of Christ's death, saying, *e.g.*, "Christ saved us from death by delivering Himself to death." [3] "We were all under sin and punishment; He by suffering punishment did away with sin and punishment. He was punished on the Cross." [4] "That He might pardon thee, God sacrificed ($\check{\epsilon}\theta\nu\sigma\epsilon\nu$) His Son." [5] "He made Him sin for us, *i.e.* He let Him be condemned as a sinner, die as one accursed. He made Him a sinner and sin who knew no sin, much less committed any. As though a King, seeing a robber undergoing punishment, should give to death his only and beloved son, laying on him not only the death, but the crime ($a\grave{\iota}\tau\acute{\iota}a\nu$), and this to save the guilty and raise him afterwards to great honour." [6] "Christ endured for us by the Cross the judgment that was our due." [7] Chrysostom, like his Latin contemporaries, brings out fully the love of both Father and Son shown in the Atonement.

*Cyril of Alexandria* combines the two main conceptions

---

[1] x. 33, Rivière, *op. cit.*, p. 199.   [2] Orat., XLV., 28, *op. cit.*, p. 867.
[3] *Gal.*, Hom. II. 8.   [4] *Col.*, Hom. VI. 3   [5] *Eph.*, Hom. XVII. 1.
[6] *II Cor.*, Hom. XI. 3–4   [7] *Eph.*, Hom. V. 3.

of Christ's work, expressing each most fully. The object of the Incarnation was indeed to instruct men; but beyond this, to renew and transform our nature, to deliver our earthly body from the corruption introduced by sin, by becoming identical with us; and to make our human soul stronger than sin, by making it His own. He has thus become the root and firstfruits of those who lead a new life. Cyril repeatedly quotes in this connection Heb. ii. 14 and Rom. viii. 3. In his Commentary on St. John, Book IX, on Jn. xiv. 20, he gives as the general object of the Incarnation St. Paul's words, Eph. i. 10, "to recapitulate—or restore—all things in Christ," *i.e.* to bring back humanity to its primitive state (a prominent idea in Irenæus; see above). The Apostle sets forth two ways of this in the two above texts—to condemn sin in the flesh and to destroy death; St. John (Jn. i. 16–17) gives a third, which includes them both—to declare us sons of God by regeneration. By becoming incarnate He who was essentially incapable of sin has raised our flesh to His divine level of sinlessness; by taking our flesh and so imparting His own life, He restores it to the life of God.

But Cyril goes on to lay stress on the Lord's death, which he describes repeatedly as a sacrifice for sins, wherein Christ is both priest and victim. He is also our ransom, an exchange for the life of all, our full equivalent ($\dot{a}\nu\tau\acute{a}\lambda\lambda a\gamma\mu a$, $\dot{a}\nu\tau\acute{\iota}\lambda\upsilon\tau\rho o\nu$, $\dot{a}\nu\tau\acute{a}\xi\iota os$); this thought and these words recur repeatedly. "Jesus Christ, the only Son of God, has redeemed us, by laying down His life (soul) for us, offering Himself to the Father as a sacrifice without blemish, giving His blood in exchange for the life of all, for He was worth more than the whole world." [1] The chief effect of the Lord's death was to destroy sin; this is done by substitution. To destroy the sin of the world He took it personally upon Himself. "God made Him to be sin, that is, made Him who had never sinned at all suffer the fate of exceeding lovers of sin; that He might declare us righteous who have accepted faith in Him . . . for One died for all, who was the equivalent of all." [2] "We have paid in Christ Himself the penalties of the sins with which we were charged. . . . But Christ having suffered for us, how is it congruent for the penalties of our transgressions to be required from us ? " [3]

[1] Ep. xxxi.　　[2] On II. Cor. v. 21.　　[3] *De Ador.*, III. 101–102.

Cyril, as might be expected, insists again and again that it is the Lord's Godhead that gives His death its value in redeeming the world.  The death of prophets or apostles could do nothing like this.  How could One die for all, and be the just equivalent of all, if this were only the suffering of a man ?  But if it is God who suffered in His human nature, then we can say with justice that the death of one is equivalent to the life of all, because it was not the death of a man like ourselves, but of God incarnate.[1]

This "Realist" view of the Atonement was the general one among the Latin Fathers, apart from the conception, equally objective, of deliverance from the dominion of the devil.  The earliest Latin Fathers, however, have little to say of the Atonement, though *Tertullian* introduced into theology the term "satisfaction," which was later on very important in this connection.  He does not, however, apply it to the work of Christ, though he attaches the highest importance to Christ's death, which is to him "the whole weight and fruit of the Christian religion" (*totum Christiani nominis et pondus et fructus*).[2]  He says in various places that this death is for our sins; it is a sacrifice; we are purchased by Christ's blood.  "Our death could not have been done away but by the Lord's Passion, nor life restored but by His Resurrection."[3]  "Who paid others' death by His own save only the Son of God ? for unto this He had come, that He, pure from offence and absolutely holy, might die for sins."[4]

Similar language is used by Cyprian.  Rivière says of these writers that their faith does not conceive of salvation apart from the death of Christ.

Coming to the great Fourth-Century divines, we find *Hilary*, who was strongly influenced by Greek thought, sharing the mystical view.  In the Person of the Incarnate Word the whole human race is mysteriously included, and thereby sanctified.  "He became man, taking the nature of flesh to Himself, that through the association there might be a body of all mankind sanctified in Him."[5]  But he recognises the essential value of Christ's *death*, laying stress upon the voluntariness of it.  His language is not always clear; but he certainly regards His death as the expiation of our sins and our reconciliation to God.  Commenting on

---

[1] *De Recta Fide ad Reginas*, esp. p. 102.     [2] *Adv. Marc.* III. 8.
[3] *De Bapt.*, 11.          [4] *De Pud.*, 22.          [5] *De Trin.*, II. 24.

Ps. lxix. 4 (" I paid that which I had not taken ") he says, " He was called upon to pay what He had not taken away; though not a debtor of death and sin, He was yet held as a debtor of death and sin. For He was called upon to pay the penalty for folly and offences which He had not committed."

*Ambrose* also is much influenced by Greek thought. This appears strongly in the emphasis laid on the efficacy of Christ's atonement depending on His Divinity. " He alone was capable of such a death as to take away the sin of the world." [1]  Ambrose repeats and emphasises St. Paul's words " He was made sin." " He did no sin but was made sin. Was then the Lord turned into sin ?  Not so; but since He took our sins He was called sin. So the Lord is also called a curse, because He took our curse." [2]  Ambrose speaks of Christ having taken the crime (*causam*) and place of man; and that because the divine decrees might not be broken, the person rather than the judgment was changed.[3]

The question of the mutual relation of the Father and the Son in the Atonement comes up in this period, being dealt with by several writers. *Ambrosiaster* and *Pelagius* lay stress on the love and devotion displayed in the Lord's death; it was this, and not the mere death, that was pleasing to the Father; for, says Pelagius, " Love is the sweetest odour to God." [4]  *Jerome* brings out the harmony of the wills of Father and Son: " neither did the Son give Himself for our sins apart from the will of the Father, nor did the Father give Him up without the will of the Son." [5]

None of *Augustine's* numerous writings is devoted specially to the work of Christ. But apart from many incidental passages and sayings, it is dealt with somewhat fully in *De Trinitate* XIII. and the *Enchiridion*. With him the Incarnation is completely conditioned by *sin*. " If man had not perished, the Son of God would not have come." He held strongly the conception of deliverance from the dominion of the devil, holding that the devil overreached himself by exceeding his rights. In *De Trinitate* XIII. he lays down that the Incarnation was not the only possible way for God to save us; but it was the most suitable, as arousing our hope by showing how greatly God values and loves us. He then comments on Rom. v. 5 f., noticing

[1] In Luc. VI. 109.    [2] *De Sac. Inc.* VI. 60.    [3] In Luc. IV. 7.
[4] On Eph. v. 2.        [5] *Eph.* iii. on V. 2.

N

how we are described as "sinners," "enemies of God,"
"weak," "ungodly." "But what is the virtue of Christ's
blood, that in it believers are justified ? " and what is the
meaning of "justified through the death of His Son " ? Is
it that God the Father, while angry with us, saw the death
of His Son and was set at peace with us ? [1] Was the Son
already so much at peace with us as to vouchsafe to die for
us, while the Father was still so wroth as not to be set at
peace (appeased) except by His Son's death for us ? How
does this fit Rom. viii. 31 ? Unless the Father were already
at peace would He have "not spared His own Son, but
given Him up for us all " ? These passages seem to contradict ; in the one, the Son dies for us, that the Father
may be reconciled to us through His death ; in the other,
as though the Father loved us first, He spared not His own
Son for us, He gave Him up to death for us. But I see
that the Father loved us not only before His Son died for
us, but before He created the world (Eph. i. 4). Nor was
the Son delivered up as though unwilling . . . because it is
also said of Him ' who loved me and gave Himself for me.'
All is alike the work of Father and Son and the Spirit of
both, equally and harmoniously."

Augustine goes on to show how we are delivered from the
dominion of the devil (see above), and then continues his
exposition of Rom. v. "Justified in His blood "—being
freed from all sins because the Son of God who had none
was slain for us. "Shall be saved from the wrath," viz. of
God, which means nothing else than just punishment ;
reconciliation with God means the end of this wrath. We
were God's enemies only so far as sins are enemies of righteousness ; on their remission such enmities come to an end,
and those whom He justifies are justly reconciled. Yet
He loved us even when enemies, since He spared not His
own Son but gave Him up for us all.

Augustine says repeatedly that Jesus, by dying, delivered
us from death—the double death of soul and body, both
the result of sin. In one place he especially brings out the
moral side, calling Christ's death a mystery and an example ;
a mystery that our old man has been crucified with Him ;
an example to face persecution and death.[2] He is far from
ignoring the moral aspect ; but this is not the main thing
with him. Elsewhere in the same work he says, "So great

---

[1] *placatus nobis.*         [2] *De Trin.*, IV. ii. 6.

a benefit has been bestowed on men, that temporal death not due was paid by the Son of God to deliver them from eternal death which was their due." [1] Elsewhere, "He vouchsafed without sin to undergo for us death, that is the penalty of sin. . . . He alone underwent for us penalty without evil deserts, that we through Him without good deserts may obtain grace." [2] "He made our offences His own offences, that He might make His righteousness our righteousness." [3]

The teaching of the *Enchiridion*, as far as relevant here, is that God willed to redeem mankind who had fallen by original and actual sin. But as they were thus under divine wrath, there was needed a mediator—that is, a reconciler—to appease this wrath by the offering of a unique sacrifice. [4] "God to whom we were to be reconciled made Christ for us sin, that is, a sacrifice for sins, by which we could be reconciled. He was made sin just as we were made righteousness." [5] He destroys thereby both original sin and all subsequent sins; men are delivered from corruption and renewed unto eternal life.

Harnack and Rivière both emphasise the following as the fullest expression of Augustine's system. "Nor should we be freed through the one mediator of God and man, Jesus Christ, unless He were also God. . . . When sins had widely separated mankind from God, it was right that we should be reconciled to God unto the resurrection of the flesh to eternal life through a mediator who alone was born, lived, and was slain without sin; that man's pride might be rebuked and healed by God's lowliness, and it might be shown to man how far he had departed from God . . . and an example of obedience be afforded to rebellious man . . . and by the Only-Begotten taking the form of a servant which had previously merited nothing, a fountain of grace might be opened, and the resurrection also of the flesh promised to the redeemed might be previously shown in the Redeemer Himself, and the devil be vanquished through the same nature which he rejoiced to have deceived." [6]

*Leo* gives a prominent place to the view that the devil by slaying Christ lost his rights over us. He has close connection with Greek thought, (1) in his strong sense of the need of Christ being both God and man : "There would

---

[1] XIII. xvi. 4.      [2] *Cont. duas Epist. Pel.*, IV. iv. 6.
[3] Ps. xxi. II. 3.      [4] *Ench.*, ch. xxxiii.      [5] ch. xl.      [6] ch. cviii

lie open to none either reconciliation to pardon or return to
life, unless the Son of God, co-eternal and co-equal with
the Father, should vouchsafe to be also Son of Man." [1]
" Unless He were true God, He could not bring us a remedy;
unless He were true man, He could not furnish an example." [2]
(2) Also in the prominence given to the renewal of our
nature by the Incarnation. But the *Death* is of special
value. He speaks of Christ offering Himself to the Father
as a new and true sacrifice of reconciliation; [3] and of our
offences being expiated because the nature, which in us had
always been guilty and captive, suffered innocent and free
in Him.[4]

*Gregory the Great* regards redemption by the Passion as
the great object of the Incarnation; its great effect is to
deliver from eternal death. " He without fault underwent
the penalty of our fault." [5] Our reconciliation with God
is twofold : (1) bringing back our hearts by penitence;
(2) appeasing God's wrath. So Christ " rebuked (*arguit*)
man from sinning and held back God from striking; He
afforded example of innocence and underwent the penalty
of wickedness." [6] Thus He is both example and expiation.

Animal sacrifices could not purify sins; a rational victim
was needed; but all men were themselves defiled. So the
Son of God took our nature, not our guilt. He made for us
a sacrifice; He presented His body without sin as a victim
for sinners, a victim which could both die by its humanity
and cleanse by its righteousness. He paid for us death
which was not His due, that the death due to us might not
harm us.[7]

Rivière, summing up the teaching of the Fathers, both
Greek and Latin, says with truth that they have not directly
treated the problem of Redemption, but have only touched
on it incidentally in connection with Scripture texts or
cognate dogmatic truths. But at the base of their teaching
we find " a fundamental principle, a truth of faith deeply
rooted in the Christian conscience—that salvation has come
to us by the Cross of the Son of God. For them all the
death of Jesus Christ is something else than an example :
it has had outside ourselves, according to the divine plan,
a real and mysterious operation, it possesses an objective

---

[1] Sermon LII. 1.    [2] Sermon XXI. 2.    [3] Sermon LIX. 5.
[4] Sermon LVI. 3.              [5] *Moralia* XIII. xxx. 34.
[6] *Ibid.*, IX. xxxviii. 61.          [7] *Ibid.*, XVII. xxx. 46–47.

and distinctive value.   Two general facts express this supernatural efficacy—the Saviour's death appeases for us the
divine wrath;  and it is a penalty, the penalty of our sins,
voluntarily undergone by the Lord in our place."

(In this essay I have commonly let the Fathers speak for
themselves without deciding what precise modern view they
best support.   In particular the distinction between representation and substitution is not clearly before their minds,
and much language can be taken either way, especially in
the case of *sacrifice*, though substitution is often more
obvious.   Nor have I troubled to set down many passages
where Christ is set forth as our Teacher or Example;  or
again, notices of the result of the contemplation of Christ's
work for us—love, devotion and holiness.   The question is
not whether these things are not included—everyone admits
this, following the clear lead of Scripture—but whether there
is *more* than these in the objects and effects of Christ's
Incarnation and Death, especially the latter.[1]   The Fathers
were far from ignoring these;  but their general teaching is
that there is much else, more fundamental.

It will be seen that I follow Rivière, *Le Dogme de la
Redemption*, somewhat closely.   In my opinion it gives quite
the best review of the doctrine in the Fathers and Schoolmen.
There is an English translation.)

[1] Cf. Dale, *The Atonement*, p. xlvi ff.

# VIII

## ANSELM'S DOCTRINE OF THE ATONEMENT

### By Arnold R. Whately

Anselm, the Italian Archbishop of Canterbury, whose name, in that long list, stands out so prominently in the history, alike intellectual and political, of the Church, was born at Aosta in 1033 and died in 1109. At Bec, where he was Abbot, he spread the fame of his monastery as an educational centre, and afterwards contended for the dominance of the Church against the claims of English kings. Whether right or wrong in his policy, he was a wonderful example of combined gentleness and strength. In his political action " he showed the same calm, the same imperturbable firmness and assurance, which are the characteristic marks of his work and of his person. Neither exile nor threats could shake him." [1]  The experience of the saint, no less than the insight of the thinker, makes a claim on the reader for sympathetic understanding, prior to all criticism.

The *Cur Deus Homo?* [2] was completed during a two years' absence from England, occasioned by his appeal to the Pope against William II. This celebrated treatise is his principal contribution to the subject of the Atonement. If not the greatest of his works, it may probably be regarded as the most epoch-making. Whether or no it deserves the epithet " unethical," which has been cast upon it, whether it is mainly a submission of religious thought to feudal and legal precedent; or is rather, with all its limitations, the victory of a spiritual thinker over the recalcitrance of his intellectual material—this question will, we hope, find some answer in the following pages.

There is nothing more important to remember, when we are studying the teaching of Anselm, than the central place

[1] Koyré, *L'idée de Dieu dans la philosophie de St. Anselm*, p. 2.
[2] Migne's *Patrologia*, Anselm, Vol. I., p. 359 ff.

held in it by the majesty and *greatness* of God. God is conceived as the infinite and complete Perfection that crowns the hierarchy of perfections, by necessity of thought. Greatness is not simply a quality of qualities, but of *God*. This is not an attitude of mind that always commends itself at the present day. We are so accustomed to concentrate upon the love of God, and to leave what seem to be mere terms of praise to take care of themselves, that we can hardly do justice to Anselm's confident resort to "fitness" as a final Court of Appeal. That appeal—as, for instance, in one passage of the *Cur Deus Homo ?*—may seem even grotesque to the modern mind. But this is of little moment. It is the general attitude that concerns us. Anselm would never be content to say, with some moderns, " This is consistent with love, therefore with the nature of God," but simply, " This is consistent with the nature of God," and even, " This, though apparently demanded by love, is inconsistent with the nature of God." " Not only unfitting, but consequently impossible," is a typical instance of his mode of inference.

It is thus that he approaches the body of doctrine received by him from the Church. There is some difference of opinion as to his view of the relation of faith to the intellect. But that in some way *both* are emphasised there can be no doubt. To give a reason for the hope that is in us—these words express the character of his ideal. If he sometimes appears to teach that the truth about God is demonstrable by reason apart from authority, he does not seem—even if he really held this—to have doubted its converse; namely, that authority does not wait upon reason. His datum is the *ordered* totality of doctrine, like the ordered whole of the Church, as he understood it and strove for it. If rational fitness and propriety hardly seem to make to us that intuitive appeal that they do to him, at least let us do justice to the significance of that appeal.

Anselm's celebrated but ill-understood " Ontological Argument," by which he undertakes to prove the unthinkableness of the non-existence of God, is an illustration of the point that readily suggests itself. This, as M. Koyré points out,[1] though in form addressed to the " fool " who " hath said in his heart ' There is no God,' " is, in logic as in purpose, directed to the confirmation of the believer. It

[1] *Op. cit.*, p. 195.

presupposes that we *really* think of God as the absolutely perfect, one "than whom no greater can be conceived." His transition from this to the necessity of God's existence cannot here detain us; but it is not irrelevant to note this fundamental place which greatness, or perfection, as such, the ordered harmony of virtues, holds in his conception of God. The Supreme Being is certainly not, for him, just the personification of love.

We now come to close quarters with his theory of the Atonement. The best course seems to be to give an exposition of this theory, and afterwards to make a few remarks on its value in relation to modern thought.

The theory makes an emphatic break with an idea that in some form or another had been prevalent, namely, that the ransom was paid to the Devil. "God owed nothing to the Devil, except punishment. . . . Whatever was due from man, he owed to God, not to the Devil." We have now to consider on what principle, according to Anselm, this payment to God is to be understood.

First as to the necessity of the Atonement. "It was fitting (*oportebat*) that, since death came upon the human race by man's disobedience, so life should be restored by man's obedience." At first, reasons for this are briefly given which to us are merely odd; but only by way of preliminary, for they do not satisfy Anselm's interlocutor in the dialogue; and the essential reason is then given—namely, that the human race, so precious a work of God, would otherwise perish, and that it was not seemly (*non decebat*) that His purpose for man should .fail. That in some way sin involves eternal death is assumed.

But might not a mere man effect this redemption? The answer rests on the assertion that the redeemed is necessarily servant to the redeemer, and that it would be beneath the dignity of manhood that man should serve a being whom the angels do not serve.

Again, why did God, who has absolute wisdom and power, save man at such a cost of suffering to Himself? Boso, the interlocutor, asserts, as an admitted truth, that God's act depends upon His simple will. And though we may plead that God suffered only in His human nature, not as God, yet we have to ask, How could God, who is both just and almighty, save the guilty by condemning the innocent?

And granted that this was not done against the will of Christ—not by actual compulsion—yet it was done by the constraint of command.

Anselm replies that God's injunction to Him was simply to save the human race, and this *involved* His death.  God's will and command was simply man's salvation, but the death was a *sine quâ non*.  This answer, even so far, seems not to be a mere distinction without a difference.  For God's direct volition of what is in itself evil, even for a good end, really does raise certain questions ; and it seems worthy of note that Anselm regards the will of God as going directly to the ultimate end.  Yet he does not venture to say that God *could* not save man without the death of Christ, rather that He did not will that it should be done in any other way.  But we must bear in mind that God's will, with Anselm, is not arbitrary, but is in accordance with reason ; and reason, for him, makes its final appeal to a certain almost intuitive sense of order, beauty, and coherence in the scheme of things.  And further, the truth is emphasised that Christ's will was itself derived from the Father.  This tends towards the view—surely a sound one —that throws back the main idea of the Atonement behind the Trinitarian distinctions.[1]

But Boso, naturally, is not satisfied yet.  He wants to know *how* this course can be shown to be becoming in God, and also how the death of Christ effects the salvation of men.  This brings us to the heart of the problem.

Sin, for Anselm, is essentially a matter of the will (*voluntas*).  Man has free choice (*arbitrium*), and this is defined as " Choice that is able to preserve the rectitude of the will, for the sake of that rectitude itself." [2]  When righteousness is lost, as it is by the Fall, free choice still remains ; but it is inoperative, because rectitude, which it can preserve but cannot win, is no longer there.  So completely is the will emphasised that he regards the transmission of sin from Adam, not as taking place by the corruption of our lower impulses, but as the transmission of a simple necessity to sin ; and this necessity is due to our fall in Adam.  All sin is unrighteousness (*injustitia*), and all original sin is sin in the fullest sense ; therefore infants, whom he feels obliged

---

[1] But he is even Monothelite.  See *Cur Deus Homo ?*, Migne, *ibid.*, p. 372 C.

[2] *De Libero Arbitrio*, Migne, *ibid.*, p. 494 B.

to regard as guilty from birth, are sinners in virtue, not of the corrupt nature in itself, but of this prospective necessity of sinning; or, in other words, of the moral impotence that their fall, in the person of Adam, has caused.

Another point is that Anselm regards unrighteousness as essentially negative : it is in itself simply the absence of that righteousness that Adam did not retain; and it is precisely this letting go of righteousness that is positive, and thus calls for punishment from God.[1] And at this point we can take up the definition of sin in the *Cur Deus Homo ?* It is simply " *not to render to God His due.*" And what is the due ? " Every volition (*voluntas*) of a rational creature should be subject to the will of God." This will is in itself pleasing to God, not only the acts that spring from it.

This, then, is the debt that man owes to God; and, since the withholding of it is in itself an affront, man must restore more than he has taken away. He must pay back the honour of which he has robbed God. That is the meaning of satisfaction.

We are now brought back to the question, why God cannot remit sins by compassion alone. We saw that God did not will it to be so; while, at the same time, God's will is not arbitrary—not even apparently so; and we must therefore ask *why* it is incongruous with our knowledge of Him that He should save man without atonement. This is answered by four reasons, which really might have been brought together into one; but each makes its separate appeal to Anselm's sense of self-evident appropriateness, and he prefers to retain their cumulative impressiveness to his mind. First, he says that merely to pass sin over would be a breach of order : sin would be left unregulated (*inordinatum*). Secondly, there would be no difference between the innocent and the guilty, and this is incongruous with what God is (*Deo non convenit*). Thirdly, righteousness is under law : that is, it is recompensed according to law; and that unrighteousness should be more free than righteousness is also incongruous. Fourthly, unrighteousness, in being free from law, would be like God, a further incongruity. We cannot very well, to-day, place ourselves at the angle to appreciate this analysis, but behind it we can feel the working of a mind to which the artistic

---

[1] *De Conceptu Virginali*, Migne, *ibid.*, p. 439 B. (*et passim*).

integrity and completeness of religious thought, and the irreducibility of moral terms, must in every aspect be maintained. In brief, the moral order, whether in relation to the order of the universe, or in respect of its subjects, or in respect of the antithesis of right and wrong, or, finally, in direct relation to God Himself, must be consistent within itself and with Him.

Two difficulties, similar to one another, are now raised. God commands us to forgive : why does He not Himself simply forgive ? This is answered by the consideration that vengeance belongs to God only. But then, as a fresh point, Boso asks, Since we pray to God to forgive us for injuries done to others, does it not seem strange that He should be unwilling or unable to forgive injuries done to Himself ? In reply Anselm does not admit that even compassion must be so interpreted as to conflict with the dignity of God and the rational orderliness of His action. Justice bars the way : love must find another outlet. For justice " is nothing less than God Himself."

But then the question necessarily arises, *How* does the punishment of the sinner minister to the honour of God, and restore what has been taken away ? If the sinner does not pay the debt of his own accord—and it will be shown that, once a sinner, he cannot do so—" God subjects him to Himself against his will by torment, and thus shows Himself to be his Lord, which man himself refuses voluntarily to confess." What man forfeits is his happiness : what God gains is, not the happiness—which He does not need—but the vindication of His honour in the *fact* of the happiness being taken away.

This violation of God's honour does not impinge upon the very being of God Himself, who is, in this sense, above injury by man. But the " order and beauty " of God's universe are disturbed ; and they are restored by the infliction of punishment. For it is not possible that God should suffer a violation of His universe without making it good.

This view, it will be seen, is not the same as if the infliction of penalty were explained in terms of the moral government of the universe. For, although God's majesty cannot really suffer loss, yet, as we have seen, sin is committed against Himself personally. Anselm might perhaps say that God *would* in Himself suffer loss if He did not repel the loss.

204 ATONEMENT IN HISTORY AND IN LIFE

That man should enter Paradise defiled with sin might well be regarded as a direct metaphysical impossibility. But that is not exactly how Anselm treats the question. It is impossible because God's allowing it is unthinkable. And that for him is the last word.

Satisfaction must be proportionate to guilt. Otherwise sin would be *inordinatum*. Now what payment can man make for sin? What *proportionate* payment? The coin in which he can pay is repentance, reformation, and voluntary suffering. But these things are not the payment of the debt, for the simple reason that they are owed to God already, quite apart from man's fall. And not only so, but sin is so stupendous an evil that the annihilation of the universe would be better than one *look* contrary to the will of God.

And since man fell when in the vigour of his unfallen state, he would need to make good this fall by a victory won in his mortality and weakness. And this he cannot do just because of that mortality and weakness.

What then must God do to make good the loss? For sin has not only, as we have seen, violated the order of the universe, but actually taken something away from it and from God. What is that? It has thwarted—or would have thwarted if allowed—God's purpose for the human race. God must therefore fill up the number of His Kingdom. But He cannot do this by means of any that have shared in the Fall. "A sinner cannot justify a sinner."

But is man unrighteous if he *cannot* pay? Yes, for he is responsible for the inability itself. Boso adds, with Anselm's evident approval, that "he is unrighteous both in not paying and in not being able to pay." This seems an illogical reduplication of the guilt; but it must be remembered that, as we have seen, "unrighteousness," with Anselm, is not identical with guilt, being in itself negative. Therefore it seems allowable to say—as a passing remark—that the unrighteousness is double; for the withholding, while it is guilt, is *also* unrighteousness, as well as the totality of sins that result from it.

The second book of the *Cur Deus Homo?* deals with the remedy which God actually employed. Man, whose nature is rational, was made holy in order to choose, love, and follow the highest good, and to be happy in so doing—in

fact, to enjoy God, and that necessarily for ever.   And
God's design must be in some way carried out.

But how ?   God will not pay the debt, because He has
no debt to pay ; man, because he cannot—he has made
himself impotent by his fall.   One Being alone could do
this, one who is perfect God and perfect Man.

Christ did not deserve to die, because He did not commit
sin.   And His not sinning is positive righteousness, for sin
was possible for Him if He had had the will.   Also He
could be perfect Man even though not subject to death ;
for mortality—as also, Anselm thinks, immortality—does
not belong to the essential nature of man.   Christ, therefore, is truly of the race of Adam, and thus, in Him, the
human race can pay its debt.

But what form shall the gift take that is given in payment of man's debt ?   It must be something greater than
anything in the possession of God.   And yet such a gift
cannot be found except in Himself.   Therefore, in apparent
contradiction, He will give Himself, or something pertaining
to Himself.   His own obedience Christ cannot give for this
purpose to God, for, as in the case of human creatures, it
belongs by right to God already.   What shall He do, then ?
What but give up Himself to death for God's honour ?   This,
since He does not deserve to die, is a gift *not* demanded.
And this satisfies the principle that, " since man has robbed
God of himself to the utmost extent, so he should give himself
to God by the greatest possible act of satisfaction."

Anselm adds that there are many other reasons why
Christ should mix with men and bear their likeness.   He
dwells briefly on the example of Christ, but soon passes on
to the main argument.   It has still to be shown explicitly
how His death outweighs even the appalling magnitude of
human sin.   He argues that the Person of Christ is such
that no degree or multitude of sins that do not touch the
Divine Person could be compared with a bodily injury
inflicted upon Christ, and that therefore the value of His
Person surpasses the enormity of these sins.   This is not
the same idea as that of the offering of Christ by Himself
for the service of God and man.   Anselm keeps to the
simple idea of the acceptance of death as an offering to the
honour of God ; and, as death is the laying down of life, he
regards the atoning value of the death as equivalent to the
value of the life.

But now the inevitable question arises, How can the death of Christ avail for those who slew Him? It avails because the sin was committed without full knowledge. The bodily injury to Christ above alluded to was supposed to be committed with full knowledge; and was merely hypothetical, having no reference to His crucifixion.

But there is one more difficulty to be considered. Can it really be said that the death of Christ was not the payment of a debt, when we consider that it was an act most pleasing to God, and surely God demands from us all *whatever* is most pleasing to Himself? Can *any* meritorious act be an act of supererogation? Anselm meets this by saying in effect that this principle is not always strictly true. Celibacy is better than marriage, yet it is not absolutely enjoined. But he seems insensibly to let go this distinction, and falls back upon the Godhead of Christ. In the light of this all that He did appears as spontaneous and above all mere authority, the surrender only of the human nature in Himself to the divine. Here, as we noted before, the thought of the Godhead tends to supersede that of interaction between the Persons.

Anselm now proceeds to insist that the Father must in justice reward the Son. But how can Christ, whose are all things, be awarded anything that He does not already possess? There is no one to receive the award. The solution is that He will bestow the award on another. And on whom should He bestow it but on those for whose salvation He became man, and to whom He left the supreme example of His death? " For in vain will they be imitators of Him if they be not partakers of His reward."

In the last passage of this treatise that it concerns us to notice, Anselm admits that there may be many reasons for the Atonement which are beyond mortal knowledge. And, moreover, God did not need to do what He did, but " immutable truth " demanded it.

We may now consider a few outstanding points of the theory which we have attempted to explain, and see if we cannot trace essential value beneath what is often at least formally obsolete.

First of all, what is the general character of the theory? Does it teach or presuppose the metaphysical necessity of the Atonement—necessity rooted in the eternal nature of things—or is it simply an act of God, taking place within the moral sphere—an act which we can understand and appreciate, but not the only one thinkable? Anselm's emphasis on "fitness," and his admission, which we have noted, that there may be other reasons for the Atonement, might in themselves indicate the more empirical and unambitious aim of the latter type of theory. But "fitness," with Anselm, when once grasped, carries final certainty. The opposite, the unfit, is contrary to that idea of ultimate perfection which belongs to the very structure of human thought, therefore unthinkable. But some metaphysical thinkers, having found *the* meaning of a doctrine, would regard the quest for further *reasons* hardly intelligible—an "unmotived" quest. But Anselm is not exactly like this. He is not set on reducing the number of first principles. His method is not so drastically deductive. The Catholic dominates the philosopher. He seeks reasons empirically; but, when found, they are not probable, but necessary.

We may now make a few comments upon his theory of sin; and, by consequence, of the satisfaction due from the sinner. Sin, we have seen, is "not rendering to God His due." And the debt that we owe to Him is explained in the sentence : "Every volition of a rational creature should be subject to the will of God." In order to appreciate this crucial definition properly, we should approach it first as it relates to God and then as it relates to man.

The stress laid upon a debt due to God must, of course, be taken quite seriously. There is nothing metaphorical, nothing sentimental, about it. And it is in harmony with that sense of God's *greatness* which controls the mind of the writer. He regards sin as a direct personal outrage upon the Divine majesty, and its visible counterpart is the infliction of death upon Christ.

Later thought has fastened rather upon the moral government of the universe, the violation by sin of the Divine order. Now Anselm does not ignore this idea : for one thing, it becomes useful to him when he feels obliged to guard the majesty of God from all attribution of suffering and loss. The order of the universe is, as it were, a buffer to bear the impact. But, none the less, the offence is against *God*, not simply against God's law or against God's love. It is not simply the thwarting of gracious purposes. It is the violation of His honour—of righteousness, which is God Himself.

Two remarks may be made upon this. In the first place,

we may ask whether our substitution of Divine office, or even of loving purpose—sound though these ideas are in their proper places—for that of direct *claim* is entirely adequate. God is love; but the demands of love are, at the very last analysis, demands for self no less than for another. Not only does it seek communion—which is possession and enjoyment—but its compassion and kindness are, in one aspect, self-regarding impulses. This question could not be fully discussed without an examination of the place held by self-regarding motive as an ultimate principle of *human* nature; but at least we may note that what is implicit in man must be explicit in God. This surely is an issue which affects our thoughts of the sovereign personality of God.

In the second place, we would suggest that the full meaning of God's claim, and of His honour, as Anselm felt it and as it is available for our thought to-day, cannot be appreciated without reference to the relation of the idea of God to His reality, as argued in the celebrated treatise to which allusion has already been made, the *Proslogion*. Whatever goes to make up the completeness of our idea of God is, as it were, *due* to the idea. And when we consider that, for our author, the idea merges into the reality—in such manner that we cannot *truly* retain the idea while denying the reality—we begin to see a ray of light that comes not merely from outside his own mind but from another chamber within it. Part of what is meant by the claim of God is the intellectual claim of consistent and balanced thought about Him.

But to turn to the human side. Sin is to withhold from God His due. And that due is the submission of the will to Him. Now here appears, on the surface, a certain tautology. Sin is undoubtedly the omission to submit the will to God; but is this not almost the same as saying that sin is sin? The fact is that the submission of the will is, in this argument, both the substance of the debt and the fact of paying it. In human affairs we say, for instance, that a certain sum of money is owed, and the payment of it is the discharging of the debt. To say that the discharge of the debt is itself that which is owed would be tautology. But the submission of the will as such is not the same thing as its particular acts of obedience. When we speak of the surrender of the will to God, we are thinking of the will—

in fact, of the very self—both as that which is paid and as that which pays. And the will as paid contains virtually —barring our subsequent failures—its right action in reference to the particular things as they occur. The submission of the will is more than obedience : it is at once the debt and the payment of it. Anselm's emphasis on the value of the good will in itself, and the absence from the structure of his theory of meritorious works, bring us to the truth that God requires the giving of the will by itself.

That the value of good works lies in the spirit of obedience is, of course, a commonplace. But even the spirit of obedience may be regarded rather in respect of the separate acts than as a whole. And when it is so regarded the thought of the Divine *claim* does not come into clear relief. For the claim is on the will in itself, the one thing that is not God's already. And this conception of the will leads at once to the thought of the self, the person, with all its affections and desires. And it is just this deepest self in us that cannot be merely used, but only possessed.

But of course we must not forget that the idea of claim contains not only the element of self-regarding motive, but also the assertion of right. It is God's honour that has to be satisfied, though love determines the form that the satisfaction shall take. And His honour is equally satisfied by the punishment and by payment of the debt. And this brings us to the serious question of retribution, which really does seem to raise a fatal barrier between the thought of Anselm and that of to-day. But a brief suggestion may help us to analyse out the essential truth ; and that is always better than the clumsier method of merely lopping off what does not appeal to us.

It is not simply God's honour, it is righteousness, that is satisfied by punishment, failing the payment of the debt. Is that a possible view to hold to-day ? When we meet this with an emphatic negative, what we have in our minds amounts to this : We think of the two alternatives as being really alternatives for God, and we conclude—rightly, indeed—that upon this view, He might conceivably have chosen to condemn. But are we really obliged, even though we say that justice must be satisfied, to think of God as at the parting of the ways ? Such a view, surely, is unphilosophical. God is not faced by alternatives as we are.

o

What He does, He simply does, and what He does not do it would be contrary to His very being to do. The justice that would be satisfied by the condemnation of the sinner would be justice without perfect love, and God is as truly love as He is justice. Each idea in the end *demands* the other.

But what is righteousness? It is conformity to the Divine law. There are many who feel that, as love is the fulfilling of the law, so law, in God, is simply love. But there are those of us—claiming to be no less modern in our outlook—to whom the moral imperative is unabsorbable by any other idea, and is grounded in the holiness of God. We who think thus are convinced that holiness and love must indeed be seen in indissoluble union, *but from the side of holiness no less than from the side of love.* The question before us concerns the claims of righteousness—which is holiness in relation to the moral law—when considered apart from love. Now it cannot *properly* be considered apart from love, for they are one in the unity of God. But still we know that we mean *something* not identical by the two words, and we who believe that law is not wholly interpretable in terms of love are able, for certain purposes, to view law, and its cognate ideas, as valid abstractions— that is, not directly in the light of God. This, indeed, we all regularly do when we speak simply of right and wrong, and accept common ground with a moral atheist. Now it would appear that, from this point of view, Anselm is strictly correct when he says that *righteousness* would be satisfied by the condemnation of the sinner. That is to say, when we think of it as an abstract principle—which fundamentally it is not—we cannot eliminate the idea of condemnation; and therefore some element that *takes account* of that idea must be recognised when righteousness is unified with love in the concrete reality of the Atonement. Antagonism to sin belongs to the very idea of righteousness, and, apart from repentance—to which we shall refer presently—can only express itself against the person of the sinner.

The thought of antagonism to sin may be taken simply to mean complete avoidance and incompatibility, or, at most, exclusion from the universe by the annihilation of the sinner. But, it must be admitted, this is not all that Anselm means. In another work [1] he says explicitly that

[1] *Monologium* (Migne, *ibid*. See p. 217).

the soul that despises the love of the supreme good cannot
be annihilated, for thus it would be in no worse position
than before it was created, and this is inconsistent with
justice.   Such a soul must suffer eternal misery.   But even
this does not bar a restatement of his general position.
For it guards, by methods of thought that are not our own,
a truth that must always abide—namely, that, on the very
ground of first principles, goodness, in the long run, is for
our good.   From the standpoint of abstract justice, apart
from the Atonement, it might be said that the annihilation
of the wicked—considered as an escape from torment—
would be equivalent to unmerited good.   Now it is true
that we do not regard unmerited favour as unjust, as we do
unmerited punishment.   But righteousness in the abstract
—moral *law*—is related to sin by way of simple antagonism :
it is not that which cures a disease.   And so considered, it
does not separate the sinner from his sin.   The essence of
Anselm's theory is not undetachable, happily, from the
traditional doctrine of future punishment, which he teaches.
But it does require the explicit recognition of an element
in belief crudely indicated by the term " condemnation,"
an element transmuted, not evaded, in the final revelation
of the Cross.   The idea of eternal *death*—annihilation—does
surely (though Anselm thinks otherwise) carry a positive
meaning, as all death does when it confronts conscious and
sensitive life ; and we naturally think of it as the goal of
final impenitence.   *Then* it is not really God's act at all.
What *God* would have done if He had not redeemed us—
this is the question that bars a true appreciation of the
theory of satisfaction.   It may seem an inevitable question, if the Atonement is to be understood, even so little
as we can understand it.   But our point is that justice,[1]
as Anselm conceives it, does require to be viewed, as we
often view it, by itself, before we can understand the Atonement ; but that, so viewed, it is abstract, impersonal,
anthropomorphically distorted : it is not God Himself doing
His second best.   He *did* redeem us, and that is enough.

But then comes in the question of repentance.   Anselm
declares that man after the Fall is impotent, though through
his own fault.   There is, however, no real difficulty here.
For even while we maintain strongly the freedom of the
will, the truth remains :  " No man can come unto Me
except the Father who hath sent me draw him."   Redemp-

[1] That is, righteousness as self-assertive (*justitia* in both cases).

tion and grace begin further back than repentance. But, we may well ask, why does not God offer the grace of repentance to all without this " satisfaction " ?  Let it be admitted that there is a real difficulty in the thought of *mere* past sin being a barrier to grace.  But, when we repent, is it of the *mere* past that we repent ?  Surely not.  The very meaning of repentance includes this : that the repentance is itself imperfect, and that the sin repented of still clings. If it is sin in general that is repented of, then it is more obvious than ever that the repentance is imperfect.

To sum up.  Sin is neither, on the one hand, mere subjective disability, nor yet, on the other, like a legal crime that is punished simply as a past event.  It belongs to the eternal sphere.  Past, present, and future meet in it.  It is a fact that challenges God Himself.  And thus *future* punishment, eternal death, is present in it, implicitly, already.

Therefore, again, we must not say that God *chooses* to save rather than to condemn, when exact language is required.  The condemnation is there already, and God diverts it—as Anselm finally almost says—upon Himself.

But one more word upon this matter.  Our minds are so inured to the idea of the Atonement as an *event*, albeit a Divine event—that we find it hard to think of it except as something that God might or might not have done.  Therefore we find ourselves persistently confronted by the thought, " If God had not performed this act, He would have condemned the sinner."  And, since even this repels us, we are tempted to explain away the ideas of law and condemnation.  But there is no " if."  The Gospel of Atonement tells us simply that God did *not* condemn the sinner. Justice in the abstract must be conceived thus, but God is not an abstraction.  And the Atonement is as truly part and parcel of God's essential being as anything else that we affirm about Him.  But just in telling us that God did not condemn man, it shows how He did not simply expose and destroy, but " *condemned* sin in the flesh."

Anselm, it is true, does not to that extent emphasise the unity of the Divine qualities.  God is supreme Perfection, and the criterion for his thoughts about Him is not that of abstract and concrete, but of fitness and unfitness.  But it is not difficult to pass from the one to other.  We know of an old-fashioned Evangelical preacher who used to picture,

in dramatic fashion, the Deity as sitting in anxious contemplation of the fallen world below Him and listening to
suggestions from angels, till at last He thinks of the true
solution of the problem.   This at least—even allowing for
rhetoric—is not what Anselm means.   He treats of alternatives, but they are alternatives rather for our minds than
for God.   And if we moderns recoil from the bald idea of
God as " subjecting the sinner to Himself by torments,"
we must not allow our sensitiveness to deter us from seeking
patiently to understand what it is that, from the spiritual
side, opens the door to such thoughts in the minds of devout
thinkers.   Granted to the full the influence of obsolete
contemporary ideas, what is it that plays upon this material,
point by point, thought by thought, and finds expression,
even though imperfect and misleading, even in its harshest
terms ?

For Anselm the objective significance of the death of
Christ was surely a vivid personal and pastoral experience.
If he did not make the thought of it the basis of permanent
assurance, the ground of that underlying " justification "
that the Reformation brought to the fore, he felt it at least
as a solid, direct, immediate reality in face of sin, the supreme
and final answer to the accusations of conscience.

" If the Lord God will judge thee [the dying man] say,
' Lord, I place the death of our Lord Jesus Christ between
me and Thy judgment : in no other way do I contend with
Thee.'   If He shall say to thee that thou art a sinner, say,
' Lord, I place the death of our Lord Jesus Christ between
Thee and my sins.'  . . . If He shall say that He is angry
with thee, say, ' Lord, I place the death of our Lord Jesus
Christ between me and Thine anger.' " [1]

[1] *Admonitio Morienti*, Migne, *ibid.*, p. 687.

# IX

# THE ATONEMENT IN REFORMATION THEOLOGY

## By V. J. K. Brook

The Reformation forced upon the thought of ordinary men the problem of the Atonement. In the beginning, of course, the Reformers were moved by practical rather than theoretical aims, but, in so far as the problem they faced was that of man's salvation and the means to it, the theory of the Atonement inevitably received much attention. At first, however, it was not the Roman system in itself so much as the abuses in it which roused opposition. Had the Pope agreed to check those abuses, apparently even Luther would have left the system, in the main, unquestioned. But his bitter controversy with Rome served to bring into clear light a divergence of thought which was really fundamental. In the practice of the Roman Church it was clearly implied that, though Christ had done much for man, He had not done all; each Christian still had to rely on a priest for absolution and on himself for true contrition and works of satisfaction or penance. Against all this Luther set his own theory—the Penal Theory of Atonement—that the death of Christ was the sole and adequate penalty for all human sins. There is therefore no need of priestly absolution, nor of good works, nor of any human action, but only of faith. Sins, indeed, deserve punishment, but all punishment has been transferred to Christ, and man is therefore free, if only he will believe it. The Theses were not posted by Luther till 1517; the definite break with Rome was even later; but the essence of this doctrine of justification by mere faith is already clear in his Lectures on the Psalms in 1513.[1] Still, it is obvious that at first he did not realise the incompatibility of his views with the Roman system.

---

[1] I owe this statement, and a good deal more, to Professor Mackinnon's *Luther and the Reformation* (I. 151 ff.).

It was the controversy over practical reform which forced him to develop his theory in full.

Quite simply, the Penal Theory consists in the belief that the punishment for all our sins has been borne on the Cross by Christ. No doubt the parallel between Adam and Christ, suggested by St. Paul, helped to commend the theory to Luther, who formulates the parallel quite explicitly. " As by another's sins," he writes, " all were made sinners, so by another's righteousness (*justitia*) all are made just."[1] And so Christ is described as " *propitiatorium nostrum* "; [2] He was " given for our sins," [3] " undergoing the penalty of sins determined by the law." [4] That is, He is not thought of as making satisfaction to the outraged honour of God, but simply as bearing the actual punishment of our wrongdoing. And that He could do because, so Luther taught, He really took upon Himself our very sins, and so could be punished for them. " Whatever sins you and we all have done, and shall for the future do, belong to Christ as if He Himself had done them." [5] Or again, " This all the prophets saw, that Christ would be of all men the greatest robber, murderer, adulterer, thief, blasphemer, etc., than whom there was never any greater in the world. . . . Not that He Himself committed those things, but that He took on His own body the things which had been committed by us to satisfy for them with His own blood." [6] Thus, " Sin, death, and hell will belong to Christ, and grace, life, and salvation to the soul." [7] Therefore, " Jesus Christ, the Son of God, dies on the Cross and bears my sin, law, death, devil, hell in His own body "; [8] " He really and truly offered Himself to the Father for eternal punishment on our behalf. His human nature behaved as if He were a man to be eternally condemned to Hell." [9] Even when all allowance has been made for exaggeration, the last quotation shows how serious Luther was in the thought that Christ had really taken

---

[1] On Gal. ii. 16 (1519). There exist two commentaries on Galatians by Luther, which I have distinguished simply by their dates—1519 and 1535.

[2] On Gal. ii. 17 (1519).    [3] On Gal. i. 4 (1519).

[4] On Gal. iv. 4 (1519).    [5] On Gal. iii. 13 (1535).    [6] *Ibid.*

[7] " On Christian Liberty," p. 112, in *Luther's Primary Works* (Wace and Buchheim).

[8] On Gal. ii. 19 (1535).

[9] I owe this quotation to Rashdall, *The Idea of Atonement in Christian Theology*, p. 400.

upon Himself our sins, not merely the punishment for them. He speaks as though He almost *deserved* eternal punishment in Hell for them.

Thus the Cross was regarded as adequate, without any merit on man's part, to blot out all sins; its benefits become available for a man as soon as he believes. Nothing else at all is needed. " Faith in Christ alone is necessary that we may be just." [1] " With constant confidence you must assume that Christ died for your sins, and that you are one of those for whose sins He was given up. This faith justifies thee." [2] " Whoso presumes to be just by any other way than by believing in Christ, he rejects Christ from himself and considers His passion and resurrection unnecessary." [3] And so, on the contrary, " it is solely by impiety and incredulity of heart that (a man) becomes guilty, and a slave of sin, deserving condemnation; not by any outward sin or work." [4] Nor is any room left for human merit or endeavour even in respect of faith. It is simply the gift of God. " It is a work of God, not of man. . . . All other works He performs with us and by us : this one work He performs in us and without us." [5] Indeed, such faith cannot be reached by man's own efforts, for it is not a deliverance of reason. There was still in Luther sufficient tinge of Nominalism to cause him at times to oppose faith to reason. Thus in the *De Servo Arbitrio* he argues, " This is the very highest stage of faith, to believe that He is merciful who saves so few and damns so many . . . if I were able by reason to comprehend . . . there would not be need of faith." [6] Man therefore cannot achieve faith by his own efforts : it must be God-given. " Our knowledge is to be known by God, who also hath wrought in us this knowledge of Himself." [7] " Before thou callest upon God or seekest Him, God must have come to thee and found thee." [8]

Moreover, time and again, the faith required for justification seems to be only the assent of the intellect to certain propositions; the mere confidence that the death of Christ sufficed, not a present trust in the power of the Risen Lord. Sometimes, at any rate in Luther, " faith " has a very

---

[1] On Gal. ii. 11 (1519).    [2] *Ibid.*, on i. 4.    [3] *Ibid.*, on i. 1.
[4] *On Christian Liberty* : Primary Works, p. 107.
[5] *Babylonish Captivity* : Primary Works, pp. 186–7.
[6] Weimar Edition of Works, XVIII, 633.
[7] On Gal. iv. 9 (1519).
[8] Quoted in Herrmann, *Communion with God* (E.T. 1895), p. 159.

much deeper meaning than this; but he does undoubtedly in places use language which suggests that a mere mental assent to the penal view of the Cross and its results is enough. " Believe that He will be your salvation and mercy, and so He will be without all doubt." [1] " The word of God cannot be received and honoured by any works, but by faith alone. Hence it is clear that, as the soul needs the word alone for life and justification, so it is justified by faith alone and not by any works." [2] Here, plainly, faith merely means believing " the word of God " as contained in the Bible. In his answer to Cajetan in 1518, Luther expressly declares, " Faith is nothing else than to believe what God promises or says." [3] Now such a definition of faith is obviously true, so far as it goes. Moreover, the benefits of the death of Christ can only become available for a man, at any rate consciously, in so far as he believes in them. But the doctrine that such mental assent alone secures justification does seem to leave entirely out of consideration the need for moral change in sinful men.

In Luther's teaching, however, the result of faith, even in the restricted sense given above, is instant acquittal or justification, not only for past, but for all, sins. If a man has that faith, he need have no fears; the only thing which can imperil his salvation is failure of belief. Nor is there possibility of any feeling of insecurity in the inner man. " Those are therefore mere tales," he writes, " that a man is uncertain whether he is in a state of salvation or not. . . . How can it be that you should not feel this faith if it is in you ? " [4]

Thus stated, in its logical form, the Penal Theory seems mechanical, external, almost immoral, for it makes no demand for any ethical change in sinners. The question inevitably arises as to how a man so obviously in earnest as Luther could have accepted it. The truth is, paradoxical though it may seem, that it was probably its very externality, its complete independence of any claim on human effort or merit, which attracted him. The depth of his apprehension of sin, his sense of its horror and enormity, simply compelled him to some such view. For, beyond all question, he was

[1] On Gal. ii. 16 (1519).
[2] *On Christian Liberty* : Primary Works, p. 107.
[3] Kidd, *Documents of the Continental Reformation*, p. 36.
[4] On Gal. i. 4 (1519).

terror-stricken by his consciousness of sin. It was that which drove him into a monastery, in the hope that strictest discipline might bring comfort and peace. But the long periods of quiet meditation and scrupulous self-examination only increased the agony of an uneasy conscience. Neither the assurances of his fellow-monks nor the sacrament of Penance brought lasting relief, for he doubted whether his contrition was sincere enough to merit forgiveness. Nor, for Luther, was any real help to be found in either of the two main views, current at the time, of the efficacy of the Cross. If its value lay, as Abelard had taught, in its appeal to the individual sinner and its power to draw him from his sin, it could not help Luther, cowed by the knowledge of his continued sinning and by the growing realisation that, do what he would, he was powerless to win free from sin. The much more widely accepted view of Anselm might have been expected to help him, for it did teach that Christ had done for man what man could not do for himself ; and there are real affinities between the Satisfaction and the Penal theories. But the Anselmic doctrine was not enough for him, though he must have been well aware of it. Primarily a man with a deep religious experience rather than a systematic theologian, he was none the less well-read. He lectured at the new humanist university at Wittenberg, and at the Leipzig Disputation in 1519 he created an impression of great learning.[1] He must have known the teaching of Anselm ; but he found peace not in it, but in long meditation on two passages in Romans— " a righteousness of God by faith unto faith " (i. 17) and " Jesus whom God set forth to be a propitiation through faith in His blood " (iii. 25). There he found a suggestion of a new righteousness not due to man's own efforts, but imputed by God because Christ had borne the penalty of sin. Such was the genesis of Luther's Penal Theory, and in it he found peace ; for according to it nothing was left dependent on his own merits or work.

It is not difficult to see that in certain respects, or at least for certain types of mind, the penal theory is more attractive than the Anselmic. In the first place, ingenious though the latter is, it does not explain why the painful death on the Cross was necessary. In view of His perfectly sinless life, Christ was entitled not to die : His voluntary

---

[1] Kidd, *Documents*, p. 48.

submission, therefore, to death in any form would have brought infinite merit. Why, then, the Cross? It *looks*, at any rate, like a punishment, and by taking it as such, the penal theory seems to explain it more adequately than the satisfaction theory.

Secondly, the Anselmic view does seem in a way to minimise the importance of sin. The idea of God suggested by it is fashioned very much after the model of a feudal prince whose will is law. Under such a prince wrongdoing is simply not doing what the prince commands; its essence is disobedience and nothing more; it is not intrinsically wrong. Significantly enough, Anselm defines sin as the failure to render to God His due.[1] That is, indeed, the real basis of the satisfaction theory : only on that supposition can the voluntary offering to God by Christ of more than was due be held to constitute a satisfaction cancelling our debt. But such an estimate of sin falls grievously short. It takes no account of the condition of men in a state of sin or of the need for the sin-infected soul to be raised out of its helplessness. That, no doubt, was one reason why it could not satisfy Luther. For he was convinced as few men have ever been of the hopeless condition of man since the Fall. Through Original Sin, he believed, all men had lost free will and could do no good thing at all. "The whole human race is nothing but *massa perditionis et maledictionis*."[2] "Of ourselves we can do nothing good, but only err, increase ignorance, and sin."[3] The Anselmic theory does nothing to meet that state of things. Nor, it is true, does the penal theory strictly interpreted (though Luther elsewhere makes good the defect). But at least it does regard sin with desperate seriousness, as evil in and for itself, deserving punishment, a load which nothing less than the death of Christ could lift.

There is yet one further respect in which the penal theory seems to go deeper than the Anselmic. It is nowhere satisfactorily explained by Anselm *why* God could not overlook the acts of disobedience which constitute sin except at the price of the Cross. Unless God Himself is subject to a higher necessity (which Anselm will not allow) it is difficult to see why He could not simply forgive our failure to render Him His due, if that is all sin is. It almost

---

[1] *Cur Deus Homo*, I. 11.    [2] On Gal. iii. 22 (1519).
[3] *Ibid.*, iv. 8.

looks as though the death on the Cross was due solely to
His arbitrary decree, as if He were a feudal princeling
insisting on his rights.   On such a view, the Cross does
lose its grandeur; it appears merely to be required by
God's "standing out" for His own dignity, and is very
difficult to reconcile with belief in His perfect love.   At
times, at any rate, Luther does seem to go deeper than
that.   To him, inheriting the scholastic idea of God as the
distributer of rewards and penalties, the Great Judge, the
Divine law is no mere arbitrary ruling, but the expression
of essential justice.   As just, God would be untrue to His
very inmost being did He not punish the breaking of it.
It is true that such a conception of God appears to differ
from the God of love revealed by Christ, who seems to
forgive sins without the exaction of any penalty from the
sinner.   Luther recognised the difficulty, but was undis-
mayed by it, thanks, no doubt, to his distrust of mere
reason inherited from the Nominalists.   He argues the point
at length against Erasmus in the *De Servo Arbitrio*.   Erasmus
is at fault, he maintains, because he makes no distinction
" between God preached and hidden—that is, between the
word of God and God Himself." [1]   "We must reason in
one way concerning God or the will of God preached and
revealed to us . . . in another concerning God not preached
and not revealed." [2]   About the hidden character of God
we are not to concern ourselves.   "In so far then as God
conceals Himself and wishes to be unknown by us, it is
nothing to us." [3]   "Human temerity, which with everlasting
perversity leaves necessary things and ever seeks and aims
at the secret will of God, must be recalled and drawn back
so that it occupy itself not in considering those hidden things
of majesty which it is impossible to attain." [4]   Once he
takes for granted this hidden, inscrutable aspect of God,
Luther has no difficulty in leaving justice and love side by
side, unreconciled.   God "does not wish the death of a
sinner, that is (as revealed) by the word, but He does wish
it by that inscrutable will." [5]   Of course, a problem is left,
but surely that is better than Anselm's mere unproved
dogma that the Cross was necessary.   Luther is full of
assurance of the love of God in Christ, and by his insistence
that the death of Christ took place because of the justice

[1] Weimar Edition, Vol. XVIII. p. 685.          [2] *Ibid.*
[3] *Ibid*          [4] *Ibid.*, p. 689.          [5] *Ibid.*, p. 685.

of God, lifts on to a high plane the whole conception of God's part in the Atonement. Had sin been forgiven unpunished, God would have been untrue to His inmost being, hidden but partially expressed in His law. But for our sake He Himself provided a victim for our sins.

It is impossible here not to feel that we are moving in the circle of Pauline ideas. Luther, like St. Paul, is not attempting to prove, almost *a priori*, why the Crucifixion must have taken place, but rather to give some explanation of the fact that in contemplation of the Cross he had found peace. Both had felt their failure to carry out God's immutable will, expressed in the law, as a barrier between themselves and God, the Judge. If the thought of the Cross brought them peace, it was not unnatural that they should regard it as the removal of the barrier, the satisfying of the claims of the law which stood between them and God's love. There is much in St. Paul's writings to suggest such a view—that God's justice was immutably expressed in the law, and that only when Christ had fulfilled the law by bearing the curse it pronounced on sin could the mercy and love of God have free play.[1] And repeatedly it is just that idea which Luther expresses : " We are offenders. God with His law is offended. And the offence is such that God cannot remit it, nor can we pay it. Therefore between God who is one in Himself and us there is a great parting. Finally God is not able to revoke His law but wishes it to be kept." [2] But because Christ has taken upon Himself our sins, He can bear the penalty which the law demands. " Then cometh the law and saith : I find that sinner taking upon him the sin of all men, and I see no sin beside, save in him ; therefore let him die on the Cross." [3] Or again, Christ " for us undergoes the penalty of sins determined by the law." [4] So He is " non legislator sed legis impletor." [5] Sometimes, it is true, Luther goes further than this and speaks as though the death of Christ really brought about a change in God, which shows that he had not fully reached the heart of the Pauline doctrine. But in speaking of the Cross as paying the penalty demanded by the law he is simply re-echoing the language of St. Paul. Therefore, like

---

[1] Cf. an article by the present writer in *Theology*, Vol. XIII., No. 78.

[2] On Gal. iii. 20 (1535).     [3] On Gal. iii. 13 (1535).

[4] On Gal. iv. 4 (1519).     [5] On Gal. ii. 17 (1519).

him, he uses " justification " in a forensic sense; it is simply the pronouncing of a sentence of acquittal because the penalty of law-breaking has been paid.

Thus it is not hard to see why Luther's teaching of the penal theory and of justification by faith met with a wide measure of acceptance. It gives the Cross the central place in the work of man's salvation; it does full justice to the seriousness of sin as deserving punishment; it bears witness both to the love of God and His sublime righteousness, while removing all suggestion of arbitrariness in His dealings with man; it makes full allowance for the dignity of God's law; and—very important to the Reformers—it can be shown to be, at any rate to a large extent, Pauline and therefore Biblical. At once it became the accepted doctrine of the Reform movement, helped to that position, no doubt, by violent objection to the trivial nature of some of the means by which the Roman Church, or its officers, seemed to suggest that peace with God might be obtained.[1] Only the sacrifice of Christ could avail to pay the penalty of sin.

But there are very obvious objections to the penal theory, whatever its merits may be. In the first place, the Atonement appears to relate solely to God, as though He had to be moved from an attitude of hostility, or at least condemnation, rather than man saved from a state of sin. It may be said that it is the law which requires the penalty, but it is difficult for us to regard that as meaning anything other than that God, the Just Judge, requires it. So it is He who is to be appeased. At times Luther explicitly says this, as in the quotation already given that God with His law was " offended," or as when he says that God sent His Son " that through this Son we might know that He is our appeased and gracious Father." [2] And references to the wrath of God suggest the same idea. Of course such language alone does not represent the whole of his thought of God : he was quite sure of His love. But the suggestion, almost inseparable from the mere penal theory, that the attitude of God to man was changed by the Cross makes that theory unacceptable to the modern mind. For it cannot

---

[1] Even Mr. Belloc admits that, by their carelessness in the matter of indulgences, the authorities " allowed the gross superstition to take root that relief from the punishment of sin could be bought " (*How the Reformation Happened*, p. 67).

[2] On Gal. iv. 19 (1535).

be argued that Luther, when he speaks of the wrath of God, or of God having been placated, only means that God is unalterably opposed to sin in man, but that, when sin is removed, God can deal with men differently, His fundamental love then expressing itself in favours rather than in corrective punishment.   On the contrary, the penal theory as logically expressed by Luther—and this is a second very serious objection to it—does not suggest that any moral change is required in man for justification.   As he repeatedly admits, even the justified continue to sin, but they are none the less justified if they have faith.   The penal theory, in a word, suggests escape for man from the punishment for sin rather than from the state of sin, which is what we want. But if any change in man's moral condition does not affect the certainty of his salvation by the Cross and his reconciliation to God, plainly the benefit won by the Cross consists in a change of the attitude of God from hostility to graciousness, independent of any moral change in man.   Nor can one help feeling that Luther, for all his emphasis on the love of God, did nevertheless feel at bottom that in God " hidden and inscrutable " the Cross had worked a change.

Besides these two objections to the penal theory there is yet a third.   The whole transaction seems to be too near akin to a legal accommodation.   It is as though, in a law court, a fine were inflicted on a man and some one else paid it, so that the prisoner was allowed to go free.   No doubt that may be the best we can manage with our human limitations.   All we can hope to do is to insist on outward conformity to the law ; the inner condition of men is beyond our control.   In a way the majesty of the law has been upheld when there has been a penalty paid for a wrong done, even if it has not been paid by the wrong-doer himself. But it does not seem to us possible to regard God as acting in such a way.   It is not consistent with ideal justice, as we conceive it, that a sinner should avoid punishment, even apparently without repentance (for faith is all that is explicitly required) because some other person has paid the penalty, even though that other person be the Son of God and though His paying of the price has been entirely voluntary.

Probably, therefore, there are few to-day who will be able to regard the penal theory as satisfactory.   But in fairness to Luther it should be added that, though he first pressed it strongly, his failure to appreciate the objections which we feel to it was not due to any unusual moral blindness on his part. Though an innovator, he was also in many respects a child of his age, and as such accepted views which were practically unchallenged, and which, if accepted, go far to destroy the objections set out above. In thinking of God, along with everyone of his day, as Supreme Judge he not unnaturally supposed that His treatment of us, though still sinners, must be changed by the payment of the penalty for our sins. And in supposing that the penalty could be paid by some one other than the actual sinners he was no different from his contemporaries. The Anselmic doctrine of satisfaction, the whole papal theory of the Treasury of Merits, rest upon such an idea. For such thoughts, then, Luther himself is not to be blamed; and they do help to explain why the penal theory so completely satisfied him, as a theory.

But the penal theory alone does not exhaust Luther's thought of the Atonement. To St. Paul, justification was merely the first stage, inevitably followed by sanctification. Similarly, Luther was firmly convinced that moral change and improvement necessarily followed justification. Strictly and formally, no doubt, he teaches that justification is independent of this change, but it is plainly unfair to Luther's thought of Atonement as a whole to leave it out of consideration.

For him justification by faith has a double aspect—the non-imputation to the sinner of his sins, for they are transferred to Christ; and the reputation to the sinner of all the righteousness of Christ's life on earth. God " honours us on account of that faith; attributing to us truth and righteousness." [1] " Let faith step in, and then sin, death and hell will belong to Christ, and grace, life and salvation to the soul." [2] But in Luther's belief, imputed righteousness is necessarily followed by the growth of actual though imparted righteousness. (For this also, like everything else in man that is good, Luther attributes solely to divine action.) In men who are justified a process is going on. " We have been and are being redeemed. . . . Do not imagine the life of a Christian is stable and quiet, but a transition and setting out from vices to virtue." [3] This

[1] *On Christian Liberty* : Primary Works, p. 111.
[2] *Ibid.*, p. 112.          [3] On Gal. iv. 5 (1519).

sanctification is, apparently, never complete in this life, for even " all the saints have sins and are sinners." [1] That does not imperil their salvation, because " the evil which is left in the body is not imputed on account of Christ." [2] So much is, of course, demanded by the logic of Luther's theory. But at times he is less cautious and writes in a way which suggests that sanctification is essential for justification. " Whoso believes in Christ is justified not yet fully in deed but in hope; for he has begun to be justified and healed." [3] Sometimes it even looks as though justification is given to man in view of the actual righteousness which God has resolved to impart. For Him, who is above time, the justification is an instantaneous act, though for us it takes time : " in the predestination of God all things already are which for us are about to be." [4] No doubt such thoughts will not fit in to his penal theory in strict logic. But they do show (as does much else besides) that Atonement was really unthinkable to Luther apart from real moral regeneration.

Moreover, such regeneration is inevitable, because " faith " really means to Luther (as to St. Paul) confidence, trust, the real throwing of one's very self on Christ. In his merely logical moments, no doubt, he does speak of it as though it were only intellectual. But he is the very last man whose real beliefs we can hope to discover in his logical moments. His real belief rather comes out when he pours scorn on the faith which is only intellectual. " To believe in Christ does not mean to believe that Christ is a person who is both God and man, for that helps no one." [5] For him, "True faith is the heart's utter trust in Christ." [6] " When faith is of the kind that God awakens and creates in the heart, then a man trusts in Christ." [7] " Faith unites the soul to Christ as the wife to the husband." [8] Therefore faith, as a real bond between man and Christ, is a constant source of well-doing. " Neither does he who has faith delay as to whether good works are ordered or otherwise, but even if there were no law, yet with this living impulse

[1] On Gal. v. 21 (1519).   [2] On Gal. ii. 17 (1519).
[3] *Ibid.*
[4] I owe this quotation to Professor Mackinnon, *op. cit.*, Vol. I. p. 203 *note*.
[5] Herrmann, *op. cit.*, p. 123.
[6] *Ibid.*, p. 172.   [7] *Ibid.*, p. 171.
[8] *Christian Liberty* : Primary Works, p. 111.

P

working and driving in his heart, he freely rushes to work, nor ever ceases to do truly holy and truly Christian works." [1] " True and living faith is that which works and urges good works." [2]   In fact, a man " believeth not truly if works of charity follow not his faith." [3]   " True faith is a work of God in us whereby we are reborn and renewed from God." [4]

In view of such passages it is not possible to say that Luther's teaching on the Atonement lacks any manward aspect.   Of the penal theory as such it may be true, but to the real Luther justifying faith is only such faith as necessarily leads to regeneration.   None the less, he is usually quite emphatic that good works, though inevitable, are not in any sense the *cause* of justification; they are its effect and are to be done not to acquire merit, but from love and joy of heart.   " Just acts do not make a just man, but a just man does just acts." [5]   What he is always afraid of is any suggestion that we can in any way win merit by our deeds, as though we wished " to turn the tables and do good of ourselves to that poor man, our Lord God." [6]   The real test of whether our acts are acceptable with God is the spirit in which we do them : if to merit justification—that is, " to deny Christ, to cast away grace and truth, and to set up oneself as an idol." [7]   They are rather to be done in a spirit of cheerfulness and love, as he constantly affirms in the tract on Christian Liberty; they are to be, as it were, the overflowing of a heart thankful for its security of justification.   " So thou seest that faith alone does not suffice and yet faith alone justifies because, if it is true, it obtains the spirit of charity." [8]

The change in man thus brought about by the only faith which justifies is due to the close union which faith (in the wider sense) creates between Christ and the believing soul. This thought is, for Luther, fundamental.   It is doubtful whether one should speak of the union so created as a " mystical union "; for there is not in Luther anything to suggest that kind of teaching of the absorption of the individual in God or Christ which we usually associate with the Mystics.   None the less, the union of the believer with Christ is to Luther a very real one, not infrequently expressed

---

[1] Introduction to Romans.
[2] On Gal. v. 6 (1535).
[3] *Ibid.*
[4] Introduction to Romans.
[5] On Gal. ii. 16 (1519).
[6] Herrmann, *op. cit.*, p. 168.
[7] On Gal. i. 6 (1519).
[8] On Gal. v. 21 (1519).

under the figure of the marriage-bond. Thus selfishness (to Luther, the real root of sin) is driven out and Christ through love controls the life of the believer, though his separate identity is maintained. "Faith unites the soul to Christ as the wife to the husband; by which mystery . . . Christ and the soul are made one flesh." [1] "This faith justifies thee, makes Christ to dwell and live and reign in thee." [2] "The justified man lives not himself but Christ in him because through faith Christ dwells in him and pours in grace by which it comes about that the man is ruled not by his own spirit but Christ's." [3] "To believe in Christ is to put Him on, to become one with Him." [4] Thus there cannot really be justification by faith without moral regeneration, though at times Luther keeps the two ideas apart. But his certainty of the believer's union with Christ has a further importance : it mitigates the harshness of the penal theory. If we are really united to Christ as wife to husband, it does not seem *quite* so unjust that He should bear the penalty of our sins. "The believing soul by the pledge of its faith in Christ . . . becomes endowed with the eternal righteousness, life and salvation of its husband Christ "; [5] nor does Luther believe that once it is really made, the union can be dissolved : "Christ cannot be separated from us nor we from Him, since we are one in Him and with Him." [6]

None the less, the fact remains that to Luther the possibility of all this wider experience of salvation depended upon the vicarious punishment of Christ. To that therefore he constantly returns, insisting on justification by faith apart from all works in a way which offends many readers. To us, however, what seems most valuable is not his logical theory, but his expression of his own experience of salvation —his certainty of God's love, of a reconciliation with God which cannot be disturbed, of a new life of moral activity and service joyfully undertaken through love of Christ and man in the spirit of freedom.

The other leaders of Reform do not call for so full a consideration. All teach justification by faith, based on a

---

[1] *Christian Liberty :* Primary Works, p. 111.
[2] On Gal. i. 4 (1519).
[3] *Ibid.*, ii. 20.  [4] *Ibid.*, iv. 5.
[5] *Christian Liberty :* Primary Works, p. 112.
[6] On Gal. iii. 29 (1519).

penal view of Christ's death. About that they have really nothing to add to what Luther says, though the ready acceptance of his theory shows how congenial it was to the age. On the other hand, none of them seems to have had so deep a spiritual experience as Luther. They do not therefore give anything like the same impression as he of the joyous liberty and triumphant strength of the redeemed in Christ. Logic tends to gain prominence almost to the exclusion of Christian experience, and the penal theory does not gain added charm in the process.

The task of first bringing some formal system into Lutheran teaching fell to Melanchthon, a young but brilliant exponent of the New Learning. His conversion to Lutheranism was due to personal admiration for Luther, not to a spiritual upheaval, and he shows little of the overwhelming happiness in believing which marked his leader. On the other hand, as a humanist, he is deeply interested in moral conduct, and insists on the need for right actions (rather than, as Luther, on their inevitability), the more so as he had to face the danger of Quietism, to which some of Luther's teaching seemed to give countenance. His *Loci Communes* grew, through successive editions, into an elaborate system of theology which greatly influenced later Lutheranism. Its definitions are clear-cut and the whole doctrine of God is systematically expounded. As a humanist, he could not rest happy in belief in the divergence of faith and reason whereby Luther managed to retain his conviction both of the love and the justice of God. Revelation therefore is regarded as only completing that knowledge of God which, in natural religion, the reason had partially grasped, and the mystery of God tends to disappear. Consequently the penal theory is set out in all its mere logical simplicity; God appears almost solely as judge, and is quite freely spoken of as being reconciled. In the Augsburg confession (drawn up by Melanchthon) Christ is described as " having truly suffered, been crucified, dead and buried that He might reconcile the Father to us, and be a sacrifice not only for original sin but also for all actual sins of men." [1] Similar sayings have been quoted from Luther : but in Melanchthon they are not balanced in anything like the same degree as in Luther by the overpowering sense of God's love. Nor, in him, is the logic of the penal theory softened by such

[1] Kidd's *Documents*, p. 263.

teaching of the real union of Christ and the believer as in
Luther.

For faith, to Melanchthon, is usually simply intellectual;
to believe is to accept those truths about God and Christ
which are revealed in Scripture and the creeds, reasonable,
though not discovered by reason. " What is faith ? Constantly to agree to every word of God." [1] And faith is
defined not as trust in Christ, but as " trust (*fiducia*) in the
divine mercy promised in Christ." [2] It is very significant
here that even *fiducia*, " trust," seems to lack any sense of
trust in a person : it rather means trust that the promise in
Christ is true : that is, even *fiducia* means little more than
hearty assent. In this tendency to limit faith to mere
mental acceptance of revealed truth there is clearly marked
the beginning of a view very obvious among later Protestants
—that the main thing required for justification is correctness
of belief. This is explicitly the view taken in the Formula
of Concord (1577), which describes the Gospel as a doctrine
teaching what men are to believe to obtain forgiveness for
their sins. Melanchthon is not so definite as that. None
the less, whereas Luther (however illogically) does insist
that justification is accompanied by a moral change, in
Melanchthon the penal theory is so presented in isolation
as to suggest that mere orthodox belief is sufficient to
obtain justification.

On the other hand, he insists even more strongly than
Luther on the necessity of good works, though he agrees
that they have no value for justification. " None of our
works justifies however good they may seem or be. But
only faith in the mercy and grace of God in Christ Jesus
justifies us." [3] Yet, he does also speak as though good
works after justification were necessary, as Luther does not.
It looks at times as though he held that when a man is
justified he must then (with the help of the Spirit) effect his
own salvation. " This, in a word, is Christian knowledge,
to know what the law demands, whence you may seek the
power of performing the law." [4] (For Luther, the law
could no longer " demand " anything : it was fulfilled by
Christ.) In the second edition of the *Loci*, he writes : " I
therefore openly and plainly declare : our obedience, that

---

[1] *Loci Communes;* in *Corpus Reformatorum*, Vol. XXI. of Melanchthon, p. 162.
[2] *Corp. Ref.*, Vol. XXI. p. 163.   [3] *Ibid.*, p. 159.   [4] *Ibid.*, p. 85.

is the justification of a good conscience, or of works which
God orders to us, of necessity should follow reconciliation.
. . . There are required not only external civil works, but
also spiritual motions, fear of God, trust, invocation, love
and such motions." [1]  Here the death of Christ is not alone
enough; the " justification of a good conscience "—that is,
good works—is further required.  In fact to Melanchthon
as much as to Luther an atonement without moral reform
is not satisfactory.  But Melanchthon, by his narrow interpretation of faith, is prevented from seeing such moral
reform as the necessary concomitant of the faith which
justifies.  He is therefore full of moral exhortations, and so
appears to return in part to the Roman doctrine of " works
righteousness."  This is not only a contradiction of his
express insistence on justification by faith, but it also
stresses the external aspect of the penal theory; man is
not changed by justification but merely excused punishment.

In Switzerland, Zwingli claimed to be a leader of reform
independent of Luther, and the claim is certainly just to a
great extent.  For as early as 1516–18, before Luther was
widely known, Zwingli had begun to protest against pilgrimages and indulgences.  On the other hand, it is certain
that he did become acquainted later on with Luther's teaching, and some things which he writes are more easily
explained as due to Lutheran influence than as his own
original thought.  He was a humanist, of a spirit very
different from Luther, and his protest was provoked by the
pettiness and folly of the Roman practices rather than by a
deep religious feeling of their inadequacy.  His conception
of God is philosophical rather than religious, and the basis
of all his thinking is the idea of the Divine Omnipotence,
and of the unquestionable right (as well as power) of God
to do what He wills with His own.  " I know that that
highest deity, which is my God, freely determines concerning
all things. . . . God who from eternity to eternity seeth all
things with one and simple intuition, hath no need of any
reasoning . . . but freely determines and disposes concerning all things, for whatsoever things are are His own." [2]
Zwingli could not doubt that such a God foresaw the Fall
and, even before it took place, had decided on a remedy.
" Although knowing and foreseeing, He formed man in the

[1] *Corp. Ref.*, Vol. XXI. p. 429.
[2] *Fidei Ratio*, given in Niemeyer, *Collectio Confessionum*, p. 18.

beginning who was to fall, equally He determined to clothe His Son in human nature who should repair the fall." [1] For it was His will that all men should not perish; but who are to be saved and who lost depends entirely on His election. No doubt this idea is implied by Luther when he teaches that only faith can justify and that God alone gives faith. But in Zwingli the idea of election is clear and emphatic—and, of course, entirely in accord with his stress on God's omnipotence. "The election of God is free and unmerited; for He chose us before the foundation of the world." [2] The real cause of salvation, therefore, is simply the will of God in election. Faith is not the cause, but at most the proof of election; for election "does not follow faith, but faith follows election." [3] Indeed, there may be some who are elect and therefore certain of salvation who have not yet faith. "They who because of their age have not faith should not be rashly condemned by us, for although they have not yet faith, nevertheless the election of God is hid from us." [4]

In view of his belief in the complete freedom of the Divine Will, it is difficult to see why Zwingli should adopt the penal theory. Presumably God could simply have forgiven man out of hand, and the more so in that Zwingli sees a clear distinction between Adam's sin and ours. "I confess that our father sinned a sin which is really a sin, that is 'scelus, crimen, nephas.' But those who were born of him have not sinned in this way : . . . original sin, as it is in the sons of Adam, is not properly sin, as has been explained, that is a crime against law." [5] It is rather, he continues, " a disease and a condition. A disease because as he slipped through self-love, so we also slip; a condition because as he was made a slave and liable to death, so we also are born slaves and sons of wrath and liable to death." [6] He does not explain why our penalty should be the same as Adam's, though our fault is different; he simply accepts the traditional view. Thus, from his main thought of God, and of the Fall, there is no need for the penal theory at all. None the less, he explicitly adopts it, and uses the ordinary language about it. Christ was a " victim making satisfac-

[1] *Fidei Ratio* (Niemeyer, p. 18).
[2] *Expositio Christianæ Fidei* (Niemeyer, p. 58).
[3] *Fidei Ratio* (Niemeyer, p. 21).      [4] *Ibid.*, p. 22.
[5] *Ibid.*, p. 20.      [6] *Ibid.*

tion for ever for the sins of all the faithful "; [1] " Christ by
His death expiated our crimes," [2] " made a sacrifice to
satisfy the divine justice for us "; [3] He " offered Himself
to the Father for us to placate His eternal justice." [4]
Further, though faith in fact, on his theory, can be little
more than assurance of election, [5] he does at times use the
ordinary language about justification by faith—" He who
believes in the Gospel shall be saved; he who does not
believe shall be condemned " [6]—a flat contradiction of what
he says about elect children—" Whoso believes in Christ,
his sins are remitted." [7]  Thus Zwingli reproduces the usual
reforming view of the Cross and of justification, but it
hardly seems to agree with his emphasis on mere election.
It almost looks as though he had taken it over from Luther,
as being the best explanation of the Cross, which, on his
own theory of omnipotence, was hardly to be explained.
Thus, in Zwingli, the penal theory, though the only theory
of atonement, remains very detached : the transaction is
entirely in the sphere of the Divine; apparently God puts
on Christ the punishment of our sins so that He may
be able to elect some to salvation; a transaction very
mysterious, and (to us) very shocking.

But what Zwingli is really interested in is the healing of
the " disease " of original sin, rather than the remedy for
its condition of guilt.  To the elect God gives faith (at least
to those who know they are elect), and that faith, to Zwingli,
at once leads to reform, for it brings union with the Divine.
Faith is a " fountain of works." [8]  " Wheresoever is true
faith, there is also work no less than where there is fire
there is also heat." [9]  And that is because true faith is not
merely " historic faith," but a faith which is " trust towards
God." [10]  Thus the elect who have faith are really changed
by Divine power : they are " through the Spirit of God
drawn to God and as it were transformed." [11]  That again

---

[1] Zwingli's *Sixty-seven Articles*, 18 (Niemeyer, p. 5).
[2] *Expositio* (Niemeyer, p. 39).
[3] *Fidei Ratio* (Niemeyer, p. 20).
[4] *Expositio* (Niemeyer, p. 48).
[5] Cf. *Expositio* (Niemeyer, p. 55).  " We have said that by faith
sins are remitted, by which we mean only that faith alone makes a
man sure of the remission of sins."
[6] Article XV. (Niemeyer, p. 5).
[7] *Expositio* (Niemeyer, p. 56).     [8] *Ibid.*, p. 57.     [9] *Ibid.*, p. 59.
[10] *Ibid.*, p. 49.                    [11] Article XIII. (Niemeyer, p. 5).

all sounds very Lutheran; but such language is not nearly so prominent in Zwingli as his insistence on the need for works and exhortations to them. The theory of atonement is lost to sight in the zeal of the moral reformer. "We preach the law no less than grace. For in the law the elect and faithful learn the will of God."[1] In one place, to "put on Christ" is explained as "to live according to His formula."[2] How great importance he attached to works may be judged from his hope that the great heroes of antiquity—Hercules, Theseus, Socrates—will be saved.[3] Thus, though he accepts the penal theory as explaining how any election is possible, his immediate concern is to rouse men to amendment of life by the example and new law of Christ, who "was given . . . that He might make us certain of the grace of God and might give us a law of living."[4]

Calvin at times speaks of Zwingli in a slighting manner, and claims rather to be a follower of Luther. This he undoubtedly was, but he was also largely influenced by Zwinglian ideas through the medium of Bucer. His importance therefore is not so much that of an original thinker. He is rather a systematiser who produced the great theological handbook of the Reformation, stoutly supporting his arguments by Scriptural appeal. This last feature added enormously to the influence of his work, for the argument from Scripture could be understood by the very simplest.

To him, as to Zwingli, the outstanding characteristics of God are power and greatness. God in His majesty is quite beyond our right of criticism and is simply a rule to Himself. "His immensity ought to inspire us with awe that we may not attempt to measure Him with our senses."[5] We are to "entertain such reverence for His secret judgments as to esteem His will the most righteous cause of everything that He does."[6] "What He wills must be considered just for this very reason, because He wills it."[7] There is tremendous emphasis on the justice of God and His wrath against sinners. But the Cross has satisfied the one and appeased the other. "Christ interposed as an intercessor; He has

---

[1] *Expositio* (Niemeyer, p. 59).　　[2] *Ibid.*, p. 40.
[3] *Ibid.*, p. 61.　　[4] *Ibid.*, p. 41.
[5] John Allen's Translation of the *Institutio* (1838), Vol. I. p. 95. All my references are to this translation.
[6] Vol. I. p. 166.　　[7] Vol. II. p. 142.

received and suffered in His own person the punishment which by the righteous judgment of God impended over all sinners; . . . by this expiation God the Father has been satisfied and duly atoned ; . . . by this intercessor His wrath has been appeased." [1] That is the ordinary penal theory. But it appears in its harshest form. There is not there the idea observed in Zwingli that the Cross is the Father's device, nor the feeling we find in Luther that it was due to His love. In places, it is true, both those ideas do occur. "If was of His mere good pleasure that God appointed Him mediator to procure salvation for us," [2] shows God's participation; His love appears in such a passage as "By a pure and gratuitous love towards us He is excited to receive us into favour. The love of God the Father therefore precedes our reconciliation in Christ." [3] But in the main it is as avenging judge that God is conceived in the transaction. He, "being a righteous judge, never suffers His law to be violated with impunity, but stands prepared to avenge it." [4]

As in Luther, justification is by faith, and righteousness is imputed.[5] But faith, much more often than in Luther, is intellectual. Sometimes, indeed, he will have nothing to do with faith which is "mere assent with which every despiser of God may receive as true whatever is contained in scripture." [6] Yet he himself says, "We shall have a complete definition of faith if we say that it is a steady and certain knowledge of the Divine benevolence towards us . . . founded on the truth of the gratuitous promise in Christ . . . revealed to our minds and confirmed in our hearts by the Holy Spirit." [7] And there is not the same sense as in Luther of personal trust in Christ and union with Him. What a man has to depend on is the trustworthiness of God rather than communion with Him ; he has to believe that God will be true to His word, and that the Cross was an adequate penalty for all sins because God so ordained.

But besides that there is, as in Zwingli, whole-hearted belief in the doctrine of election, and its logical corollary, reprobation, is frankly recognised. "That He may the more illustriously display His liberality in so eminent a gift, God deigns not to bestow it promiscuously upon all, but by a

---

[1] Vol. I. p. 401.    [2] Vol. I. p. 420.    [3] Vol. I. p. 402.
[4] Vol. I. p. 401.    [5] *E.g.* Vol. I. pp. 577–8.
[6] Vol. I. p. 439.    [7] *Ibid.*

singular privilege imparts it upon whom He will." [1] His
choice is made " totally irrespective of human merit," [2]
but we may not question the justice of this. " We deny
that He is liable to be called to any account : we deny also
that we are proper judges." [3] In fact, " this diversity dis-
covers the wonderful depth of the Divine judgment." [4] All
this is reminiscent of Zwingli rather than of Luther. His
real attitude towards works, too, is rather that of Zwingli
than of Luther. It is true that he does in places use
language like that of Luther—" we never dream of a faith
destitute of good works," but " we attribute justification
not to works, but to faith." [5] He even, like Luther, claims
that they are done in voluntary obedience, without compulsion from the law. [6] But there is not really the same
genuine joy and spontaneity about works as one finds in
Luther, and Calvin's real feelings, one suspects, really come
out much more clearly when he says of " pure and genuine
religion " that it " consists in faith, united with a serious
fear of God, comprehending a voluntary reverence and producing legitimate worship agreeable to the injunctions of
the law." [7]

Thus, it is true to say that, so far as theory is concerned,
all the Reformers agree in accepting the penal view of the
Cross as being the sole sufficient cause of reconciliation
between men and God. But no one of them gives a satisfactory explanation of why God should have required it;
indeed, the more logical they are, the more unsatisfying
does their theory seem. On the other hand, although it
does not really fit their own theory, all agree that a moral
reform in man is the necessary concomitant of justification.
But whereas this amendment in Luther is shown to be
necessarily consequent upon the kind of faith which wins
justification, in the other Reformers, in spite of explicit
assertions to the contrary, it is difficult to avoid the feeling
that somehow man's final salvation depends in part at least
on his works and not merely on the Cross.

[1] Vol. I. p. 465.    [2] Vol. II. p. 128.    [3] Vol. II. p. 143.
[4] Vol. II. p. 120.    [5] Vol. II. p. 24.    [6] Vol. II. pp. 54–5.
[7] Vol. I. p. 37.

## X

## THE ATONEMENT IN POST-REFORMATION WRITERS

### By E. C. Essex

OUR examination of Post-Reformation doctrine concerning the Atonement can only indicate lines of thought which may be considered characteristic of the theories of certain outstanding writers, who have had influence on the people of their own and succeeding generations. We shall try to show wherein they appear to have contributed towards a truer expression of the doctrine, either by their determined opposition to what they regarded as faulty or mistaken, or by their constructive thought advocating strongly some important aspect which they held should be emphasised.

The Reformers had proclaimed the absolute necessity that God should punish sin. Outraged justice and offended Majesty must demand satisfaction, and by enduring the pains of death Christ bore the punishment, satisfied offended Deity and procured pardon. But they have been grossly misjudged and misrepresented, as if that dominant note in their theory of the Atonement were their whole theme. Calvin (*Institutes*, Book II. Chap. XVI.) quotes with approval these words of Augustine :

" God did not begin to love us when we were reconciled to Him by the blood of His Son; but He loved us before the creation of the world, that we might be His children, together with His only-begotten Son, even before we had any existence. Therefore our reconciliation by the death of Christ must not be understood as if He reconciled us to God, that God might begin to love those whom He had before hated; but we are reconciled to Him who already loved us and with whom we were at enmity on account of sin."

*Socinus* flatly denies any inherent necessity for God to demand satisfaction. " To forgive sins and to receive satisfaction for sins are plainly contradictory and cannot exist together." There can be no need of forgiveness if someone has paid the debt. God has the right to pardon or punish any affront to His Majesty. In exposing the weakness of the argument of the Reformers, Socinus is betraying his own error of judgment. He claims an arbitrary freedom for God to forgive if He chooses, and is thus in danger of weakening the essential ethical character of God, while the Reformers, by over-emphasis of the necessity of retributive justice, were perilously near to contradicting the inherent nature of Eternal Love.

" Not on the Cross, but in heaven," says Socinus, " is Christ's perfect oblation made. He continually intercedes with God for us, that is, by the authority and power given to Him by God ever frees us from all ills, and so makes perpetual expiation of our sins." Here he is ignoring the power of the Atoning death, in order that he may prove that the risen and ascended Lord is making effectual that work in the heavenly sphere.

In so far as his shrewd intellect reveals the imperfection of previous exposition, he is doing Christianity a service, but his dialectical skill is chiefly used for destructive criticism.

We are in a totally different atmosphere with *Grotius*.[1] His is a mediating position between Calvin and Socinus. He opposes Socinus' contention that there cannot be satisfaction made for sin, and also remission, by showing that the one is antecedent to the other. Yet he is far removed from the Reformers, for he denies the necessity of the punishment of sin, and the death of Christ is to him practically only a penal example or incentive.

God is not so much offended Majesty as supreme Governor, who must preserve law and order. Christ, as Head of the Body of which we are members, is punished for the maintenance of authority. But he brings out quite clearly the love and goodness of God :

" God, being moved of His goodness to be signally beneficial to us, but our sins, which deserved punishment standing in the way, He appointed that Christ, who was willing

[1] *Defensio Fidei Catholicae de Satisfactione Christi.*

of His love towards men, should, by enduring grievous torments and a bloody and ignominious death, pay the penalties due for our sins, that, without prejudice to the demonstration of the Divine righteousness, we, by the intervention of true faith, should be freed from the penalty of eternal death."

" If Christ suffered such severities that ye might obtain the pardon of your sins, having indeed obtained it by faith, ye ought to beware of sinning in the future."

We see here an advance on some earlier statements, for Christ's sufferings are viewed as the loving act of an essentially loving God, whose loving Son voluntarily offers Himself to bear the penalty of our past sins, and this offering acts as an incentive to future holiness. By dwelling on the moral value, he is released from any quantitative aspect of exact equivalent. To him the sufferings of Christ meet the moral ends of penalty by preserving the authority of righteous government, revealing and bearing the ill desert of sin and deterring from future offences.

Stevens feels that there is a certain artificiality in the views of Grotius :

" A kind of apparatus of government . . . intervenes between God and man and conditions their relations."

but he says that the book he wrote was " a praiseworthy effort to find a point of view more satisfactory " than that of the Socinians and the Calvinists.

The Socinian and Grotian theories exercised a considerable influence over later writers. Many who held tenaciously to the doctrine of penal satisfaction expressed their views in a modified form. During the next two centuries there is little progress towards a more profound interpretation of the nature of the Atonement. Perhaps we should note two who, in this period, displayed an originality of outlook.

*Robert Barclay*, the Quaker, so strongly emphasised the spiritual work of Christ in the believer's life that his followers fell into the grave danger of minimising the vital importance of the historical fact of the death on the Cross. But surely he was right in maintaining that man is made just by the inward birth of Christ in the heart. Spiritual life is imparted. There is no need to speak of a merit belonging to someone else being imputed to us. God does not pretend that we are what we are not, but by grace through faith actually makes us sons of God and inheritors of His Kingdom.

*Jonathan Edwards, Senior,* of America, is one who combines with some Calvinistic teaching a great deal of the Grotian element. The ethical aspect is prominent. Christ's sympathy causes Him to suffer for our sakes. He suggests that if man could offer to God a repentance proportional to the greatness of the majesty despised punishment would be unnecessary, but man is incapable of such a repentance. Thus he prepared the way, unconsciously enough, for the grander conceptions of the Atonement presented by M'Leod Campbell and Moberly.

In the latter half of the nineteenth century many earnest thinkers devoted themselves to the study of the subject.

A retrograde step is taken by *Shedd.* He ascribes to the sufferings of Christ the character of a penal satisfaction or judicial appeasement of distributive justice, and to him justice is the unconditional necessity to punish. God's tenderness and pity are optional.

Retributive justice is necessary in its operation. The claim of the law upon the transgressor for punishment is absolute and indefeasible. The eternal Judge may or may not exercise mercy, but He must exercise justice. The wrath of God is constitutional, but His mercy is voluntary. The Divine wrath issues from the necessary antagonism between the pure essence of the Godhead and moral evil. But the Divine compassion issues from the voluntary disposition of the Deity. As justice is impersonal, God can fairly let the punishment fall upon a substitute, who is vicariously punished.

How mechanical and repellent this sounds ! It is as if justice and law were things apart from the Being of God, and as if the punishment of sin were the chief desideratum in the Mind of God. There is a sharp distinction between justice and mercy. They are contrasted, opposite and even, possibly, antagonistic factors in the character of God.

*A. H. Strong*[1] develops his earlier theory on much the same lines. God may be merciful, but must be holy. Love may be exercised, but holiness must be. Justice is " a principle of God's nature, not only independent of love,

---

[1] *Systematic Theology,* esp. pp. 138, 139, 412–416.

but superior to love." Yet God loves the sinner and cannot see him perish. " Guilt was not simply imputed to Christ, it was imparted also."

He appears to depart from his original position in *Christ in Creation and Ethical Monism*.[1] Christ is the root and substance of humanity and suffers by identification with humanity. " His is the all-including consciousness." Later still he pronounces that we can no longer hold " the old mechanical and arbitrary conceptions of the Atonement. Christ's doing and suffering is not that of one external and foreign to us. He is bone of our bone and flesh of our flesh." It is impossible to relate these statements to his earlier forensic penal theory.

*Dale* [2] shows that the New Testament is full of emphatic statement concerning the transcendent significance of the death on Calvary, regarded as the unique atoning sacrifice for the sins of mankind. But is he quite fair to some presentations of the moral theory when he makes the dogmatic assertion :

" The Pauline conception of the relation between the death of Christ and the remission of sins is irreconcilable with the moral theory of the Atonement, whatever form that theory may assume " ?

Are there not elements in the apparently contradictory theories capable of a true synthesis ?

As an ardent champion of the fact of the Atonement and a staunch upholder of its objective value, we honour Dale for his devoted allegiance, while we feel that the truth was too profound for him to make a successful attempt to rationalise it. Moberly [3] questions the validity of some of his expressions which, to say the least, are unfortunate :

" This enduring by Christ of the punishment of sin consti- tutes a reason why God can and does forgive us."

" Christ is the Propitiation for our sins and therefore He has allayed the Divine anger, so that God, for His sake, is willing to forgive us."

" God's hostility to our sins has received adequate expres-

[1] Stevens, *Christian Doctrine of Salvation*, footnote, pp. 180, 181.
[2] *The Atonement.*
[3] *Atonement and Personality*, pp. 389-96.

sion in the Death of Christ, and now He is ready to confer on us the remission of sins for Christ's sake."

" The remission of sins brings to the man who has received it a sure and permanent escape from the hostility and wrath of God."

Prominence is given to punishment, anger, hostility, escape, submission to justice, destruction of sin. But this is the view of guilty man oppressed with the thought of offended Deity. Should not the language of redeemed mankind also present the other side more joyously ? The most merciful Father's all-conquering love fighting victoriously for His children, exalts to holiness and to communion with Himself through His gift of the Son of His Love, at infinite cost to Himself.

Moberly notices that Dale does not include Pentecost, and leaves out the eighth chapter of Romans, " the crowning glory of St. Paul's exposition." But in fairness to him we must bear in mind that his chief object was to fight against the dangerous latitudinarian views of his day as put forward by Jowett, and he certainly proved a powerful adversary by maintaining the authority of the Bible as indisputable witness to the value of the Atoning Sacrifice of the death of Christ.

Dale attaches great significance to our Lord's cry upon the Cross : " My God, my God, why hast Thou forsaken me ? " Commenting on it he writes : " Immediately before His death He was forsaken of God. . . ." That sinful men, even though they have been transformed into saints, should sometimes lose the sense of the Divine presence and the Divine love is explicable, but how was it that He, the Son of God, was forsaken by the Father in the very crisis of His sufferings ? He speaks of saints " losing the sense of the Divine presence and love." Was this the experience of the truly human Jesus ? An actual experience of the sense of desertion, the loss of the serene joy of the Father's Presence, is a poignant part of the vicarious suffering of all who pass under the dark shadow of that guilt of loved ones which they take into their inmost being and make their own, through the indwelling of the Spirit of Christ in their hearts. How much more profound to Him, who completely identified Himself with us in the bearing of our sin, is the sense of the withdrawal of the light of His Father's

Q

countenance. Actual desertion by God is unthinkable. A wrong conception of the wrath of God and of His inflicting a penalty as satisfaction of offended justice is responsible for such an interpretation of this saying of Christ on the Cross.[1] This text could at most only be corroborative of the doctrine which Dale holds that it illustrates. We have far stronger and more certain grounds than this for maintaining that our Lord did actually bear the burden of human sinfulness.

*Denney* [2] teaches penal substitution. Christ died the sinner's death. In that death a Divine sentence was executed upon the sin of the world. Our Lord's Passion is His sublimest action. Jesus ends His life by an act of sacrifice which has as its purpose and effect the liberation of the forfeited lives of many. Atonement was originally " outside of us," a finished work in which God in Christ makes a final revelation of Himself in relation to sinners and sin. In the work of Christ His distinction from men rather than His likeness to men should be in the foreground. He therefore prefers " substitution " to " representation."

(Would he have been willing to use " presentation," for ought he not to have allowed that Jesus presents as an acceptable sacrifice to God the ideal new Humanity His holy work creates, and of which He is Himself the consecrated first fruits in humanity ?)

Denney maintains that in His death Christ bore our sins, and through His death forgiveness is mediated. The propitiation which God provides in Christ is the final proof of His love. A doctrine of the Atonement must treat sin with the seriousness with which it is treated in the New Testament. Propitiation, in the sense of an absolutely serious dealing with God's condemnation of sin for its removal, is essential to forgiveness as long as we regard that condemnation as an absolutely real and serious thing. This does not involve a " forensic " doctrine of Atonement. " There is nothing which I should wish to reprobate more wholeheartedly," says he, " than the conception which is expressed by these words " [3] (*i.e.* " legal," " forensic ").

---

[1] Moberly's note on pp. 134–5 of *Atonement and Personality* fairly presents the varying views, and urges the impossibility of any certainty with regard to the significance of the words on the Cross to the mind of our Lord Himself.

[2] *Studies in Theology ; The Death of Christ ; The Atonement and the Modern Mind.*

[3] *The Atonement and the Modern Mind,* p. 69.

Denney feels that there is " something unrealisable and even impious " in Calvin's view that " Jesus endured in His soul the dreadful torments of a condemned and lost man." [1] He emphasises the value of the moral side of the Atoning work of Christ, which is " A demonstration of love made at infinite cost, powerful enough to evoke penitence and faith in man." It is through Christ we get the know-ledge of God's character, which evokes penitence and faith and brings the assurance of pardon to the heart. " In all real forgiveness there is a passion of penitence on the side of the wrong-doer, and a more profound passion of love on the other, bearing the sin of the guilty to win him through reconciliation to goodness again."

We feel that Denney has climbed to greater heights than many former exponents of the penal theory. But is it not true of him, as of Dale, that the triumphant note of victory through exaltation to the life of holiness is not sounded loudly enough ?

The prelude in the minor key, with its theme of sin and guilt and punishment, is not God's main theme. Christ comes to resolve it into the major key, that the sad music of sinful humanity may be turned into the eternally joyous song of the ransomed. Would not the reverent and serious contribution of these writers to Christian thought upon the Atonement be grander still if to their wholesome medicines had been added the invigorating tonic of Du Bose's virile doctrine of salvation ?

Fellowship with God and with one another in love is to *Ritschl* the goal of humanity. Christ consciously pursued that end and fully realised it in His human life. He is the complete revelation of God—the Word of God in human flesh. He maintained in life and in death an unbroken fellowship with God, and it is the one great object of His work to lead men into the same consciousness of God's love and Fatherhood, and unto the same fellowship which the Son enjoyed. Fulness of fellowship with God, the final goal of all religion, is realised in Christ alone. He founds and builds up on earth the Kingdom of God. The Church promotes the Kingdom when its members are actively engaged in deeds of love. By introducing men into the same relation to God which He enjoys, He procures for them forgiveness of sins, making them members of the Christian community. Only by participation in the life of

[1] *The Death of Christ*, pp. 63, 64.

the Christian community can the salvation of the individual be realised. By the death of Christ God's forgiving love is secured beforehand to those who belong to Christ's community. God's satisfaction of justice can mean only the realisation of His eternal purpose of love.

The Atonement is the restoration of each soul to its proper place in the Kingdom. Justification is the forgiveness of sins and rests on the work of Christ. There is no necessity or even possibility for a satisfaction of justice considered as a penal element before forgiveness can take place, or as a condition of its bestowal, for God's justice and righteousness are the persistency of His purpose of grace. It is unbiblical to assume any opposition between God's grace or love and His righteousness. Christ's sufferings and death were experiences which lay in the path of His duty in revealing God and living the perfect life. He steadfastly endured all suffering and held true to His vocation.

The work of Christ did not make God willing to forgive. Christ reconciles sinners with God, but the penal view is to be rejected, for punishment implies guilt, and Christ was guiltless. The forensic view conflicts in every respect with the religious interest of the Christian. Christ revealed the guilt and hatefulness of sin by revealing and realising the holy life. His revelation of the guilt of sin was the negative aspect of His revelation of holiness. He sets the evil of sin in the light of perfect goodness, and this is its condemnation. Thus for Ritschl we see a great ethical purpose animating the life of Christ, and this purpose is primarily and ultimately the salvation of the community. We need to be reminded of this great truth of the unity of the Body increasing unto the edification of itself in love, till we attain unto the Perfect Man.

*Stevens* [1] has no room for the penal idea in any form : " It is because the eternal will of God is a will of love, that Christ who came to realise the Father's will saw the meaning of His own life in self-giving." It was at once the Father's commandment and His own choice that He should give His life in absolute self-devotion. The command and the choice were not two, but one for His consciousness. The Cross represents what is most characteristic in Christ because it expresses what is deepest in the heart of God.

Humanity is not in its essential character totally depraved, yet all need healing, for none is righteous. Man is

[1] *The Christian Doctrine of Salvation.*

by nature a child of God, even if he be a lost and wandering and sinful child. But there is no such thing as man's unaided powers independently attaining to perfection. Christ's is the perfect realisation of the true, Divine ideal of human nature. The influence of Jesus Christ as the incarnation of the immanent God in our humanity is the most potent and practical power which ever does or ever can touch our life. "For myself," says Stevens, "I believe that we have scarcely begun to appreciate the significance and saving power of such a personality and such a life as that of Jesus Christ in our world." [1]

The righteousness of God is His holy love. It includes benevolence and purity. To define righteousness as retributive justice, the necessity to punish, is radically unscriptural. Christ reveals and satisfies God Himself in His saving, holy love. His Passion is the consummate revelation of the Divine love, showing what love wills to do in order to save. It reveals what sin is, since it shows how a sinful world treats perfect love. The Passion of Christ thus exhibits the sinfulness of the world on the background of perfect holiness.

Salvation is from sin, and implicit in this is salvation from its penalty, and it is to holiness. To emphasise escape from penalty is too negative, for this is a subordinate aspect of salvation. The death of Christ is not the ground of forgiveness, but its outcome and expression. It is not the cause, but the method of grace.

" Christ lived, laboured, suffered and died not to make God willing to save, but to show how willing He is, and to make His willingness effective—really to accomplish what God in His holy love desires to do.

" Christ atones for sin in the sense of judging, condemning and abolishing it. He is substituted for men in the sense in which perfect love takes the place and bears the burdens of its objects. He gives the ransom which love always pays in its vicarious devotion. But this is no mere transactional procedure done outside of us. We must enter into its meaning and make it our very own."

" His work avails by our appropriation of His Spirit."

" The sinner in his sins can see in God only the wrathful Judge. Jesus reconciles men to God, and transforms Him *for their consciousness* from the angry God whom alone the

[1] *Op. cit.*, pp. 487, 533.

sinful conscience can see, into the God of love, whom
repentance and faith embrace." [1]

Jesus secures for us the forgiveness of sins and the favour
of God by enabling us to see and to know God as He truly
is—at once holy and gracious.  He moves us to a repentance and faith which change for us the face of God.  We
are enabled to see and acknowledge the Lamb in the midst
of God's Throne—the love that is at the heart of His power
and sovereignty.

The death of Christ is a transcript of the eternal passion
of the heart of God on account of sin.  Salvation is no
mere acquittal.  It is a recovery to God-likeness, from
alienation into fellowship.  Christ perfectly fulfilled the life
of sonship to God, and the progressive realisation of that
same sonship and of human brotherhood by humanity in
the spirit of Christ is the Atonement, which is a continuous
and progressive work.[2]

*Du Bose* [3] is positive, forceful and startling in his aphor-
istic appositeness.  Man has a capacity for the spiritual
which is his essential nature, realisable, but not realised.
Sin hinders, limits, contradicts the full expression of our
personality.  Jesus is not only the example, but also the
cause of holiness.  He is holiness communicated to, and
realised in man, not the infection, but the *potentia*.  He is
the *res* of our salvation.  He warns us not to regard reconciliation as objective and sanctification as subjective.  Both
are accomplished for us and these in us.  Sin is what we
are when God is not in us.

To be " out of God " is death.  Sin and moral disobedience are synonymous with death.  They are the reason or
cause of physical death, and the abolishment of them shall
be the abolishment of it.  What we call death would cease
to be death apart from sin.

The wrath of God, properly understood, so far from
being in conflict with the love of God, is the highest expression of it.  How can God love my good without hating my
evil ?  " Our God is a consuming fire," but the fire of the
furnace, which is hatred to the dross, is love to the gold.
God's wrath against sin is not only love, but the only love
to the sinner.  He is never so much our God as when He is
consuming us.  Sin carries the wrath of God in itself.

---

[1] *Op. cit.*, p. 534.　　　　　[2] *Op. cit.*, p. 535.
[3] *The Soteriology of the New Testament.*

He regards the Cross as that sole instrument of human salvation. By our Lord's perfect crucifixion of the flesh of sin He condemned sin in the flesh, broke the power, abolished the sway, abrogated the law, and did away with all the consequences of sin in the flesh. We must, by a birth from above, be what God is, before we can do what God does. Even God cannot save us, or be our obedience and righteousness without us, because whatever He might be in us without us would not be our obedience or righteousness. Du Bose makes the humanity of Christ an intense reality.

Christ works out first His own redemption in working out that of humanity. He was what He was, as man, by faith not in Himself, but in God. Grace is prior to faith, but received by faith. Objectively it is already given : subjectively it is not received until faith appropriates. What Jesus Christ is, by our faith in what He is, will make us what He is. We were as really spiritually in the redemption wrought by Him as we were physically or naturally in the loins of Adam. God in Christ only calls and treats us as righteous because in Christ He makes us righteous. Our obedience is the consequence of our Sonship through grace.

If Christ's death " propitiated " God, it is because Christ's death was in itself potentially and in us actually the extinction of that which, in the nature of things, renders it impossible for God to be propitious or favourable towards us. By the penal death of our Lord, a death inflicted on Him instead of on us, and because inflicted on Him not to be suffered by us, something has been done, a satisfaction rendered to God's nature or to God's law, or to the Divine administration of the world, an expiation or atonement made for our sins, which enables God to be gracious or favourable, and so makes our salvation possible. An objective salvation which remains objective only is only a salvation for us, and not in us.

*M'Leod Campbell* [1] made a great contribution towards our understanding of the Atonement. The Fatherhood of God is his chief theme, the perfect Sonship of Christ shown in the whole of the Incarnate Life is expressed in the key-text " I come to do Thy will, O my God. I delight to do it. Yea, Thy law is within my heart." To him the wrath of God against sin is a reality, and he holds that satisfaction

[1] *The Nature of the Atonement.*

was due to Divine justice. Christ, in dealing with God on behalf of men, must be conceived of as dealing with the righteous wrath of God against sin and as according to it that which was due.

That " equivalent sorrow and repentance " which Edwards felt might be adequate as satisfaction of justice, but which was not forthcoming from mankind, Campbell sees in Christ. That perfect confession, only possible to perfect holiness, was offered by Christ to the Father. He thus substitutes vicarious repentance and confession for vicarious punishment.

But to do him even partial justice we must note that in his peculiar use of the word " confession " lies a whole continent of meaning. The confession is the life lived in complete filial obedience, and the death undertaken to acknowledge the justice of God's judgment on sin.

When he denies that the sufferings of Christ were penal, he is simply stating that they were not inflicted on Him by an external judge, but voluntarily chosen by the Son. " The sufferer suffers what he suffers just through seeing sin and sinners with God's eyes, and feeling in reference to them with God's heart. Is such suffering a punishment? Is God, in causing such a Divine experience in humanity, inflicting a punishment? . . . What he suffered was not— because from its nature it could not be—a punishment." [1]

To him the word punishment evidently means retributive vengeance. Moberly contends that to deny that our Lord's sufferings were penal in that sense is one thing, but it is another and more doubtful matter to deny that they can be called penal in any sense at all.

" What a vindicating of the Divine name and of the character of the lawgiver are the sufferings now contemplated, considered in themselves the manifestation in humanity of what our sins are to God, compared to that to which they are reduced if conceived of as a punishment inflicted by God." [2]

" That oneness of mind with the Father which towards man took the form of condemnation of sin, would in the Son's dealing with the Father in relation to our sins take the form of a perfect confession of our sins. It is a perfect Amen in humanity to the judgment of God on the sin of

[1] *Op. cit.*, p. 102.         [2] *Op. cit.*, p. 116.

men. It has all the elements of a perfect repentance in humanity for all the sin of man—a perfect sorrow—a perfect contrition—all excepting the personal consciousness of sin; and by that perfect response in Amen to the mind of God in relation to sin is the wrath of God rightly met, and that is accorded to Divine justice which is its due, and could alone satisfy it." [1]

Is not this an objective view? A satisfaction is offered to Divine justice rightly meeting the wrath of God through the sorrows of holy love endured in realising our sin of misery, and this offering is made by Christ in humanity for humanity.

" A condemnation and confession of sin in humanity which should be a real Amen to the Divine condemnation of sin, and commensurate with its evil and God's wrath against it, only became possible through the incarnation of the Son of God. But the incarnation of the Son of God not only *made possible* such a moral and spiritual expiation for sin as that of which the thought thus visited the mind of Edwards, but indeed caused that it *must be*." [2]

The loftier range of his ethical concept over that of the exponents of rigid penal theories is shown in the following statement :

" There is much less spiritual apprehension necessary to the faith that God punishes sin, than to the faith that our sins do truly grieve God. Therefore, men more easily believe that Christ's sufferings show how God can punish sin, than that these sufferings are the Divine feelings in relation to sin, made visible to us by being present in suffering flesh. Yet, however the former may terrify, the latter alone can purify." [3]

" The necessity for the Atonement was moral and spiritual, arising out of our relation to God as the Father of spirits; and not merely legal, arising out of our being under the law." [4]

Moberly criticises certain phrases which might be inter-

---

[1] *Op. cit.*, p. 117.  [2] *Op. cit.*, p. 120.
[3] *Op. cit.*, p. 122.  [4] *Op. cit.*, pp. 161, 162.

preted as apparently separating the Son from ourselves. In speaking of " the Son's dealing with the Father in relation to our sins " as also of Christ's Atonement on Calvary as " His expiatory confession of our sins," there is a suggestion of distinguishing between the Son and humanity. But this is far from Campbell's intention, as is abundantly proved by other statements.[1]  We ourselves feel compelled to set Christ's perfect humanity over against our imperfection, and in this sense He is other than ourselves. His is unique Sonship in all the glory of perfect holiness.

We must agree with Moberly that in his eagerness to oppose the view of Dale concerning the significance of the cry on the Cross, M'Leod Campbell has grievously erred in the other extreme.  By no possibility could we say less than that the cry is one of pleading remonstrance in the sense of being forsaken by God.  The sense is real, whatever interpretation we may put upon it, and it cannot be explained away.

To M'Leod Campbell : " An atonement to make God gracious, to move Him to compassion, to turn His heart toward those from whom sin had alienated His love, it would, indeed, be difficult to believe in ; for if it were needed it would be impossible. . . . The Scriptures do not speak of such an atonement . . . they represent the love of God as the cause, and the Atonement as the effect." [2]

He maintains that the atoning elements in the sufferings of Christ are the holiness and the love :

" To men believing the sufferings contemplated to be strictly penal, the pain as pain should be the chief object of attention, being indeed that for which alone, on this view, a necessity existed."

The foremost blessing is deliverance from SIN, rather than from the punishment of sin.  Deliverance from punishment is secondary.[3]  Atonement is conceived as directly related to the gift of eternal life, manifested in the life of Sonship.  The righteousness of Christ is imparted to us, and not only imputed.  Christ is the perfection of the beauty of manhood.  This is to be reproduced in us through the power of Christ.  " It seems difficult," says Moberly, " to

[1] See Stevens, *op. cit.*, footnote, p. 214.
[2] *The Nature of the Atonement*, p. 17.      [3] *Op. cit.*, p. 165.

estimate too highly the debt which Christian thought owes to that reverent spirit." [1]

Through the spiritual warmth of the personal element introduced by Moberly into his book *Atonement and Personality*, we feel he is getting near to the heart of things. Perfect penitence is only possible to the personally sinless.[2] Therefore Christ alone can be perfectly penitent. His illustration of this in the sympathetic self-identification of a holy and devoted mother with her erring son, and her actual bearing of the shame of his sin, rings true to experience, for they are spiritual beings, and in the spirit realm she is in him and he in her. He dwells on the true penitence of that which realises and vitally experiences within itself the alienation of sin, and the penal averting of God's face which wrings from Jesus the cry on the Cross. There is no element of infliction or endurance of vengeance. This is too shocking and too blasphemous even for thought. The consummation of penitence carried with it the straining to their breaking of the vital faculties, the dissolution of the mortal instrument. That dissolution was also the consummation of righteousness by inherent power finally victorious through and over the utmost possibilities of sin.

Yet we feel there is something lacking. Has he carried his illustration far enough? We may carry it farther. The penitence is for sin of a loved one against God, holiness, righteousness. The loving Father's relation to mother and son is wanting. The son's sin is against a devoted father, the profound depths of whose LOVE for the erring son can only be known by the beloved wife who knows she is dearer to her husband than life itself. She volunteers to die to rescue and reconcile son to father, for that is her dearest desire, and the only way in which the son will awaken to the fulness of the love of the Father whose very heart is torn in voluntarily yielding his wife to save his son, and whose anguished penitence will be in exact proportion to his comprehension of the love of his mother, who at so great a cost saved him, and of the love of the father, who had what seems to be the harder task of yielding up to suffering the best beloved, to whom he is spiritually united as one, for the sake of the beloved son. Penitence is now only a subordinate factor, while yearning, sacrificing, victorious, doubly-saving love is the dominant force.

[1] Moberly, *Atonement and Personality*, p. 402.   [2] *Op. cit.*, p. 117.

The Father is saved from the loss of the love of the now penitent son.

The Son is saved from the loss of the enjoyment of the now realised love of the Father.

He says " Christ does not ' deal with the Father in relation to men ' by way of vicarious expiatory confession of sin, in Campbell's phraseology " (here, of course, he is striving to correct M'Leod Campbell), " for Christ *was* humanity perfectly penitent, and His perfect penitence involved death, not in any way as the endurance of punishment, but as its own consummation.   In bitter humiliation of a self-adopted consciousness of what sin—and therefore of what the damnation of sin—really is, He bowed His head to that which, as far as mortal experience can go, is so far, at least, the counterpart on earth of damnation, that it is the extreme possibility of contradiction and destruction of self." [1]

He is not very clear in this much-qualified statement of Christ's bearing of the penalty of sin, and Rashdall seems to have proved him to be somewhat confused and inconsistent at times.

Moberly shows the vital connection between the Atonement wrought for us objectively through the vicarious penal sacrifice of Christ, and that selfsame Atonement made effective through the operation of the Holy Spirit within ourselves.   This is one of his chief contributions to a fuller declaration of the doctrine of Atonement.

To *Forsyth* [2] the Cross is the central fact of history.   He claims that we have emerged from the " moral theory," not where we went in, and certainly sees in the Cross of Christ an objective value.   He fearlessly and deliberately uses the old words substitution, penalty, and satisfaction, but with an enriched and loftier significance.   He sees that the Church has slowly but surely progressed in her spiritual struggle to comprehend the mystery.   Through the illumination of the Holy Spirit we learn what to cast away and what to retain as precious truth.   We shed the husk that we may grow the tree.

Amongst the ideas outgrown are : [3]

---

[1] *Op. cit.*, pp. 133, 142.
[2] *The Cruciality of the Cross ; The Work of Christ ; The Atonement in Modern Religious Thought.*
[3] *The Atonement in Modern Religious Thought*, pp. 64 et seq.

(1) That God has to be reconciled; for the satisfaction made by Christ flowed from the grace of God, and did not go to procure it.

(2) That the Redemption cost the Father nothing, for the Son could not suffer without the Father suffering, and a forgiveness which cost the forgiver nothing would lack too much in moral value or dignity to be worthy of holy love or rich in spiritual effect.

(3) That Christ took our punishment in any quantitative sense. What fell on Him was the due judgment or condemnation of sin.

His was not merely sympathetic suffering, but an actual bearing of sin's condemnation.

A vicarious repentance for His holiness was impossible.

He who was made sin for us could never be made sinful, nor, being made a curse for us, was he accursed.

(4) That God can ignore sin. Much of the sentimental talk about the Love of God is dishonouring to Him. By the very nature of God and of human dignity He cannot lightly overlook sin. The Parable of the Prodigal is not a complete exposition of God's relation to the sinner. The punishment of the sinner is not an arbitrary ordinance which can be dissolved at pleasure by a kind God, for the law which ruins the sinner is as eternal and holy in the nature of God as the passion to make Him a saint.

" The dignity of man would be better assured if he were shattered on the inviolability of this holy law than if for his mere happy existence it were ignored." [1]

(5) That forgiveness was impossible till justice was appeased and mercy set free by the blood of Christ.[2]

(6) That satisfaction was made by Christ either to God's wounded honour or to His punitive justice. The obedience of Christ is of more importance than the suffering which is a condition of the Atonement. Not the mere act of dying, but the spiritual manner of it has saving value. Obedience unto death, and that the death on the Cross, showed the completeness of the

[1] *The Atonement in Modern Religious Thought*, p. 66.
[2] *Ibid.*, p. 67.

beloved Son's submission and sacrifice. Therefore we must not separate the life of obedience from His expiatory death. Each miracle cost a small Passion. He was inwardly in death's presence oft before the supreme pouring out of His soul.

Any adequate treatment of this solemn theme cannot rest on personal experience alone, but the experience of the Church must also be used, and the Bible must save the Church from wrong interpretations. Our forgiveness has an objective ground, and is inseparable from the death of Christ. Socinus' pronouncement that expiation and forgiveness are mutually exclusive would be true if the quantitative and equivalent idea of payment of the debt of sin be still held. But grace is still sovereign when God offers pardon to those who own in the Cross the *kind* of penalty their sin deserved. Jesus is the Revelation of God the Father in all His Love.

But this Revelation includes in its spiritual necessity judgment upon sin, as an accomplished and exhibited moral fact. We may have an adequate sense of the love of God in Christ without an equally real sense of His actual condemnation of sin. The revelation of holy love was itself such a judgment on sin as brought it to its utmost crisis and its final judgment. Forgiving love reveals its moral majesty. A due repentance contains an adequate sense of the evil done, and to this alone can there be forgiveness. This recognition of the majesty of the law of holiness is made by a conscience unblunted in its moral perceptions, because perfectly obedient, yet identified in sympathy with the sinful race. It is not repentance in Christ's case, but it is the source of repentance in us who are joined with Him.

The two polar experiences, joined in one spiritual and organic act of mystic union, form the complete type of Christian faith. The repentance is ours alone; the penalty is not, the judgment is not. The penal judgment or consequence or curse of sin did fall on Christ, the penitential did not. The awful atmosphere of guilt was His, He entered it and died of it; our chastisement was on Him, but God never chastised Him. Our saving repentance is not due to our terror of the judgment to fall on us, but to our horror of the judgment we brought on Him. The end and intent of the judgment on Him was our judgment of ourselves in Him.

" Where did the difficulty lie that was to be overcome by Redemption ? " [1] asks Forsyth. " Was it in God or in man ? Was He dealing with a human attitude or a Divine relation ? We must answer both. The antithesis is but on the surface. . . . That which produces forgivable penitence in man is the expiation to law which bore first on God. Love's awful moving cost in satisfying the broken law and maintaining its holy and inviolable honour is the only means of producing such a sense of guilt as God can forgive. The difficulty of true repenting is the difficulty of realising that God took the broken law of His Holiness so much to heart that it entailed the obedience in agony and death of the Holy One."

No one, after carefully studying Forsyth, should be able to go back again with approval to the somewhat superficial and dissatisfying arguments of many who hold in an attenuated and diluted form what they imagine to be a purely ethical view. Their failure seems to be due to their imperfect doctrine of the Person of Christ, to their minimising of His essential Divinity. If Forsyth errs, he errs reverently on the other side, by laying such stress on the Divinity of Christ as might lead to a depreciation of the essential manhood of Him who was " very God and very man of a reasonable soul and human flesh subsisting," in one indissoluble unity of person, as, for instance, when he says, " When Christ did what He did, it was not human nature doing it, it was God doing it. . . . It was not human nature offering its very best to God. It was God offering His very best to man." [2]

To him Christ is supra-historic, supra-human and premundane. " None but a Christ essentially Divine could do what the Church . . . knows the Cross to have done for its soul." [3] In Christ God not only comes near to us, but by an eternal act makes us His own. Christ in His humanity is the Sacrament of Godhead. God does in Christ the one thing needful for the holy redemption of the race into the Kingdom. Christ approves Himself as a Divine Reality by His revolutionary causal, creative action on that inmost reality whereby man is man. Christ is more

---

[1] *The Atonement in Modern Religious Thought,* pp. 77, 78.
[2] *The Work of Christ,* p. 24.
[3] *The Cruciality of the Cross,* p. 30.

precious to us by what distinguishes Him from us than by what identifies Him with us.

Yet in this last statement Forsyth is not necessarily relinquishing the perfect humanity of our Lord. For such an expression is true of a strong, noble elder brother—albeit spiritually imperfect—as contrasted with a weaker, erring younger brother, who is full of admiration of the qualities he perceives in the elder, altogether wanting in himself. How much more, then, should we feel the distinction between Christ in His holiness and ourselves in our sinfulness ?

"In Christ alone," says Forsyth, "I have forgiveness, reconciliation, the grace of God, and therefore the very God." The Parable of the Prodigal Son shows the love of the Father running to meet, but the act of Jesus dying on the Cross shows Him dying to save. It was a creative act oɪ God, whereby man was brought to a new relationship with the Father and the whole race's relation to God is changed.

"In presenting Himself Christ offers implicitly, proleptically, the new Humanity His holy work creates." [1] The Cross is the crowning moral act both of God and of *humanity in Christ ;* it set up a new covenant and a new humanity. " As it was the Cross that universalised Christianity, so also it is the Cross which is the permanent and creative thing in it." [2] Only a study of his books can reveal the eager and profound reverence of Forsyth for the crucified Saviour, whose holy love redeems us.

After this brief and imperfect survey of Post-Reformation views concerning the Atonement we conclude with some reflections and suggestions as to the necessity and the nature of the redeeming work of Christ.

By God's creative act man is fitted to hold correspondence with God. This is implied in the demand that man should act in accordance with the Will and in conformity with the character of God. This alone accounts for the justice of the indignation of God, which is His personal holiness, burning on behalf of man for the removal of that which either wittingly or unwittingly man is doing and becoming, which is " indignus," unworthy of the proper being of true man. He is not egotistically indignant against man for

---

[1] *The Work of Christ,* p. 192.    [2] *The Cruciality of the Cross,* p. 170.

offending against His august majesty, His sublime holiness, or His impersonal law or government. But His fires of purification are the heat of personal love removing from humanity all that is inconsistent with the truth of human nature at its best, all which therefore hinders or prevents perfect reciprocal relationship between our Father and His loved children.

Viewed in this light, the burning indignation hot against sin can no longer be regarded as a curse, but is one of God's greatest blessings; for the positive dross, the active principle of evil, is being burnt away, lest it defeat the end for which man was created—namely, that he and his Father might take mutual delight in their spiritual fellowship. This claim that man is normally fitted for communion with God is most certainly *not* the assertion that some inherent power of spiritual perfection belongs to man independent of, and apart from, the Grace of God. It is God's highest gift in creation.

Personality cannot express itself without relationship to other personality, and all its powers are derived from the great personal Being, the Father-God who has endowed His children with these potentialities. This relationship, which exists by virtue of God's created act and power, can be increasingly exercised by the interpenetration of personality through influence of voluntary wills willing to cultivate ever more perfectly this growing power of intercommunion, which we are only just beginning dimly to comprehend.

In His ardent longing for the development to perfection of this loving fellowship and co-operation amongst His children, God has endowed us with the God-like power of freedom to will. God uses every spiritual power and effort consistent with His own essential Being and man's created likeness to woo and win man into ever closer intimacy with Himself. The only compulsion, therefore, can be love. This love is agonistic in its ardour, majestic in its awe-inspiring perfection of the holiness of pure Being, and antagonistic in its purifying indignation against all which impairs or mars or breaks that closest fellowship which is the desire of the heart of God, and the only satisfaction for which He yearns and victoriously labours.

Without this full communion He cannot rest content, for without it man's personality, his affinity in spirit with his Heavenly Father, cannot become complete; with it

R

full delight of fellowship is attained, for man can then fulfil the one purpose for which he was created—namely, to glorify God and to enjoy Him for ever. Jesus is God assuming humanity for this loving purpose, and for ever glorifying it, by presenting before the amazed and adoring eyes and heart of spiritually perceptive man the glory of perfected humanity in all its Divine loveliness.

Jesus is man in perfect correspondence with His Father, delighting to will His Will, always doing those things which are pleasing in His sight, and thereby bringing joy and peace to their perfectly inter-related spirits.

All the agony of the life and death of Jesus is caused by man's inability and refusal, through the moral evil of sin, to become like his Father. He brings into humanity through the whole of His incarnate life of love a new dynamic which shall overcome this evil, and triumphantly completes the voluntarily undertaken task in the crowning act of love by His death, which is the fullest evidencing of God's love, and therefore the greatest spiritual force which God might use in His work of salvation.

He plants in the soil of humanity the seed of the Incarnate Word, causing it to germinate into vigorous life through the noonday ardour of the sunshine of that love poured forth from Calvary. Higher life through self-sacrificing death to the lower self is the mysterious law of the spirit world. We cannot understand the mystery of vicarious suffering, but we can humbly thank the Redeemer God that He Himself has shown its power to save, through the shame it engenders in the heart of the penitent son, who now hates the sin which caused the agony of God's best-beloved son.

Tennyson in his "Northern Cobbler" tells how the drunken husband in his insensate fury kicks his patient, loving wife, but when he comes to himself he says :

"An' when I waaked i' the mornin' I seead that our Sally went
    laamed
'Cos' o' the kick as I gied 'er, an' I wur dreadful ashaamed."

He repents and becomes a sober man. Her suffering love had been made visible, and caused him to hate himself for the sin which wounded her. Thus love became victorious through suffering.

Sin is failure to hold perfect communion with God. It is

caused by ignorance of the character of God and of our relationship to Him, and also by wilful refusal to act in accordance with spiritual impulses towards the realisation of that relationship. Perfect ignorance causes total failure to appreciate and develop latent spiritual powers, a lamentable lack of all response to the Spirit of God. Wanton disobedience causes actual decay of these powers, and when completed inevitably leads to spiritual disease and death.

Our past sins were indications of our sinfulness of heart, and each yielding to temptation has its immediate consequence within ourselves in deterioration of character, and also on the community, whose spiritual vitality is impaired by the evil influence of a degraded person within it. What we have been makes us what we are. God forgives persons and not deeds. God forgives by converting our hearts and transforming the person, so that he now hates what he loved, and loves what he hated, and is empowered to do the right.

There is NO forgiveness without change of heart and restoration to health of spirit.

God's forgiving grace causes change of mind and gives power of obedience. It is creative, and not transactional.

In forgiving me He is forgiving all the sinfulness of the past which is within me, and restoring to health the society whose vitality I have impaired.

His forgiveness of me is never only individual, for it includes all whom I influence for good through my conversion.

The word influence is to be taken in all its literal fulness.

Our lives actually flow into other lives more really than tributaries into a river.

In what real sense can we say that the penalty of our sin fell on Jesus, "who His own self bare our sins in His own body on the tree that we being dead to sin should live unto righteousness"? (I Peter ii. 24). Can we attach a significance to this statement which shall ring true and have nothing fictitious or even only metaphorical or symbolic in it? I think we can.

Surely the penalty of sin is that holiness dies. Love is slain by hatred, forgiveness by vengeance. The spiritual is slain by the worship of the temporal and material. We despise, reject and finally kill goodness through enthronement of evil, and this is the death which is DEATH indeed.

Now Jesus was the embodiment of holiness. He was love incarnate. He was forgiveness personified. He was goodness made visible. In other words, He was God manifest in the flesh.

By submitting to be slain He was actually bearing in Himself at one and the same time the judgment which falls on sin as it affects both God and man. This terrible just judgment of God was actually wrought out, not only in the heart and mind of the Saviour who agonised throughout His whole ministry for the sinful souls of men, but also visibly in and on the Saviour in the condemnation of sin which fell on His sacred Body. He is therefore the appointed voluntary bearer of the Wrath of God on sinful humanity. He is the manifestation in human flesh of what happens to man repeatedly sinning against the light. Here is revealed both the effect of personal and of corporate guilt.

But He is also the visible embodiment of the penalty of sin as it affects a suffering God, for this terrible judgment actually also affects God. In the process of sin's victory over man it is a defeat of God. He is banished from His rightful inheritance—man-soul, He loses the loyal obedience of His beloved children.

When Christ dies there is a triumph of redeeming love. Grace works the stupendous miracle of the Cross. Man is released from the bondage of corruption into the glorious liberty of the Sons of God. God is enabled to welcome home to His heart of love His self-banished rebellious ones, while man welcomes to his now loyal and gratefully obedient heart the God whom he, in deep contrition and humble penitence, recognises as his eternally loving, forgiving Father, who is also still as Father his righteous Judge and his wise and holy Governor in the spiritual Kingdom into which he is now uplifted.

Why was the death of Christ necessary?

(1) That there should be burnt into the heart of man for ever the consciousness of the depths of depravity to which man sinks through sin. But this could only be accomplished by the Son of God, the Lord of Love voluntarily taking on Himself to be done to death by sinners.

Adequate knowledge of the enormity of sin in its hatred of goodness could alone be shown in the rejecting and crucifying of the Holy Jesus and alone could lead to the due loathing of sin and to an adequate repentance.

Without the Cross there could not come this knowledge of the heinousness of sin and its awful effect on the soul of man, nor such a hatred of it as should lead to a true conviction of God's abhorrence of it. An effective penitence is created. SIN IS CONVICTED and DETHRONED.

(2) That the perfect love of God should be declared in the only language man can understand, namely, in an actual life lived in the flesh, perfect God becoming perfect man and pouring forth that love in self-sacrificing life of death.

The only way in which God's Name could be hallowed was through the holy Child Jesus living God's life in humanity, and in His death showing the heights to which holy love can go in humility, patience, forgiveness and self-sacrifice. A true understanding and a deeper reverence for holiness are created. In the Person of Jesus the God of holy love is revealed as exalted and enthroned. A true understanding of God is created.

(3) That man should be proved to be a spiritual being created for perfect communion with God who is his Father, and to this communion man can attain, for Jesus, who is very Man, has attained to it by perfect communion and obedience. The highest act of communion and obedience was in the perfected obedience in His death. In the Person of Jesus man becomes spiritually exalted and enthroned. A true understanding of the high destiny of man is created.

(4) That it should be fully actualised in human life that man lives in and for his brother man. There is no such thing as individual, isolated life. The life which is life indeed is wholly altruistic in its outlook and has no place for egotism. In pouring out His life entirely for others, Christ gained the fulness of life, and thereby enriched His brethren by the wealth of His love. Only a heart embracing the whole of humanity and loving to completion in a holy, forgiving love for His murderers could reveal this truth in all its fulness. A perfect knowledge of the relation of man to man is created.

(5) To show that God's will is to win His Kingdom and the voluntary allegiance of His children without the compulsion of physical or mechanical force, but only by the spiritual over-mastering force of wooing and winning love, shown in lowly service.

He wills to gain the willing loyalty and obedience of intelligent children whose only motive shall be reverent and grateful love to their all-holy Father; and that man can win the same Kingship and be seated on the Throne of God only by the same humble ministry. The refusal of Christ to claim an earthly kingdom is one of the chief reasons for His death. Love begets love and love alone has eternal lordship. A knowledge that the loftiest Kingship is attained by the lowliest service is thus created.

(6) To teach man how relatively unimportant is the changing scheme of the outward, material, visible and temporal when contrasted with the permanent, abiding reality of the inward spiritual, invisible eternal. " It is expedient for you that I go away." Here lies one reason for the sacrifice of the wounded body of Jesus in the early prime of vigorous manhood. There is created in man, through the death of Christ and resurrection to the higher life, a consciousness of the reality and supreme importance of the spiritual.

(7) That God's children should realise the cost to our holy Father's heart of the sacrifice of His well-beloved Son in ignominious death upon the Cross. There is a greater sacrifice of love even than the sacrifice of one's own life—namely, the voluntary yielding up of one's best beloved to death even for those whom we love, but especially when they are in open defiance and hostility of hatred.

" God so loved the world that He gave His only-begotten son."

There is created in this yielding up of His Son for us a new understanding of what is implied in " Our Father."

(8) That a regenerating, recreating, invigorating power should stream into man's life to lift him from the degradation of sin into which humanity had fallen

into all the fulness of spiritual life and restored communion with the Father.

All other miracles of Jesus pale into insignificance before this greatest of all miracles, the healing, life-giving power of the Cross. It is this alone which can bring the prodigal to himself and to the consciousness of the seeking and saving power of the Father through the Son.

By this sublime consummation of the Life of Jesus in the poured out life blood, mankind can say, " I am saved ; I am being saved ; I shall be saved."

There is generated in the Cross an Eternal Power of God unto Salvation for every man who comprehends and apprehends for himself the Truth as it is in Jesus. Within that life the salvation is effected as he lives the life of holy sonship to God and humble service to his fellows.

Each Christian who is empowered to pour himself out in selfless love is hastening this fulfilment of God's plan.

When a Christian nation, or a Christian Church, as a united body, in the power of the Spirit of Jesus, instead of using worldly weapons for the preservation of its existence or the upholding of righteousness, yields itself up for the redemption of the spiritual life of the world, our Lord will be one stage nearer to reaping the reward of the travail of His Soul and being satisfied in the increase of His Love, for they will thereby prove themselves to be very members incorporate in the mystical Body of Christ.

[The writer of this essay acknowledges his special indebtedness to the works of Stevens, *The Christian Doctrine of Salvation*, and of J. K. Mozley, *The Doctrine of the Atonement*, which he has used throughout the earlier portion of the essay.]

# XI

# ATONEMENT AND THE PROBLEM OF EVIL

## By The Archbishop of Armagh

For the Christian thinker, Atonement, however it be conceived, is the bringing of sinful man into a right relation to God. The Being of God, His perfect righteousness, our responsibility to Him, and the fact of Sin : these are assumed. They form the postulates of all discussion. " God is light and in Him is no darkness at all." That is declared to be the essential Faith. There is no evil in God. If there were, the evil in His creatures would need no other apology. He has placed us here, and given us the knowledge of the good and the power of choice : we must answer for our use of these gifts. We know that we have not used these gifts aright, and that human life throughout is corrupted by sin. As the necessary result, we discern that the Divine purpose for the moral universe has not been realised. Through sin, the Kingdom of God has not come as He designed.

So we may describe, in simple language, the situation, the moral and spiritual situation, which all generations of men who have grasped these fundamental ideas have felt to demand an Atonement. Indeed, the history of religion shows that the need of Atonement has been crudely felt and expressed in various ways by men of many races and cults who never approached the clear-cut moral conception of the relation between God and man which has been described. The need of Atonement lies deep in the heart of humanity.

We see therefore that the problem of Evil is very profoundly involved in any real consideration of the subject before us. Yet theologians have often failed to realise this : they have presented conceptions which evaded the main issue, seeking a solution in notions which have to do with human law or custom. It is not within the scope of our inquiry to examine the various theories which have been set forth. Though it may prove impossible to avoid reference to some of them, the subject of this essay is too great, and its limits are too narrow, to leave space for discussion of them.

The first task which presents itself is to ask, What is meant by evil? There are, it is commonly said, two forms of evil : physical evil, or pain, and moral evil, or sin.

As regards the first, while it is clear that it cannot in itself be regarded as an object of reprobation, the history of human thought shows that there is an almost inevitable tendency to connect physical and moral evil as somehow interdependent. The history of punishment, and the various doctrines connected therewith; the impulse to regard suffering as penalty inflicted by superior powers, witness the Book of Job; the idea of *Nemesis* in Greek thought; the Eastern conception of suffering and degradation as the result of sin in a former incarnation : all these reveal a conviction in the mind of man that sin and suffering cannot be separated. So universal in human experience is this relating of the two forms of evil that it might almost be called instinctive. Dr. Westermarck, indeed, finds the origin of punishment in resentment against injury, the reaction which makes a man desire to inflict pain on another who has been the cause of pain.[1] But why pain for pain, instead of the mere annihilation of the cause of injury? No reasonable man would try to inflict pain upon a stinging fly because it had hurt him, though he might destroy it as dangerous. It is the discerned moral quality of the relation between sin and suffering with which we have to do. It is only when there is a conviction that the offence has been committed by a being possessed of will, a being who has chosen to do the injurious action, that punishment in the true sense begins. Then there emerges that conviction which is wide as humanity, that the suffering of pain is the appropriate consequence of the doing of evil.

A very important criticism of this ancient doctrine has been forcibly expressed by Dr. Wildon Carr in a recent work, *Changing Backgrounds in Religion and Ethics*. He writes, " The old philosophy regarded the relation between physical evil or pain, and moral evil or sin, as direct and self-evident, and theology found it impossible to admit a doubt." The problems arising out of this doctrine, he continues, " tormented the human spirit in the pre-evolution period. There

[1] *Origin and Development of the Moral Ideas*, Ch. I and II.

was, moreover, the further difficulty that the lower animals
are certainly subject to physical evil, although in no sense
responsible for moral transgression.  This, indeed, proved a
serious stumbling-block to the theological interpretation,
yet until the theory of evolution there was no rational
explanation of the suffering of animals (if, which many were
driven to doubt, they do suffer pain), and it was relegated to
the inscrutable mysteries of Providence." [1]

The solution of the problem Dr. Carr finds in the discovery
that " pain is a vital product as specific as sight, hearing, or
touch, and, like these sensations, is to be judged by its
utility."   " Pain is not punitive; it is a form of consciousness with distinctive quality and positive value.  It is a
mode of sentience contrived for an economic function and
having a distinctly utilitarian end."   " Over the whole
surface of the body it has been discovered that there are
terminal neurological organs beneath the outer cuticle which,
when stimulated, produce sensations of four differently
qualified kinds.  They are named the heat, cold, touch, and
pain spots.  This discovery that pain is a specific sensation
with a specific sense quality, ultimate and unanalysable, the
direct result in consciousness of the stimulation of a definite
sensory receptive nerve terminal is of the highest significance."   And what is that significance ?  It is that " pain
is a biological factor with a distinct psychical function.
It is not superposed or inflicted." . . . " It is not dis-
ciplinary.  It enters as a specific and positive element into
the psycho-physiological scheme of living activity."

The truth of this account of pain as an effective element
in the development of animal life cannot be questioned.
In our own experience, the sensation of physical pain is, in
most cases, a warning.  Our limbs and other bodily organs
are in constant danger of injury, from which we escape
because the sharp sting of pain bids us beware.  Pain is
indeed, for every sensitive creature, a means of deliverance,
a way of salvation.  It is not, however, to be denied that
the sensitiveness which, on the whole, is a useful element in
animal life, can become a means of severe suffering which
passes beyond its proper function.  This is mere matter of
experience; and it is, surely, this excess of pain in the world
which creates the real problem.  Also, it is a problem which
becomes more and more urgent as we ascend from lower

[1] p. 197 ff.

forms of life to higher forms.   It would seem that there is
but a limited capacity for pain among creatures of lowly
organisation, and that the volume of animal suffering in
Nature is not nearly as great as we imagine it to be when
we read our own more developed consciousness into the
experience of animals.   It is in man that suffering assumes
its more intense and poignant forms, because in him there is
a power of reflection which looks before and after, and also
because, in him, on account of his far higher development of
nervous organisation, even physical pain must reach a greater
intensity than with creatures of lower kinds.   But the worst
sufferings in man are not physical at all : they are hurts of
the soul, disappointments, fears, social injuries.

When we turn from physical evil to moral evil we find
ourselves confronted with an even deeper and more tremendous problem.   The seat of moral evil is in the Will.
" There is nothing," said Kant, " in the world, or even out
of it, which can be called good without qualification, except
a Good Will."   This is the truth which our Lord teaches us,
throughout all His moral instructions—that good and evil
proceed out of the heart, they are not qualities of merely
outward actions.   And to the inwardness of the good
corresponds the inwardness of the evil.   Just as the good
will is good in itself, so the evil will is evil in itself.

When we so speak of the will we think of the single
decision, the act.   The act is qualified by the motive :
indeed the motive is just the inner side of the act, and its
quality characterises the act.   But acts may become
habitual, and so there come into being virtues and vices.
Virtue, as Aristotle taught us, is " a habit of choice "—that
is, habitual will to do the good.   Vice is also habitual will,
a habit of evil choice.   Evil in the moral sense may therefore
be the quality of a single definite act, or the quality of a
character that has a disposition to commit evil acts.   This,
we shall find, is important.

The problem of evil is the distressing thing that it is for
our thought, because it overthrows all the mental construc-
tions by which we try to think out a universal scheme of
things.

Philosophy is an endeavour to think of the Universe as a
rational whole.   Evil is an irrational element which we
cannot eliminate.   Theology is the endeavour to uphold a
Divine administration of the Universe.   Evil makes a

breach in every systematic attempt to preserve the Divine sovereignty. If the Universe is ultimately irrational, as some of our recent thinkers seem to suggest, then there is no problem of evil, nor is there, in the last resort, any consistent thought on any subject. If we believe in God, but fail to believe that He is ultimately sovereign in the Universe, then is there no reason to believe that He will finally overcome the forces which oppose Him. The dilemma is a terrible one. It seems to strike at the very root of faith, the faith that helps us to live and work and hope, the faith that, in the end, God must prevail, and the good be triumphant.

In our own day this dilemma pressed with terrible force on minds that never attempted to think in the terms of theology or philosophy. " Can God," men said, " be indeed a God of love when He allows the awful evils of the Great War ? " Or, " If he be a God of love then He must be a God of very limited power : He can be in no sense omnipotent."

Such questions as these lead to sceptical habits of mind, and they underlie much of the frivolous abandon of the years which have followed the War.

And so the problem of evil is a puzzle not for the student of theology only : it is, consciously or unconsciously, a potent agent of agnostic suggestion in the minds of the seemingly thoughtless men and women of our time.

A very daring effort has been made by the movement called Christian Science to solve this problem by denying the reality of evil. Both sin and pain are, according to this teaching, illusions belonging to " mortal mind." If by a great act of insight we can rise to the conviction that God is all and that God is good, these unrealities, sin and suffering, will vanish into nothingness, the afflicted soul and the afflicted body will both pass into a condition of health and happiness.

This doctrine was expressed in a manner which called down the judgment and often the ridicule of critical minds. But it must be confessed that, in essence, it is a solution of the problem which seems to resemble very closely one that has commended itself to many of the greatest thinkers. St. Augustine, in a well-known passage in his *City of God*, affirms that evil must be traced to a *deficient* cause, not an efficient cause. " Let no one therefore seek the efficient cause of the evil will—it is as if any one should wish to see darkness or hear silence." [1]

[1] *De Civ.*, xii. 7.

An affluent, but hardly consistent, thinker, Augustine's doctrine here is difficult to reconcile with the theological system which he built up in his controversy with Pelagianism. It would seem that he took refuge in this denial of the positive reality of evil in order to avoid attributing it to the design of the Creator. This has indeed, in one form or another, been the common device of the puzzled theologian.

John Scotus Erigena, whose greatness as a Christian thinker is being more and more recognised, holds that evil is, properly speaking, causeless. The Free Will cannot be evil. Evil is the irrational motion of the will, and therefore contrary to its freedom. He goes even further. Like St. Augustine, he compares evil to shadow in relation to light. The dark shadow in the picture contributes to the beauty of the whole. From the Divine point of view there is no such thing as evil. As the shadow of the earth, which we call night, does not extend infinitely into space, but reaches its apex at a certain distance and is then swallowed up in the glorious rays of the sun, so evil must finally be merged in the perfection of God. Mr. Bett, in his valuable study of Erigena, identifies his doctrine with that of Origen, John of Damascus, Anselm and Aquinas. Certainly the last named follows Augustine in describing evil as *defectus boni*.

This doctrine, wherever it appears, is an abstract construction, designed to avoid attributing the responsibility for the existence of evil to the Creator. It is not based on the facts of experience. The modern scientific conception of evolution yields a doctrine which may be placed side by side with it. According to this view, evil is a survival of qualities and modes of action which belonged to more primitive stages in development. Actions which are natural and free from blame at such stages become evil when the living creature reaches a higher level. Evil, it may be said, is the persistence of brute instincts in the life of man. And, as man progresses, it is the emergence of lower tendencies in the lives of those who have reached the higher stages. For example, the slaying of the clansman of another tribe is regarded as a good deed at a certain stage in social order. So it is among Wazirs and Mahsuds to-day, on the north-west frontier of India. Among people who have attained to a higher ethos, such an action is the crime of murder. Relying on these facts, there are those who regard them as proof that morality is mere matter of custom, that there is no absolute right and wrong.   If what is right at one period is condemned as the worst of crimes at another, how can there be an eternal standard ?   We are back again, by another path, at the idea that sin, if not an unreality, is entirely relative to the thoughts and habits of men.

Against all these views there are very serious objections. It is to be observed that, whether with the philosophic theologian or the modern evolutionist or the Christian scientist, the doctrine of the unreality of evil rests upon certain abstract considerations.   There is no sufficient examination of the facts.   Moreover, some of the arguments depend on physical illustrations which have no validity. Good and evil are not like light and darkness : they are not physical facts, but qualities of personality.   Darkness is the absence of light, but is sin merely defect of goodness ?   It seems clear that when we come to consider qualities of character, virtues and vices, good deeds and evil, we are dealing with things very different from the mere negation of a physical quality.   Can an evil character contribute to the ultimate perfection ?   Can it, like the shadow in a picture, help to the beauty of the whole ?   If God's design in the Universe is the full realisation of His Kingdom, surely we must believe that every good deed and every good character helps towards that great end, and every evil deed and every evil character hinders it.   Or, to examine the actual facts, it would seem that an evil deed or an evil character is just as positive an existence as we can imagine.   An act of cruelty or injustice is certainly a positive reality.   And even though repentance and consequent forgiveness may help to lift the sinner out of his degradation, they cannot undo the past or make the evil deed to be a good in itself.   Still more evident is it that a character hardened in evil is a positive element in the moral world, working mischief continually, and, though change of heart may come, and the crust of evil habit be broken through, the evil influences of the past cannot be undone.

There is a further consideration concerning this whole doctrine of the nature of evil which must be mentioned here. Adopting the imagery of Augustine and Erigena, and viewing evil as the shadow which contributes to the beauty of the whole, it becomes clear that there is a confusion of thought.   For the shadow, as part of the picture, is not an unreality.   It is an essential element in the whole.

Abolish the shadows and the picture ceases to be. Strictly speaking, what we have here is the doctrine that evil is an essential element in the whole system of things. It is part of the Divine intention, a contribution to the perfection of God. Also, on this view, there is no reason to think that evil will ever cease to be, because if it is now an element in the totality of the Divine order of things, why should it ever be eliminated ?

Turning now to the evolutionary doctrine which regards evil, as we find it in human life, as a survival of a more primitive order, it would seem that there is a confusion of thought here also. Because, while it is quite true that actions which are permitted in one state of society are forbidden in another, it is also true that, at every stage of social progress, there is a good and evil relative to the moral condition of the social order of the time. To get at the moral quality of an action or a character, you must consider it in relation to that condition. The action of Jael in enticing Sisera into her tent with lying promises and then killing him in his sleep seems to us a specially base treachery. It did not appear to be evil to the tribal morality of her time. It was a splendid, a heroic action. But, according to that same morality, a similar action, committed upon one of the warriors of her own tribe, would have been evil indeed in the sight of her people. At every stage of society, when the distinction between the morally approved and the morally disapproved has once been apprehended, there is always a better and a worse, a good and an evil. The evil man of to-day may refrain from deeds which the good man of five thousand years ago would have done, because the standard has risen, but that does not change the fact that the good man of old was good relatively to the position in which he stood, and the evil man of to-day is evil relatively to the standard of his own time. To affirm this does not involve the denial of an absolute moral standard. The absoluteness of morality can mean nothing but this—that there is a final perfection towards which all that we call good is less or more an approximation. We get therefore no nearer to a solution by shifting the problem from the conditions of the present day to those of a remote past.

We have seen that the source of evil is in the will; and that just as the good will is intrinsically good, so the evil will is intrinsically evil. Also we have now seen that the evil will and the evil character are no mere unrealities : they are not mere defects or negations : they are positive and real.

Good and evil emerge as the will comes to itself in the exercise of that power—that freedom—which properly belongs to it.   If there is such a thing as the power of choice, it means that the will can choose between several courses of action. Here emerges the old controversy about the nature of this choice.   It was said long ago that whatever choice a man makes, he selects that which seems to him to be the good. Therefore no man is ever willingly evil, and all man needs for goodness is knowledge.   But the argument forgets the influence of passion and of habit, which delude the mind so that it chooses as its good that which, in times of calm reflection, or in better moments, as we say, is discerned to be evil.   If action could always be with a " single eye," no doubt it would always be good so far as the illumination of the conscience extended ; but sometimes the light that is in the man is darkness : then how great is that darkness !

There is then the choice between good and evil, and it is just this which creates the moral situation.   It is this also which constitutes the discipline of life by which character is formed.   Now the choice of the good implies the possibility of evil.

This conclusion has been contested, and on two grounds : first, that it implies that, of Good and Evil, " we cannot have one without the other."   But this is exactly what it does not imply ; for it is the very nature of the moral, as distinguished from the physical, to leave open diverse courses of action.   Secondly, a saying of Augustine is said to formulate the truth : " It is a great liberty to be able not to sin ; but the greatest liberty is to be unable to sin." This saying, no doubt, expresses a truth, but does so in a very inaccurate manner.   For the word " unable " here can mean nothing but a will so formed that without effort it resists and overcomes temptation.   Such a will is indeed the mark of the highest moral liberty.   But, so far as our human experience goes, no such will exists anywhere except in those who by continued victory over temptation have attained to it ; and even then, when fully formed—if such a condition be supposed in any merely human being—it is still " Will," and therefore not rightly to be described as " unable " to exercise choice.[1]

It is this possibility of evil involved in the very nature of

[1] See von Hügel, *Essays and Addresses*, Second Series, pp. 202, 203.

will which creates the chief difficulty of the whole tremendous problem. For it seems to mean that the whole course of history, and the realisation of the Divine purpose, are at the mercy of the will of man. Also, as a matter of fact, we find that, so far as we can trace the course of things, God's purpose for the world has actually been defeated. Moreover, if this power of choice remains, there is no security, it would seem, that Supreme Will, aiming at the perfection of the whole, will ever be able to overcome all oppositions. In the face of such a fact, how can we maintain an unshaken faith that God and goodness must, in the end, prevail ?

This is no new problem : but it has certainly been accentuated by the history of creation as unfolded by modern science. In days when men thought of the world as created only a few thousand years ago, and as formed by the Creator, and left by Him in a state of perfect happiness and moral purity, and then defiled by a definite act of rebellion, from the effects of which it was soon to be cleansed by a great Divine interposition, the problem of evil could be regarded as an unhappy incident, a passing phase, in the eternal history of the Universe. But we are taught by a whole cycle of the sciences that the world is many millions of years old, that living things have existed upon it for millions of years, that man himself, though relatively a newcomer, can be traced back for probably hundreds of thousands of years, and that all through that great history living creatures struggled with one another, devoured one another, inflicted and suffered pain; and that, when man appeared, he dwelt in no happy sinless Eden, but fought, a creature of dawning powers, among wild beasts, until he gradually won for himself some degree of security, and of what we now call civilisation. In this tremendous story we find pain far more deeply rooted in life, and sin far more seemingly inevitable, than in the old story of our childhood. The Creator, if there be a Creator, seems far more directly responsible for the sufferings and sins of His creatures than He appears to be in the Biblical account. For, in the scientific account, the fierce competition which brings pain and sin is part of the order of things from the beginning.

What can we say in answer to this question ? How can God whom we describe as a good and loving Father have brought into existence a world in which the fierce strife of one living creature with another was inevitable ?

It is certainly impossible to answer this question in any

s

complete or conclusive way; for we know not the meaning, scope, or implications of the original creative activity. But we can see that, out of this strange, and in some respects terrible, history, has arisen a race of beings endowed with intelligence, will, moral faculty, æsthetic powers, and all those qualities and characteristics which we sum up as the spiritual attributes of humanity. This human race, with all its imperfections, possesses the gifts which can form the foundation of a moral order, and which can even enable it to respond to the moral character, the holiness and love, of the Creator. Yet, man's moral powers being what they are, there can be no certainty, so far as we can see, that such a result will be attained. The uncertainty arises from the very nature of the moral choice as we find it in ourselves. It follows that to bring into existence a world in which feeling and thinking beings could enter into moral and social relationship, and in which they could be fitted to know and love God, a tremendous risk had to be taken : moral freedom had to be launched upon its age-long adventure, and gifted with the power of choice between good and evil, in order that, by a right use of its opportunities, it might ultimately attain to harmony in a moral and social order under the rule of God. There was and, from the nature of things, there could be, no other way. Here we have the true meaning of the narrative of the Fall as we read it in the book of Genesis. The truth there expressed is the fundamental principle of all life.

It is profoundly interesting to observe that biological science is now tracing a primitive indeterminateness, a spontaneity of individual conduct, very far back in the Life series. Recent observation of the movements of those microscopic animated jellies which are termed *amœbæ* has shown that these primitive creatures are no mere automata. They exhibit, in their pursuit of one another, a power of selection and of the adaptation of means to ends in view of changing circumstances which it is hard not to describe as conduct. And this spontaneity of action can be traced from this lowly beginning up through the long history of developing life until we reach its highest point in the will of man. Feeling, thought and will, the elements of our psychic life, blended in the unity of our conscious existence, have come to themselves as the result of a long history which began when first sentient life made its appearance.

This consideration is of the utmost importance for our

present purpose, because it shows that pain and sin, the two forms of evil, spring from the same root. In order to feel the attraction of aims corresponding to the circumstances of its life, the living creature had to acquire sensitiveness, some degree of awareness, and some inward urge depending upon feeling. Out of this state sprang all that we call mind and will. Pleasure and pain, desire and satisfaction, hope and attainment, fear and disappointment, are all involved. These elements, beginning in the crude impulses of lower beings, find their full realisation in man's life. And, as they emerge, they bring to light, first the tremendous fact of suffering aware of itself, and then the distinction between good and evil.

Nor does it at all affect this conclusion that suffering is built upon the foundation of a psycho-physical mechanism which first came into being in order to serve a biological purpose. The same is true of the higher life of man in every department.

Linked thus in their origin, these two elements, suffering and evil, interact in their history. The emergence of the distinction between good and evil puts man upon his trial as a moral being, and the essential quality of moral discipline is the enduring of suffering in order to do the good, or to overcome the evil. Through the conflict which thus arises the moral life of humanity is created. Here also is the sphere of the great problem of Atonement which fills so large a place in the religious experience of mankind.

While all this is true, it is a mistake to darken too much the shadows. Life in itself is happy. Every living thing attains the bliss of at least one adventure. Most of the pains of animal life are short : most deaths are painless. It is the sentimentalist, not the man of science, who thinks of the age-long struggle as an age-long agony. To man, it is true, suffering brings a keener sorrow, for he looks before and after. But that is the cost of his higher calling, the mark of his greatness.

It is in choosing the good and rejecting the evil that the will finds its highest exercise ; and the conditions which enable this choice to be made involve as their very essentials the sentient life of pleasure and pain, and the moral elements of good and evil. The actuality of pain and the possibility of evil form the school of discipline in which man is made.

Christianity adds the affirmation that God has not left

man to struggle alone, but has entered human life in order to enable him to overcome, enduring the pain, with him and for him, and giving power for the conquest of evil.

From this natural history of suffering and sin, we gather that moral evil is not an essential element in the total scheme of things, nor, on the other hand, is it an unreality. It is a state of human life arising, though not necessarily, from the contingency which must belong to any order of things in which moral and spiritual attainment is possible.

Here arises the question whether this tracing of evil to the contingency which is an essential condition of moral life sufficiently accounts for the enormous development of evil, for the corruption which enters so deeply into human character, and for the cruelty, vice, and degradation which mar the history of mankind. Whence came all this ? Is it only to be explained by some doctrine of original sin, some inbred evil tendency in human nature ?

This is an old question, and has been attracting a great deal of attention in recent years. Two important works especially have dealt with it : Dr. Tennant's *Origin and Propagation of Sin*, and Dr. Williams' Bampton Lectures, *The Ideas of the Fall and of Original Sin*. The former regards the sinful tendency in man as the survival, the persistence, of the crude animal tendencies which, in his animal ancestors, were natural, but which, after the emergence of man's moral nature, became the source of evil. Dr. Tennant does not regard these instinctive tendencies as themselves evil : they become the source of evil when, by their brute strength, they impel man to turn aside from the path marked out by that higher nature to which he has attained. This is a very reasonable theory, and is in complete accord with the modern evolutionary view of Creation.

Dr. Williams' view seems to approach very closely to a revival of a doctrine which the Church rejected as a Gnostic heresy in the early days of Christianity. He thinks that evil goes far more deeply into the sources of our life than Dr. Tennant admits ; and that it must be traced to a pre-mundane Fall of the *Anima Mundi*. The *Anima Mundi* is conceived by him as the Life-Force imagined by some recent thinkers. Created by God and entrusted with the process of world-evolution, this being fell, and imparted to all created living things from the bottom up some share of its own fallen nature.

It is our old acquaintance, the δημιουργός, so well known in the Gnostic and Neo-platonic speculations of the first centuries.

This speculation seems to be too fantastic to secure our adhesion. Dr. Tennant's view, though some criticisms are possible, seems far more in accordance with experience and sound judgment.

Whatever view we adopt, we are now confronted with the certainty, as it seems, that the creation of beings capable of moral faculty and moral conduct involved the possibility of evil. And this means that by calling into existence a world of spiritual beings in whom He could find a moral and spiritual response to His own nature, the Creator took a gigantic risk. God is revealed as the Supreme Adventurer. From the point of view thus reached, there is no certainty that this great venture will be justified. It may, so far as we can see, end in failure. But this we can see—that the venture thus made reveals a far higher degree of moral nature and also of creative power in the Supreme Being than would belong to the character of a Creator who created either : (1) a world of mechanised beings who could act only in a way previously determined for them, or (2) an order in which the sufferings and sins of His creatures were only the shadows in the picture necessary to make its perfection complete. If we believe that the highest thoughts about God are the truest—which is surely the very essence of faith—then it becomes clear that the conception of an Adventurer God is infinitely more worthy of our acceptance than is the idea of a Supreme Being who makes us to be all that we are, whether good or bad, in order to promote his own glory.

The following conclusions seem to result :

(1) The end of the universal process is not settled beforehand.

(2) Though the ultimate perfection must take the form of a universal order in which the supreme blessing must be one and the same for all—that is, a perfect social order—a Kingdom of God—this is a form which may include an indefinite variety of contents.

(3) Victory over the oppositions of evil wills must be attained by moral force, not by physical or non-moral means.

(4) The only moral power known to us which would seem adequate is Love—Love as the attribute of God. For, more than any other spiritual power, it can conquer an opposing will without destroying it. It overcomes and at the same time realises to the full the highest powers of its object.

The objection which at once springs into being as we consider this view of the Universe as a great adventure is that it seems to leave us with a final uncertainty as to the outcome of the whole process. The Divine Adventurer may fail, the evil may prove too powerful to be overcome, even Divine Love may not ultimately succeed in triumphing over the oppositions of evil wills. So it would seem.

To deal with this question, we must get back to our pre-suppositions. The basis of the old theology and also of the old philosophy was that the reason which belongs to our own mental system is the perfect clue to the whole system of the Universe. The final rationality of the universal plan was the fundamental pre-supposition. In justification of this principle it would appear that the reason we find in our mental constitution is the best instrument we have got, and, if it fails, there is nothing more to be said. But philosophers, from Plato onwards, recognised a higher and lower use of reason. And in a series of great thinkers, from Plato to Hegel, it may be observed that the conception of degrees of reality is, if not actually expressed, yet implicit.

In our own time, a great movement, affecting both science and philosophy, is revealing the fact that the various spheres of our knowledge are defined, it might be said constituted, by processes of abstraction. Thus geometry deals with the pure abstraction of space; arithmetic with the abstraction of number; physics with the abstraction of measurable quanta of energy, defined as the capacity of doing work; biology with organic creatures who have what we call life; psychology with mental phenomena; philosophy seeks the principles involved in our experience as a whole and therefore must take account of all the things we know and do, or, at least, of our way of knowing and doing. The boundaries so indicated are to some degree breaking down at the present time, but the principle remains.

It will be seen that this series rises from the thinnest abstractions, space and number, until it includes all experience. Philosophy deals with experience as a whole. It seeks rational principles which give system to experience as a whole. In this search, it cannot be said to have attained any real agreement. But it can hardly be denied that this is a fair description of its aim.

Now there is one final problem which confounds all the systems of the philosophers and theologians : that problem is the relation of the individual mind and will to the whole. There is no principle in reason, so far as we can discover, which can get rid of the individual point of view by merging it in a universal system. The disagreements of philosophers are a perpetual witness to this fact. But it is really quite obvious when we consider that the world of experience, though we must assume, as the basis of our intercourse, that its framework is similar, or identical, for everyone, yet is presented to everyone from a unique point of view. What thus becomes clear from the side of Knowledge, becomes startlingly evident when we turn to Will. The individual will confronts the world with an independence which is all its own. It may yield to persuasion, to fear, to enticement, to love; but it has also the power to refuse all yielding. This is the very quality which makes it capable of good and of evil.

From all this follows the conclusion that the unifying power of reason reaches its limit when we ascend to the consideration of the multitude of spiritual beings possessed of mind and will. There are degrees of reality below this level which can be unified by our reason, but here this power fails. Yet we cannot believe that the Universal Scheme of things breaks down where *our* reason finds itself limited. The whole analogy of our Experience points to at least *one supreme degree of Reality beyond us*. For God, there must be a final Unification. This final unity may surpass our thought, but we must believe in its existence. We may, indeed, venture to think that what we call the Love of God, embracing all His creatures, is the best and fullest expression of the ultimate truth. We can even hold that we can know as an experience what is beyond our thought.

Here, it would seem, is the essence of the Christian doctrine of the Trinity, which means just this—that in God there is a principle of Unification higher in kind than any known in our experience. We cannot think this out, but we can see that it is inevitable. And it is just here that we get some indication of the relation of God to the problem of human suffering. To suppose that His attitude to sinful, suffering humanity is one of mere pity, mere sympathy, seems to affirm a remote transcendence, and to be contrary to every line of the New Testament. Very different is the view which sees in Christ God entering into human life, sharing our sorrows and, through that suffering, effecting our redemption. And yet, with this very faith, our belief in an ultimate Reality, beyond our thought, enables us to hold that in the highest height of being is a realm of Eternal blessedness where sin and sorrow can never enter.

We venture to say these things on so tremendous a subject, as St. Augustine says, " not that we may speak, but that we may not be silent."

If this way of regarding the problem as a whole be sound, we find that we have a real explanation of the reason why the problem of evil has shown itself to be, for every philosophy, an insoluble problem. Evil cannot be rationalised, because it has to do with just that point where the categories of rational thought have reached their limit. But it does not follow from this that we are wholly unable to grasp, by means of some analogy, the method of Divine Atonement. It may have to be admitted that ideas which were found satisfying at certain epochs in the history of Christian thought are now unsatisfying, perhaps misleading. Nor can we be sure that ideas which seem to approach the truth more nearly, owing to their relationship to the thought and experience of our own day, will be ultimately found more permanent. Yet we may venture to note the following points : they arise naturally out of our discussion.

(1) In the individual life, the overcoming of evil is accomplished by means of the enduring of suffering in the struggle against the temptations which spring from passionate desire or ingrained habit. All such struggle is itself a form of suffering. There is a great saying which the writer owes to a thoughtful friend,[1] that a world subject to sin but free from pain would be a worse world than this. Such a world would lack the moral discipline by which true character is formed, and by which strength for moral conquest is gained. If the conclusions we have reached above, as regards the purpose of God in Creation, express

[1] The Rev. T. B. Brown.

the truth, no matter how imperfectly, Atonement must be restoration. It may even be the winning of a more perfect fulfilment. Now the condition of the moral world being what it is, the only true restoration, or fulfilment, of the original Divine purpose, can be no other than such re-making of the character of each member of the social order under the headship of God that His Kingdom may come. Can such re-making be attained otherwise than by a discipline involving suffering?

(2) If this be interpreted to mean that, through the moral discipline of all individuals, whether here or hereafter, the Kingdom of God can come, the difficulty arises that no amount of such discipline can undo the lost opportunities, the sinful acts committed, the evil habits created, the evil influences exerted upon others.

But can we discern, or even imagine, any power which can undo these evils? Certainly no human effort, nor human merit—if there be such a thing—can help here. But, be it remembered, that, as we have seen, there must be in God a unifying Life which, passing beyond the grasp of our thought, can best be expressed as Love.

(3) In human life, Love has a strange transforming power which is all its own; though here it is subject to the limitations which belong to our nature. Yet human love, when it is pure and true, can, in a sense, undo the past. It can transform the lost opportunity, the old sins, the evil habits, even the evil influences which dragged down others, into objects of pity, and out of them create strong bonds of sympathy and occasions of self-sacrifice by which to raise up the fallen. We do not realise the miracle of transformation by which the most hateful things in our experience become, when grasped by the saving love of a mere human being afire with Christian pity, potent forces for salvation.

(4) This being so, it is surely within the range of our imagination to gain a vision, however dimly, of the effect upon the whole of human life of the entering into it of a Divine Person, sharing the Universality of Him in whom we live and move and have our being, and grasping in His Divine pity all the sins of all the generations. It is clear that such a Divine-human life must take into itself the tremendous discipline of suffering, suffering in relation to the whole of human sins, which must result from the contact of such an all-embracing life with the moral degradation of humanity.

The conception of the Divine Nature which results from this mode of regarding the mission of Christ is the loftiest, morally speaking, which it is possible to imagine. As the author of the Epistle to the Hebrews puts it, in a moment of supreme vision, " It became Him for whom are all things and through whom are all things, in bringing many sons unto glory, to make the Author of their salvation perfect through sufferings."

(5) For the soul which discerns the Love of God in the sufferings of Christ as Divine Saviour, that Love is experienced as a transforming power. The old sins, revealed in their new character as wounds inflicted on the love of Christ, are renounced, and at the same time so transfigured in the light of His self-sacrifice as to become fresh proofs of His goodness. Here is the actual experience of the Atonement. It is this experience which has carried the belief in Atonement through all the centuries of debate, and set a fresh problem for the theologians of every age.

In setting forth this series of considerations, it is not intended to form any complete theory, any doctrine, of the Atonement. The view here presented is that, in the last resort, theory is impossible, because the solution of the problem of evil lies beyond the limits of our thought, but that the nature of Love as known in our best experiences enables us to realise in fact what cannot be completely worked out in the terms of a rational theology.

## NOTES

I. The late Dr. Rashdall, Dean of Carlisle, in his great work, *The Idea of Atonement in Christian Theology*, Appendix I, criticises the appeal to Experience, on the grounds that it is (1) vague and (2) subjective, never giving knowledge of any objective fact except the fact that a certain feeling is felt. " Subjective emotion may enable a man to say that he no longer feels the guilt or the power of sin since he believed such and such things . . .; but when he declares that this experience of his is due to the objective fact that God has forgiven the sins of those who entertain such and such beliefs, this is something which he could not possibly know by immediate experience." But surely he can know that, when he discerns the love of God in Christ and in His work for man, there enters into the soul a power which

transforms all the conditions of the life; and it is not unreasonable to believe that this result is caused by a real
objective truth rather than by a delusion. After all, it is
true of every force that it is known only by its effects.

II. In the above essay, the various theories which have
been proposed for the Atonement have not been considered :
there was not space for such a discussion. Briefly, however,
it may be said that the difficulty which has prevented the
acceptance of these theories is the same in every case : it is
not clear how the atonement offered by one, no matter what
its nature may be, can be available for another. To
summarise this difficulty, so as to include all the more
prominent doctrines, it is impossible to show how the punishment, or confession, or obedience of Christ can serve instead
of the punishment, or confession, or obedience of the sinner.
Dr. Moberly, in agreement with the thought of Bishop
Westcott, put forward, in his *Atonement and Personality*, the
daring view that " Christ as man offered to God on the Cross,
not only the sacrifice of utter obedience . . . but also the
sacrifice of supreme penitence." But vicarious penitence is
as hard to justify as vicarious punishment. Indeed it is
much less within the bounds of moral experience; for if
there is anything which must proceed from the depths of the
unity of the personality, and from no other source, it is
penitence. There is only one solution of this problem. If
it can appear that Christ, as universal in relation to mankind, includes all men, His work will be seen to possess a
universal validity. And surely when we regard Christ as
the very Incarnation of that Love which is the ultimate truth
of the Divine Nature, we discern most clearly the real inner
quality of the Atonement.

III. The philosophical conceptions involved in the fore-
going discussion are more fully discussed in the writer's
*God and Freedom in Human Experience*, and, in a more
popular manner, in his *Christianity and the Supernatural*.

## XII

## THE ATONEMENT IN PERSONAL EXPERIENCE

### By L. W. Grensted

"Jesus died for me." All the wonder of the Atonement is in those four short words, and they are written large upon the lives of the Saints of every age. They are the common ground which underlies all the theories, and their direct appeal has undying power, power which has often been weakened rather than reinforced by expositions and explanations. For the various theories of the Atonement depend in each case upon the thought of the age, its practical problems, its political and social outlook, its moral and intellectual standards. But the personal experience of Atonement is in its essence one and the same in every place and age, and for every race of man. The differences are differences of exposition rather than of life, and when we criticise the Ransom theory of the fourth century as crudely superstitious, the Penal theory of the sixteenth century as involving a conception of God's wrath impossible to us to-day, the Moral Theory of the nineteenth century as a mere emotional subjectivism, we have to remember that men holding these different theories have alike found in the Cross the key to the problem of life, have felt the bondage of sin and what it is to be free, and have known that this deliverance is not of themselves but of God.

The devotional language of the saints is one in every age however widely their professed theologies may differ. It is very striking to note the similarity, for example, between Anselm and Abelard when they are not writing formal theology. Set side by side this, from Anselm's Meditations :

"But, O Lord, Thou that didst endure death that I might live, how shall I rejoice in my freedom, seeing it cometh but of the chains that bound Thee ? How shall I take pleasure in my salvation, since it is wrought but by Thy sufferings ? How shall I be glad of my life, which cometh only by Thy death ? " [1]

and this, from his prayers :

" Even as a mother, when her only son is taken from her, sitteth weeping and lamenting continually beside his sepulchre, even so I also, as I can, not as I ought, having in mind Thy passion, Thy buffetings, Thy scourgings, Thy wounds, remembering how Thou wast slain for my sake, how Thou wast embalmed, how and where Thou wast buried, sit with Mary at the sepulchre in my heart, weeping." [2]

with this, from Abelard's letters to Heloissa :—

" Gaze upon Him as He goes out to be crucified for thee, laden with His own cross. Be thou of the people and the women who were bewailing and lamenting Him. . . . Suffer thou with Him who suffered willingly for thy redemption, and be thou pierced with Him who was crucified for thee." [3]

The spirit of the two writers is identical. Both alike have found in Jesus a personal and individual Saviour. Because they are theologians they try to explain the meaning of what He has done for them, and they explain it differently. But redemption comes before theology.

Never has this personal experience been more finely expressed than in the *Dies Irae* of Thomas de Celano :

> Rex tremendae majestatis
> Qui salvandos salvas gratis
> Salva me, fons pietatis.
> Recordare, Jesu pie,
> Quod sum causa tuae viae
> Ne me perdas illa die.
> Quaerens me sedisti lassus
> Redemisti, crucem passus ;
> Tantus labor non sit cassus.

We may go back to the fourth century and we find Gregory of Nazianzus crying :—

---

[1] *The Devotions of St. Anselm. Meditation IV* (ed. C. C. J. Webb).

[2] *Ibid.*, Prayer I.          [3] *Ep. V.*

" He has ascended the Cross and taken me with Him, to nail my sin upon it." [1]

Or we may go forward to the seventeenth century and hear Traherne :—

> 'Tis death, my soul, to be indifferent;
> Set forth thyself unto thy whole extent,
> And all the glory of His passion prize,
> Who for thee lives, who for thee dies.

And the deepest devotion of the present day is touched by such hymns as

> Glory be to Jesus,
> Who, in bitter pains,
> Poured for me the life-blood
> From His sacred veins.

or Toplady's

> Rock of ages, cleft for me,
> Let me hide myself in thee.

Perhaps the most vivid example of all is to be found in Bunyan's *Pilgrim's Progress*. The story is an allegory, and Christian is, or ought to be, a lay figure. But Bunyan's amazing art, resting upon his own personal experience, has made Christian live and, reading, we share his adventures, his trials and his triumph. And in the scene where his sins fall from his shoulders and roll away to the foot of the Cross we are conscious that this is no mere allegorical representation of a piece of theology. It is an individual and a personal happening. Jesus died to save mankind. That is true enough, but it has no meaning until its truth is applied to our own case. Jesus died for all. Wonder of wonders, that means that He died for me.

And so we come back to our original formula : Jesus died for me. The theologians have been greatly concerned with the preposition. What exactly does that " for " imply? Does it mean " instead of " or " on behalf of " ? Is there a substitution involved, a victim offered where I ought, by every rule of justice, to have suffered for my own sin? Or does Jesus act as, in some sense, my representative, entering into the suffering that sin brings upon itself and so pleading for man before the Father's throne? The history of the doctrine of the Atonement is in effect a history of the interpretations of that one short word.

[1] *Or. XXIV.* 4.

But the word " for " is not the word that we naturally stress in the sentence. The emphasis is upon " Jesus " and upon " me," and upon the ever-new marvel that the two words can be uttered in a single sentence at all. Herein is summed up the experience of the saints. They grow in the knowledge of Jesus, that is, the knowledge of God in Christ. And in the light of that knowledge they grow in the knowledge of themselves.

In detail and in order the form of their experience varies. In some cases, and these perhaps the most striking, the beginning is with themselves. There is unrest, bitter dissatisfaction and self-criticism, an unsolved conflict between will and desire. The good that they would they do not, and the evil that they would not, that they do. Augustine, Francis of Assisi, and Luther stand as types of a great company, led by St. Paul himself, who have sought peace and have sought it long in vain. It is here that we find sudden conversions, sometimes accompanied by ecstasy or vision or a sound of words spoken, and followed by changes of character that all may see. We must distinguish this experience of conversion from the wider experience of redemption, of which it is a part. Conversion is very largely coloured by the temperament or disposition of the person concerned, and in many cases shows marked pathological features. And often these very features, explicable enough to the psychologist, have been regarded as miraculous, authenticating the conversion itself. But the real authentication lies beyond the moment, in the newly-ordered life, in the unified self which has replaced the old divided self, in an experience of redemption which is enduring, resting as it does upon a new sense of God in Christ. Here the knowledge of the self comes first, and then, with the knowledge of Christ, that knowledge is changed and enlarged, until, in the most triumphant cases, it almost ceases to be knowledge, for the self forgets itself in God.

For others, perhaps the more normal type in times of a settled Christian tradition, it is the knowledge of Jesus that comes first. Understanding comes slowly, but the facts are there, in the pages of the Gospels, in the preaching of the Church, in the lives of men. And as understanding grows, the conviction of sin grows too. They see themselves in the light of Christ, and more and more their unworthiness of His example, their unfitness for His friendship, is brought home to them. And so they too come to the wonder of the experience of atonement. They find themselves at the foot of the Cross and know that He who hangs there, the sinless One, the Lord of all life, God and Man, hangs there for them.

And so, for both types alike, the word that falls next for emphasis is the word "died." There can be no question among men that death is the supreme and final sacrifice. "Faithful unto death " [1] is the highest praise that we can bestow. "Greater love hath no man than this, that a man lay down his life for his friends." [2] But man, even at his best, is apt to make bargains. The cause must be a good one. He for whom we would shed our blood must be a friend, or at least one helpless, and innocent in his help-lessness. "Scarcely for a righteous man will one die : for peradventure for the good man some one would even dare to die. But God commendeth His own love towards us, in that, while we were yet sinners, Christ died for us." [3] Helpless we are indeed, in the struggle with sin, but innocent we are not. It is by our own fault that we are in such sore straits. We could understand the help of such another as ourselves. Sinner may well help sinner, pitiful and unavail-ing though that help must be in such a warfare. But that such a Friend should stand with us in our need, sinless Himself and with the victory already won, dragged down by His loyalty to us to that broken, shattered death, dying as robbers and murderers die, and even in His dying lifting the robber at His side to a courage and hope that could look beyond the grave, that touches our very heart. It is not until we have grown in grace and understanding that the amazing condescension of the Incarnation itself over-whelms us, as at the very close of his life it overwhelmed St. Paul.[4] But the condescension of the Cross strikes home at once. We may not understand it, or be able to frame a theology about it at all. And when we do attempt to give an account of its meaning it all seems pitifully cold and meagre. The language of devotion serves us better than that of scientific theology. "Ye are not your own, for ye were bought with a price." [5] To explain such a sentence in terms of detailed and human analogies is to destroy its

---

[1] Rev. ii. 10.        [2] Jn. xv. 13.        [3] Rom. v. 7, 8.
[4] Phil. ii. 6–11 has no parallel in the earlier Epistles.
[5] I Cor. vi. 19, 20.

power. The overwhelming immensity of the cost enthrals
our emotion and breaks down our self-love and our pride.
Later on we may, if we have the philosophical mind, seek
for an exposition of the analogy, or even challenge its exact
suitability, but that is a secondary and not a primary
reaction. Faith comes before understanding, and faith is
born of love.

> The very God ! think, Abib; dost thou think ?
> So, the All-Great, were the All-Loving too—
> So, through the thunder comes a human voice
> Saying, ' O heart I made, a heart beats here !
> Face, my hands fashioned, see it in myself !
> Thou hast no power nor may'st conceive of mine,
> But love I gave thee, with myself to love,
> And thou must love me, who have died for thee ! ' [1]

If we ask, then, what is primary and essential in this
experience, the answer is that it is just its externality, its
objectivity, what von Hügel has called its Givenness. Not
of ourselves, or of our seeking, hardly even of our desiring,
cometh our redemption. All is of God and of His giving.
No effort and no desert of ours is worthy of such a gift.
In this truly religious and evangelical estimate of self, to
use Ritschl's phrase, all the saints agree. It is no prerogative of Protestant orthodoxy, but is as Catholic as
salvation itself. And herein is the truth of the preposition
" for," the last word of our formula to claim our attention.
That which is done is done for us and not by us, and it is
done by God Himself, at a cost such as we can dimly feel
but may never wholly understand. " Herein is love, not
that we loved God, but that He loved us, and sent His Son
to be the propitiation for our sins." [2] This is the key to
the strange power of the doctrine of election, as we meet
it in St. Paul, in Augustine, or in the Calvinists. Logically
it should be no better than the barest scientific determinism,
or the fatalism of Islam. To all appearance it should make
moral effort absurd and mission preaching an almost cruel
appeal to those for whom appeals can have no ultimate
meaning. But in fact the preaching of a Jonathan Edwards
or a George Whitfield has moved men as men are seldom
moved by any preaching to-day. The uneducated, almost
uncivilised, colliers who were swayed by Whitfield's words

[1] R. Browning, *An Epistle.*    [2] I Jn. iv. 10.

T

as by a very wind of God, were not thinking of the logical consequences of the doctrine which he preached. For them it was enough and more than enough that God had taken into His own hands the issues of sin and death. The Cross had set them free.

When we come to inquire more closely what is implied by this objectivity, this givenness, of the Atonement, the logic of our investigation moves in two directions. The fact of Atonement is grounded as a fact of history, with a definite, a complete, and a final occurrence in time and place. And at the same time Atonement, if it is to be my Atonement, and all our analysis has gone to show that this is fundamental to my experience, must be here and now. We may take these points in turn.

Christianity is distinguished from all other world-religions by the unique stress which it lays upon its historical setting. It does not start as an idea, or a principle, or a universal truth. It starts from a particular happening, the life of one Jesus of Nazareth, who revealed the possibilities of human nature in a character uniquely balanced, uniquely strong to help His fellow-men, and uniquely sure of God. And this life ended in shameful disaster. For no reason other than His sheer goodness, because He would make no compromise with the standards of His day, He was put to death in that manner which most completely marked man's condemnation. And on the third day He rose again. All this is history, and just because it is history it is particular, objective, and unchanging. It is like a sentence spoken, a poem written, a picture painted. As a fact each of these is unchanging and complete. The significance may change, with new knowledge, new circumstances, new powers of interpretation. But interpretation cannot create the facts which are its object-matter, and this externality of the facts is that which secures the interpretations from the danger of relapsing into mere impermanent fantasy. "What is truth?" asked Pilate, little thinking that his own act was about to secure truth for ever from that charge of subjectivism which his question implied. It is just because the Cross is a fact of history that we are set free from the possibility that our deliverance is no more than a dream, an imagining to which no reality corresponds. These things happened, and to interpret history apart from them—and we are part of history—is as absurd and unscientific as it

retributive justice. The God of Grotius is a benevolent ruler. The God of the nineteenth century was a loving but rather Victorian father. The movement in the twentieth century seems to be at present in two directions. The conception of the Fatherhood of God is being broadened out on popular and democratic lines into that of the good friend or loyal comrade. And, by a not unnatural recoil of feeling, there is a wholly new stress upon God's unapproachable and dominant holiness. To every phase its own theory of Atonement, all partial and all witnessing to the truth. But it is noteworthy that the one statement of the doctrine which has tended to persist throughout, concurrently with the changing theories, is its statement in terms of sacrifice. For the thought of a sacrifice offered blends with the thought of a sacrifice made, and the utter objectivity of God's self-giving is set forth in terms of cost, a cost so great as to pass human understanding.

Our analysis of the personal experience of Atonement has been elementary enough from the point of view of technical theology. The one advantage of this method of approach is that it has served to throw up in relief those features in the picture which make a strong and, as it seems, unfailing appeal to men of every type and age. And so far as many, perhaps the majority, of Christians to-day, or in any period, are concerned, this analysis probably sufficiently covers the facts. They do not think clearly, but they feel deeply. They know that Christ has set them free, and that this thing is not of themselves, but of God. Beyond that their thought is confused, if they think at all. Nevertheless at two points we may press the analysis further without going outside that which is at least implicit in any Christian experience of Atonement. These two points are the identification of Jesus with God and the individual conviction of sin. We have already touched upon both in our discussion of the two main ways in which men have entered upon the experience of Atonement. We may now consider them rather more fully.

To the ordinary man, untrained in philosophical thinking, the word "God" has no very direct meaning. It comes down to him with the general tradition of the most solemn and ultimate things, and his attitude towards it is perhaps best expressed by a circular argument. His God is that which moves him to worship, and it moves him to worship because it is his God. Obviously this is not logic, but there are deeper things than logic, and this attitude of submission, reverence and, in the end, trust, is one of them. It is the acceptance of a general position with regard to life and its problems, a position from which they are viewed as worth while, as having meaning and hope, even though that meaning and hope are for the moment hidden. And for the ordinary man his own life and his own individual problems are inevitably the starting-point. It is only later, as sympathy and knowledge grow in him, that his own problems are seen to be one with the problems of the world. When any fact, be it a fact of history or of science, is accepted as especially significant, as a clue to the solution of these problems, man makes an assertion about God. The laws of science are such assertions in the field of knowledge, and though they do not claim validity beyond their own special subject-matter, the scientific attitude of mind is inherently a religious attitude. But a law of science is at the best only a generalisation, an abstraction, and cannot completely cover the significance of any of the particular facts upon which it is based. The case is very different with the fact of Christ. To accept that fact as final and supreme does not mean merely an assertion about the nature of God, though the proposition " God is love " is, indeed, an inevitable conclusion. Our very acceptance of it as final means that as a revelation of God it is for us complete. We may not wholly understand it. We may be wholly unable to remodel our lives by its standard. But we have made our choice. For us, and, we believe, for all if they could but see, God has revealed Himself once and all-sufficiently in Christ. The fact is more than the theology.

That there has been, and indeed is, such a fact as this is the great certainty upon which Christianity is founded. It is this and nothing less that lies behind the conviction of personal Atonement : Jesus died for me. To make this assertion, with this particular and individual reference, is at once to rest upon history and to go beyond it in a single act of faith. The revelation of God in Christ is not bound to the time and place from which it goes forth to man. That Jesus died is an event dated " under Pontius Pilate," that He died for me is a truth of immediate experience now. And I do not merely mean by this that the historical effects of His death, the new spirit which has been slowly transforming civilisation, or the great fellowship of His Church are available for me. I mean something much more immediate and personal, something that no dead Christ could mean or do. He it is that takes my life in its weakness, its transience, its failures and its disloyalties, and brings it into touch with its Maker again. The Jesus of Calvary is the living Christ, and the conviction that this is true is implicit in the experience of all those who lay their burden at the foot of His Cross. But if that is so, the revelation of God in Him is not limited to a moment of history. It lives in all history as the living Christ enters into the lives of men, suffers there and is betrayed, is crucified there, and there once more conquers sin and death, rising to a newness of life that is beyond their power. But this eternal miracle of regeneration is for us the very key to unlock the mysteries of the universe. So, and so alone, the God whom we would worship becomes the God whom we can worship. Apart from Christ we can fall down before the altar of the Unknown God, but our adoration is a mere crying in the void. In Christ we worship with a new certainty, for we know that what He has done for us is to make available for us such life as His own, perfectly one with God. And so side by side with the impulse to worship God goes the impulse to worship Christ Himself. And in this we feel no disloyalty. The two impulses are a single impulse. In the life of worship Christ is God and theology does but confirm that which we already know.

The saints have differed, and will differ, in the expression which they give to this truth. For some, and those the more philosophically minded, the thought of God Himself becomes more and more dominant as they reflect upon their experience. Christ has been for them the Way to God and the Truth of God, and God is now all in all. The classical example of this is to be seen in Augustine's *Confessions*, the most clear-sighted religious autobiography ever written. It comes almost as a shock to us to note how little is said in the book about Christ. God is everything, and if there is but little said of Christ it is because in Christ Augustine has found God and has lived, since that great moment in the garden when the voice said "Take and read," amazed and overwhelmed at the splendour of that discovery.

But for others it is the thought of Christ which becomes

more and more dominant. These are not the thinkers, and their experience is perhaps nearer to that of every-day men and women. As a type we may take Francis of Assisi. Christ had found him and held him, and his whole life becomes more and more one with that of the Master whom he follows. For him the human figure of Christ crucified grows until it fills all his horizon. The pattern of the life of Christ is stamped upon all that he does, and all life finds its meaning in Christ, until at the last upon the mountain of his vision all nature and all being seem to him merged in that stricken figure upon the Cross, and the stigmata upon his hands set the seal of God upon his life. Francis is as full of Christ as Augustine is full of God. And there is no conflict between the two types of experience. Jesus and God are one.

In both these cases we see that full faith in Jesus as God is a climax, as well as a beginning. Logically such faith is prior to the experience of Atonement, but " justifying faith " is only the first step in the Christian way. In life the meaning of the Cross for us and faith in God grow upon us together. There may be a moment of overwhelming conviction when our pride gives way and we fling ourselves at our Saviour's feet. And this is faith. But day by day and year by year throughout the Christian life that faith develops to new understanding and new devotion. At the outset of our pilgrimage we cry, " My Lord and my God," and at its close we have no more to say. Those few short words have grown in meaning until all time and all eternity are within their scope. Life's riddle is answered. There is no more bondage. The sons of God are free.

As the experience of Atonement brings us to knowledge of God, so also it brings us to knowledge of ourselves. It is the paradox of sin that we only come to understand it in its full horror when we look away from it to the holiness of God. The sinner may or may not be aware of conflict and distress, but it is just in so far as he ceases to be a sinner and yields to the love of Jesus that he learns what sin really is. And thus there is both truth and falsehood in the widely established belief that if we would be saved we must come to salvation by the way of the conviction of sin. The experience of Atonement humbles us indeed. But it is not by the contemplation of ourselves, however honestly undertaken, that we know ourselves as we are. To gaze into a

mirror is to see darkly.   Only as we come face to face with
Jesus can we know, even as also we are known.   To see
ourselves we must look away from ourselves.

And here the Cross of Christ is the supreme test.   It is
not simply as an atrocious crime wrought in the name of
justice that it awakens our sense of sin.   There have been
many and terrible crimes in history, and each of them tells
us something about human nature.   That there should be
men in whom these things are possible is tragedy enough,
but the horror of their guilt passes me by.   There is, indeed,
some satisfaction in the thought, " I could not have done
such things as these."   But in the Crime of Calvary it is
not the evil done that stirs my conscience, but the triumph
of good over evil.   I do not compare myself with Judas and
Pilate and Caiaphas, but with Jesus.   In the light of His
constancy, His courage, His patience, His love, my weakness and failure, and worse, stand revealed.   And so I come
to the conviction of sin.   For here is God, and what am I,
even to stand afar off and look upon Him ?

To start from the conviction of sin, as so many preachers
have done, is to start in the wrong place.   Denunciations,
however well delivered and however well deserved, will
arouse not penitence, but anger.   It is in the experience
of Atonement that conviction of sin is reached, and even as
we know our sin we know that it is put away.   The sinner's
penitence and his peace are one.   And this conviction is an
abiding part of the Christian life.   It marks its opening
stages, and it continues throughout.   For it is simply the
obverse of the conviction that Jesus is God, and of that
truth even the greatest saints have never penetrated to the
end.

What has been written in this essay is not an attempt to
frame a theology of redemption, but rather to express those
elements which have been generally implicit in the experience of the Atonement.   The few quotations which have
been given might have been multiplied indefinitely.   The
one question of importance which emerges is whether such
an experience as we have described is as typical of Christianity to-day as it has been in the past.   Undoubtedly there
is a weakening in the hold of traditional theology.   Many
are prepared to take Jesus as a great Example, but hesitate
to make assertions about His Godhead.   And side by side
with this we find what purports to be a wider charity, but

is in effect a refusal to accept the conviction of sin. No age has been so ready as the present with its excuses. It is impossible to escape the feeling that a great deal of our current Christianity has lost assurance and depth alike. We cannot do without the preaching of the Cross, a preaching by men who are not ashamed to say very simply and very directly, " Jesus died for me."

# XIII

## THE ATONEMENT AND SOME TENDENCIES OF MODERN THOUGHT

### A SERMON WITH AN INTRODUCTORY ESSAY

### By C. J. SHEBBEARE

THE late Dr. Bernard Bosanquet, shortly before his death, spoke of a recent " change in the fashion of philosophical argument." " A new rank," he said, " has been given to those primitive and indestructible instincts and emotions by which our sense of our incompleteness, in religion, in knowledge, and in social life, is made irrefragably clear."

By a " new rank " Dr. Bosanquet clearly meant a " higher rank," and he writes of the change sympathetically. He welcomes the new respect accorded to the primitive emotions. He would not, indeed, " abandon old arguments in which man embodied his sense of his unity with and in a Universe that excelled himself." But the modern method of " examining on all sides unities and discrepancies of concrete experience," of " exploring actual experience by appreciative analysis," appears to Dr. Bosanquet to be part and parcel of that " better and fuller logic," which modern philosophy devotes to its problems.[1]

In these remarks Dr. Bosanquet shows himself an accurate observer of facts. He shows also a profound insight into certain far-reaching tendencies which can be illustrated from facts—the writings of Continental theologians—which are hardly likely to have come under his own notice. Further, is he not probably right on the whole in approving the change which he describes ?

A great rôle in the drama of religion has been played in the past by doctrine which implies this " sense of our own incompleteness " of which Dr. Bosanquet speaks—man's

---

[1] See *The Meeting of Extremes in Contemporary Philosophy*, p. ix.

helplessness, weakness, need, failure, dependence, guilt,
impurity : and just now the doctrines of Sin, Grace, Redemption, Atonement, Election, the Fall, which had fallen somewhat into the background for at least a generation, are
receiving renewed attention.   The pulpit has perhaps hardly
yet returned to its old language : it hardly yet speaks of our
" offended God," our " lost and ruined world " ;  but there is
certainly an increased respect for those emotions to which the
doctrines of the need of Grace and Atonement are congenial.
Moreover, we are inclined to respect these emotions just
because, in Dr. Bosanquet's words, they are " primitive " and
seem " indestructible."   While the first effect of our discovery that conceptions such as that of " Eating the God,"
the "Dying God," belonged to certain savage religions was to
throw suspicion upon the corresponding Christian beliefs, our
present tendency is rather to argue that it would have been a
defect in Christianity if it had wholly failed to meet cravings
and requirements which seem native to the religion of
mankind.   Anthropology is now freely spoken of—pre-
maturely, perhaps, but confidently—as " confirming " the
Christian doctrines of the Incarnation and the Eucharist;
and such a conception is not wholly unconnected with those
elements in Dr. Bosanquet's thought which led him to
approve the "change of fashion" which his words describe.
He approved it partly because it furnished an antidote to
what is still, in his opinion, very common, " the specifically
ethical and non-religious attitude " [1] for which—to quote the
old humanistic paradox—" the end is progress."   Is there,
then, something in religion of which the " specifically moral "
conception of human life must fail to take account ?   In
particular, is there something narrow and inadequate in the
purely moral and " exemplarist " conception of the Atonement ?

The problem which Dr. Bosanquet's words set before us is
to form a correct judgment on this " change of philosophical
fashion."   The connection of this problem with theology
and with religion is obvious ;  and I suggest that the true
answer falls under two headings.   In the first place, we ought
to have nothing but approval for the tendency to return to
those aspects of religion which the " specifically ethical
attitude " has led us to overlook—the sense of guilt, the sense
of weakness and dependence, the need of grace and puri-

[1] *Meeting of Extremes*, p. viii.

fication. The more anti-Pelagian our theology becomes, the more it speaks of Sin, Guilt, the Fall, Election, Atonement, Grace, the better both for theology and for religion. But, secondly, this salutary " change of fashion " has involved loss as well as gain. Connected with this deepening of religious insight there has been a tendency to lose some of the ground which Hegel and Rationalism had won for us. With the revolt against the *shallowness* of Liberalism there has gone also a revolt against its *sanity*. There has been a tendency to return to something like the Roman doctrine of authority, the Roman antithesis of Reason and Revelation.[1] There has even been a tendency to assert that religion is, on its most characteristic side, irrational : that there must be in it something " given," in the sense of something not in any sense developed by reason from its own resources.[2]

Both these aspects of the change of outlook—both its " anti-Pelagianism," and its " Irrationalism "—may be illustrated by passages picked almost at random from that remarkable book, Karl Barth's *Commentary on the Epistle to the Romans*.[3]

Barth is not an easy writer to expound or to understand, and his Commentary will probably need to be worked through and thought through more than once before any reader will have gleaned from it all that it may teach him. Yet even a cursory study is enough to show that the book is a great book, and of vastly higher religious and intellectual value than Otto's *Idea of the Holy*, from which (on one side at least) the recent changes in theological outlook may also be illustrated.

Take, first, the doctrines which imply man's sinfulness, helplessness and need. God's " message of salvation," says Barth—and this is his standing translation of εὐαγγέλιον—must be received with " fear and trembling." [4] It is no story of the " divinity or deification of man," but the message of a God " of whom man as man can neither know nor have anything," and from whom, " for that very reason, man's

---

[1] See *Summa Theol.*, Part I, Question 1, Art. 1, conclusion.
[2] Wallace, *The Logic of Hegel*, 2nd ed., p. 8 ; German edn., 1840, p. 8.
[3] *Der Römerbrief*, 8–11 thousand. 1924, Munich. Barth has been accused of returning to original Protestantism and of returning to St. Thomas. The two charges, he remarks dryly, are not quite the same.
[4] *Der Römerbrief*, 1924, p. 4. For the phrase *der ganz anders ist*, see below, p. 308, note 3.

salvation comes." Man cannot save himself : " What is of man cannot save man." Our eventual righteousness must consist in our "fundamental renunciation of our own righteousness."[1] Man is fallen. In Jesus Christ—the " historic Jesus " who died about A.D. 30—" two worlds meet and part." Two planes cut one another : one known, the other unknown. " Our world " is the known : the world of " the flesh," of " men, time and things." It has been " created by God, but is fallen from its original unity with Him, and therefore needs redemption." [2] To this world man belongs. Sin, therefore, is the " specific gravity of human nature as such." [3] It is no " event or state, or sum of events or states," no " historical or psychological accident." It goes deep into the essential universal character (*Bestimmtheit*) of all human events and states. It is found " always and everywhere." " Sin is not a fall, or a series of falls, in the life of man ; but *the* fall," which is already present in human life from the beginning. Sin is there " even before it shows itself in the consciousness or subconsciousness of this or that individual man. Sin is a power even before it has become the will or disposition of any human person. Before the law Sin was in the world." Thus " man in this world is a prisoner." God's power is power of " redemption." We are " further from God than we imagine." Man's " creatureliness is his fetter ; his sin in his guilt ; his death is his destiny. His world is a Chaos, heaving formlessly to and fro—of natural, psychical and other forces." " To wish to conceive such a world as this as one with God, is *either* religious arrogance, *or* the ultimate insight which comes from God." But to get the " ultimate insight " we must " withdraw the penultimate insight from circulation." " As long as false money circulates, the true comes into suspicion." [4] The " penultimate insight " of which Barth here speaks is presumably that of the type of Hegelian philosopher who, without Barth's sense of the immense distance of man from God, of human life from the Divine standard of holiness, is ready to conceive God as fully realising Himself in the dialectical rough and tumble—rightly apprehended—of

---

[1] *Op. cit.*, pp. 39, 82, *Nur von Gott, immer wieder nur von Gott aus gibt es eine Gerechtigkeit des Menschen*, is a good example of his style.
[2] *Römerbrief*, p. 5.
[3] *Op. cit.*, p. 151. Cf. Wallace, *The Logic of Hegel*, 2nd ed., p. 56 ; German edn. (1840), p. 58 top.   [4] *Op. cit.*, pp. 12, 13.

nature and history. Such an identification of God and the World (*diese Welt in ihrer Einheit mit Gott begreifen zu wollen*) seems to Barth mere irreverence and spiritual pride.[1]

The difficulty of Barth's style proceeds partly from the fact that, amid free use of philosophical terms and frequent allusions to modern literature, he has the habit of throwing at the reader's head without explanation phrases and epigrams such as one meets with in sermons and devotional books. " Grace is the inconceivable fact, that God can be well-pleased in man, and that man may rejoice in God. Grace is grace only if it is apprehended as inconceivable." [2] " The man who believes, loves with Job the God who, in His unsearchable height, is merely an object of dread, loves with Luther the God who hideth Himself. To him the righteousness of God reveals itself. He—only he—is redeemed." [3] " Only the captive becomes free; only the poor becomes rich; only the empty is filled; only the Nothing becomes Something." [4] " Against all disobedience and ungodliness—literally " lack of reverential awe " (*Ehrfurchtslosigkeit*)—" on the part of men there is revealed the wrath of God." " The wrath of God is the judgment under which we stand so far as we do not love our Judge." This judgment is a " fact, quite apart from our attitude towards it ": it is, indeed, " the most significant fact for our life." " Man is lost, even if he knows nothing of redemption." [5] If " the captive remains a captive," then " in the place of the Holy God comes Destiny, Matter, the Whole, blind Chance, blind Necessity." But still " it is always God whom we really encounter. Even unbelief comes up against God. . . . God's wrath is the righteousness of God revealed to unbelief, for God will not be mocked. God's wrath is God's righteousness seen out of, and apart from, Christ." [6]

To those of us, however, who are accustomed to Evangelical theology—and especially to Evangelical religion—many of these epigrams will present no difficulty when once we have become accustomed to their unfamiliar setting—they agree so remarkably well with the customary language of old-fashioned Evangelicalism.

Take, for example, some of Barth's sayings about " good

[1] *Op. cit.*, p. 13.   [2] *Op. cit.*, p. 7.   [3] *Op. cit.*, p. 18.
[4] Quoted from Luther.   [5] *Op. cit.*, p. 18.
[6] *Op. cit.*, p. 19. Cf. the use of the word " Krisis " (= κρίσις), which seems to be the mark of all this school.

works." That Evangelical language should appear, to those who know it only from without, to be antinomian in tendency, to put religious belief and religious sentiment above right will and conduct, is not particularly surprising; and this is not the place to correct the error, as it is singularly easy to correct it, with a mass of documentary evidence.[1] It may suffice to point out that in the *Marked New Testament*— issued some few years ago by an Evangelical Committee— among the six passages in the Epistle to the Romans to which (among others marked less prominently) special attention is called by a pointing finger in the margin, there stands the text, " Shall we continue in sin that grace may abound? God forbid. How shall we that are dead to sin live any longer therein? " This text stands side by side with other texts similarly marked—" To him that worketh not but believeth on him that justifieth the ungodly, his faith is counted for righteousness." " There is no difference, for all have sinned "—but the prominence given to the disavowal of the intention to sin so that Grace may abound should make it clear that it is possible without antinomianism to love those texts in which the hope of justification through good works is repudiated. There is, indeed, perhaps no better question which an interpreter of this Epistle can ask himself than this : Why, even in St. Paul's own day, was it necessary to guard the Pauline theology against an antinomian interpretation? The answer will bring out the difference between believing (as Luther did) that God commands good works, and believing that we can ever do enough of these to satisfy the severity of His judgment. " In its own time," says Luther, " we shall handle this subject that the law and good works must be done; but here, where we are on the subject of justification, we cast away good works." To " ascribe justification " to these is to " take away the glory from Christ and give it to works."

In older Evangelicals, then, it awakens memories of familiar language when Barth speaks of what does, and what does not, justify a man in the sight of God. What justifies the Gentile of Romans ii. 14 is not what " man's judgment " would approve in him : [2] not the " good heart," the " idealism," the " religious dispositions," which the religious world might be willing to grant that he possesses. Nor, again, is it anything of the sort which Modern Civilisation (*der*

[1] I have given some of this evidence elsewhere.
[2] *Op. cit.*, pp. 42, 43.

*Mitteleuropäer*) chiefly values—personality, inwardness, character, mental maturity, breeding. It is not anything of this kind which " gives joy in heaven " : which God rewards (Romans ii. 6. 7) with everlasting life. What gives more joy in Heaven than the ninety and nine righteous—this " work of the law, which God has written in the Gentile's heart "— is something which only God can see.[1] Barth, following Scripture,[2] calls it repentance. But he is exceedingly anxious to distinguish it from anything that the " world " or the " Pharisee " would describe as " moral." " It is not the last, highest, finest act of man's righteousness for God, but the first basic (*grundlegende*) act of God's righteousness for men." [3] It is *God* who has written this work in their hearts. It is God's work, not man's; man's relation to it is passive rather than active. " Perhaps in the hour of death a mere state of terror before the mystery . . . perhaps something better and fairer. It matters not. In Heaven there is more joy over one sinner than over ninety and nine righteous." " Who hears the voice of conscience," he continues,[4] " as it speaks even in the lawless and godless ? Who sees through the dialectic of God and Destiny, Destiny and Guilt, Guilt and Atonement, Atonement and—God, in which men stand ? *God* hears. *God* sees. To Him speaks the silent, scarce conscious, thought. . . . God has before Him just that evidence in man's favour of which the human judge is ignorant. He knows that which we know not. Hence the incomprehensible possibility that the lawless come into judgment and are yet acquitted." [5]

Consonant with this attitude to " good works " are some of Barth's remarks about saintliness and piety. Barth shows to the full what the hostile critic of Evangelicalism may describe as the " Protestant animus against the Saints." This aspect of Protestantism is, of course, very unfairly judged, because the frame of mind from which it proceeds is misunderstood. I venture to think that I have myself known more Evangelicals who could keep Saints' Days with devotion than I have known non-Evangelicals who could

---

[1] *Op. cit.*, p. 43.        [2] Luke xv. 7.        [3] *Op. cit.*, p. 43.
[4] *Op. cit.*, p. 43, commenting on Rom. ii. 15.
[5] The elder generation of Evangelicals will remember well such sayings as " Do not assume of anyone that he is in Hell. We can set no limits to God's power to work secretly on the rebellious soul even in the moment of death."

U

preach with passion and conviction on the text " There is no difference, for all have sinned." Yet what text brings out so clearly that for the Christian preacher the great dividing line is between the " penitent " and the " non-penitent," the " converted " and the " unconverted "—not between the good and the bad, not between those who have made greater or less progress along the path to holiness ? For Barth faith is " never identical with piety "—not even with piety of the finest and purest sort.[1] For him, it is not the charming qualities, not the spiritual gracefulness, such as we justly admire in the Saints, which " avails before God ";[2] but rather the inward restlessness, convulsion, and awe (*Beunruhigung, Erschütterung und Ehrfurcht*), the sense of amazement and astonishment, of respect for that which is above us, an insight into the transitoriness of all that is human, a humility, an awed submission before God.[3] He speaks of the sense of being " broken down " (*Gebrochenheit*)[4] as identical with the " sense for God." In commenting on those who, " not having the law, do the things contained in the law "[5] Barth says nothing about their good deeds, in the ordinary sense of the words. He speaks solely of their uncomfortable inward feelings (*nörgelnde Unrast*), which, in spite of their original unpeacefulness, none the less point the way to the peace which passes all understanding. It is, of course, a vital question—when we are speaking of this humility, and " brokenness," and " awed submission "— what we are in awe *of*, and what we submit *to*. If we are in awe of the " eerie," the " weird," the " uncanny," the non-morally numinous—if we are in awe of something that cannot in the end be identified with the Moral Law, then we need the warning of the prophet who calls us away from "wizards that peep and mutter," and bids that God alone be " our fear and He our dread." In a world that contains a Rudolf Otto, it might have been well that Barth should have been more circumspect in his use of language. Yet, if we read him with sympathy and charity,[6] we shall find, surely, no

---

[1] *Op. cit.*, p. 15.   Note a number of similar expressions, pp. 4, 16, 31, 35, 36, 37, 38, 43, 84.

[2] *Op. cit.*, p. 41.                        [3] *Op. cit.*, p. 41.

[4] *Op. cit.*, pp. 41, 42.                   [5] Rom. ii. 14.

[6] It is to be remembered not only that Barth confessedly changes his language from edition to edition (see *Vorwort zur zweiten Auflage*), but that his theology is still in a state of development. Thus whether it will ultimately crystallise itself in a more or less rational direction is still perhaps an open question.

essential antinomianism in his thought, but chiefly a profound grasp of the lesson taught in the Parable of the Pharisee and the Publican and in Romans iii. 22, 23. "There is no line between Saint and non-Saint." [1] There are no visible circles of Saints, "exempted persons," Heroes, Supermen, Righteous, formed through the possession of Law, of the record of Revelation, of character, of Morality, of Sacrament.[2]   Of St. Francis he remarks—and even those who regard St. Francis as the disciple who of all others has walked most nearly in the footsteps of his Master must feel that something of this sort has needed to be said—that St. Francis so far surpasses Jesus in "love," childlikeness, and strictness [3] as to be (though, of course, unconsciously) "a living impeachment of Jesus." Whether we err, then, on the right hand or on the left, "all have come short." Degrees of saintliness exist and have their importance; but they must not be so dwelt on as to obscure the truth that there is no true righteousness but one, and that of each individual it can be said that he either possesses it or is definitely without it.[4] The saint needs pardon as much as the grossest sinner.

> "There may I, as vile as he,
> Wash all my sins away."

That side by side with the anti-Pelagianism of Barth's teaching—anti-Pelagianism of a distinctively Evangelical type—goes a certain "irrationalism" (which is perhaps not really vital to it [5]), will have been seen from some of the quotations already made. It is enough to point out that valuable as paradox may be in calling attention to aspects or presentations of truth which appear antithetical, but which have to be reconciled—important as it is to prevent the philosopher thinking that he has reconciled the oppositions, when in truth he has not done so—a philosophy which is contented to leave its oppositions as oppositions and its paradoxes as paradoxes is self-confessedly imperfect. It is all very well to say that God must be "known" as the

---

[1] *Op. cit.*, p. 32.
[2] P. 49. *Ausgenommenen*, used apparently in some sort of technical sense, is not quite easy to understand.
[3] *Op. cit.*, p. 32; see *The Mirror of Perfection*, Chapters II, IV, etc. (esp. the story of the brother who wants a Psalter).
[4] See *Römerbrief*, p. 17.
[5] See note 6 on p. 306.

" unknown." There is, doubtless, a sense in which this is true. But the problem is not solved for the philosophical theologian till he has shown clearly what that sense is.[1] The paradox left to itself is the statement of a problem, not its solution. It is all very well to say that the Gospel must be received with fear and trembling. But to say that man as man can know nothing about it, that no " experiences "— not even if they were of the highest rank—can do anything for us in this respect, but only simple objective knowledge of that which " eye hath not seen, nor ear heard," suggests a broad line of division between our thought and experience and something which comes wholly from above.[2] After all, " objective knowledge " is itself an experience : and if it leads me to think something different from what I was led to by some previous experience, there must be some attempt made to weigh and decide between the respective rights of the two. Such decision can only be the work of thought; and this implies that—however sharp be the opposition between Flesh and Spirit—there can be no absolute division between them. The unity of reason implies the unity of that world of reality with which reason deals, and which it knows. However much God may differ from man—or anything from anything else—the very difference is a relation, and the differing elements fall within a Whole (even if the Whole has to be identified with God). The one element may be so much to be contrasted with the other as to justify (at least for purposes of rhetorical expression) the use of Barth's distinction [3] between that which is merely " very different " and that which is " quite different," but there can be no difference without any unity at all, since difference itself is a relation. No two things can be so different as to be quite unrelated. So far as Barth means his assertions of complete difference to be taken with absolute seriousness, his system may be fairly called " Irrationalist."

What has been said above must not be taken as even a sketch of Barth's whole system or of its relation to other movements. There are various streams of tendency to be recognised. For example, Barth in some respects illustrates

---

[1] While there is probably no living musician who could satis- factorily finish the *Unfinished Symphony*, there are thousands competent to detect the inadequacy of any suggested ending. We know enough of what a satisfactory ending would be to recognise those that are *not* adequate. The adequate ending is known to us as unknown.

[2] *Op. cit.*, pp. 3, 4.     [3] *Op. cit.*, p. 431.

the remark of Dr. Bosanquet with which this essay opens.
Yet with much of what Barth writes Dr. Bosanquet would
have had little sympathy.  We have seen enough, however,
for the immediate purpose with which we are concerned.
There exists in the modern world a really strong reaction
against some aspects of theological Liberalism; first,
against its predominantly ethical conception of religion, and
secondly, against its impatience of paradox.

If from recounting the facts we are to pass to a judgment
upon them, it is clear that a revolt against liberal theology
can only be of intellectual or religious value after full justice
has first been done to the truth which Liberalism expresses.
The elements of Liberalism which chiefly concern us here are
its insistence on the absolute claims of morality, and the
absolute claims of clear thinking.

The problem, then, that confronts the modern theologian
seems to be this—Can we, while remaining true to the
recognition which Liberalism has accorded to the claims of
morality and the claims of clear thinking, learn the lessons of
the theological movement of which Barth is a prominent
representative ?

Dr. Bosanquet spoke—as we saw—of the advantages of
" examining on all sides unities and discrepancies of concrete
experience," and of " exploring actual experience by appreciative analysis."   Barth's distinctions, first, between those
rival ideals—" Nature " and " Culture "; " Materialism " and
"Idealism"; "Imperialism" and " Democracy"; " Church "
and "World" [1]—which he regards as falling *within* this present
world, and, secondly, the great contrast between the whole of
this present world and that unknown world of the Spirit
which lies *outside* of it and judges it, help to reveal to theology
the nature of its task.   If we are to extend our " appreciative analysis " to " all sides " of actual experience, our
task as theologians is a vast one.   We must judge and put in
its place each member of those pairs of conflicting ideals
which are such a familiar and yet such a characteristic
subject of modern thought.   We must judge the rival claims
of Mysticism and Rationalism; the rival claims of the
Classical and the Romantic : of the natural and the artificial;

---

[1] *Op. cit.*, p. 28.  We may be thankful for the insight which sees that
the opposition between the "ecclesiastical " and the " civil,"the Church
and the World, are not at all the same opposition as that between the
" Spirit " and the " Flesh."    Cf. p. 50, *jenseits aller Gegensätze.*

the relations between the Protestant and the Catholic elements in Christianity, and so forth.

But behind all these problems there lies a single and comparatively simple one. Can Barth's passionate sense of the sharp opposition between Nature and Grace, Flesh and Spirit, be reconciled with that belief in the unity of the world which is vital to a rational theology? Can we, with Hegel,[1] recognise the fall of Man as in one sense a "fall upwards"—a step in the onward progress of our race—and at the same time perceive the violent alienation from God which sin involves? Can we recognise the "negative moment" as a necessary part of the process, and yet keep loyal to what our moral consciousness reveals to us as to the evil of the bad will? That some disciples of Hegel have dropped into the worldly view of life against which Barth is in protest must be admitted. Yet Hegel himself, while rightly refusing to allow philosophy to be overawed by religion, speaks with respect of the "doctrine of original sin and man's consequent need of succour."[2] Surely the answer to our question is that when we have once recognised the opposition and contrasts which the movement of the Universe, the development of the Divine plan, necessarily involves, the mere sense of the qualitative sharpness and violence of these oppositions adds no new intellectual difficulty. The man of profound moral insight will see more clearly than others the "loss," "ruin," "estrangement from God," which sin brings with it. But he, too, will see more than others the glory of redemption. His clear sense of the reality and the depth of our downfall is perfectly consistent with his recognition that this utter downfall is the necessary condition of salvation; that the Fall is no game, or sport, or experiment; that God "shut up all into disobedience"[3] as the only conceivable means by which men could come to their highest good; that all is in "deadly earnest," for God as for man.

So much, then, to give the theological context in which the following sermon should be read. One remark may be added on the argument of the sermon itself.

---

[1] It is not always certain that Barth is thinking of Hegel whenever he uses language which in England we call "Hegelian." There seems, however, to be a genuine Hegelian revival in Germany.

[2] Wallace, *The Logic of Hegel*, 2nd ed., p. 54; German ed., p. 55.

[3] Rom. xi. 32 (R.V.). Cf. Beza's *Conclusit in contumacia*.

" The emotional demand," said a friendly critic of the sermon,[1] " for a doctrine of the Atonement I fully understand and can enter into.   My difficulty is with a rational statement of the doctrine in relation to the Fatherhood of God and the Person of our Lord.   I am willing to admit that there is a ' set off ' with regard to sin in the death of Christ, but I cannot see *how* it was so."

The criticism clearly is of the right kind.   Yet I suggest that it treats as one two distinct objections.

The first is compressed into the underlined "How ? "   I ask then, " What does this ' how ' mean for one who understands the ' emotional demand ' ?   What kind of further enlightenment is he desiring ? "[2]   If a man could say, " I feel clear that what is alleged to have happened on Calvary, in the general context in which it is alleged to have happened, would, if the whole story is true, satisfy my demands for

[1] The late Archdeacon Derry.

[2] I do not imply that there is no further question of any kind to be asked; for, in fact, at this point a very curious problem arises.   In the first place, moral and æsthetic judgments are judgments of *necessity*, not of contingent fact.   To say, " A treacherous intention is *de facto* shameful, but this might quite well have been otherwise," is palpably absurd.   But, secondly, a necessary truth is one that cannot be denied without open or hidden contradiction.   What other definition is adequate ?   To *show* a truth to be necessary we show the contradiction involved in denying it.   Moreover, the distinction between " It is " and " It must be " lies just in this— that in the latter case we are asserting that if we had sufficient knowledge the contradiction involved in denying the statement could be shown.   If no contradiction is involved in denying a truth, in what sense is the truth necessary ?

Now between moral judgments and certain other " judgments of necessity " there are two marked differences : (1) The contradiction involved in denying moral judgments cannot be shown *more geometrico*. We may hesitate to say that moral judgments are less certain than mathematical judgments, but, at least, we cannot " see into " their necessity in quite the same way as we do in mathematics.   (2) Insight into moral judgments involves a certain state of *emotion*.   Unless I feel some emotion of horror or dislike at a base act, I do not understand its turpitude.   Similarly, if I do not feel the incongruity of two jarring colours I cannot *see* this incongruity (see p. 317 below).   Since, then, our moral insight cannot be independent of this emotional state, we are supposing, as the condition of complete moral knowledge at each point, a state of emotional consciousness possessing a particular kind of clearness which, as a fact, our emotional consciousness never has.

This problem arises with every one of that class of judgments which it is now customary to call " judgments of value."

the cleansing away of sin and the general neutralisation of evil; and I see this clearly in just the same sort of way in which (see below, p. 315, Sermon, § II end) I know that the ' resolution ' for which the chord of the dominant seventh ' cries out ' is supplied by the chord of the keynote "—if he could add, " In each case I feel equally clearly that the emotional demand is thus satisfied to the full "—he would, surely, have no need to look further afield for an explanation. The only further enlightenment that he could wish for would be a fuller assurance [1] of the correctness, the justice, the objective validity, of his emotional demand.

Secondly, the critic desires a rational explanation of the Atonement with express reference to the personal relations of the Father and the Son.[2] Now here a theory which removes arbitrariness from the conception of the Atonement does at least something to ease the difficulty. If the Father and the Son are conceived as fully agreed that the cleansing sacrifice must be made, is it not as fitting that the Father should accept and demand it as that the Son should offer it ?


A SERMON PREACHED IN GREAT ST. MARY'S CHURCH,
CAMBRIDGE, ON MARCH 7TH, 1926.

" A fountain opened for sin and for uncleanness."—Zech. xiii. 1.

THIS text, understood by Medieval writers [3] as a prophetic reference to Christian Baptism, is probably associated in the minds of modern Anglicans rather with the doctrine of the

---

[1] See previous note, p. 311, note 2.

[2] The difficulties seem to be increased rather than lightened by the suggestion that Jesus went to Jerusalem deliberately seeking death; that He believed on religious grounds that His death was necessary, and therefore adopted a policy which must ensure His own condemnation. Would not such an intention be rightly described as fanatical ? The Gospel story suggests rational grounds for the visit to Jerusalem. Was it not a simple act of mercy to give the rulers of His people, at all risks, the chance of accepting His leadership ? The prayer in Gethsemane suggests that He regarded this chance as unlikely but not utterly negligible. It is, at any rate, one thing to recognise that God is fulfilling deep and hidden purposes, and quite another to guide life, not by duty to one's neighbours, but by supramundane considerations which take no account of immediate and obvious good.

[3] See *Summa Theol.*, Part III, Question 68; art. 4. cf. Luther on I John v. 6.

Atonement : of the cleansing sacrifice of the Cross.   At any rate it is well fitted to guide our thoughts on that subject.

The modern world regards this doctrine of the atoning blood with mixed feelings. " If anywhere there is religion which is genuine "—so a man will often say—" it is among the extremists : among those who preach the Atonement most crudely.   Their preaching, at least, bears fruit ; and if *I* could believe what *they* believe, the belief, I think, might transform me as it has transformed them."   " But then," he will continue, " *can* I believe it ?   Is not their doctrine either unmeaning, or else barbaric—and, indeed, even frankly subversive of morality ? "

These questions are so often asked that it seems well that we should consider carefully the various types of criticism with which the doctrine of the Atonement is assailed.   Two types of criticism are especially prominent : that which proceeds from the Naturalistic or Secularist unbeliever, and that which proceeds from the Liberal Christian.

I. The unbeliever's criticism of the Atonement is forcible. "What a monster," he says, "you make of God.   The Eastern tyrant is said to care little who is punished, so long as adequate punishment is suffered by someone.   But what satisfaction could a good God find in punishing the innocent ? " [1]

It is hardly a sufficient answer, though it is partly true, to say that this criticism is directed against a *caricature* of the Christian doctrine.   The criticism brings out difficulties inherent in the doctrine itself.   Nor is it sufficient to say, though this also is true, that the critic of this type commonly takes for granted all the presuppositions of an extreme individualism.

It is, however, entirely fair to point out, first, that the popular conception of an angry Father, conciliated towards mankind by a more placable Son, is alien to the whole spirit and letter of official Christian theology.   That theology declares the Son to be the " express image of the Father's person," whose relation to the Father is indicated in the comparison with it of the relation of the seal to its impress, of the flame to its light.   Again, this theology is not " official " only : it is implied in just those conceptions which are most in the mind of the simple believer.

Thus the conception of Christ as suffering *punishment*

[1] Cf. Shelley, *Queen Mab*, VII.

—especially punishment arbitrarily inflicted—has not been the prevailing form of this doctrine.

In the main, the Father and the Son have been represented in Christian literature as engaged, with entire mutual agreement and at great cost to themselves, in an absolutely necessary enterprise, in a work for man which was in the nature of things inevitable if man was to obtain salvation. " Love eternal, free and boundless, forced the lord of life to die." Father and Son alike are the " victims of pure love." It is involved in this conception that the work is due to no arbitrary requirement on the part of the Father, but is somehow a necessary condition of man's full salvation which God, who wills that salvation, must see fulfilled. Such a conception needs development and explanation. It may be assailed by many criticisms. But it cannot be said to represent God as harsh or cruel. It represents Him rather as afflicted to the utmost in the affliction of His people.

II. So much, then, for a type of objection which rests mainly on misunderstanding.

By far the gravest difficulties of the doctrine come to light when we consider the objections of the Liberal Christian. " You represent the Atonement," he says, " as a *transaction :* legal or quasi-legal in form." But no transaction of any sort is necessary in order that God may forgive the sins of the penitent. God *must*, by the necessities of His nature, forgive the penitent. The Divine forgiveness, on the fulfilment of the one necessary condition, " so acts as if it were self-acting."

With the latter part of this statement every Christian preacher must agree. What it asserts is the very essence of our Gospel. There is—there can be—no such thing in the world as an unpardoned penitent. But is this relevant as an objection to the whole conception of an Atonement ? Questions of this type, it is obvious, can only be dealt with in relation to those moral and religious ideas and experiences which call them into being.

Suppose, then, a common case. Suppose that with a long memory of flagrant sins behind me I come to true repentance. If I am penitent, then—however gross my sin and however recent—I am right in being assured of full forgiveness. But is there no place for shame at all ? Is there no stain upon my past ? Ought I to look back—can I look back—to my past sins without any sense of a defilement that they have left behind them ?

A preacher of the last generation raised the question whether the saved would for all eternity be tortured by the memory of their past sins. We could not, he said, wish to forget the history of our salvation : and yet, he felt, the memory of sin must for ever be acutely painful. A similar problem, as we know, exercised the mind of Dante.[1] No one, I think, can reasonably maintain that these questions are evidence of a morbid sensitiveness. Surely sin does leave, and ought to leave, a consciousness of defilement—the sense that a stain lies upon our past life : a stain which neither penitence nor any other action of our own can remove.

But if we are serious (and surely every penitent *must* be serious) in these two convictions—viz., that a stain lies on our past and that we can do nothing ourselves to remove it—then at least in a *general form* the conception expressed by the prophet in the text will have meaning for us. " A fountain opened for sin and for uncleanness." To wish passionately for such cleansing is in a sense to conceive it—even if we only longed after it as something that seemed too good to be possible. There is always a certain intellectual clearness in what is emotionally distinct : and with many of us this sense of the stain of past sin, and the consequent desire for cleanness, are very distinct feelings indeed.

Here, then, we have ground for one definite conclusion : that the Christian demand for atonement may reasonably be regarded as at least the expression of a valid need. The first objection, you will remember, was that the doctrine is un-meaning. To say that sin has left a stain is, as we now see, at least not nonsense. I repeat that I do not believe that many people will, if they reflect, regard this sense of defilement even as morbid. When Lady Macbeth[2] says, "Out, out, damned spot," we should hardly speak of this cry as a sign of undue sensitiveness. A man may say that he personally does not feel that his past " cries out " for cleansing, just as another man may say that he does not understand how to the musician a discord " cries out " for resolution. But neither is justified in saying more than that this conception is obscure to himself. Those to whom such conceptions are clear seldom doubt that they bear witness to something really and objectively true.

III. The objector, however, may not unnaturally ask

---

[1] *Purgatorio*, XXVIII. 127.
[2] *Macbeth*, Act V, scene i.  Cf. Act II, scene ii.

whether this figurative expression of a moral need is not in truth the sole contribution of the doctrine of the Atonement to a rational theology. " The orthodox statements," he will say, " appear to allege that the sins of to-day are cleansed, or neutralised, or cancelled—or whatever metaphor may be preferred—by an event that occurred some nineteen centuries ago. This notion that the offensiveness of an act may be removed by some occurrence in a remote period of time is at least extremely difficult, and the strangeness of the conception should be frankly admitted. We must not disguise the fact that, in traditional theology, elements of truth are sadly mixed with remnants of barbarism."

Now, if the modern theologian uses language of this sort, it should not surprise us. Yet we may rightly ask whether it is true that the notion of moral " neutralisation " (as it has been called) is wholly unfamiliar and its application to human sin wholly without parallel. Schopenhauer speaks (without approval) of the common juristic conception that in punishment a wrong is " atoned for " and " neutralised " (*gesühnt : neutralisiert*).[1] The comparison of the atonement with legal punishment is not, I think, the aptest of all comparisons. It might lead to the conception of the Atonement as primarily an act of vengeance. But legal punishment is at least an evidence that the general conception of an evil act as having its offensiveness removed by something separated from it in space and time is familiar to mankind. Obviously this conception is not peculiar to jurists. It is the basis of feelings shared by the most unreflective persons. When Haman is hanged on the gallows fifty cubits high, " then," we read, " was the King's wrath pacified." [2] The presumptuous act still remained true—a fact in the undying past. But though the act remains, its offensiveness has been done away. Not always a particularly amiable feeling, but perfectly intelligible.

Thus against the familiar objections of certain schools of liberal Christianity, it seems right to maintain that the notion of an act " cleansed," " robbed of its offensiveness " by some occurrence outside itself, is not in a general way unmeaning. Those to whom a religious trust in God, and the optimistic view of the Universe which results from it,

[1] Schopenhauer, *Die Welt als Wille und Vorstellung*, § 62, p. 411. (Leipzig, 1891.)
[2] Esther vii. 10.

seem to be established on a rational basis, will naturally seek
to work these conceptions of moral purification and the need
for it into the framework of a rational theory of the Universe
in general.  Such optimistic faith will justify, for one thing,
the kind of argument always prominent in simple minds when
they begin to think of their beliefs.  God—they say—will
fulfil the needs He has created in us.  If mankind not merely
*desires* some gift, but *needs* it—needs it for the realisation of
its highest good—a good God will supply it.

IV.  " But these reflections," you may say, " though they
meet in some degree the familiar criticisms, do not go far
towards establishing the traditional doctrine.  Why should
this general notion of *some* fact or facts in the Universe,
adequate to remove the offensiveness of sin, be associated with
death, with bloodshedding, or with Christ ? "

In answer to this question it is worth while to consider
certain conceptions that have played their part in old-world
religion, Pagan or Jewish, and to seek to enter into these
conceptions by emotional sympathy.  Philosophers have
discussed, and sometimes denied, the cognitive value of
feelings.  But, obviously, there are cases where feelings give
knowledge.  If we do not *dislike* æsthetic incongruity—bad
harmonies or badly matched colours—we shall not know what
æsthetic congruity or incongruity is.  Here reason and
feeling are inseparably blended.  And, surely the cognitive
value of feeling is as evident when we are asking, "What does
the soul need ?  What would a satisfactory Universe contain ? " as when we are asking, "What is needed for artistic
congruity or perfection ? "

It ought not to be quite impossible to us to understand, for
example, the Old Testament conception of purification by
fire.  The Lord shall purify the blood of Jerusalem by the
Spirit—or the blast—of burning.[1]  Our own dislike of bodily
filth and defilement is not merely prudential : it is partly
æsthetic.  Thus I imagine that most of us if we had been
oppressed by the presence in our neighbourhood of loath-
some and insanitary dwellings, would experience a distinct
emotional satisfaction if these had been destroyed by fire—
distinct from what we should feel at the removal of the
uncleanness by quieter methods, though from the sanitary
inspector's point of view these latter might be equally
effective.  It is hard to say how many people would feel

[1] Isa. iv. 4.

this distinction acutely : but it is very closely connected with the evident fact that we loathe uncleanness directly and are not merely aware that it is a danger to health. Those who do feel the distinction acutely will also enter into the spirit of Isaiah's phrase.

It is harder for the modern mind to grasp the notion of purification by the shedding of blood. Yet to enter into this conception is not beyond the power of the scholar's imagination, even if some of the capacities for emotion that found exercise in antiquity have in us become dormant through atrophy. When Lord Roberts issued to his soldiers a prayer that Christ might wash them in His blood, a Unitarian Minister asked why the General wished the men to use this " disgusting language." This criticism could hardly have been made by one who had ever fallen under the magic of that fine verse of Æschylus : [1]

μήλοισιν αἱμάσσοντας ἑστίας θεῶν

" drenching with the blood of sheep the hearths of the Gods."

When Shakespeare makes Venus, after the death of Adonis, " stain her face with his congealed blood," [2] the same critic might call this a " disgusting line." Men deficient in the stronger passions will always fail to understand the violent expression of them. They may even resent their violence. No one but the passionate lover can judge fairly such an action as that which is attributed by Shakespeare to Venus. Similarly it requires a sympathy with certain religious passions to understand the Mithraic " bath of bull's blood " : or the conviction of the writer of the Epistle to the Hebrews that, though the blood of bulls and goats cannot take away sin, such sacrifices may sanctify to the purifying of the flesh.[3]

V. What is the bearing of these reflections on the doctrine of atonement by the blood of Christ ? If we once admit that the general conception which Schopenhauer expresses by the word " neutralisation "—the taking away of the offensiveness of an occurrence by another occurrence, separate in space and time from the first—is not unmeaning; if we recognise certain examples of this moral or æsthetic or quasi-æsthetic neutralisation which have seemed clear to certain minds in primitive times; if, further, we are prepared to

---

[1] *Seven against Thebes*, 275.    [2] *Venus and Adonis*, 137.
[3] Heb. ix. 13.   Cf. x. 4.

believe that these experiences were not mere examples of perverted taste; then the question whether we may conceive of something which might in a similar sense be felt, and rightly felt, to remove the stain which sin has made upon the world, will not be without interest for us. It may indeed be for us a matter of passionate concern, if we feel as acutely as some do the sense that the world and our own past suffers from this defilement, and are also convinced (as we well may be) that this sense of the defiling power of sin is a correct and rational apprehension. Its passionateness is not in itself a proof of irrationality.

Can we develop and specialise this purely general conception? If this neutralisation is at all possible, it is obvious that it must be accomplished either by certain physical facts or by certain mental facts—for there are no other kinds of fact—or by some combination of the two.

The traditional doctrine suggests at least as much as this : that God has provided satisfaction for a desire which He must feel more acutely than we do : that if we knew (as we may know it in the end in Him) all the whole range of physical facts and mental experiences which the Universe contains, and had also the feeling and insight to appreciate all these in their true significance and relations, we should then see the Universe as indeed very good ; since though defilement is real we should in this wide experience have had direct contact with those facts by which the offensiveness of this evil is done away.[1] The suggestion that it is in part through suffering, through intense love and sorrow and pain that this purification is accomplished, is at least in accordance with the analogies that have occurred to us. It is through facts which provoke emotion that wrath is pacified. The Jewish and Pagan sacrifices, whatever their origin, could hardly have continued so long as they did if they had not stirred the emotions of many generations of mankind.

Mr. Bernard Shaw has said that the Christian conception of the Atonement presents us with an " insane vengeance and a trumpery expiation." If we have seen that the sense of the

---

[1] It seems obvious that if the words "neutralisation of the offensiveness of sin " have meaning, there must be a conceivable group of facts which would accomplish this, just as if " perfection " has meaning there must be some conceivable group of facts which would deserve the name. I can remember no discussion of this point.

defiling power of past sin is rational and *not* insane, we may perhaps come also to see that the question as to what occurrences would be adequate to expiate it depends upon our insight into the nature—in part into the emotional nature—of those occurrences. Can we reasonably conceive that if we knew in full (as God knows them) all the volitions, the emotions, and other experiences which came to their head in the death on Calvary, we should (if our moral and æsthetic valuation of their significance was adequate) see in them something sufficient to neutralise—just as minor wrongs are neutralised for our feelings by just punishment—the sins of the whole world ?

Under this general question it would be well worth while to reflect carefully upon certain special conceptions of theologians of past days—upon the Pauline thought, developed by some Greek Fathers, of Christ as " equivalent " [1] to, and including within Himself, the Church, or mankind, or the Universe ; again upon the passages in which St. Paul speaks of Christ as the head of humanity,[2] and speaks of himself as filling up [3] what is lacking in the sufferings of Christ. Can we, I ask, think that the sufferings of mankind (as including and interpreted by the suffering and voluntary self-sacrifice of Him in whom humanity has attained its consummation) may conceivably possess the capacity to " neutralise " the admitted evils of the world ? This mass of tragic suffering can, at least, not be reasonably spoken of as a " trumpery expiation."

It may be objected that these suggestions are out of harmony with the requirements of a professedly rational theology ; that they are a reversion to the theory that we may accept upon authority that which we do not ourselves understand. But this accusation is not just, except as against those who say more than they have a rational ground for alleging. If we say merely that sin is rightly felt to leave a stain on the past which even the sincerest repentance of the individual sinner does not wholly remove ; further, that faith in God's goodness inclines us to believe that He will in the end somehow do for us what we cannot do for ourselves ; and, lastly, that there is something correct in the instinct which has led traditional Christianity to associate the meeting of this need with the sufferings and death of Christ—we are speaking

---

[1] Cf. Rashdall, *Idea of Atonement*, pp. 313, 315, 316.
[2] Col. I. 1 and II. 19.    [3] Col. I. 23.

of what may fall well within our individual knowledge. There is nothing irrational in suggesting in a general way how a need may be met, even if we admit that we cannot work out in fulness of detail a completely adequate theory. If we are candid about our own uncertainties, there is no obvious harm in using liturgical language in which what seems to us a sound instinct is imperfectly, even if at the same time too confidently, expressed.

But it is not on the note of uncertainty that I wish to close. Whatever qualifying clauses we may wish to add when we are discussing the doctrine of the Atonement as a whole, we may, I think, express without any qualification at all our conviction that sin brings, not only guilt, but also defilement; that the pardoned penitent must ever look back to a sin-stained past; that he can never expect to view the world with a soul satisfied and at rest unless indeed God has fulfilled for him what is expressed in the vigorous metaphor of the prophet, and opened for us in some sense and by some means a fountain for sin and for uncleanness.

x

# XIV

## THE PREACHING OF THE CROSS

### BY C. M. CHAVASSE

" The preaching of the cross is to them that perish foolishness; but
unto us which are saved it is the power of God."

I Cor. 1. 18 (A.V.).

I cannot understand the woe
Which Thou wert pleased to bear,
O dying Lamb! I only know
That all my hope is there.

ST. PAUL, in his first Epistle to the Corinthians,[1] has
described " the Preaching of the Cross " as foolishness to
them that are perishing, but the power of God to them that
are being saved. That is, the Cross cannot be understood
apart from a personal acceptance of what it offers. And this
he further amplifies from his own experience of preaching
Christ crucified [2]—that it was a " stumbling-block " to the
Jews and " foolishness " to the Greeks.

The whole history of the doctrine of the Atonement from
his day down to this present volume would support his words.
No satisfactory theory has ever been discovered to explain
the precise working or the real necessity of the Cross.
Pictures have proved inadequate to express it. And each
successive generation has therefore repudiated the analogies
which satisfied its parents. But yet the preaching of the
Cross and its practical effect has all down the centuries
changed lives, brought peace to troubled hearts, and inspired
men and women to serve and to suffer to the utmost.

Many have therefore been content to accept the Gospel
preached by the Cross without seeking to penetrate its
mystery. They agree with Spurgeon that the Atonement
" was wrought in darkness because its full meaning could
not be beheld with the finite mind," and they are satisfied
with Bishop Butler's verdict, " How, in what particular way,

[1] I Cor. i. 18.     [2] I Cor. i. 23, 24.

322

Christ's death was efficacious, there are not wanting persons who have endeavoured to explain; but I do not find that Scripture hath explained it." They have felt that—as indeed with all the greatest facts of life, such as human nature, free will, and personality—the truths of the Atonement are not so much for the intellect as for the heart, and that Calvary cannot be understood like a map, but only apprehended like a picture. Argument, they say, and controversy, and the demand for proof, are out of place here. The Cross is a fact and a force to be verified by personal experience, and it preaches a Life to be known and a Person to be loved.

But many more are impatient of the secrets of mystery. They would pierce the veil with their understanding, and they cannot rest content unless they can explain to their satisfaction what the Saviour has effected for them. The attitude is right and wholesome up to a point. The spirit of reverent inquiry is responsible for throwing much light upon the Cross; for correcting errors which threatened to divide the Godhead into a " wrathful Potentate " and a "pitiful Redeemer "; and for bringing home to our wondering gratitude how great is the mystery of our salvation. But the adventurous spirit of inquiry courts disaster if it refuses to allow anything beyond what it can understand, and terms as unreasonable that which is beyond reason. It does not solve a mystery to declare that no mystery exists, nor can manifest difficulties be unravelled by cutting the Gordian knot and explaining away Christ's words as a gloss, or by the presumption that we know more about the Saviour's own death than His sayings would seem to show that He did. To a very great extent such students of the Atonement, though they stigmatise so-called conservative views as immoral, yet, in practice, rest all their hopes upon the facts which such views imperfectly enshrine; and they sing the old hymns " There was no other good enough to pay the price of sin," and they repeat the old texts " The blood of Jesus Christ, God's Son, cleanses us from all sin," with hearts full of thankfulness and peace.

For the Cross is always preaching; it is not only being preached. The Revised Version gives the truer rendering when it speaks of " the Word of the Cross," where the Authorised Version translates " the Preaching of the Cross," [1]

[1] I Cor. i. 18.

and thereby attributes to the Cross a living utterance with a message that is its own commendation and carries its own conviction. Like an ancient monument it cries—" Sta viator "; first it arrests attention and then declares its own Gospel. So that the fact remains that wherever Christ is lifted up and the Cross is preached in its own language, and the words of the Saviour and of His Apostles are quoted as showing (to use Bishop Lightfoot's summary) that it is " the ordained instrument of salvation "—there lives are changed and what seems foolishness is yet the power of God unto salvation.

The first Epistle to the Corinthians is for all time the great record of the Preaching of the Cross, its message, and its results; so that it has been called " The Epistle of the Cross in its social application."

The city of Corinth seemed the most unlikely soil in all the world for the Gospel. With its two harbours fronting the seas of East and West, it was rich and cosmopolitan, and was as wicked as its buildings were gorgeous. It has been described as " the Empire in miniature." It was as if at Corinth the Empire were reduced to a single state in which European civilisation only intensified some of the grossest features of Oriental worship. It was [1] " the Vanity Fair " of the ancient world, " conspicuous for its depravity even amid the depraved cities of a dying heathenism." Its very name was a byword for profligacy. " A Corinthian drinker " and " a Corinthian banquet " were current proverbs for shamelessness; and the word " Corinthian " has survived almost to our own day as a description of profligate ideas. It was from this city that St. Paul wrote his terrible indictment against paganism.[2] And this Epistle itself is one which is forced to deal with immorality as an all-pervading atmosphere which produced unbelievable scandals even in the Church itself.

The Apostle approached this gorgeous Gomorrah with feelings akin to terror. He was with them " in weakness and in fear, and in much trembling." [3] And the more so because of his recent failure to make the slightest impression upon Athens, which was to Corinth what Oxford is to London or Liverpool. There he had experienced a rebuff that had shaken him to the very soul. After immense pains, he had

[1] Farrar, *Life of St. Paul*, pp. 557 ff.
[2] Rom. i. 21–32.  [3] I Cor. ii. 3.

surpassed himself in setting forth the new teaching of Christianity before the doctors and professors of what was the centre of the world's wisdom.  His approach had been through their own reasoned philosophy of life to the manifestation of God in Jesus Christ risen from the dead.  But at mention of the Resurrection his audience had dispersed in laughter.  No Church was ever founded at Athens.  No Epistle is called after its name.  And St. Paul departed from its lovely buildings and noble traditions crushed with a sense of failure, never to set foot again within its famous walls. Wherein lay the fault, with himself or these flippant scholars ? Chiefly he blamed himself.  The Resurrection was the climax of the life and death of Christ, and he had erred in supposing that it could be understood apart from them.  How, then, would he and his message fare in the far more hostile atmosphere of Corinth, the seat of business, pleasure and vice ? But on one thing he was determined.  No more eloquent sermons !  No more dependence upon rhetoric to win men to Christ through their intelligence !  The Cross should henceforth preach its own gospel !  Christ, and Him Crucified, alone should be his theme !  He would attack not the intelligence, but the heart and conscience by lifting up the Saviour, and so suffer Him to draw all men unto Himself. So it is that throughout this Epistle we constantly come across evidence of how the wretched experience of that black day at Athens had seared itself deeply upon the Apostle's soul.  " Christ sent me . . . to preach the Gospel, not in wisdom of words lest the Cross of Christ should be made void." [1]  " We preach Christ Crucified, unto Jews a stumbling-block, and unto Gentiles foolishness ; but unto them that are called both Jews and Greeks, Christ the power of God, and the wisdom of God." [2]  " I came unto you . . . not with excellency of speech or of wisdom, proclaiming to you the mystery of God.  For I determined not to know anything among you save Jesus Christ, and Him crucified.  And my speech and my preaching were not in persuasive words of wisdom, but in demonstration of the Spirit and of power." [3] " For the wisdom of this world is foolishness with God," [4] and so on throughout the first four chapters.  Thus did he settle down to make his assault upon the wicked city.  And he remained there for eighteen months ; to conduct one of

[1] I Cor. i. 17.          [2] I Cor. i. 23.
[3] I Cor. ii. 1, 2, 4.    [4] I Cor. iii. 19.

the most successful missions of his life; and to build up a
Church that should become his glory. As Bengel shrewdly
remarked, " The Church of God in Corinth [1] is a great and
joyful paradox." But it actually came to pass through " the
preaching of the Cross."

The preaching of the Cross, therefore, as St. Paul discovered, had two results. First as regards the preacher—a
great peace filled his troubled heart, and he gained a mighty
self-confidence by learning to rely on his Master's message
rather than upon his own powers of persuasion and reasoning.
So did his Lord appear to him in visions of the night. " Be
not afraid, but speak, hold not thy peace : for I am with thee,
and no man shall set on thee to harm thee : for I have much
people in this city." [2] And then, secondly, his hearers were
affected, for there is the witness of the Holy Spirit of
Conviction in every heart to apply the Gospel of our Saviour.
Inquirers crowded in, were baptised, and changed their lives.
And who were these decent men and women with shining
faces, steadfast eyes, and arresting lives, who flocked into the
house of Titus Justus to hear the Apostle, to sing their hymns,
and join in the breaking of bread ? St. Paul reminds them in
this Epistle.[3] It is a terrible list, which includes thieves,
rogues, drunkards, prostitutes, fornicators, and even worse.
" Such," he says, " were some of you : but ye were washed,
but ye were sanctified, but ye were justified in the name of
the Lord Jesus."

It was an amazing congregation, which had made trial of a
Christ who had not failed them, so that they attracted others
by the conversion and consistency of their lives. No wonder
that the whole city was moved ; or that Crispus, the ruler of
the synagogue next door, joined himself to their company !
And they were the fruits of " the preaching of the Cross."
Christ Crucified had been lifted up before them, and they had
been saved.

Then what Gospel did the Cross preach at Corinth which
effected this astounding revolution ? Was it that teaching
of which we hear so much to-day—that the death of the
Saviour was not a payment for sin, but only a demonstration
of love to the uttermost; and that forgiveness was not
purchased at Calvary, but that there we were shown how full
and free is that forgiveness with which a Heavenly Father is
always ready to welcome back sinners without the enforce-
ment of any penalty ?

[1] I Cor. i. 2.      [2] Acts xviii. 9, 10.      [3] I Cor. vi. 9, 10, 11.

But if Christ had only died the death of a martyr, and Calvary was only the appropriate conclusion to a life of self-sacrifice—then there is nothing of foolishness in such a preaching of the Cross to affront the learned. Plato was never accused of foolishness by these same Greeks for describing how the great Socrates was done to death. In this same Epistle [1] St. Paul " makes known " the Gospel of the Cross which he preached to the Corinthians and by which they were saved.—" For," he continues, " I delivered unto you *first of all* that which also I received, how that Christ died for our sins (that is, on account of our sins) according to the Scriptures." It is clear from St. Paul's corresponding declaration in this same Epistle concerning Holy Communion [2] that when he says that he " received " this Gospel, he means that it was handed on to him by the Apostles, who themselves heard it from the lips of the Saviour Himself. Now one of the chief purposes of the ministry of the great forty days after the Resurrection was that Christ might teach His Church " the things concerning the kingdom of God." [3] And in his Gospel St. Luke further informs us that this teaching was largely concerned with His atoning death.—" Thus it is written that the Christ should suffer . . . and that repentance and remission of sin should be preached in His name." [4] And what is this but a reiteration of His own statements before His death, that He gave His life " a ransom *instead of* many " [5] and shed His blood " unto the remission of sins " ? [6] That is to say, according to the teaching of the Saviour Himself, both before and after His Resurrection, His death was central to His whole earthly ministry. That death was not simply a fitting conclusion to a life of self-sacrifice and obedience to the uttermost, but He was born to die, and His death " effected something vital for our salvation, which His earthly Incarnation, had it ended in some other way, could not have secured for us." [7]

This, then, was the Gospel of the Cross which St. Paul preached, not because he invented it himself (as is sometimes affirmed), but because he had himself " received " it of the Lord through those who heard it from His own lips. And, moreover, it is the same Gospel which the other Apostles preached even as they had received it; as, for example, St.

---

[1] I Cor. xv. 1, 2.   [2] I Cor. xi. 23.   [3] Acts i. 3.
[4] Lk. xxiv. 44, 45, 46.   [5] Mt. xx. 28.   [6] Mt. xxvi. 28.
[7] Dr. K. E. Kirk in *Essays Catholic and Critical* (from whom I have quoted more than once).

Peter, who describes Christ as, in His own self, bearing our sins in His own body upon the Cross,[1] and St. John, who affirms that " the blood of Jesus Christ His Son cleanseth us from all sin." [2]

Now it does not fall to my province to attempt to show how such a theory of the Atonement, even if we cannot wholly understand it, yet provides the only satisfactory explanation which meets all the otherwise baffling questions which surround the meaning of the Life and Death of the Son of God.

Why did our Lord anticipate His death from the first days of His Ministry,[3] and expect it with increasing foreboding as the doom of the Cross cast its shadow ever more darkly across His path ? Why did He model His ministry upon Isaiah's Suffering Servant, even as John Baptist pointed to Him as the Lamb of God, bearing away the sin of the world ? [4] And why did He yield Himself so voluntarily into the hands of His murderers, when He knew the danger which threatened, and could so easily have withdrawn from it, even as He had escaped before ? If the Cross was not a necessary act of rescue, then it was a rash act of suicide on the part of a sentimental fanatic ! Why also did He shrink unduly in Gethsemane from physical suffering, if it was only bodily torture that He anticipated ? Even the two robbers would have spent their last night on earth more calmly ! Or, again, what actually caused the disruption of His soul and body ? It was not the pain of Crucifixion, which, as is shown in the case of the two robbers, was designed as a lingering death, so that Pilate marvelled and required confirmation that his Victim had succumbed in six hours.[5]

All such considerations point to some deeper cause, some dark experience which spoke in the great cry of desolation and can only be explained by it, and which St. Paul has ventured to describe to these very Corinthians as "the ministry of reconciliation given him by God, to wit that God was in Christ reconciling the world unto Himself. . . . Him who knew no sin He made to be sin on our behalf; that we might become the righteousness of God in Him." [6]

This "ministry of reconciliation," as effected and taught by our Saviour and preached at His bidding by His Apostles, has been wonderfully summarised by Dr. Routh, the famous

[1] I Pet. ii. 23.   [2] I Jn. i. 7.   [3] Jn. ii. 19 and iii. 14.
[4] Jn. i. 29 and Lk. xxii. 22.   [5] Mk. xv. 44.   [6] II Cor. v. 18 ff.

centenarian President of Magdalen of the last century. When he was nearly ninety years old Dr. Routh penned the following letter to a member of a Quaker family known to him, who had been sentenced to death for an atrocious murder. " Sir, this comes from one who, like yourself, has not long to live, being in his ninetieth year. He has had more opportunity than most for distinctly knowing that the Scriptures of the New Testament were written by the Apostles of the Saviour of mankind. In these Scriptures it is expressly said that the blood of Jesus Christ cleanses from all sin, and that if we confess our sins, God, being merciful and just, will forgive us our sins on our repentance. Think, say, and do everything in your power to save your soul before you go into another life."

Further than such a setting forth of the Gospel of the Cross, as preached to the Corinthian Church, it does not concern us to go in this essay.

Rather we are constrained to inquire why such a Gospel works with so potent an effect upon men's hearts and lives, from the days of the Corinthian Church down to our own. And it is from this viewpoint of man's need that we may best be led to comprehend, even dimly, something of the necessity for the "transaction" on Calvary. We have in the past been inclined to ask what difference the Cross made in God's relations towards ourselves. Thus the second Article declares that Christ " truly suffered, was crucified, dead, and buried, *to reconcile His Father to us.*" But this is not the teaching of Scripture, which never speaks of God being reconciled to us by the Cross, but always of ourselves thereby being reconciled to God ; and of God indeed (as we have seen) as Himself accomplishing this reconciliation through Christ —" God was in Christ reconciling the world unto Himself." [1] There is then some barrier on our side to remove which it was necessary for our Saviour to endure all that the Cross involved. And every individual heart will confess what it is —namely, the conviction within us all that sin must bring punishment, and that there can be no forgiveness apart from retribution. This fact is well brought out in the Parable of the Prodigal Son. The Parable is often advanced as containing our Lord's own explanation of the manner of Divine forgiveness. In it we are reminded that there is no penalty enforced, whether vicarious or otherwise. But that the love

[1] II Cor. v. 18, 19.

of God, like that of a Father, is depicted as always going out more than half-way to welcome sinners who come to themselves and return with penitence. But what is the significance of the Prodigal's cry, "Father, I have sinned *against heaven* and in Thy sight "? [1] What does it mean " to sin against heaven " ? If the phrase possesses no meaning, then it is the only one in the parable which expresses no spiritual truth. But, on the contrary, we have here an acknowledgment by the returned prodigal that he had not only sinned against a Father's love, which was open to receive him back, but also against a Divine Order, inexorable in its working, and beyond even the power of love itself to override.

There is, then, a world of meaning in the cry " I have sinned against heaven," and by it sinful man confesses himself judged and condemned by the moral law of the Universe, that law which is as inviolable and unalterable as Natural Law.

It may be said that the Almighty Lawgiver Himself is not bound by His own laws, and that He can overrule the Moral Law, if He wishes to forgive without the due penalty being paid. But would such an easy solution build up a righteous character in His children, or effect (what a true atonement must involve) that God and man should be " at one mind " regarding sin ? Would it not rather be to translate to the skies that fatal easiness of a good-natured parent which has been the ruin of so many sons ? There is no problem in the world so difficult as that of forgiveness ! How to remit punishment without cheapening sin ! How to pardon a wrong and yet to vindicate the right ! How to restore the guilty and yet to teach the offender to hate his offence ! It has been well called " a problem fit for God." And even if we cannot fully explain its meaning, yet the Cross does offer a practical solution which satisfies all requirements.

On the one hand, it proves beyond all question the love of God for sinners ; even as St. Paul wrote from Corinth, " God commendeth His own love towards us, in that, while we were yet sinners, Christ died for us." [2] On the other hand, it has convicted the world of sin ever since its sinister rood was first raised against the skyline on Calvary ; even as St. Paul reminded the Corinthians that they were not their own, but bought with a price [3] and again wrote from Corinth that even

[1] Lk. xv. 21.  [2] Rom. v. 8.
[3] I Cor. vi. 19, 20.

as Christ died unto sin once, " even so reckon ye also your-selves to be dead indeed unto sin." [1]

But, chiefest of all, the Cross, by the immensity of its sacrifice, convinces the sinner that he is forgiven, and that, despite his violation of the Moral Law, yet, in God's sight, the past is as if it had never been. I do not think that we sufficiently take into account how hard it is for a sinner to realise that he is forgiven. Man lives upon an earth where the Laws of Nature hold inviolable sway, and where conse-quence must follow cause in inexorable sequence ; so that he who attempts to break Nature's laws is himself broken with-out hope of redress. There is also that within man which tells him that the principles which govern the earth are parables of heavenly truths, and that by reason of the Almighty Simplicity of the Divine Mind the same system of law runs through all—nature and the moral order alike. We know therefore that the law of "cause and effect" applies also to the spiritual world, although the phraseology is changed to "sin and punishment" and "right and reward." And, apart altogether from arbitrary punishment or the outward consequences of wrong behaviour which we may or may not escape, yet we are fully aware that any breach of the Moral Law is visited with a corresponding and proportionate injury to character.

Our human system of justice is indeed an acknowledgment of these truths, for it is retributive in its origin and essence, and an attempt to reproduce in society what we observe in nature and experience with regard to our souls. The Law Court was not, as many suppose, primarily designed as a deterrent against wrong-doing or to reform the offender. Punishment is only reformative and a deterrent in so far as it is first retributive, and thus vindicates righteousness and builds a warning barrier against evil. Human justice, then, would attempt to make the punishment fit the crime, and so confesses that by the breaking of law something is owed to the law, and that payment must be made. And what does this mean but that man according to his own theory of justice believes himself incapable of being forgiven, until by punish-ment he has wiped off the debt ? No sinner therefore can rest content with forgiveness made easy, or by an atonement which costs nothing.

At the recital of certain crimes the voice of public conscience

[1] Rom. vi. 11.

is heard crying out, " Death is not enough." This is a
sentiment uttered by Christ Himself, the Representative of
the human race, when He spoke of millstones and deep seas
in connection with crimes against children.   If therefore we
are tempted to affirm that it would be easy for God to forgive
without demanding a penalty, we forget that what we call
the " wrath of God " finds its answering echo in the human
heart; that the demand for expiation is deeply rooted in the
instincts of man's being; and that our whole system of
Justice is an expression of its truth.   All this is pictured in
the prodigal's cry of despair, " Father, I have sinned against
heaven "; and it explains the development of the whole
elaborate system of the Confessional, in that it is against
nature for a sinner to believe that forgiveness is possible.
Thus, with all reverence, we may affirm that it is man
rather than God who demands the full, perfect and sufficient
satisfaction of the Cross, and that he cannot conceive of
himself as forgiven unless he actually beholds the price of
sin paid either by himself or by Another.

It is, then, a gospel of peace to the guilty soul that the Cross
preaches with saving power.   And if we rest (in old-fashioned
phrase) on " the finished work " of Jesus Christ, then we may
understand that it was " naturally fitting " that Christ should
die, for if in the Universe " all bills must be paid," Christ
" pays the bill Himself "; [1] which is only to paraphrase His
own explanation that His death was a ransom instead of
many and a remission of sins.   In a word, then, upon the
Cross our Lord paid homage, as it were, to the Moral Order,
and thus vindicated the righteousness of God, even while He
expiated our sin against heaven.

Now such a gospel works !   It is still to-day " the power of
God and the wisdom of God," even as when it was preached
by St. Paul at Corinth.   And without it we have no message
for those who are under deep conviction of sin.   Just as the
Jew of old could only believe himself forgiven as he watched
the scapegoat bearing away his sins out of the Camp, so we,
taught by our deepest and truest instincts, are still burdened
with the guilt of sin, till by a transaction on Good Friday,
which we are bound in loyalty to our Lord's own phraseology to describe in some sense as " substitution," we
behold Him on whom the Lord hath laid the iniquity of us

[1] Canon Streeter, *Reality*, pp. 230, 231 (to whom I am indebted for
much in this Essay).

all, the Lamb of God, bearing away the sin of the world. With such a gospel there is no conscience so stricken but that it may find assurance and peace, even if the mind cannot grasp the full explanation of the mystery of redemption.  And the very horror of the sacrifice offered up on Calvary, from which the mind so recoils that it is tempted to explain it away, is proportionately the very assurance of that salvation upon which the guilty heart can rest its only hope.  Archbishop Cranmer has wonderfully expressed its power when he poured forth his soul in prayer in St. Mary's Church, Oxford, before his burning, and craved the forgiveness of God for his re-cantation of the Reformed truths he had taught.  With many tears he cried out, " Thou didst not give Thy Son unto death, O God, for our little and small sins only, but for all the greatest sins of the world, so that the sinner returns unto Thee with a penitent heart, as I do here at this present." And the late Bishop of Durham, Dr. Moule, in some striking lines has emphasised the same truth—namely, that because the mystery of the Cross is unfathomable, therefore the measure of forgiveness it offers is limitless.

> The gloomy Garden, blood-bedewed,
> The midnight scene of shame and scorn,
> The scourge, the wreath of rending thorn,
> The tortures of the dreadful Rood;
>
> There were the billows of Thy death,
> The storm-tossed surface; but the cry—
> Thy Spirit's woe, " *Sabacthani* "
> Rose from the ocean underneath.
>
> Man has no line that sea to sound,
> The abyss of night—whose gulfs within
> Now lies entombed our weight of sin
> Forgotten, never to be found.[1]

It may be thought that I have enlarged too much upon one aspect of the preaching of the Cross, at the expense of its other great voices—its assurance of Divine love, its promise of power, and its inspiration to service.  But all these follow naturally from its central work of forgiveness, and they are exhibited in other ways by the Incarnation and Resurrection, while forgiveness can only be found at Calvary itself.

Moreover, it is this aspect of the Cross which needs em-

[1] *Christus Consolator*, p. 66.

phasising at this particular time; and Evangelicals especially need to reassert it.

As Dr. J. S. Simpson has tersely said, "Catholicism has a teaching, Liberalism a temper, but Evangelicalism a message." And if Evangelicalism loses its message, for what does it stand ?

The word Evangel or Gospel was one coined during the misery of the Babylonian Captivity; and, as Isaiah proclaimed, the first work of the Servant of the Lord was to preach " Good News " of deliverance to exiles.[1] This work Our Lord, in the synagogue at Nazareth, claimed as being at length fulfilled in Himself,[2] save that the deliverance was a greater one from the bondage of sin.  When therefore, at Nazareth, He accepted this very word " Gospel " as expressing His Ministry, the context shows that He came to preach " Good News " to those who were exiles in the " far country " of alienation from God; and His own description of His redemptive work as a "ransom instead of many " is explained from this picture, ever in His mind, of the exiled children of God.  The burden of His message was therefore one of Atonement—that is, a return home and a reunion with God which would in itself involve the knowledge of a Father's love, and a sharing of His power which should manifest itself in uprightness of life and service for others.

But this gospel of deliverance was not that there was no need of deliverance, or that the exiles were really at home without knowing it.  It was, instead, the good news that the deliverance had been wrought for them ; the ransom had been paid ; and they were redeemed by a salvation which a lone Saviour had effected for them.

To-day we are in danger of preaching an emasculated doctrine of the Atonement, and a Cross with no Saviour that hangs thereon.  But such was not the preaching which founded the Corinthian Church, and it produces no effect of changed lives to-day.

It behoves, therefore, the preacher of the Cross to listen to the hymn of praise and supplication which, from the day of Pentecost itself, has ever risen from the hearts of the redeemed as they worshipped the Lamb that was slain—

Thou art the King of Glory : O Christ
Thou art the Everlasting Son of the Father.
When thou tookest upon thee to deliver man :

---

[1] Isa. lxi. 1.    [2] Lk. iv. 18.

Thou didst not abhor the Virgin's womb.
When thou hadst overcome the sharpness of death :
Thou didst open the Kingdom of Heaven to all believers.

We therefore pray thee, help thy servants :
Whom thou hast redeemed with thy precious blood.
Make them to be numbered with thy saints :
In glory everlasting.

And then to add once more, as a finale, his own personal petition, resting (as does the writer) all his hope upon the Cross which he has preached to others—

O Lord, in thee have I trusted :
Let me never be confounded.

# INDEX

PRINTED IN GREAT BRITAIN BY RICHARD CLAY & SONS, LIMITED,
BUNGAY, SUFFOLK.